I0644874

Young Faculty in the Twenty-First Century

SUNY series in Global Issues in Higher Education

Kevin Kinser, Jason E. Lane, Philip G. Altbach,
and Ş. İlgü Özler, editors

Young Faculty in the Twenty-First Century

INTERNATIONAL PERSPECTIVES

Edited by

Maria Yudkevich
Philip G. Altbach
Laura E. Rumbley

SUNY PRESS

Published by State University of New York Press, Albany

Printed in the United States of America

For information, contact State University of New York Press, Albany, NY
www.sunypress.edu

Production, Diane Ganeles
Marketing, Kate R. Seburyamo

Library of Congress Cataloging-in-Publication Data

Young faculty in the twenty-first century : international perspectives / edited by Maria Yudkevich, Philip G. Altbach, and Laura E. Rumbley.
pages cm. — (SUNY series in global issues in higher education)
Includes bibliographical references and index.
ISBN 978-1-4384-5727-7 (hc : alk. paper)—978-1-4384-5726-0 (pb : alk. paper)
ISBN 978-1-4384-5728-4 (e-book)
1. College teachers—Employment—Cross-cultural studies. 2. College teaching—Cross-cultural studies. 3. Universities and colleges—Faculty—Cross-cultural studies. I. Yudkevich, Maria, editor of compilation. II. Altbach, Philip G., editor of compilation. III. Rumbley, Laura, editor of compilation.

LB1778.Y68 2015
378.1'2—dc23 2014034932

10 9 8 7 6 5 4 3 2 1

Contents

Illustrations

Figures

Tables

Acknowledgments

This volume, and the research project from which it stems, is part of the continuing collaboration between the Laboratory for Institutional Analysis at the National Research University–Higher School of Economics, Moscow, and the Boston College Center for International Higher Education. The original idea for this work came from Professor Maria Yudkevich, vice rector for research at the Higher School of Economics, who was convinced that the challenges faced by Russian academics were not unique and that cross-national research would yield some useful insights. This project is a continuation of our earlier work on academic remuneration and contracts, which resulted in two publications: Philip G. Altbach, Liz Reisberg, Maria Yudkevich, Gregory Androushchak, and Iván F. Pacheco, eds. *Paying the Professoriate: A Global Comparison of Compensation and Contracts* (New York: Routledge, 2012), and Philip G. Altbach, Gregory Androushchak, Yaroslav Kuzminov, Maria Yudkevich, and Liz Reisberg, eds., *The Global Future of Higher Education and the Academic Profession: The BRICs and the United States* (New York: Palgrave, 2013).

We were able to assemble an able group of researchers from ten countries to work from a common template to analyze their own university systems. The research group met in Moscow to discuss the research, and the chapters in this volume reflect their insights. We are indebted to the Higher School of Economics for funding for this project. At Boston College, Dr. Laura E. Rumbley, associate director of the Center for International Higher Education, managed the project and also edited the chapters. At the Higher School of Economics, we appreciate the assistance of Alexander Novikov for data analysis and Elena Erlykova for excellent logistics support at HSE. Our major debt of gratitude goes to the researchers who have worked with us and who are the authors of the case-study chapters presented here.

Maria Yudkevich
Moscow, Russian Federation

Philip G. Altbach
Chestnut Hill, Massachusetts, USA

Laura E. Rumbley
Chestnut Hill, Massachusetts, USA

Introduction

The Logic and Organization of the Book

The Centrality of the Theme

For young graduates, the decision to start an academic career is determined by both individual preferences and the realities of higher education in terms of job markets, conditions of work, and other factors. To attract the "best and brightest" to academe, national higher education systems must provide competitive remuneration and career prospects. At the same time, the success of all higher education institutions requires the quality, qualifications, and commitment of the professoriate—those who do the actual teaching and research. Without question, the academic profession is in crisis almost everywhere in the world—affected by the challenges of massification, the expansion of the private sector in higher education, the privatization of public universities, globalizations, and an array of other forces. Those responsible for higher education policy, in government and in the universities, seldom pay attention to the changing realities of the academic profession. Often—when the professoriate is considered at all—it is subject to criticism for failing to adapt to the "new realities" of mass higher education, commercialization, increased competition, and other challenges. Governments and academic managers increasingly see the professoriate as employees rather than as a community of scholars.

Many who read these words will say that adjustments to the new realities are mandatory, and the academic profession simply needs to meet the challenges. It is certainly the case that the realities of the contemporary university have changed. But our belief is that, even in challenging times, the professoriate is the core of the university and that it must continue to be a community of scholars with a strong sense of commitment to the values of higher education. Academics serve as more than just employees.

This book concerns a key but so far largely ignored segment of the academic profession—younger entry-level academics. If the best and brightest young people are not attracted to the academic profession, the entire future of the academic enterprise is bleak. It is true that a career in higher education has never offered the remuneration of a career in the professions or industry, but data show that the gulf between work in academe and professional opportunities for similarly trained people outside higher education is great and expanding.

Young academics also need a clear career path—some kind of assurance that it will be possible, assuming satisfactory performance, to build a successful career as an academic. For a growing number of academics in many countries, building a career is increasingly difficult; more are employed part time or on limited contracts. There is increased competition for jobs. At the same time, a large number of countries is facing severe shortages of university teachers. This is particularly the case in developing countries and places, such as India and China, which have seen rapid expansion in higher education enrollments in recent decades. In most of the world, many senior academics are of retirement age, and there is a need to replace these scholars with younger colleagues.

One thing is clear—if universities do not offer an attractive career path and appropriate working conditions for young faculty, no amount of marketization, adjustment to "twenty-first-century realities," or managerial guidance will produce high-quality teaching or research. Luring the best and brightest to the academic profession is difficult under the most favorable of circumstances—and current realities are far from optimal.

The Organization of the Book

This volume has two distinct aims—to provide a general perspective on the challenges facing young academics as they start their careers, and to indicate how the realities in specific case study countries illustrate the broader themes. In addition, the case studies, which are at the heart of this volume, show in detail how national academic systems affect young faculty, how the academic labor market determines opportunities, and if indeed it is possible to develop a stable career in academe.

We have chosen ten countries for analysis. These countries reflect a range of regions with varying academic realities. In all of these cases, it is possible to discern aspects of the "crisis of young academics." Although the cases differ in scope and details, there are common themes. We chose countries that illustrate a range of national experiences but with a focus on countries with fairly robust academic systems. Thus, no low-income developing countries are included—we felt that neither the universities nor the academic profession were well enough entrenched to provide relevant data. We have included all of the BRIC countries—Brazil, Russia, India, and China—as well as South Africa. In addition, the book presents the experiences of a range of European countries, from major academic systems such as Germany and France, to smaller countries including Norway and Portugal. The United States—as a large and centrally important academic system that employs many scholars and scientists from around the world—is also included. Thus, there is representation from almost all continents and from academic systems with different characteristics.

The case study chapters follow a common template in order to provide a common perspective for comparison and understanding. A brief introduction to the higher education realities of the case country is provided. The focus of this book is on young faculty, and the bulk of each chapter describes and analyzes the conditions of academic work for this key segment of the academic profession. Each chapter discusses the broader academic labor market, the arrangements or hiring and promotion, issues of salary and remuneration, and related themes. Each researcher was asked to focus on these common themes, but the specific realities and conditions in each country shape the narrative of each chapter.

Common themes, patterns, and generalizations are discussed in the first and last chapters. The first focuses on broad issues highlighted in research literature on the academic profession, while the final chapter focuses on key themes that emerged from the case studies.

Although this volume is not a "guide" for young academics, we hope that it will provide a useful overview and analysis that will contribute to thinking about an academic career. We are convinced that we must understand the realities facing young academics in order to make good decisions, both for individual careers and for improved public and university policy. In a globalized world, these realities must also be considered in global perspective.

Chapter 1

Building an Academic Career

A Twenty-First-Century Challenge

Philip G. Altbach

There is general agreement that the academic profession is in crisis worldwide. Without a successful professoriate, higher education is itself in crisis, for the academics are at the heart of the university—the teachers, researchers, and indeed creators of the intellectual and scientific life of higher education everywhere. If the "best and brightest" are not attracted to academe, not only are world-class universities impossible to achieve, but the academic system as a whole will be second-rate. Despite this situation, neither policy makers nor most academic leaders recognize either the centrality or the deep problems facing the academic profession. The concern here is to outline some of the structural problems that exist and to illustrate some of the particular challenges facing a specific but highly important sector of the academic profession—the younger generation now entering the profession.

Academics everywhere are part of a profession that has common elements worldwide. A small segment at the top of the profession is part of a globally mobile academic workforce. Most academics, however, are tied to their home countries and, in general, to a specific academic institution, since interinstitutional mobility for most is limited or impossible. There are additional distinctions created by institutional variations. For example, working conditions are quite different for professors in research universities than for teachers in a university devoted exclusively to teaching. There are variations by field and discipline as well. As Burton Clark has pointed out, the academic profession is composed of "small worlds, different worlds" (Clark 1987; Becher and Trowler 2001). Thus, global generalization is difficult—yet, common realities are facing the professoriate.

Of special importance are the people in the younger generation of the academic profession. They are not only the future of the entire academic enterprise, but they have special significance because in most countries the academic profession in general is aging and large numbers will be leaving the profession in the immediate future. Further, postsecondary education has expanded dramatically in much of the world in the past thirty years, creating the need for larger numbers of new academics, while in many countries, there have been insufficient numbers of appropriately trained postsecondary teachers. The overall quality and levels of preparation of the academic profession in much of the world has declined in recent years, creating even more pressure on higher education. Indeed, while there are no accurate statistics, it is likely that the majority of teachers standing in front of a class at a postsecondary institution now has the equivalent of a bachelor's degree! This is not the case in all countries and certainly not in the industrialized world, but it is reality in many places—especially in parts of the world that have seen recent rapid expansion.

One would expect that the market demand for young academics would improve salaries and working conditions in an effort to attract bright teachers and researchers. However, this has not happened. Indeed, in much of the world the terms and conditions of academic work have deteriorated. Even in the United States, fewer than half of new appointments to colleges and universities are on the traditional "tenure track" that leads to a career track (Cummings and Finkelstein 2011). Although statistics are scarce, it is clear that a growing proportion of the academic profession worldwide has part-time or otherwise unstable appointments. While the numbers of academics have expanded to meet growing student demand, the nature and conditions of appointments have become less satisfactory. The situation for those who are entering the profession tends to be least satisfactory—in terms of salaries, terms and conditions of service, contractual arrangements including security of tenure, building a career, and participation in the governance of the university.

Although without accurate statistics, most agree that the overall qualifications of twenty-first-century academics have declined in response to massification and the dramatic expansion of enrollments and access everywhere (Altbach, Reisberg, and Rumbley 2010). Fewer academics hold a doctoral degree. As a proportion of the total, fewer are engaged in research of any kind. More hold part-time appointments and fewer hold career-track academic appointments. Most academics globally cannot live a middle-class lifestyle relevant to their country with their academic salaries alone—thus, moonlighting and other remuneration are necessary. These realities hit younger academics particularly hard.

The Global Policy Environment

Debates and policies—relating to higher education generally, to the academic profession, and to younger academics—are unfavorable to the professoriate and especially to younger academics. Indeed, with no discussion of the role of the academic profession, there seems to be an assumption that higher education does not need to be concerned with how the academic profession fits into the changes envisaged by policy makers. There is a general consensus that significant change is needed in higher education. The themes that can be discerned in international and national debates are among the following:

- The financing of higher education must be significantly altered, so that academic institutions and students pay for most of the costs of education. Impelled by enrollment expansion that most countries find difficult to support and a changing philosophy of higher education that stresses the "private good" benefit to students, the state seeks to reduce expenditure for higher education.
- Linked to financing reforms, universities are asked to become more "marketized," earning income in various ways, charging more tuition, and in general becoming less dependent on public sources of income.
- Postsecondary studies and degree structures should be increasingly based on employability.
- Research should be "practical" and preferably funded by links with industry.
- Learning outcomes should be measured and quantified and used not only to measure student accomplishment but also the effectiveness of the academic profession.
- The use of information technology should be expanded, mainly as a cost-cutting strategy.

- Increased accountability is necessary to control costs and measure effectiveness of academic institutions and systems.

These are examples of trends in contemporary policy discussions, and many of the changes that have taken place in higher education in recent decades have reflected these and similar concerns. Regardless of the necessity or usefulness, these initiatives are largely negative for the academic profession. They place constraints on academic autonomy, ask for increased "productivity," reduce emphasis on research autonomy and often funding, and deemphasize basic research. Increased emphasis on the use of information technology for delivering courses and degree programs place burdens on academics to develop and deliver new programs, many of which may end up eliminating jobs. Although these and other initiatives affect all parts of the academic profession equally, younger academics likely must shoulder more of the burdens—for example, of online learning—than their senior colleagues, because they typically have less autonomy in their careers. Further, young scholars may choose not to join the profession at all due to deteriorating working conditions.

Salaries and Remuneration

Salaries have not kept pace with competing remuneration in fields requiring similar skills. In a study of academic salaries and contracts in 28 countries, with significant variations among countries, in no nation did academic salaries compare favorably with competing fields (Altbach, Reisberg, Yudkevich, Androushchak, and Pacheco 2012). And in many cases, salaries for younger scholars were much lower than for those in senior ranks—low enough so that a middle-class lifestyle could not be maintained.

Increasingly, other career options are attractive for well-educated and bright young people—even more than is the case for senior academics—and thus academe is increasingly unappealing. Other emerging fields such as information technology, biotech, consulting of all kinds, and finance pay much more attractive salaries—and seem more exciting and welcoming.

Academic salaries are not only in general fairly unattractive, but starting salaries have probably deteriorated more than senior remuneration. Further, in an increasing number of countries, the gulf between starting salaries and top salaries has become greater—part of a trend toward inequality in many societies and in academe as well. Younger academics may have to wait a long time to reach the top of the salary scale.

Further, in many countries academic salaries are not linked to "market conditions"—that is, university salaries in high-demand and well-compensated fields such as management or information technology cannot compare with what is offered by employers outside of academe. In these cases, academic salaries are the same for all fields and all universities, making it more difficult to recruit top candidates to highly compensated fields and disciplines. Further, there was little or no differentiation of salaries among universities with different missions or locations. Research universities often provided the same salary structure as teaching-oriented universities, even though academics in the research sector have greater earning capacity—both within the country and internationally, than their colleagues at less prestigious institutions. And there was little recognition of varying living costs, based on location or other variables. Again, the absence of market-based salaries affects younger scholars most, because they enter at the bottom of the scale and are also most likely to be recruited by nonuniversity employers.

Perhaps the most serious salary problem for younger academics is the inability to enjoy a middle-class lifestyle with an academic salary—particularly important for people establishing families. Academics after all do not generally enter the profession to earn high salaries but must be able to live appropriately according to the standards of their societies. In the 28-country salary survey, fewer than half of the countries offered middle-class salaries (Altbach, Reisberg, Yudkevich, Androushchak, and Pacheco 2012).

Mobility—Local and International

From a global perspective, job mobility for academics is unusual. With no accurate data, anecdotal evidence suggests that very few academics are mobile either within their home countries or internationally. Thus, for most beginning academics, the job that they obtain is likely to be the only position they hold during their careers. Although there is some mobility, it is likely to be within the same category of institution. Thus, extraordinarily few academics can move from an unselective teaching-focused institution to a research university. Obtaining a suitable and appropriate initial position is, therefore, of great importance. In an increasingly difficult academic job market, obtaining a position that matches an individual's interests and qualifications is not easy—and mobility from that job can be quite challenging.

Even in countries with a reputation for interinstitutional mobility, such as those in North America and western Europe, mobility is often limited to the upper segments of the academic system and in any case often happens early in the academic career (Huang, Finkelstein, and Rostan 2013). Once settled, most academics stay put. Those who are highly mobile tend to be well-known scholars and scientists who publish a lot and have reputations beyond their home institutions.

International mobility is even more unusual. Although a good deal of global academic mobility exists, much of it is among senior professors. There are several rather distinct kinds of global mobility. The best known is among top scholars who are hired away from their home countries, often for large salaries. This occurs mainly among the top universities in the developed countries, although occasionally "stars" will be hired from other institutions. A few places, such as Hong Kong and Singapore, hire internationally to obtain a diverse and high-quality academic cadre. Much larger numbers of academics are hired by universities in countries that do not produce a sufficient number of academics for themselves. Examples include Saudi Arabia, where a majority of academics are non-Saudis, mostly from the Islamic world, and most of the Arabian Gulf nations, which hire more broadly. A number of African countries hire nonlocal faculty, as well.

Although there is no information concerning the age of globally mobile academics hired by countries such as Saudi Arabia, they seem to be of all ages. Many younger academics who cannot find good jobs at home go onto the international market. In many cases, foreign faculty are not offered permanent jobs and must settle for renewable contracts.

Closed Labor Markets and Inbreeding

In many countries, academic hiring markets are not open, creating special problems for younger faculty, who are unlikely to be known by the professional community in their fields during their early careers (Altbach 2003). Open positions may not be widely advertised. Hiring may be done through informal contacts among senior professors or through the use of various types of personal influence. In China, *guanxi* (personal influence) is widely practiced in academic hiring and promotion as well as more broadly in society. In some countries, it is well known that universities will hire graduates only in a small circle of similar institutions. In the

United States, for example, research universities typically hire graduates with PhDs from other research universities and seldom from elsewhere in the system (Caplow and McGee 2001).

In some cases, especially in Latin America, the situation is different but still creates problems. In some countries, such as Argentina, available academic positions must be widely announced and applicants subjected to a formal "contest" for each position. The process is generally quite lengthy and public, creating stress for candidates. In practice, on many occasions the positions are already reserved for identified candidates and the contest is symbolic.

A common practice among academic systems worldwide is inbreeding—appointing faculty members from among the graduates of the hiring university. This practice is surprisingly common globally and might well be a factor in close to half of the world's academic appointments. Most agree inbreeding is detrimental for a vibrant and open academic profession by closing academic labor markets, ensuring that younger academics are dependent on their senior colleagues, and limiting new ideas from academic departments and faculties. Inbreeding creates a kind of client relationship between junior and senior academics that may last throughout the academic career.

Career Structures

Younger academics are especially concerned about building a successful career in academe. They want assurance that they can enter the academic profession and build a successful career. One of the attractions of the American academic system is the "tenure track" arrangement, which permits entry into the profession as an assistant professor and a clearly defined path for promotion up the ranks, with rigorous evaluations at several stages, and typically the award of tenure (permanent appointment) after promotion to associate professor on the sixth year. Although standards and requirements for promotion vary substantially by institution, patterns are similar throughout the system. In recent years, the proportion of tenure-track appointments in the United States has declined substantially—fewer than half of new appointments—with the rest being full-time contract appointments or part-time jobs, creating deteriorating conditions for young academics. Current estimates are that fewer than half of those teaching in American higher education today are on the traditional "tenure track" (Schuster and Finkelstein 2006).

In some countries, such as Germany, career structures are highly complex and offer many barriers for younger academics, who must frequently change jobs and wait for a small number of senior positions to open. In general, academic systems with a "chair system," in which a very limited number of senior positions exist at the top of departments or faculties, provide fewer opportunities for young scholars and are less attractive.

A substantial but declining number of countries retain a civil service model of academic appointments. Typically, this means that when a person is appointed to a junior academic position, he or she receives an immediate permanent appointment with promotions and salary increases largely based on time in place rather than performance or productivity. New appointments thus have substantial job security, but little incentive for productivity, and universities have few ways of rewarding effective performance or punishing poor productivity.

Without question, a clearly articulated career structure encourages new entrants to the academic profession, by making it clear that productivity will be rewarded and promotion and increases in salary are integral to employment and the culture of the university. Many countries lack such career structures, thus making the professoriate less attractive to young academics. Senior scholars have somehow maneuvered the system to achieve a measure of success and thus are less concerned.

The deterioration of career structures for young academics is without question—one of the most serious problems facing new entrants to the profession—and a key deterrent to making a decision to enter the academic profession. In many countries, the path to a stable career in academe is simply unclear.

The Rise of the Private Sector

Private universities are the fastest-growing segment of higher education worldwide. Although the proportion of private enrollment has remained fairly stable in North America and Western Europe, numbers have expanded dramatically in much of the rest of the world. Latin America now has more than half of its students in private higher education. East Asia has traditionally been dominated by the private sector, and Southeast Asia has a rapidly growing private sector. In general, the new private sector serves a "mass" clientele and is relatively low quality. Much of the sector is for-profit, even in countries where there are restrictions against profit-making higher education. Typically, students prefer to study at public universities.

Unsurprisingly, the terms and conditions of academic work in the new private higher education institutions are inferior to what is found in the public sector, creating special problems for younger academics. Very few of these institutions offer secure full-time appointments or opportunities for promotion. They often hire young faculty and also some retired older professors, but do not keep them employed for a long time. Salaries tend to be low, and there are few benefits. The very large majority of people who are hired are part-time instructors who receive small stipends for their direct teaching.

There are some exceptions to this rather bleak picture: there are a small number of nonprofit private universities, including the traditional Catholic universities in Latin America, the older private institutions in Japan and South Korea, and a few new nonprofit private institutions in Turkey and several other countries. In general, however, the private sector has created an underclass of teachers who cannot make a career by working in these institutions. Private universities, where they existed, were traditionally nonprofit, high quality, and widely respected. While these institutions continue to exist, the nature of the private higher education sector has dramatically changed and, along with the change, has come vastly deteriorated prospects for a stable and productive academic career.

Trends in Graduate Education

Like much else in higher education, the gulf between high-quality and substandard preparation for the academic profession has grown, creating problems for younger academics. Expanding enrollments have created a need for more academics to teach, particularly in the new institutions catering to mass enrollments—with students who are much more diverse in backgrounds, social class, and abilities, than the small number of elite students traditionally attending universities. As was noted, graduate education (termed postgraduate in the United Kingdom and some other places) has lagged far behind the demand for teachers in postsecondary education worldwide. Thus, graduate education is rapidly expanding in many countries (Nerad and Heggelund 2003).

Traditionally, the large majority of academics had graduate training—either a master's degree or, in many countries, a doctorate. These academics were largely educated in respected research universities, which chose students fairly carefully and where quality was generally maintained. To meet mass demand, graduate education has expanded significantly. Almost a century ago, American universities that were not experienced in offering advanced degrees and had no significant research profile began to offer graduate degrees—creating second- and third-tier PhD producers, and even a wider range of master's offerings. Graduates of these institutions typically could not aspire to jobs at top universities, but usually obtained positions at institutions mainly focusing on teaching. Thus, a pecking order developed among universities offering advanced degrees. In the twenty-first century, graduate education, particularly at the master's level, has expanded to the Internet, and degrees in many fields are offered through distance education. Some "professional doctorates" are now offered online, as well.

In many countries, all institutions with the title of university were expected to focus on research and offer advanced degrees. This is the case in much of Europe. Universities that traditionally offered only small graduate programs expanded them to meet the new demand. Thus, the quality of universities offering advanced degrees became more diverse, and the quality on average probably declined. This vastly more complex marketplace for graduate education has created challenges for young scholars and scientists in terms of choosing the appropriate university, and ensuring that the degrees offered will yield success in employment. In some countries and fields, there has recently been an oversupply of doctorates, while in many others there are severe shortages.

Graduate education, even more than higher education generally, has become internationalized. The proportion of international graduate students attending top global institutions is much higher than for undergraduate students. Many academic departments, particularly in science, technology, engineering, and mathematics fields, depend on international students to maintain enrollments. Doctoral graduates, particularly from top universities, find jobs globally. English is increasingly the medium of instruction at the graduate level in some parts of the world, further internationalizing institutions, and student populations. Young scholars look globally for the best departments and universities—and for the most attractive scholarship opportunities.

There are basically two models of graduate education at the doctoral level: the American pattern of what the British call the "taught doctorate" and the European "research doctorate" orientation. The American system requires a considerable amount of course work as well as a dissertation, while the European arrangement mainly consists of a dissertation written under the supervision of a faculty mentor. The European system assumes that the student will have a detailed background in his or her field, because of the specialized pattern of most European undergraduate programs. Some European universities are moving to require more course work. Other parts of the world have adopted one of these models or a combination of both. An additional complication exists in a few countries such as Russia and Germany, which require a second doctoral thesis for appointment to senior positions.

These trends affect younger academics. Competition for entry to many of the top universities has become stiffer. A differentiated graduate education system means that those who obtain degrees from lower-tier graduate schools typically cannot find jobs in research universities. Changing patterns in doctoral curricula are sometimes difficult to understand. Budgetary problems in many universities have meant that the attention paid to students has decreased—and the quality of programs has to some extent declined. The job market was at one time fairly simple—senior professors were expected to find jobs for their students. This paternalistic arrangement, perhaps practical for small and elite systems, has for the most part disappeared. Further, the cost of graduate education has gone up in some countries, and scholarship and other financial support have decreased.

Governance and Autonomy

Traditionally, one of the attractions of the academic career is participation in academic decision making and enjoying a sense of autonomy. Several general trends may be observed globally in the organization of universities that affect governance and both institutional and personal autonomy. It must be noted first that in many countries and academic institutions there has never been a great deal of faculty involvement in governance or individual autonomy; and in these cases, the status quo has not changed.

Indian undergraduate colleges, of which there are more than 30,000, have never enjoyed much institutional or academic autonomy. They are highly bureaucratized, with most power and authority concentrated in the hands of the principal. Further, because most colleges are affiliated to a university, much academic authority over curriculum and other matters is in the hands of university authorities (Agarwal 2009). Many academic systems, while differing in the details, offer little institutional or academic autonomy—and the academic profession has little autonomy or creative freedom to develop the curriculum.

In general, research universities and other postsecondary institutions at the top of the academic ladder have more institutional autonomy and offer academic staff more freedom in their teaching and research. In most cases, research universities have governance arrangements that provide significant authority to the academic staff, and often "shared governance" in which academics share authority with administrators, and in some countries, especially in Latin America, with students. Typically, academic senates or other representative bodies of the faculty exercised considerable authority over academic matters.

The traditional European pattern of governance gave most authority to the senior professors, enhanced by the election of the rector for a fixed term by the faculty. This pattern of academic authority was predominant in much of continental Europe until the 1960s, when university reform movements gave some power to students and younger academics. The American research universities shared governance between administration and faculty—with external boards of trustees holding legal authority, but typically devolving much of it to academic authorities.

Young academics had little authority in the European universities that were dominated by senior chair-holding professors. This arrangement, stemming from the origins of the research university in Germany in the early nineteenth century, gave immense power to the senior chair-holding professor who dominated each discipline. The disciplines were organized around the chair, who had authority to hire junior scholars, and typically dominated them. This organizational pattern came to dominate much of continental Europe and Japan. The American system was more democratic, with its department-based structure that provided participation to all faculty members on most issues, and thus some participation by junior academics. The British arrangement was somewhere between these two models and was influential in South Asia and Africa (Shils 1997).

The "golden age" of governance has, for almost a half century, been under pressure from massification, demands for accountability, and increased authority exercised by state authorities. In general, faculty authority has been weakened, and administrative power along with governmental influence has increased. All of this has decreased autonomy as well as the influence of faculty over academic decisions—with deterioration in the attractiveness of academic work, as a result.

The impact of these forces on younger faculty has been particularly acute. As noted, in many institutions and countries, young academics have limited authority in any case. What power that has remained with the professoriate is largely in the hands of senior faculty.

Attitudes and Young Academics

With the litany of woes that have been discussed here, it may seem surprising that anyone would choose to join academe now. Yet, the Changing Academic Profession international survey of academics in nineteen countries shows that the academic profession in general, and younger academics in particular, are, in many countries, not terribly dissatisfied with their chosen profession (Teichler, Arimoto, and Cummings 2013). The survey offers two kinds of evidence related to the satisfaction of academics with their jobs and careers: one item requiring respondents to rate their level of overall job satisfaction on a five-point Likert scale from low to high; another item asking respondents for their level of agreement with the statement: "If I had it to do over again, I would not choose an academic career again." Career satisfaction is defined as disagreement or strong disagreement with the statement.

There are substantial differences in overall job satisfaction among the nineteen Changing Academic Profession countries, ranging from 87 percent satisfied in Mexico and more than 70 percent in the Netherlands, Japan, and Korea; to barely 40 percent in the United Kingdom; and barely half in Australia and Portugal. Overall, satisfaction levels seem to track fairly closely with financial pressures, especially government funding cuts, on the system—such as in the United Kingdom and Australia. In most cases, job and career satisfaction are related—with the United States serving as one of the clearest exceptions. In the American case, career satisfaction is considerably higher than overall job satisfaction, reflecting perhaps high satisfaction with the high predictability of the U.S. tenure system.

The differences in the levels of satisfaction expressed by senior and junior academics seem rather small, related to the other "objective" indicators of career opportunities for the two subgroups—with the possible exceptions of places like China, where the opportunity structure for new entrants is quite favorable. Thus, junior academics tend to express levels of satisfaction that are significantly higher than their objective prospects. Ultimately, it may be that new academics—those who have managed to earn some kind of foothold in the system—are relatively grateful or sanguine about their prospects. Thus, it is no doubt the case that many academic systems, especially in the advanced economies, are losing young doctorates who ultimately succumb to the discouragement at their prospects.

Conclusion

In the twenty-first century, the academic profession does not offer an alluring future for young scholars and scientists. Access to the job market, levels of remuneration, career prospects, and terms and conditions of academic work are all problematical everywhere. Although the academic profession in general can be considered to be in crisis worldwide, the difficulties for young academics are especially serious. The challenge is especially grave in the emerging private higher education sector—where the chance for a normal career is largely absent.

All of this is problematic for several reasons:

- Massification has created a need for many more postsecondary teachers.
- In many countries, particularly in the industrialized nations, large numbers of academics are retiring, thus creating shortages.
- The emergence of the global knowledge economy has created a need for a cadre of creative research-oriented academics to staff the research universities located at the top of academic systems worldwide—a "special breed" of highly educated young scholars and scientists.

Although higher education is, in many countries, a topic of major debate in the media and in policy circles, such topics as accountability, cost reduction, university-industry collaboration, and others are themes of debate. There is much discussion about "disruptive innovation" and the need for postsecondary education to provide training for employment. And there is some criticism of the academic profession for its alleged conservatism and unwillingness to change. But there is no recognition of the needs of the academic profession or the necessity for an effective and committed academic workforce to serve the needs of higher education.

Despite all this, young people continue to enroll in graduate programs and aspire to work in universities. The lure of "the life of the mind" remains strong despite all of the evident difficulties. This is, perhaps, the hope for the future—the indomitable spirit, intellectual commitment, and curiosity of a sufficient number of young people to commit themselves to an academic environment that hardly deserves them.

Acknowledgment

I am indebted to Martin J. Finkelstein for data and analysis of the Changing Academic Profession survey that is reported in the "Attitudes and Young Academics" section.

References

Agarwal, Pawan. 2009. *Indian Higher Education: Envisioning the Future.* New Delhi: Sage.

Altbach, Philip G., ed. 2003. *The Decline of the Guru: The Academic Profession in Developing and Middle-Income Countries.* New York: Palgrave Macmillan.

Altbach, Philip G., Liz Reisberg, and Laura E. Rumbley. 2010. *Trends in Global Higher Education: Tracking an Academic Revolution.* Rotterdam, Netherlands: Sense.

Altbach, Philip G., Liz Reisberg, Maria Yudkevich, Gregory Androushchak, and Iván F. Pacheco, eds. 2012. *Paying the Professoriate: A Global Comparison of Compensation and Contracts.* New York: Routledge.

Becher, Tony, and Paul R. Trowler. 2001. *Academic Tribes and Territories.* Buckingham, UK: Open University Press.

Caplow, Theodore, and Reece J. McGee. 2001. *The Academic Marketplace.* New Brunswick, NJ: Transaction.

Clark, Burton. 1987. *The Academic Life: Small Worlds, Different Worlds.* Princeton, NJ: Carnegie Foundation for the Advancement of Teaching.

Cummings, William K., and Martin J. Finkelstein. 2011. *Scholars in the Changing American Academy: New Context, New Rules and Roles.* Dordrecht, Netherlands: Springer.

Horta, Hugo. 2013. "Deepening our understanding of academic inbreeding effects on research information exchange and scientific output: New insights for academic based research." *Higher Education* 65: 487–510.

Huang, Futao, Martin J. Finkelstein, and Michele Rostan, eds. 2013. *The Internationalization of the Academy: Changes, Realities and Prospects.* Dordrecht, Netherlands: Springer.

Nerad, Maresi, and Mimi Heggelund, eds. 2003. *Toward a Global PhD? Forces and Forms in Doctoral Education Worldwide.* Seattle: University of Washington Press.

Schuster, Jack H., and Martin J. Finkelstein. 2006. *The American Faculty: The Restructuring of Work and Careers.* Baltimore: Johns Hopkins University Press.

Shils, Edward. 1997. "The Academic Ethos under Strain." In *The Order of Learning: Essays on the Contemporary University*, edited by E. Shils, 137–162. New Brunswick, NJ: Transaction.

Teichler, Ulrich, Akira Arimoto, and William K. Cummings. 2013. *The Changing Academic Profession: Major Findings of a Comparative Study.* Dordrecht, Netherlands: Springer.

Chapter 2

Brazil

Opportunities and Challenges for the New Generation in a Diverse Academic Environment

Elizabeth Balbachevsky

In the last decade, higher education in Brazil experienced massive expansion, going from fewer than 2.1 million students enrolled at the undergraduate level in 2000 to more than 6.7 million in 2011. In the same period, the number of academic positions available grew 91.3 percent, from 197,700 to 378,300. Growth in numbers was followed by new dynamics that utterly changed the country's higher education landscape, creating a new, more complex scenario for the new generation of scholars who are now entering in Brazilian higher education.

The main challenges faced by the new generation come from three different sources: first, the strong fragmentation of the academic profession in the country, which is a consequence of the size and relevance of private higher education. Next is the intense differentiation that characterizes both the private and public higher education sectors. Third, there are the pressures posed by government policies and society's expectations for higher education massification. This chapter intends to analyze some of the most relevant changes faced by the new generation of academics in Brazil. It starts with a brief description of the country's higher education landscape, describes some of the most relevant policy dynamics that impact higher education, and analyzes how these changes create new demands for the new generation of young scholars in the country and frame the opportunities open to this new generation.

Data used in this analysis come mainly from two sources: information collected in a nationwide representative survey of academics carried out in 2007, as part of the efforts of the international research network "The Changing Academic Profession"[1] (CAP), and the official data on Brazilian higher education collected by the statistics office of the Ministry of Education, INEP, with special attention to the Brazilian Census on Higher Education, carried out annually by this institute since the mid-1980s.

Brazilian Higher Education: Main Traits

The Brazilian Census of Higher Education shows that, in 2011, Brazil had more than 2,300 higher education institutions. Although by law all these institutions are supposed to provide similar undergraduate instruction—all of them being entitled to grant bachelor degrees—the differences among them are immense. In order to grasp the nature of these differences, one should first consider the massive size of the private sector in Brazil. In fact, private institutions comprise 87 percent of all higher education institutions and absorb 73.7 percent of all undergraduate enrollments in Brazil.

The huge size of the private sector means that most of the opportunities open to the new generation of young academics are to be found in private institutions. In fact, in 2011 these institutions were responsible for 60 percent of all academic positions in the country. The private sector also experienced the sharpest growth in the last decade. From 2000 to 2011, the number of academic positions open in the public sector grew 71.2 percent, while the number of academic positions in the private sector grew 107.5 percent. Although most of the full-time contracts are in the public sector (67.5 percent), this kind of contract also experienced a sharp growth in the private sector. In 2000, only 21 percent of all academic positions offered by private institutions were full-time contracts. In 2011, 32.5 percent of all academic contracts in the private sector offered full-time employment. In spite of the improvement indicated by these figures, contract conditions in the private sector are still grim: academics working in the private sector have no prospect for tenure or any kind of job stability, and most of them (67.5 percent) have access only to part-time or hourly contracts. For young scholars, these conditions are still worse. Inside the private sector, access to full-time contracts tends to be a prerogative of seniority, which means that almost all positions open to young scholars are hourly teaching positions, that offer little support for research activities or any other academic benefits.

The public sector is responsible for 26.3 percent of the undergraduate enrolments and offers 44 percent of the academic positions in the country. The great majority of these positions (81.3 percent) are full-time, stable contracts. Employment in the public sector also improves the opportunities for support for research activities. Access to public sector employment is regulated by tenders, which are open nationally. These tenders tend to be quite competitive, especially for the young scholars now entering the academic profession. In the last decade, holding a doctorate became a must for the young scholar looking for a position in the public sector. In 2011, 66.5 percent of all positions filled by academics with doctorates were in the public sector.

Patterns of Institutional Stratification

Brazilian higher education is not only diverse, it is also highly stratified. In the public sector, the main dividing line is the one created by graduate education. In the 20 *public research universities*, graduate enrollment represents more than 30 percent of total enrollment, and together with a few Federal Research Institutes, they are responsible for more than 85 percent of all doctoral degrees granted in the country (CGEE 2011). These universities attract many PhD holders, and thus are also able to capture the public resources to support research. Federal Research Institutes are specialized institutions, each devoted to a field or a subject. These sixteen institutes are highly relevant to graduate education, and offer a number of programs at the master's and doctoral level (for more detail, see: http://www.mct.gov.br/index.php/content/view/741.html?execview=). The remaining institutions are classified as *regional public universities* and are characterized by their focus on undergraduate education. These institutions play a relevant role as a regional source of skills and knowledge.

Inside the private sector, differences are also vast. At the top, a small number of *elite private institutions* cater to students from wealthier families. These institutions have the ability to engage a large proportion of PhD degree-holders on their academic staff, using academic credentials as a source of prestige for the institutions. *Mass-oriented private institutions* represent the great majority of Brazilian higher education institutions. They hold the lowest position in this stratified system, and are confined to a kind of commodity-like market of mass undergraduate education, where they compete for students by offering the least expensive education possible.

The stratification of institutional environments creates important differences regarding the conditions of academic work. Table 2.1 explores

Table 2.1. Work conditions and academic experience by sector

	Type of institution				
	Public research institutes	Public research universities	Public regional universities	Private elite institutions	Private mass institutions
Full-time employed	95.9%	90.3%	79.7%	51.8%	22.2%
Have contract with another academic institution	16.3%	7.1%	14.5%	24.0%	39.0%
Work experience outside the academic market	24.5%	18.8%	30.7%	50.9%	66.7%
Have done research in the last 2 years	95.9%	93.9%	83.1%	71.9%	61.0%
Have access to external support for research	73.5%	57.9%	30.1%	27.5%	8.6%
Have generated academic products (last 3 years)	93.9%	88.3%	75.3%	63.7%	55.2%
Have international research connections	65.3%	37.6%	22.0%	27.5%	9.0%
Teach only at undergraduate level	15.4%	46.1%	62.5%	64.0%	92.9%

Source: Brazil 2007—CAP survey

some relevant aspects of this situation, using the information provided by academics interviewed in the last national survey on the Brazilian academic profession, carried out in 2007 under the international research network "The Changing Academic Profession."

Full-time contracts are the norm inside the research institutes and the public research universities, which is not the pattern to be found in many other public Latin American universities. Research-oriented institutions also present a more competitive environment, calling for greater commitment to academic activities. For example, inside these institutions there are only a small number of academics with working commitments outside their walls, and the proportion of academics who are also active researchers (doing research and publishing, with external support) is bigger than what is found in other institutions. Public regional institutions and private elite institutions have a more modest profile, but also do well in all dimensions considered here: they still have a great number of academics committed solely to the institution, and have a fair proportion of active researchers among their academic staff. The most relevant difference between them is the proportion of academics with work experience outside the academic market—academics with this profile represent 50 percent of the faculty employed in the private elite sector, but only 30 percent at the public regional universities. This figure does not come as a surprise, because institutions in the private elite sector usually boast their competence in providing excellent education oriented toward the job market, both at the undergraduate and graduate level. For them, faculty with sound, up-to-date experience of the job market is an asset, not a failure. Private mass-oriented institutions provide the poorest academic environment: they usually operate with part-time teachers,[2] many of them with commitments to other institutions or outside the academic market. Being teaching-only institutions, the teaching experience of their academics is usually confined to undergraduate instruction.

Young scholars entering each of the institutional environments described earlier will face diverse circumstances, typical of the kind of institution in which their professional lives begin. Most important, each institutional environment tends to emphasize different roles and to reinforce a different mix of competences.

Brazilian Academic Markets: Main Traits, Challenges, and Opportunities

Academic markets are complex not only because they tend to be highly formalized, but also because they are partially regulated by written laws and rules, and partially regulated by informal norms and customs known by all stakeholders but rarely articulated by anyone. When analyzing the modes of organization of the academic market in Europe, Christine Musselin (2005) proposes a typology based on the interplay between four factors or dimensions, some of them formal, others informal. Together, they create the roadmap for understanding career patterns in different countries.

The first factor is related to the selection device that organizes access to a specific academic position. In this dimension, Musselin (2005) defines two opposite mechanisms: the *concours*, where many candidates apply for a position open to recruitment or promotion, and situations in which selection depends on meeting specific criteria, and selection (or promotion) is decided without competition.

The second factor is related to the length and role assigned to the pretenure period. In this dimension, Musselin (2005) identifies two contrasting processes: pretenure as a way to reveal competencies or pretenure as a time for apprenticeship. When the pretenure period is regarded as a way to reveal competencies, the division of work between tenured and nontenured positions is less marked than when the pretenure period is regarded as an apprenticeship (Musselin 2005).

The third factor relates to the balance between internal and external labor markets. Musselin (2005) proposes using the terminology *internal academic markets* for situations when career development occurs within a university and when internal rules and incentives "organize" such a development. On the other hand, *external academic markets* describe situations when ascent in the career depends on successfully being hired for positions open in other institutions.

Finally, the fourth factor relates to how and who is in charge of establishing the prices in the academic market. As noted by Musselin (2005), in few countries do those in charge of selecting new academic staff also have room to negotiate salaries, medical insurance, housing, and so on, with a job candidate. In other higher education systems, those in charge of selecting the new staff are never in charge of negotiating prices, mostly because salaries are fixed by bureaucratic rules applied uniformly through all institution.

The typology proposed by Musselin (2005) is useful also for understanding how academic markets are organized in Brazil, considering the differences from sector to sector and the different kinds of institutions. But one relevant point differentiates academic markets in mature and emerging countries and should be stressed here: in Brazil, as in many other emerging countries, the relationship between institutional rank, academic degree and prestige is far from linear.

Brazil, like many other emerging countries around the world, has been constantly plagued by shortcomings derived from the small pool of qualified academics from which to recruit faculty for its higher education institutions. Since 1930, when the first University Act was enacted in Brazil, the number of professionals holding doctoral degrees has been low, the same applying to those with international experience and competence for proposing and directing relevant research projects. Although this situation puts a premium on degrees, it also creates pressures for mitigating the need for a degree for ascending the academic career ladder. Even today, in some institutional environments, academics without a doctorate can be promoted to the rank of associate professor or even ascend to a full professorship, as long as they can provide "evidences of a satisfactory performance," in the eyes of their peers inside the particular university where they are employed. More relevant, this rule weakens the meritocratic norm that is usually supposed to constitute the core of any academic market. Although some young scholars may enter at the bottom of the career ladder when already holding a doctoral degree, in their professional life, they will usually encounter older colleagues with lesser formal qualifications (in terms of degrees held) but occupying positions of superiority within the institutional hierarchy. Also, it will not be unusual to find colleagues with lower academic performance occupying higher positions on the career ladder. The only way to accommodate the tensions that go with this situation is to mitigate the relevance of hierarchy inside the university, assuming that different career steps have no other relevance except for differences in earnings.

Notwithstanding, given the recent growth of the graduate layer inside the public sector and the complex process of internal differentiation that has taken place in both public and private sectors, the situation described above has disappeared in some institutions. This is clearly true inside the ones classified here as research universities. Here, one will usually find the expected linear relationship between expertise, academic performance, and career. But, even here, institutional hierarchies are much less marked. More important, these differences are assumed to be of no relevance when it comes to configuring the prerogatives and the autonomy academics have for organizing their daily professional life.

Career Prospects in the Public Sector

In the public sector, access to academic positions is always regulated through a competitive process organized under uniform rules. It starts with a written examination, includes a public inquiry into the candidates' academic background, which, in more competitive environments, includes an assessment of the candidates' research interests, followed by a formal lecture presented by the candidates to a selection committee. Because the appointment is supposed to last for the hired individual's entire academic life, the academic staff from the hiring department fiercely controls the entire process, from selecting the committee members to defining the themes covered by the written exam and the lectures.

Although the competitive hiring process always follows the same rules, the degree of competition is highly variable depending on the university's profile and the department's reputation. In order to be successful in a competitive search to fill an academic position in a highly prestigious department inside a research university, young candidates should have a competitive curriculum vitae, mostly measured in terms of their competence in raising funds for research and their publishing experience.

In order to improve their chances, it is common that after finishing their doctoral training, the would-be candidates undertake a long period of informal "internship," working as assistant researchers linked to a substantial research project under the responsibility of a university professor. In most cases, this period is covered with a postdoctoral scholarship. Postdoctoral scholarships are provided by science foundations, both at the federal and regional levels, and are open to newly graduated doctors (up to five to seven years after finishing the degree). Major research projects usually include a number of postdoctoral scholarships in their budget. Thus, using Musselin's (2005) typology, one could say that public research universities tend to recognize an apprenticeship period, partially covered by postdoc fellowships. During this period young scholars will develop their research activities under strict supervision of a senior researcher, usually as part of a research team that is highly structured and hierarchical. This is also the time when young scholars aspiring to a position in a prestigious university improve their portfolio of funded research and published materials.

Once successful in being hired to an academic position, by law, young scholars across the public sector are supposed to fulfill a probationary period before being entitled to all rights of a stable civil service contract. In research universities, during this period the young scholars assume responsibilities for teaching at the undergraduate level (which is a duty shared by all academics), and starts advising candidates at the master's level. Only after successfully advising a master's thesis to its conclusion and defense, will they be entitled to advise at the doctoral level.

As a member of the academic staff in a research university or a research institute, the young academic faces a competitive environment that tends to subsume the role of teacher to the role of researcher. Even when personally more inclined to teaching, young academics in this environment are pushed toward a more active role in research as a requisite for climbing the career ladder. In research universities, research tends to be institutionalized in collective structures, such as laboratories and research centers. Inside these collective research environments, young scholars have access to support, equipment, and assistance needed for doing successful research and for maximize recognition of their research products. On the other hand, young scholars tend to accommodate their personal academic interests to the ones defined by their seniors as central to one of these collective research structures.

In less competitive environments, like the ones found in most public regional universities, access to an academic position is less competitive. Although it is still organized through a competitive process, other issues may count more in favor of candidates than their actual academic profile. In regional universities situated in more remote areas, one relevant issue is the probability of the candidates settling down in the region and remaining at the university. Thus, holding a PhD may be important, but not decisive. A high profile in research outputs is not as relevant. In some cases it may even speak against the candidates, because it may be read as a clue of a low probability that the candidate will settle down and build their academic life in that university.

Inside regional universities, the young scholars newly hired are usually required to be in charge of the activities that are regarded as mere bureaucratic formalities by their older peers. Surprisingly, these activities may even include the position of head of the department, because, in such environments, this position is weak and devoid of any real decision-making power. For young scholars, the duty of being responsible for the department's bureaucracy represents a real burden. It severely constrains their commitment to academic work, in particular research and publishing, because of the long hours required to attend to all demands. Teaching at the undergraduate level also tends to dominate academic life for the majority of the academics at regional universities. Teaching at the graduate level is less usual. Regional universities tend to sustain few programs at the graduate level, and even these programs usually are limited to the master's level. On the other hand, compared to the situation faced by young scholars in research universities, more entrepreneurial young scholars in a regional university have more independence to pursue their own research interests and develop their own personal projects, even if on a more modest scale.

Inside a regional university, the young scholar will face a conflagrated academic environment, produced by contrasting values, worldviews, and aspirations held by different parts of the academic staff (Balbachevsky 2000). Inside these universities there is a strong subculture characterized by the primacy attributed to teaching vis-à-vis other academic commitments. This is a self-referent culture where "the professional identity is not defined by the individual's achievements as an independent scholar and researcher but by affiliation to an institution and a group with whom she/he shares daily problems, achievements, and routines of academic life" (Schwartzman and Balbachevsky 1996, 271). The young scholar entering this environment will have to make a choice between either a professional culture centered on the values of academic achievements or one centered on the egalitarian values supported by part of the local community.

This choice is not an easy one: inside regional universities, research is less structured and garners less support. Public universities in Brazil are not used to setting aside institutional funds for research, which means that the young scholar will need to compete for external support without access to the same kinds of networks that are available to the young scholars at research universities. For many young scholars in regional universities, research becomes an individual endeavor, limited by the lack of funds and institutional support, resulting in products of small impact and minimal recognition. For these young scholars, the best (but less accessible) alternative is to attach their project to a collective research effort organized inside a major national research network supported by the federal science agency. But, opportunities for this kind of networking are rare and tend to be concentrated in the fields and themes that are regarded as strategic by the relevant funding agencies.

On the other hand, accepting the predominant egalitarian culture may jeopardize the academic future of the young scholar. The faulty academic profile—measured in terms of research products—that is usually found among the academics supporting the egalitarian perspective creates a vicious circle where past poor performance precludes access to the means that could improve future results.

The public higher education sector in Brazil is marked by the prominence of internal markets. Once nominated as part of the academic staff of a public university, the young scholar has access to a de facto lifelong stable contract from the first day. Dismissing a colleague during the probationary period is something almost unheard of. Inside regional universities, progression in career is mostly determined by seniority. When the academic is hired before holding an academic degree, finishing the graduate studies may speed progression up the career ladder; but, if the young academic already holds a doctoral degree at the time she or he wins a competition for an academic position in a regional university, progression in the career is only a matter of time. In research-oriented universities, academic profile is a relevant issue, and progression in the career is a matter of both seniority and a portfolio of academic products and successfully funded research projects that should be presented when applying for a promotion.

Until 2012, the federal universities—the more relevant part of the public sector—were allowed to choose between opening new academic positions at the beginning of the career ladder (such as for teaching assistants, when candidates are not required to present a degree above the bachelor level) or opening these at the mid-career level, when the university could ask for a doctoral degree as a minimal requirement. The latter option was usually chosen by research-oriented universities. The practice of opening new positions at this level created a relevant external market in the public sector—many young scholars could start their academic career in a regional university and move to a more research-oriented institution after accumulating enough experience and research products.

The new law regulating the academic career in the federal system (law 12722/2012) closed this external market. Since December of 2012, the federal universities have been forbidden to open new mid-career positions. The only entry position is now as teaching assistant. The law also reinforced seniority as a necessary requisite for career progression, even inside research-oriented universities. Even PhD holders must enter as teaching assistants, and even if they are entitled to an increase in salary, they still will need to wait years before reaching the position of associate professor.

In all public sector institutions, the only position with a restricted number of places is the full professorship. Access to this position is done through a competitive process. But in many departments informal rules impose seniority as the main criterion for deciding who, among the associate professors, is entitled to apply for a new opening for a full professorship. In the federal system, until 2012, this competitive hiring process could also be open to external candidates (something that seldom happened). But the new law also closed this alternative. Since then, the contest for a full professorship is a closed process, open only to academics already in the university's career track. Nevertheless, one should also note that aside from an increase in salary, full professorship status creates no relevant prerogatives in the federal system.

State-owned institutions have room to organize their career patterns in different manners, but in general they tend to follow the pattern established by the federal system. The only major deviation from this norm is seen in the three universities belonging to the richest state in the federation, the state of São Paulo.[3] In these universities holding a PhD is a formal entry requirement to the academic profession. These universities also impose a postdoctoral degree, the *livre-docência*—an adaptation of the old German *Privatdozent*[4]—as a mandatory requirement for all candidates aspiring to the rank of full professorship.

Finally, in the public sector there is no negotiation regarding salaries or other benefits. The salaries are fixed by bureaucratic rules, and increases follow the strict and universal rules that apply to all academics.

Career Prospects in the Private Sector

As previously explained, the largest academic market in Brazil is found in the private sector. Access to a position in the private sector is mostly achieved through informal procurement. Usually it is the program coordinator who chooses the new faculty. Candidates are chosen if they fulfill some requirements, which may vary from one position to another and from one institution to another. The private sector does not offer tenure contracts, but each institution offers full-time contracts to a restricted number of academics, usually ones with major responsibilities inside the institution. Careers in the private sector mix academic performance and administrative responsibilities: young scholars improve their position as they assume more responsibilities in the institution's management. Promotion up the career ladder depends on performance—mostly as a teacher—but also as a manager. Most of the promotion in the private sector is done through the external market—it is by moving from one institution to another that young academics move up the career ladder and improve their contract conditions

Elite private institutions offer a more dynamic and diverse academic environment for young academics, but the contract conditions may vary a great deal. Positioned outside the benevolent umbrella of the public sector, private elite institutions cannot afford to offer the same generous terms of contract one finds in the public sector. Nevertheless, in order to be attractive to the families of the upper-middle class, they have to sustain a rich and dynamic academic environment. To accommodate these divergent needs, these institutions tend to diversify contract conditions across their academic staff. They usually have an academic core composed of well-regarded teachers, distinguished scholars, or acclaimed professionals. These professionals have access to well-paid positions that assure time for research and other academic activities. In some institutions, there is even a kind of "division of labor." Some academics are hired as researchers, with their performance measured by the number and quality of articles published; others are hired as lecturers, with their performance measured by their popularity among students; and finally, others are hired as consultants, with their performance measured by the number of contracts won.

Young scholars entering these institutions face a much harder situation than the one faced by young scholars in the public sector. Usually, they are hired as hourly teachers. Access to the institution's career track is negotiated on a case-by-case basis with the head of the department or program coordinator. Access and promotion depend on the young scholars' performance and the reputation they are able to build up as a teacher, a researcher, and/or as a consultant. If the young scholar is hired as a teacher, the large teaching load will be an obstacle for improving performance in the first years of employment. If hired as an assistant researcher or as junior consultant, the diverse experiences and contact with graduate students will create better career prospects. Even so, competition is high in the first years of employment and the choice between different roles and kinds of contract do not always depend on the candidate's profile—sometimes it simply depends on the profile of the positions available at the institution.

Inside private elite institutions, there is a minimal threshold for salaries and other benefits, but the candidates may negotiate increases in salary and other benefits, including the degree of support they expect to have for research-related activities. These negotiations are usually conducted by the one in charge of recruiting the new academic, but are supervised by the institution's chief executive officer.

Young scholars hired by institutions operating in the mass-oriented private sector face the worst contract and working conditions. These institutions offer the same terms of contract to almost all academics—an hourly teaching contract, with no career prospects. Even the largest private for-profit universities have to abide by the same ironclad rule: to charge the lowest possible tuition fees for the education they provide. Because most of their students come from poorer families and have to pay for their studies, the enrollment numbers experience sharp increases when the country's economy grows and deep declines in harsh times.[5] In these circumstances, the academic market functions as a cushion, softening the movement between the expansion and contraction cycles. It is easy to see that these conditions do not provide an environment conducive to a proper academic life.

For-profit universities have a career ladder, and hire some academics with full-time contracts, but access to these positions is very difficult. The career track is mandatory by law, but the proportion of academics accepted into the career track or holding a full-time contract is usually very small. Access to these positions is less influenced by actual academic performance than by the faith the institution has in the individual's commitment to the needs of the institution.

In spite of all these negative signals, the academic market inside the mass-oriented institutions experienced relevant changes in the past ten years. In response to the new pressures exerted by the federal regulatory body, these institutions opened their doors to young academics coming from the ever-expanding public graduate education system. The new professional profile has entailed differentiation and brought new tensions into these institutions. The graduate experience creates expectations of a more active academic life among the young scholars, which these institutions are not in a position to fulfill. Some of the tensions are being alleviated as some institutions develop a more entrepreneurial profile and explore alternatives in the market for skill training and lifelong learning. For other young, more ambitious academics, the contract as a lecturer in these institutions is supposed to be a transitional placement while waiting for an opening in the public sector or a move to an elite private institution. In the larger metropolitan areas, it is not unusual for young scholars, once finished with doctoral training, to combine evening lectures in mass-oriented private institutions with a fixed-term, part-time contract as an assistant researcher on a research project directed by a senior academic in a public university. Although this is regarded as an acceptable alternative, the large teaching load may prevent the young scholar from gaining enough research experience and outputs to build up a competitive profile that is needed for success in the competition for access to more dynamic academic environments.

Recent Trends and Policy Dynamics

The last decade of the twentieth century and the first of the twenty-first century were years of intense change across the Brazilian higher education landscape. Some of these movements produced convergent dynamics between private and public markets, while others pushed for stronger differentiation.

From the 1970s until the early 1990s, the private and public sectors coexisted with almost no point of contact.[6] Operating under different rules and with diverse goals, one sector almost ignored the other and recruited professionals in segregated markets. Private institutions recruited their academics among their own alumni, but here academic credentials did not matter. Thus, instructors enlisted by the private sector were poorly qualified and totally ignorant of the rules of academic life. Public universities also relied on their alumni, but had the public graduate system to help meet their need for qualified faculty. At that time, there were plenty of scholarships available for candidates both at the master's and doctoral level.[7] Teaching at a private higher education institution, while working on a dissertation, signaled a disadvantage rather than an advantage in the curriculum of a would-be academic.

This picture started to change in the beginning of 1990s, when a new education act, the *Lei de Diretrizes e Bases da Educação* (LDB), was enacted. The new regulatory framework required the private sector to increase the academic credentials of their staff. The new requirements opened a new market for young scholars coming out of the ever-expanding public graduate education sector. This happened at a time when stiffer rules, enacted by the federal government as part of the toolkit for fighting the high inflations rates, temporarily closed the doors for young academics to employment in the public sector.

The new regulatory framework was followed by large initiatives for evaluating undergraduate education and reinforcing the evaluation of graduate education already in place. In the same period, the leading agency for funding science and research, CNPq, introduced significant reforms in its program portfolio. The reforms established a competitive environment for research support in general and concentrated resources in some major initiatives favoring consolidated research groups working in networks with emerging ones. The new, more demanding environment was noted by academics of all institutions, both in the private and public sectors. When, in 1989, the first national survey on the academic profession, asked if teaching performance was evaluated by the institution, 44 percent of the respondents gave a negative answer. In the 2007, this proportion dropped to only 6.5 percent (Schwartzman and Balbachevsky 2013).

Since the 2000s, expanding access to higher education has become another issue in Brazilian higher education's already overloaded policy agenda. In 2002, the government launched the program "University for All," directed toward the private sector. The program exchanged institutional tax rebates for tuition exemption for low-income and minority students. Public universities were also encouraged to implement quota programs in order to lower the entrance threshold for candidates coming from public high schools and minority groups.[8] In 2012, a bill reserving 50 percent of the enrollments in federal universities for students from low-income families and minority groups faced no relevant opposition in the Congress and was enacted by the executive branch in record time.

In 2007, the federal government launched a major program for the federal universities. The program—known by its acronym REUNI—provided support, funds, and new academic positions to encourage expanding enrollments, opening new bachelor programs and, in particular, establishing evening courses targeting nontraditional students. Under REUNI, enrollments in the federal system increased 35.6 percent in three years and the number of positions for incoming freshmen in bachelor programs in federal universities grew 108 percent, but the number of academic positions grew only 25.4 percent.

A note must be added regarding the situation of the most prestigious universities in the country, the three universities owned by the richest state in the country, São Paulo. In 1987, these universities reached a comfortable situation of ample and unrestricted autonomy. From that year on, the three universities had guaranteed access to 8 percent of the major state revenue, a tax applied to all commercial or service transactions occurring inside the state. This autonomy, coupled with a dynamic academic environment, provided room for the growth of a strong academic culture geared toward research and graduate education. Nevertheless, these universities are also under pressure from society and the government to expand access at the undergraduate level.

Relations between the private sector and government have been characterized by an adversarial relationship and legal confrontations. The government's initiatives toward this sector have a permanent *leitmotif*: to push strict control and restrictions. The instruments for steering the private sector are increasingly formalized, focused on micro-level regulation,[9] and tending to become almost unintelligible. Such developments have reinforced trends for consolidation inside the mass-oriented private sector, with the growth of mega teaching-only institutions, catering to students with poor academic profiles. In these private for-profit universities, scale pays for the luxuries imposed by the federal rules. The growth of these mega for-profit universities also introduced new dynamics in the academic market. One common feature of undergraduate instruction inside these institutions is its commoditization—all courses are framed in the same way, and organized around a fixed number of classes. Course content is standardized in handouts distributed to all students attending similar courses. The only role left to the academic staff is to lecture students following the fixed content and to perform the necessary evaluations. As one may expect, the growth of for-profit universities contributed to lower salary levels for instructors and increased the level of turnover in the academic market of the private sector.

In short, the dynamics outlined above reveal contradictory tendencies. The new legal framework pushes for more convergence and is responsible for creating relevant channels of contact between the academic job market in the public and private sector. For the first time, hiring academics holding a graduate degree became a goal for the private sector, and mobility between the private and public academic markets was strengthened. But, other policy dynamics tend to amplify the gaps that separate different academic trajectories. This situation makes decisions made early in the professional life crucial for defining the alternative paths open for young scholars.

In the public sector, increased competition and stringent performance exigencies for access to public funds for research call for a greater degree of professionalization in these activities. Young scholars interested in attaining a position inside a research university face increased pressures to enhance their portfolio of research products, which means spending some years after finishing the doctorate in an informal internship, sustained by a postdoc scholarship.

On the other hand, the pressure for quick growth of undergraduate enrollments at the federal universities created new tensions between the older academic cohort and the new staff hired to deal with the increased size of undergraduate body. The young generation hired to meet the needs of the expansion has extended teaching loads and works in much more precarious conditions. Many of the new campuses and programs are installed in provisional buildings with no infrastructure. Until recently, these tensions were eased by generous resources distributed through the REUNI initiative and other programs. This is not true anymore. Many young, well-qualified young scholars hired during this last expansion now realize that their expectation of becoming a full-fledged academic with good work conditions is a fraud. The extended strike that paralyzed all federal universities for more than three months in 2012 shows that tensions are already building up inside the federal sector.

The next section explores how the changing policy dynamics in Brazilian higher education have impacted the prospects faced by the new generations of scholars that are now entering the academic profession.

Mobility in the Academic Market

No official data are available regarding academic mobility between different institutions and market niches. Nevertheless, anecdotal evidence and personal observation by the author points out that academic mobility is quite low in Brazil, even if this picture has experienced some changes in the last few years. Changing institutional affiliation is more common in the first years of the academic career, when young scholars are in search of an institutional environment suitable for their academic ambitions. But, it is a very rare experience for mature academics to move from one institution to another. In the public sector, the uniform career standards and the fact that a relevant part of the academic salary comes from seniority gains make moves very costly. Among the more research-oriented public universities, mobility is almost zero. Once accepted into one of the most prestigious universities in the country, the probability that a young academic moves to another university is almost nil.

Mobility at the beginning of the career is more usual in public regional universities. Many young academics start their career in regional public universities and, after accumulating some experience, apply to a position in another institution regarded as more active in the relevant field, or even to a research university, searching for a more supportive environment for their ambitions as researchers and scholars.

Even this small amount of mobility inside the public sector tends to be curtailed in the later years, especially at the federal universities, as discussed above. Mobility from a private elite institution to a well-regarded public university is common. It is facilitated by the fact that private elite institutions tend to be geographically concentrated in the same regions where the research-oriented public universities are situated.

Mobility between different elite private institutions is also quite common. Here, it seems to affect more mature academics. In fact, there is some evidence of a kind of proto-academic market operating among private elite institutions: cases of an institution attracting a well-regarded young academic from another elite private institution, by offering better working conditions, better contract or higher salary, are becoming more frequent since the last decade. Moves from the public sector to the private sector are almost unheard of, especially among young scholars. It seems that, until now, the conditions of work offered by the public sector and the stability of employment that went with the civil servant status, provided good enough perspectives for the young scholars able to find a position inside a public university.

Finally, while changing institutional affiliation is a very frequent experience for academics working in mass-oriented private institutions, ascending to positions in institutions better positioned in the country's landscape is a much rarer event. The poor academic environment and the bad conditions of work faced by these professionals prevent them from enriching their academic curriculum in order to become competitive enough to successfully apply for positions in more highly regarded institutions.

Data collected in the CAP survey of 2007 corroborates these impressions. In the survey, 43 percent of respondents answered that the institution where they were interviewed is the one where they started their career. Another 32 percent indicated that they worked fewer than five years in other institutions before being accepted to their present institution. This pattern of response holds true even for the older academics who started working prior to the 2000s. The only exception is to be found among those employed in the private mass-oriented sector. Here almost 75 percent of the older academics declared they had worked more than five years in other institutions prior to entering the present institution. On the other hand, when asked if they are considering a move to another institution, 68 percent of all respondents gave a negative answer. This figure is higher among the academics at the research universities (80 percent), and lower among those employed in the private mass-oriented sector (60 percent).

The Changing Relationship Between Graduate Education and Academic Career

Officially, Brazilian graduate education recognizes three different kinds of degrees: the "specialization" degree, the master's degree, and the doctorate. Specialization is a professional degree, deemed to offer alternative postgraduate studies for professionals working in the general market. Its main objective is to create an opportunity for deeper understanding of selected aspects of professional training, and develop competences needed by the professional labor market. In this sense, it resembles what is known in other countries as a lifelong learning program. Master's and doctoral programs have a strict academic orientation.[10] They cater to candidates interested in academic research. Since the 1960s, when such programs were first officially acknowledged in Brazil, their main goal has been to provide intensive training for the young generation of Brazilian researchers. The master's degree is an intermediate stage in the training for an academic life, while the doctoral degree finishes the academic training. Applicants to doctoral programs are supposed to have finished a master's program. This holds true even in professional fields like law and engineering. To successfully conclude the master's and the doctoral studies, candidates are supposed to attend a prescribed set of courses and to present a thesis (or a dissertation) in a public defense before a board of examiners—the board consists of three examiners in the case of a master's degree and five for the doctorate. In both cases, it is mandatory for the board to include academics from outside the candidate's program (for a better description of graduate studies in Brazil, see Balbachevsky 2010).

Figure 2.1 provides a strong indication of how the demand for academic qualifications has increased in the last decade. First, one can see that the proportion of academics with only a bachelor's degree has dropped both

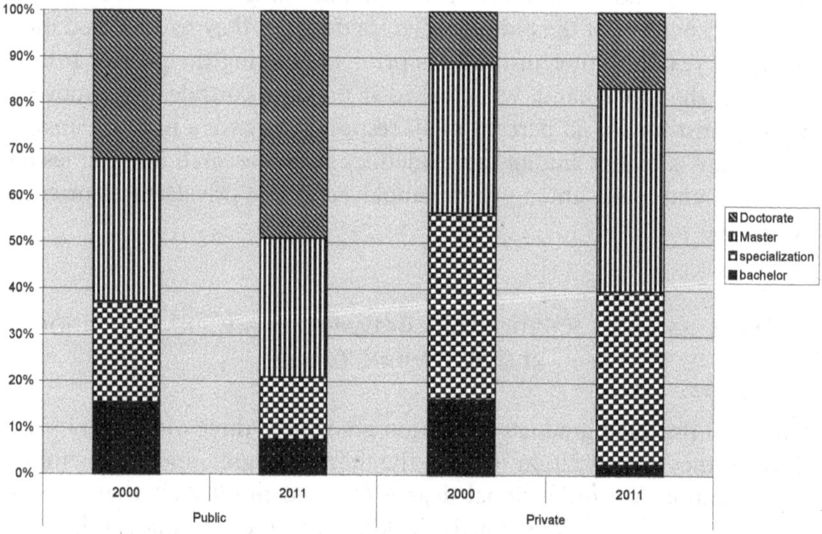

Source: Brazil, National Census of Higher Education, 2000 and 2011.

Figure 2.1. Brazil, 2000 and 2011: Academic qualification of academic staff, public and private sectors.

in the public and private sectors. In the public sector, 70 percent of the new positions opened in the last decade were filled by academics with doctoral degrees, and those holding master's degrees filled 28 percent of the openings in this sector. (The remaining 2 percent of positions were filled by those holding another type of qualification--a bachelor's degree, a specialization credential, etc.) Thus, while the doctoral degree holders represented only 32 percent of all academics employed in the public sector in 2000, they now represent 49 percent. In the private sector, 49 percent of the new positions were filled by academics with a master's degree, and another 19 percent were filled by academics with doctorates. As a result, the proportion of academics with a master's degree employed in the private sector grew from 32 percent to 44 percent between 2000 and 2011, and the proportion of academics with doctorates grew from 11 percent to 16 percent.

The challenges posed by these dynamics for young scholars are presented in Table 2.2. Academics in the sample of the 2007 national survey were grouped into three different cohorts. The cohorts are defined by the year in which the respondents indicated they first secured an academic staff position.[11] The columns provide information about two different aspects related to the relationship between the graduate studies and the academic career: the first column reports the average time, in years, elapsed between when the respondents finished their master's program and the year they reported getting the first job as an academic. The second column reports the average time, in years, elapsed between when the respondents finished their doctoral degree and the year they secured a job as an academic, for those reporting holding a doctoral degree. Negative values indicate that the respondent started working as an academic staff member before finishing the degree considered.

As one can see in Table 2.2, for the older cohort, graduate education was, typically, an experience that came *after* being recruited as an academic. While in research-oriented institutions the gap between starting the academic career and finishing the first graduate program was small—a bit more than two years, on average—it was bigger for academics employed at the more undergraduate-oriented institutions (from four to seven years on average, depending on the type of institution). When one considers the doctorate experience in more detail (last column in Table 2.2), typically, older academics would start their study at this level years after securing their first job as an academic. This observation holds true for the older generation in all kinds of institutions. This finding means that in the past, even in Brazilian top universities, the practice of hiring academic staff without a doctorate was a common one. In fact, in 1989, when the first national survey on the Brazilian academic profession was

Table 2.2. Time, in years, elapsed between the conclusion of the first graduate program and the PhD program and the first position as an academic, by academic cohort* and type of institution

		Master's degree		PhD degree	
Type of institution	Academic cohort	Average time, in years, spent between finishing the degree and securing the first academic position**	Std. Deviaion (in years)	Average time, in years, spent between finishing the degree and securing the first academic position**	Std. Deviation (in years)
Public research institutes	Pre-1990s	−2.0	5.7	−10.6	7.4
	1990s	2.8	3.9	−1.2	4.9
	2000s	7.6	3.3	2.2	1.3
	Total	.96	6.2	5.7	8.2
Public research universities	Pre-1990s	−3.0	6.7	−12.4	6.5
	1990s	1.9	4.8	−5.5	4.6
	2000s	4.3	4.9	.9	2.5
	Total	−.6	6.6	−9.0	7.2
Public regional universities	Pre-1990s	−3.9	6.7	−15.8	6.5
	1990s	.5	5.3	−6.3	4.2
	2000s	2.0	3.6	.2	2.1
	Total	−1.0	6.2	−10.4	7.7

Private elite institutions	Pre-1990s	–4.6	8.7	–14.5	8.2
	1990s	–.8	4.8	–7.6	3.8
	2000s	3.2	5.5	–.9	2.4
	Total	–1.9	7.5	–9.8	7.9
Private mass institutions	Pre-1990s	–7.4	7.9	–19.5	6.7
	1990s	–.3	5.3	–6.6	3.4
	2000s	2.0	4.3	–1.9	3.1
	Total	–1.0	6.7	–9.8	8.3
Total	Pre-1990s	–4.5	7.5	–14.6	7.3
	1990s	.2	5.3	–6.2	4.2
	2000s	2.5	4.4	–.4	2.8
	Total	–1.0	6.7	–9.5	7.8

*Academic cohort is defined based on the year reported by respondents when they secured their first position as an academic staff member in an institution.

A negative value indicates that academic career have began **prior to finishing the graduate program considered.

Source: Brazil, CAP survey, 2007

carried out, the proportion of academics without doctorates working in public research universities was fairly large (37 percent), and the proportion of academics with a similar profile inside regional universities represented the great majority: 75 percent. At that time, the main difference between these two groups was that while 83 percent of the master's degree holders employed at research universities reported that they were already working for a higher degree, this proportion dropped to 36 percent among the master's employed in regional universities (Balbachevsky 2000).

The 1990s was a turning point inside the public sector. Since then, requiring at least a master's degree of the candidates for an academic position became common practice. In the 2000s, the requirement of a doctoral degree also became usual in the public sector and among elite private institutions. On average, the academic cohort of the 2000s employed in these institutions reported securing their first academic placement only *after* finishing the doctoral degree. Institutions in the mass private sector were slower to require faculty to hold some graduate degree. It was only in the 2000s that this requirement became more widespread among these institutions.

Thus, our data support the argument that the new generations are facing increasing competition for employment as an academic in Brazil, even considering the strong increase of new academic positions opened in all kind of higher education institutions. Finishing a graduate program is a necessary condition even for those seeking a position in institutions of lower prestige.

Although a doctoral degree is not a formal exigency posed by the rules that organize access to a place in the public sector, holding a doctoral degree is a relevant advantage. It is also, increasingly, a major advantage for securing a position in the private sector, especially at elite private institutions.

This reality is a novelty in Brazil's academic market. Conditions for access are harder now than before, requiring longer years of hard study and dedication from the young generation. The increased interest in research at expense of teaching manifested by the new generations of Brazilian academics (Schwartzman and Balbachevsky 2013) may well be explained by the increasing number of young academics with such scholarly backgrounds. Nevertheless, to declare that one's priority is research does not say much about how this research is being done, and the intensity of this research work.

In the 2007 survey, 42 percent of the scholars who obtained a PhD degree were still unable to secure a stable, full-time appointment. Without securing a full-time job, PhD holders also tend to have diminished opportunities for access to increasingly competitive public funds for research. Thus, while reporting strong interest in and commitment to research, a significant number of Brazilian scholars with PhD degrees also reported having no access to external research funding (40 percent). This situation is one of the major sources of tension among young Brazilian scholars.

Pathways to the Academy

With such a wide diversity of institutions and sectors present inside the Brazilian higher education system, one should expect the existence of diverse pathways leading to different niches inside the academic market. The survey shows that it is actually the past experience as undergraduate student, and not the postgraduate experience, which is the best predictor for different trajectories leading to diverse niches inside the public and private higher education sectors.

In the public sector, 80 percent of all academic staff has also done their undergraduate studies in a public university.[12] What is more impressive, among the academic staff in public research universities, 50 percent have received their bachelor degree from the institution where they are employed. These data provide an indication of the strength of the forces closing access to the premium academic market in Brazil.

Surprisingly, when considering the academic experience at the postgraduate level, the data indicate a less closed pattern of recruitment: only 34 percent of the academic staff from the research universities have done all postgraduate studies in the university where they are employed. This figure drops to 18 percent among academics from the public regional universities. At the private elite institutions, 30 percent of the academics have this profile. Together this information reveals the real nature of the inbreeding issue in Brazilian universities. It is not so much about the classic inbreeding problem as described in the international literature (Eliot 1908; Wyer and Conrad 1984; Horta, Velloso and Grediaga 2010). It is, rather, a kind of market segregation. The best public universities clearly favor applications coming from their former bachelor students above other candidates coming from other universities.

Considering now the graduate experience of the different cohorts employed in diverse types of institutions, the data from the CAP survey show that the public sector experienced small changes in the last decade. Today, as in the past, public universities favor academics who have done all their graduate studies in the public system. Among the older cohort, 81 percent of the academics employed in the public sector have completed all of their graduate studies in the public sector. Among the younger generation hired by these institutions, this figure is 79 percent.

The main shift is to be found in the private sector. Here, among older cohorts, the predominant profile is of academics who have done all of their studies within the private sector. Among academics working in the elite private sector who started their academic careers before the 1990s, 62 percent declared to have done all of their graduate work in the private sector. This figure is 56 percent for academics in the mass-oriented private institutions. Among the young scholars, the proportion of academics coming from public postgraduate programs experiences a drastic increase. In the elite private sector, 61 percent of the younger scholars have done at least part of their graduate studies in the public sector. In mass-oriented private institutions, the tendency is similar: 64 percent of all young academics employed in this sector have done some graduate studies in the public sector.

These data provide a clue regarding one of the most important dilemmas faced by the young generation of scholars in Brazil. The expansion of graduate education (master's and doctorate programs) and changes in the regulatory framework described earlier tend to raise the threshold for access to premium positions in the academic market. As competition increases, demands for qualifications and performance also become tougher. In order to compete for an academic position inside a top research university, young academics now face the challenge of improving their academic background, authoring a number of academic pieces, and building up strong connections in their field. All of these things take time, require concentrated efforts, and imply timely career decisions. Still, the odds of success are increasingly small. Many young, well-qualified academics are forced by circumstances to find employment in less-than-adequate academic environments, in the mass private sector. Once there, the burden of long hours, low hourly pay, and the lack of incentives make changes in the career path almost impossible.

Even for those who found employment in the public sector in recent years, the picture is not as bright as it used to be. Federal government policy is heavily focused on encouraging the growth of undergraduate enrollments in the federal universities. In the 2000s, sixteen new federal universities were established, most of them situated in remote parts of the country. The number of undergraduate enrollments in federal universities grew 66.4 percent but the number of new academic positions opened within this sector increased only 45 percent.

The REUNI program has steered growth but has not provided adequate resources for sustaining quality. Under the double pressure of growing enrollments at the undergraduate level and expanding access to minorities and children from low-income families, many federal universities have chosen to open new programs and add new campuses without securing sufficient resources. Poorly equipped and improvised facilities become the norm in these universities. The new academics hired to staff these new initiatives, even if formally entitled to similar legal contracts, do not enjoy the supportive environment that was usual in the past. Scattered evidence that emerged with the media coverage of the 2012 strike[13] at federal universities has provided insight into the stark conditions faced by the academics working in the new campuses established in recent years. Some of these problems include entire campuses precariously accommodated in abandoned buildings originally designed as primary schools; small, overcrowded classrooms with no ventilation; the absence of libraries and laboratories; extended teaching hours; and few prospects for engagement in research and graduate programs.

In the data collected by the 2007 survey, these issues were not yet clearly delineated, because some of the most relevant programs to steer growth in the federal system were not in place. Nevertheless, some issues were already present. For instance, in this survey the association between rank and commitment with research in regional public universities runs against the expected pattern. Although only 6.3 percent of the full professors display a profile that could be described as mature and internationalized, this percentage grows to 18.2 percent among the associate professors, falling to 4.3 percent among the junior staff. Furthermore, while virtually all (94.8 percent) associate professors hold a PhD degree, only 39.6 percent of the full professors have similar degrees. These figures provide some clues with regard to the challenges faced by federal universities when trying to accommodate the new, better-qualified young academic cohort into its old rank system, where seniority is still more relevant than actual academic performance.

Conclusion

Two different forces have changed the landscape of Brazilian higher education in recent years: the new demands for access coming from society, and changes in the regulatory framework that imposed adjustments by institutions when selecting new academics. Access creates pressure for growth in both the public and private sectors. With growth comes new job opportunities and changes in the general conditions of employment and work for the academic staff. The new regulatory framework was brought by the Brazilian Education Law of 1997, and afterward unfolded in a myriad of new decrees and norms. It imposed a new threshold for academic staff qualifications and opened up new job opportunities for the growing number of graduates formed by the expanding system of graduate education.

In more recent years, the changes in the rules for access to the public sector have contributed to new opportunities for growth within the elite private sector. Since the beginning of the 2000s, all institutions from the public sector have been under strong pressure to expand quickly in order to meet the needs for access coming from the lower middle class. In 2012, all federal universities were required by law to reserve at least 50 percent of all freshmen seats for children from lower-income families. One side effect of this movement is the decline in the conditions of academic work, as described earlier. Larger, increasingly overcrowded classes in the public universities are perceived as a loss in the quality of education provided by the public sector. On the other hand, the access measures that favor lower-income candidates also sharply increase the competition for access among the children from middle- and upper-middle-class families. These changes create a new niche for the growth of the elite-oriented private institutions. It is too early to assess how this change will impact the prospects open to the new generation of academics.

Combined, all of these forces create contradictory dynamics. In the last decade, the number of new academic positions open in Brazilian higher education grew fast, but the requirements for filling these positions have increased drastically. Although in the past graduate education was typically an experience that came after employment, the would-be academics now must finish graduate studies before applying for an academic job. If their interest lies in the public sector or in an elite private institution, holding a doctoral degree is necessary. In addition to a doctoral degree, they will need to work hard to improve their academic profile with published materials, research experience, and good connections with senior colleagues. The efforts are massive, and imply dedication over a large span of years, but still the odds are against the candidate. Many young, well-qualified academics will fail to secure a place in a nurturing academic environment that could support their development.

While mobility in the Brazilian academic market has increased in the last decade, it is still an experience confined to the first years of the academic career—and the new law from 2012 regarding the academic career in the federal sector creates strong barriers for mobility even in those early-stage years. It is in these first years that young academics must make some crucial decisions regarding their academic placement. The window of opportunity that could lead to a placement with good prospects is very small. Once locked into a path leading to a poorly endowed academic environment, changing the trajectory is extremely hard. The dynamics of segregation present in the better universities impose further barriers for alternative routes. Thus, many of the young PhD holders formed by the strongly subsidized graduate system in the public universities will be locked into positions that will not allow them to develop as academics or researchers.

Acknowledgment

The author would like to acknowledge the financial support given by FAPESP, *Fundação de Amparo à Pesquisa do Estado de São Paulo* (2006/03329-0).

Notes

1. For more information on this project, see http://www.uni-kassel.de/wz1/cap/international.ghk.

2. The most common contract in the private sector is a part-time arrangement with payment according to work tasks. This may include teaching, coordination of programs, advising students, and even doing some research.

3. The three universities are the Universidade de São Paulo (USP), the Universidade Estadual de Campinas (UNICAMP), and the Universidade Estadual Júlio de Mesquita (UNESP).

4. *Privatdozent* (or PD, for short) is both a title and a position in the European university system, especially in Germany. In Germany, PD-ship is conferred to academics holding the PhD degree. In order to achieve the PD title, candidates must write another thesis, working under supervision of a full professor, as well as giving a number of lectures, a procedure that takes, in all, about six years. In the German system, the PD is a necessary step for access to the rank of full professor.

5. This situation is in sharp contrast with the numbers for graduate education offered by the public sector. As in many other countries, enrollments at this level tend to expand in times of economic crisis because graduate education may function as a buffer for upper-middle class children when unemployment is high. Public graduate education is tuition-free and sustained by a generous offer of scholarships from the federal and regional governments.

6. The only exception in this picture is the *Pontificie* Catholic universities, which traditionally had a profile similar to the public universities and catered

to the needs of children from upper-class families interested in differentiated education.

7. Even in the worst days of the Brazilian debt crisis of the 1980s, scholarships for graduate students were relatively abundant. Because of a trick in the Brazilian Public Budget Bill, the best way the Federal Science Agencies had for preserving their share of the Public National Budget was to convert most of their resources into scholarships. By Brazilian law, scholarships as well as salaries cannot have their resources cut from one year to another.

8. In Brazil, access to university is limited by a *numerus clausus* principle. The universities are required to publicize in advance the total number of positions open for each bachelor program. Students to fill these positions are selected through a competitive examination. Until 2009, each university was responsible for organizing its own entrance examinations. Since then, the federal government proposed a nationwide entrance examination that was adopted by all federal universities and some state universities. For a detailed analysis of this issue, see Balbachevsky, Kerbauy, and Santos 2010.

9. We use the expression "micro-regulation" to describe the tendency to focus the evaluation on insignificant formal indicators. These are presented to the institution in the form of a disconnected list of indicators that the institution is required to respond to, regardless of its relevance. In order to better understand the regulation and steering regimes of Brazilian higher education, see, Castro 2012, 2013.

10. Since 1997, CAPES also recognizes (and supervises) professional master's programs. This variant of the traditional master's program envisages a hybrid training that combines an academic orientation with an applied one. The main difference is that while in the traditional master's programs all advisors are supposed to have a doctoral degree and are evaluated by their academic performance, in the case of a professional master's there is the possibility of engaging professionals with recognized expertise outside the academy as part of the program's faculty. Nevertheless, since this model was proposed, it has experienced strong resistance inside public universities and the number of such programs grew very slowly. In 2012, there were 104,000 students enrolled in traditional master's program against 12,200 in professional master's programs. The professional master's degree is included as a graduate degree in this study.

11. In Brazil, as a rule, doctoral candidates are counted as students. The difference between apprenticeship experiences as part of a doctoral program and a job as an academic is clearly delineated in our respondents' life experiences.

12. This information is even more impressive if one considers that the public sector accounts for only 25 percent of all undergraduate enrollments.

13. The 2012 strike was the longest strike faced by the federal system. It started on May 17 and ended only at the end of September. Almost all federal universities were affected by the movement.

References

Balbachevsky, Elizabeth. 2000. *A Profissão Acadêmica no Brasil: As Multiplas Facetas Do Nosso Sistema De Ensino Superior*. Brasília: FUNADESP.

Balbachevsky, Elizabeth. 2007. "The Changing Patterns of the Brazilian Academic Profession in the Era of Globalization." In *The Professoriate in the Age of Globalization*, edited by Nelly Stromquist, 65–86. Rotterdam: Sense Publishers.

Balbachevsky, Elizabeth, Maria Teresa Miceli Kerbauy, and Vanessa Mattos dos Santos. 2010. "Brazil." In *Getting into Varsity: Comparability, Convergence and Congruence*, edited by Barend Vlaardingerbroek and Neil Taylor, 253-270. Amherst, NY: Cambria Press.

Balbachevsky, Elizabeth, and Simon Schwartzman. 2010. "The Graduate Foundations of Brazilian Research." *Higher Education Forum* (7): 85–100.

Castro, Maria Helena de Magalhães, forthcoming. "The Role of the National State and Regional Authorities in Regulating and Steering the System as a Whole, Including Both Public and Private HE Providers: The Brazilian Case." In *Higher Education in the BRICS: Investigating the Pact Between Higher Education and Society*, edited by Simon Schwartzman, Ròmulo Pinheiro, and Pundy Pillay. Dordrecht: Springer.

CGEE. 2011. *Doutores 2010. Estudo da Demografia Da Base Técnico-Científica Brasileira*. Brasília: Centro de Gestão e Estudos Estratégicos.

Horta, Hugo, Francisco M. Velloso, and Rócio Grediaga. 2010. "Navel Gazing: Academic Inbreeding and Scientific Productivity." *Management Science* 56(3): 414–429.

Musselin, Christine. 2005. "European Academic Labor Markets in Transition." *Higher Education* 49(1): 135–154.

Sampaio, Helena. 1999. *Ensino Superior no Brasil: O Setor Privado*. São Paulo: FAPESP/HUCITEC.

Sampaio, Helena. 2011. "O Setor Privado De Ensino Superior no Brasil: Continuidades e Transformações." *Revista Ensino Superior* 2(4): 28–43.

Schwartzman, Simon, and Elizabeth Balbachevsky. 1996. "The Academic Culture in Brazil." In *The International Academic Profession: Portrait of Fourteen Countries*, edited by Philip G. Altbach, 231–280. Princeton, NJ: Carnegie Foundation for the Advancement of Teaching.

Schwartzman, Simon, and Elizabeth Balbachevsky. 2014. "Brazil: Research and Teaching in a Diverse Institutional Environment: Converging Values and Diverging Practices." In *Research and Teaching in a Comparative Perspective*, edited by Akira Arimoto, William Cummings, Jung C. Shin, and Ulrich Teichler, 221–235. Dordrecht: Springer.

Wyer, Jean C., and Clifton F. Conrad. 1984. "Institutional Inbreeding Reexamined." *American Educational Research Journal* 21(1): 213–225.

Chapter 3

Conditions and Opportunities for New Faculty in Higher Education in Mainland China

Qi Wang, Yi Li, and Nian Cai Liu

Introduction

Young faculty have become a major force contributing to higher education development in Mainland China. They are regarded as the future of academia, and it is believed that the capacity of young faculty has a direct impact on competitiveness of higher education in the global market (Austin, Sorcinelli and McDaniels 2007; Altbach 2011). Chinese higher education has undergone rapid transition in the past three decades, including massification, marketization, and employment reform. The shifting landscape of the academic workplace has brought both opportunities and challenges to young academics.

This chapter provides a detailed account of young academics and the career paths they are experiencing. It aims to analyze the quality and conditions of academic work for young faculty entering academia and to reflect on the challenges facing Chinese higher education to attract the best young academics. This chapter focuses its analysis on young academics under the age of 35 appointed to a faculty position at public universities in Mainland China.

General Characteristics of the Higher Education System in China

Higher education expansion in Mainland China has led to a rapid increase in the numbers of new faculty to serve the demand of growing student enrollment. These early career academics are generally young, highly educated, knowledgeable, and motivated in their work. They take on a large teaching and research load, and have become a major force in university development. A series of policies and reform strategies have been implemented both at the national and institutional level to encourage and support young faculty's professional development. However, research shows that, for many historical, cultural, and economic reasons, young academics are in a rather disadvantaged position in the academic workplace and feel increasingly pressured (Chen 2003; Yang 2005; Zhang 2008). This section discusses the current development of young academics in the socioeconomic context of Chinese higher education. It starts with a description of the differentiated higher education system in the country and demographic analysis on new faculty.

Expansion and Differentiation

The economic transformation of China over the last thirty years is well known. Annual GDP growth rates of around 10 percent have been maintained for at least two decades. The continuous economic growth has raised tremendously China's demand for highly educated workers. Education is regarded as an investment for individuals and families to secure high-income employment opportunities and social status (Li, Morgan, and Ding 2008). It is under these twin demands that the Chinese higher education system has been compelled to expand at both undergraduate and postgraduate levels since the late 1990s. Total undergraduate enrollment increased from about 5.6 million in 2000 to more than 22.3 million in 2010, and the gross enrollment rate for young people between the ages of 18 and 22 increased from 12.5 percent in 2000 to 26.5 percent in 2010 (Ministry of Education 2012a).

Chinese higher education institutions can be classified into different types in terms of governance structures and qualification granted. Most higher education institutions are public in nature, administered by a government body. Among these, some are considered national higher education institutions, administered by the Ministry of Education and other ministries; others are local higher education institutions administered by provincial or municipal governments. The number of universities governed by national ministries remained steady at 111 from 2004 to 2010; the number of provincial or locally controlled universities increased from 1,394 to 1,573; and the number of private universities increased from 226 to 674.

China has a diversified and differentiated higher education system. Different types of institutions enjoy different status, which may differentiate the market for academics. Public universities, in general, enjoy higher social status and are considered to provide higher quality education than private universities in China, mainly because private universities primarily serve to supplement public institutions' efforts to satisfy the demand for access to higher education. Private institutions often enroll students who failed to enter public institutions (Yu, Stith, Liu, and Chen 2010). The governmental funding schemes to develop teaching and research excellence, namely the 985 and 211 Projects, have provided concentrated financial support to develop the overall capacity of selected public universities, and in turn have strengthened the status of these universities. The differentiated status of Chinese institutions is a fundamental factor shaping the country's academic labor market.

The unprecedented expansion has made China the world's largest higher education system, in terms of the number of university students enrolled. The system also serves the demand for a high-skilled workforce in the socioeconomic transition underway in China. However, the expansion also leads to issues and concerns about overeducation, devalued postgraduate degrees, as well as quality assurance (Li and Chen 2006; Hong et al. 2012).

Graduate Education in China

Graduate education in China is provided at two levels—master's and doctoral. The length of study for a master's degree program is normally two to three years (a full-time student at this level is expected to graduate at the age of 24 to 25), and three to five years for a doctoral program (a full-time doctoral student is expected to graduate at the age of 28 to 30). Both master's degree programs and doctoral programs consist of taught and research components. To receive a doctoral degree, students need to complete taught courses, sit for a qualifying exam, conduct original research for a dissertation, and pass an oral defense of the dissertation. In addition, doctoral students at all institutions are required to publish research papers during their studies.

Graduate education in China typically takes place in universities and research institutes, with the vast majority of graduate education delivered by universities. Indeed, 96.4 percent of all postgraduate students are educated at universities, while only 3.6 percent are educated in research institutes. More specifically, only 8.7 percent of doctoral students and 2.6 percent of master's students are enrolled in research institutes (Ministry of Education 2012b). (See Table 3.1.)

Public universities offer most of the graduate education programs and admit the largest numbers of postgraduate students (Yu et al. 2010). In 2010, there were 481 universities providing graduate education, among which 98 universities were national higher education institutions and 383 institutions were supervised by local authorities. Although national and local higher education institutions award almost the same number of master's degree (164,080 and 162,533 respectively), the majority of doctoral degrees—79.8 percent, or 34,472 out of a total of 43,214—are issued by national higher education institutions (Ministry of Education 2012b). It is worth mentioning that, alone, 39 leading universities selected in the 985 Project award more than half of China's new doctoral degrees each year (The 985 Project Research Team 2009).

Research institutes in China are large academic (but nonteaching) units. They are entitled to issue postgraduate degrees, and include such entities as the Chinese Academy of Sciences, the Chinese Academy of Social Sciences, the Chinese Academy of Engineering, as well as other research institutes and centers affiliated with various ministries. With top-notch scientists, abundant research funding, and up-to-date facilities, research institutes provide an innovative environment for graduate education. Students enrolled in these programs tend to have more opportunities than their peers in university settings to participate in cutting-edge research projects (Ni et al. 2005; Zhao 2007).

A continuous expansion has been taking place in the graduate education sector, within which master's enrollment enjoys a slightly higher increase than doctoral enrollment (see Table 3.1). In 2010, the total number of postgraduate students is 1.54 million (including both universities and research institutions), more than a four-times increase since 2000. Among them, 83.2 percent of the total postgraduate students are pursuing master's degrees, while 16.8 percent are pursuing doctoral degrees. The proportion of female postgraduate students has been increasing from 33.3 percent in 2000 to 47.9 percent in 2010, reaching gender parity. In the context of expansion, quality of graduate education has been a major concern in China. Efforts have been made to enhance teaching, to develop

Table 3.1. Graduate education enrollment in China (2000–2010, selected years)

	2000	2002	2004	2006	2008	2010
Total number of graduate students	301239	500980	819896	1104653	1283046	1538416
Total number of master's students	233144	392243	654286	896615	1046429	1279466
Total number of doctoral students	67293	108737	165610	208038	236617	258950
Percentage of graduate students at universities	94.2	94.5	95.1	95.6	95.9	96.4
Percentage of graduate students in research institutions	5.8	5.5	4.9	4.4	4.1	3.6
Percentage of female graduate students	33.3	37.3	41.6	44	45.7	47.9

Source: Educational Statistics Yearbook of China, 2000/2010 (Ministry of Education 2012b).

infrastructure and to improve learning and research environment, so as to cope with the increasing student demand.

Growth of Young Faculty Numbers

To serve the ever-increasing student demand and fill out the faculty shortage in the context of overall system expansion, the university faculty population has increased massively in the last decade, through recruitment of new graduates and employment of part-time teaching staff.

The total number of full-time university faculty increased from nearly 463,000 in 2000 to 1.3 million in 2010. Out of the total faculty population, the percentage of young faculty (i.e., those under age 35) has remained steady in the last ten years—47.3 percent, on average. In other words, young faculty are a major force in higher education. In terms of gender, statistical data show that full-time faculty in China have nearly achieved gender parity in recent years. The percentage of full-time female faculty has risen from 38.2 percent in 2000 to 46.5 percent in 2010. Gender parity is also observed among young faculty, with women accounting for a total of 54.8 percent of young academics under the age of 35 (Ministry of Education 2012a).

Chinese university faculty quality has improved in terms of academic backgrounds and qualifications. The percentage of total faculty holding a doctoral degree increased from 6.1 percent in 2000 to 14.9 percent in 2010, while the percentage of those holding master's degrees as their highest qualification grew from 23 percent to 35 percent (Ministry of Education 2012a). The number of all faculty members with doctoral degrees is higher at the 39 leading research universities selected by the 985 Project, reaching 70 percent. To improve faculty quality, higher education institutions (particularly top universities) have emphasized recruitment of doctoral degree holders in recent years. In addition, full-time faculty members without a doctoral degree are encouraged to conduct doctoral studies on a part-time basis (and given a maximum period of seven years to complete the degree). The number of faculty holding a doctoral degree is expected to increase in China in the coming years.

When Chinese higher education first began to expand, Chinese universities increasingly employed fresh graduates as faculty members at both undergraduate and postgraduate levels. Among full-time faculty, the percentage of new graduates employed was 5.2 percent in 2000. After reaching the highest point of 8.8 percent in 2004, this percentage began decreasing and dropped to 4.1 percent in 2010 (Ministry of Education 2012a). Due to the limited number of postgraduate degree holders, more bachelor's degree holders were employed before 2004 to fill up the faculty shortage. For example, in 2000, 64.2 percent of new graduates entering university faculty positions held only bachelor's degrees and 35.8 percent held postgraduate degrees. As the graduate education sector has expanded and been able to provide more staff to the academic labor market, 83.1 percent of the new graduates entering faculty positions in 2010 held postgraduate degrees, including both master's and doctoral degrees (Ministry of Education 2012b). In spite of their more advanced credentials, young faculty are said to lack teaching and research experience, which may compromise the quality of these activities at universities (Sun and Wang 2010). This point is analyzed more deeply later in this chapter.

Meanwhile, statistical data may suggest a declining demand for new faculty. While the total number of faculty is still increasing, a decline in the total number of newly recruited faculty (including those changing jobs) has been observed since 2006. As mentioned earlier, the percentage of new graduates in relation to the total number of faculty has also been decreasing since 2004, as a faculty quota system limits the number of faculty that can be recruited (see the "Promotion and Evaluation" section of this chapter). With the increasing rate of postgraduate enrollment, however, the competition for academic jobs may become more intensified.

In addition to recruiting new graduates, employing part-time faculty serves as another strategy to tackle the faculty shortage in the context of higher education expansion in China. According to the government regulations in 2002, part-time faculty are defined as teaching experts from outside the host university who teach at least one subject. The number of part-time faculty, as a percentage of the total faculty population, increased from 4 percent in 2000 to 21 percent in 2010 (Ministry of Education 2012a). Part-timers are mainly retired professors, specialists, and experts from enterprises and industry, as well as renowned researchers from various research academies. In terms of academic qualifications, part-time faculty have a similar profile to that of full-time faculty, and teaching quality has been improving. It is argued that employing part-time faculty can improve teaching quality, facilitate development of new courses and subject areas, and promote collaboration with industry. However, there is a lack of systematic mechanisms to manage part-time faculty. (See Table 3.2.)

Table 3.2. Full-time university faculty in China (2000–2010, selected years)

	2000	2002	2004	2006	2008	2010
Total number of full-time university faculty	462772	618419	858393	81403	1237451	1343127
Percentage of young faculty under the age of 35	47.59	46.23	47.27	48.34	47.78	46.22
Total number of new faculty entering universities (including changing jobs)	68162	112738	162260	152878	115759	984438
Percentage of new faculty entering universities (including changing jobs)	14.73	18.23	18.90	14.21	9.35	7.33
Percentage of new graduates recruited as new faculty entering universities	5.21	6.99	8.78	8.08	5.25	4.09

Source: Educational Statistics Yearbook of China, 2000/2010 (Ministry of Education 2012b).

The Labor Market for Young Academics

The massification of China's higher education system and the resulting transformation of various aspects of higher education in the country (including student and faculty numbers and profiles, institutional management and governance, and the role of universities in society) have introduced further changes in academic markets and careers (Lai 2012; Goastellec et al. 2013).

Due to the limited number of faculty vacancies set up by the national faculty quota system mentioned previously, a doctoral degree alone can no longer secure job opportunities in universities, particularly for young academics. Issues of supply and demand, as well as salary and prestige, tend to influence young academics' career choices and perceptions of academic work. Building on the previous section on the Chinese graduate education system and young faculty demographics, this section provides an analysis of the university job market and young academics' career paths, taking into consideration the unique features of the Chinese academic profession.

The Changing Demand for Young Academics

The unprecedented higher education expansion in China (which has proceeded at a rate even greater than that of the country's overall economic expansion) has led to various consequences, including the consideration of higher education and its degrees as a positional good; the emergence of graduate unemployment; and the increased stratification of esteem and status among universities (Wang and Lowe 2010). These three factors can also be reflected in the labor market's demand for young academics, which further intensifies the competition for academic positions.

As undergraduate enrollment continues to expand, more and more students are forced to pursue postgraduate degrees, to stand out in the battle for seeking employment. For example, the number of graduates who received doctoral degrees was just over 2,000 in 1990. This number increased to 13,966 in 2002 and 47,407 in 2010 (Ministry of Education 2012a), with an average annual increase of nearly 17 percent. These developments to some extent enable China to achieve the strategic goal of developing an elite workforce for the country's socioeconomic reform.

However, as the population growth rate slows down, along with a decrease in university-age students, higher education expansion (in particular at the undergraduate level) has also been slowing down. Such a declining growth rate can also be observed in terms of university faculty members. As mentioned earlier, despite an increase in the number of graduates at the postgraduate level, a decrease in the percentage of new graduates entering university faculty positions can also be seen (see Table 3.2). This is largely caused by the faculty quota system, which limits the total number of faculty, as well as the number of faculty at different ranks, which a university or an individual school or department may employ or promote. The number of faculty allocated depends on a range of factors, including university goals and a vision for development, student numbers, schools and departments' specialized fields, teaching and research loads, and the existing faculty quality. Therefore, while the overall quality of teaching among Chinese faculty is still low in terms of many working professors' academic backgrounds (as shown in the previous section), the faculty quota system mostly affects the job opportunities for young academics.

A doctoral degree has been generally considered as an entry requirement to the academic world at universities. Furthermore, the status or prestige of the university from which a candidate's degree has been awarded plays a significant role in screening for new hires, that is, whether a candidate holds a doctoral degree from a 985 or 211 Project university, or an overseas world-class university. It is worth mentioning that recruitment and hiring has been a different story for renowned professors and researchers. Not only universities but also the government have promoted various policies to attract high-level academics and scientists to work at universities in China. Talent schemes, such as the Chang Jiang Scholars Program and the Recruitment Program of Global Experts, have been created to recruit top researchers and ultimately to enhance teaching and research quality in Chinese universities.

The Academic Career and Alternative Job Opportunities

The tension between supply and demand for university faculty positions has led to a diversified career route for doctoral students, including options at universities and research institutes, as well as within industry and government organization. Graduates can freely choose their career routes based on their interests. It is worth mentioning here, despite the lack of data, that there is graduate mobility between universities and research institutes. Research institutes, such as the academies, do not exclusively recruit their own graduates. Based on a nationwide survey on doctoral students in 2007, a report on doctoral education quality in China shows that, between 1995 and 2008, 43.9 percent of doctoral graduates chose to teach and research at universities, 10.8 percent worked in research institutes, and 2.9 percent participated in postdoctoral study. That is, about 60 percent of doctoral graduates start their careers in teaching and research, forming a major force for research and knowledge innovation. Alternatively, 15.2 percent of graduates holding doctoral degrees enter industry, 5.2 percent governmental organizations, and 2.9 percent pursue careers abroad.

Further analysis shows that the number of graduates taking on jobs in universities and research institutes, and seeking postdoctoral appointments, has tended to decrease since 2002, while more students have started their careers in governmental organizations and industry. As demonstrated earlier, due to the decelerating expansion of the sector, the number of academic positions for new entrants to the profession shows a slight slowdown. The increase of job opportunities in research institutes is also compromised by the fast-growing supply of graduate students.

Thus, the academic and research job market for doctoral graduates is getting increasingly competitive, which has forced more graduates to look for alternative employment opportunities in governmental organizations and industry. In terms of geographic preference, most graduates tend to seek employment in big cities and in the eastern regions of China ("Doctoral Education Quality in China" Research Group 2010).

These findings are mostly echoed by another study conducted in fourteen higher education institutions on new doctoral graduates' employment prospects (Zhao et al. 2010). Zhao et al.'s research also finds that the average monthly salary received by doctoral graduates was RMB 4,814—about US$764 per month if converted directly to U.S. dollars and more like US$1,114 per month if a purchasing power parity (PPP) conversion is applied. Furthermore, Zhao et al. (2010) found that the wage difference between academic and nonacademic jobs was significant. Doctoral graduates working in industry received RMB 7,184 per month (about US$1,135 using a straight currency exchange rate, or about US$1,663 by using PPP conversion), while those working in research institutes earned RMB 4,709 per month (about US$747 using a direct currency exchange rate), and those working in academia earned the least per month, at RMB 3,932 (about US$624 via a direct currency exchange rate, or about US$910 using a PPP conversion). The average monthly salary received by graduates working in the east of China was RMB 1,000 (about US$159 using a direct currency exchange rate, or about US$231 as measured against PPP) higher than those working in the western regions of China. Here, it can be argued that the academic employment route might lose its attraction in the face of limited economic returns.

The above-mentioned two studies ("Doctoral Education Quality in China" Research Group 2010; Zhao et al. 2010) also reveal that doctoral graduates from different backgrounds—based on factors such as gender, specific discipline, graduate school attended and its location—tend to have different approaches to selecting their employment route. When it comes to gender, female doctoral graduates were more likely to choose to work in universities than their male peers. Meanwhile, doctoral graduates in science, humanities, and social sciences subject areas were more likely to work in universities, while engineering graduates chose to work in industry. Social sciences graduates are likely to prefer job opportunities in big cities, while engineering graduates are more likely willing to work in the less developed western regions in China.

Postdoctoral Training as a Transition Stage to an Academic Career

Postdoctoral training experience is regarded as one alternative route, or transition stage, for doctoral graduates looking to start their academic careers. The postdoctoral training system was implemented in China in 1985 to increase the domestic supply of highly skilled researchers and improve research quality. One can apply to take a postdoctoral position after receiving the doctoral degree. The postdoctoral experience usually lasts two years, with no subsequent degree or title awarded. Though postdoctoral researchers are regarded as staff in Chinese higher education and research system, they are not considered to be in a professional or faculty position. In other words, postdoctoral position is considered work rather than an educational experience (Stith, Liu, and Xu 2011).

The number of active postdoctoral scholars has been increasing each year; however, the population is smaller compared with that of recent doctoral graduates. For example, there were 10,559 active postdoctoral researchers in China in 2010, which represents about 22.3 percent of the total number of doctoral graduates that year (China Post-Doctoral Researchers Committee 2012). One can argue that this proportion of postdoctoral researchers to doctoral graduates had been generally decreasing before 2008, but has shown a slight increase since then. One of the possible causes is that domestically trained doctoral graduates are pushed to a disadvantaged status in employment battles for faculty positions against their peers who have returned from abroad. Although domestically trained graduates are an important group of highly skilled scientific talent, the quality of graduate education in China is not considered to be on par with that received by overseas returnees, and the domestic research and training environments are also generally perceived to be inferior to those abroad (Wong 2009). Such perceptions have been reinforced in China's attempt to attract senior scholars internationally to boost teaching and research excellence. To secure their career prospects, domestic graduates tend to pursue postdoctoral training after graduation to demonstrate ingenuity and productivity (Stith, Liu, and Xu 2011).

Ways to Enter the University Job Market

An employment reform has been implemented in Chinese universities since the early 2000s. Under this reform, all faculty positions are long term and contract-based, and can be renewed based on performance evaluation (Lai 2012). The employment reform aims to transform the "all-tenure" or "iron rice bowl" system to a performance-based system. That is, competent people can be hired and promoted for the right posts regardless of one's title, while even a full professor may not be kept if they are not competent (Chen 2003). In other words, as a result of employment reform, the Chinese academic profession has no concept or practice equivalent to the "tenure track," as understood in the United States. This competitive employment mechanism has had an impact on the ways faculty enter and develop in the university job market.

Academic Post System and Faculty Hierarchy

In general, the academic post system in Chinese higher education consists of a four-rank hierarchy—that is, teaching assistant, assistant professor, associate professor, and professor. An academic career starts at the rank of teaching assistant or assistant professor, depending on the candidate's qualifications and experience.

One of the key components of the employment reform in China can be seen in the faculty classification. Underpinned by the concept that the fundamental missions of higher education are teaching, research, and public service, faculty appointments are classified into three types: teaching-oriented faculty who spend most of their time delivering basic courses, such as mathematics and English, and possibly engaging in some research work at the same time to improve their teaching; research-oriented faculty who spend most of their time conducting cutting-edge research; and teaching-and-research combined faculty who usually divide career development between teaching and research. Due to the nature of these three categories, faculty positions in teaching-oriented universities are mainly teaching-oriented, while research universities provide more positions for research-oriented and combined teaching-and-research faculty members.

Another key development in the employment reform is to further classify the four-rank hierarchy into a 13-level faculty rank system, which parallels the traditional post system. Generally, full professorship consists of four levels with a member of the Academy of Science considered as the top rank (Level 1–4). Associate professorships (Level 5–7), assistant professorships (Level 8–10), and teaching assistantships (Level 11–13) each consist of three levels. Faculty members are categorized into one specific post level, based on their qualifications, teaching and research experience, and competence, which further links with an individual's salary level.

A Full-Time Career Path for Young Academics

A standard full-time career path for new academics in China starts after a postgraduate degree is received. Increasingly, most higher education institutions in China require a doctoral degree as a basic entry-level credential for teaching and research posts; this is the case at both national and local universities.

The most likely positions for new faculty under the age of 35 are assistant professor and teaching assistant, depending on the academic degree held by the candidate. The teaching assistant post is focused on assisting teaching and research in universities, and is seen as a transition role from students to teachers, and from receiving knowledge to delivering knowledge. It is the first entry level to an academic post. Teaching assistants are usually required to have a master's degree in a relevant field. Doctoral students may also serve as teaching assistants or research assistants under the guidance of a faculty member.

In China, graduates with a doctoral degree are most likely to start their academic career trajectories as assistant professors. Furthermore, an increasing number of universities, such as the 985 and 211 Project institutions, have placed emphasis on a doctoral degree from top-quality overseas universities. This policy to some extent has complicated domestic doctoral degree holders' employment possibilities and marginalized their status in the academic job market. In turn, increasing numbers of domestic doctoral degree holders may have to participate in postdoctoral training as a transition stage to enhance their employability before embarking on their academic careers as assistant professors at those leading universities in China; however, postdoctoral training experience is not a prerequisite for such employment.

Open Competition and Inbreeding

Available teaching and research posts and academic vacancies, including postdoctoral positions, are usually advertised on the websites of universities and relevant schools and departments. However, it is interesting to note that there are, as yet, few recruitment websites collecting information on academic vacancies in China. Applicants need to scan different universities' and departments' websites in search of opportunities. Theoretically speaking, the search for academic talent is international in nature and open to applicants from different parts of the world. Both domestic and international candidates will compete together for positions and have to go through the same application processes. However, due to differences in contract conditions, working environment, language issues, and so on, entry-level academic jobs have not drawn much attention from international academics. Nevertheless, increasing numbers of Chinese doctoral graduates from overseas universities have been returning to China and competing with domestic doctoral students for entry-level academic positions, and these numbers are expected to increase. Once receiving an application, the department will organize a committee to assess and screen the application material according to the department's specific requirements, invite the candidate for an interview and a trial teaching session, and then make an employment decision.

It is true that academic employment procedures are open competitions; however, various studies and statistics show that academic inbreeding is fairly common in Chinese higher education (Sun and Wang 2010; Zhang and Jiang 2010). In particular, during the recent period of higher education expansion, the practice of recruiting faculty from among one's own graduates has been a common approach by universities to cope with the faculty shortage. This internal approach to employment has led to low academic mobility, lack of competition, and lack of innovative thinking. For example, Gu (2006) found in his study that 604 out of 987 young faculty in seventeen Chinese universities worked at the same institutions after their graduation. Yan (2011) conducted a large-scale survey among fifty top graduate schools in China and found that 37.1 percent of the total 6,253 faculty respondents received both their undergraduate and postgraduate (including both master's and doctoral level) education at the universities where they were currently employed, and 47.4 percent received either their undergraduate or postgraduate education at the universities for which they were currently working. Another study on full-time faculty's career development in Chinese higher education (Lin 2009) found that more than half of the faculty members in research universities graduated from the same institution where they were also employed, a higher percentage than their peers at local teaching-oriented institutions. Faculty in the fields of science, engineering, agriculture, and medicine are more likely to stay on at the same institution than their peers in the social sciences.

Nevertheless, having realized that high levels of academic inbreeding may be detrimental to teaching and research quality, and to some extent even undermine academic freedom, Chinese universities have promoted academic mobility. A series of policies have been adopted at institutional levels to prevent universities from recruiting their own graduates and encourage more focus on international recruitment (Jiang and Shi 2008). This policy change has been reflected in some statistics that show that young academics tend to have much lower rates of academic inbreeding than their senior peers (Lin 2009). In addition, faculty members are encouraged to participate in various domestic and international visiting scholar programs for a period of time. Special funds for such programs are available at both institutional and national levels.

Promotion and Evaluation

In general, faculty promotion relates to two factors, namely, the available faculty positions and the applicant's teaching and research performance. First, the faculty quota system limits the number of faculty who can be employed and promoted. Young academics with little experience are unlikely to be employed or promoted if there is no vacancy in the department. However, the quota system does not restrict efforts to attract highly reputed professors and researchers. A 2007 employment regulation on faculty positions at national higher education institutions administered by the Ministry of Education and other ministries suggests that a university should adhere to a 20 percent quota for full professorships, and limit associate professorships to 30 percent, assistant professorships to 40 percent, and teaching assistantships to 10 percent.

Second, a promotion decision will be made based on the applicants' teaching and research performance. Once there are vacancies available, faculty members can apply for promotion to a higher rank, such as from teaching assistant to assistant professor and from assistant professor to associate professor, after a required period of time, which usually is a minimum of three years or based on individual universities' regulations. The faculty member's performance will be assessed through peer review processes for such promotion. Once found to have met the departmental requirements and achieved adequate progress, the scholar will be awarded a higher rank post. The scholar's performance will be evaluated again after several years. If one makes significant teaching and research contributions, the faculty member can be awarded the rank of professor. Based on statistics from the Ministry of Education (2012a), the largest group of teaching assistants is those under the age of 30. Similarly, the largest group of assistant professors is in the age range of 31 to 35, while the age range of 36 to 40 years is most common among associate professors, and 46- to 50-year-olds are most prevalent among those who hold professor posts. We estimate that, on average, it takes five years for an assistant professor to be promoted to an associate professor post, and about ten years in total to be promoted to a professor post.

Contracts at Entry-Level

As mentioned earlier, there is nothing equivalent to "tenure track" posts in Chinese higher education. Currently, young faculty appointments take place in the context of a system based on posts and contracts, which is considered a reflection of the Chinese academic profession's evolution from a predominantly bureaucratic culture to a competitive corporate culture. This implementation of market mechanisms has brought about greater academic freedom, attention to quality, and transparency of promotion in the academic profession (Chen 2003; Yang 2005; Lai 2012).

There are both full-time and part-time faculty positions in Chinese universities. However, as mentioned in the previous section, part-time faculty members are mostly senior professors and renowned researchers and experts in each field. Thus, entry-level young academics usually have a full-time position at the university with a contract for a certain employment period, which can be from one to three years. In addition to regular legal terms, universities and departments articulate clear job responsibilities and criteria for each position (in terms of teaching, research, and public service), which are explicitly outlined in the contract once a young faculty is employed. Specific job responsibilities and criteria may vary among different institutions, faculties, or departments. Faculty members' performance will be evaluated based on these criteria on an annual basis and at the end of the contract term within the department, the results of which will be reported to the human resources department. After the first contract is completed, a second contract can be renewed based on the faculty's performance evaluation, if the faculty wishes to continue at the employing university for the longer-term. If the faculty fails to meet the requirements as stated in the contract, the contract will not be renewed.

The teaching and research loads that young faculty should take on are not regulated or fixed, and vary according to institutional, faculty, or departmental practices or policies. In general, young faculty (including associate professors, assistant professors and teaching assistants), take on greater teaching loads and public service work than their senior colleagues in both research and teaching-oriented universities, while professors take on more demanding research loads. It is worth mentioning that professors and associate professors are required to supervise postgraduate students in the Chinese higher education system. As a result, teaching assistants and assistant professors may need to teach more classes to cover the university's or departments' needs in this area.

A performance-based salary system has been in place in Chinese higher education since 2006, as part of the employment reform. The new wage system intends to link faculty salary with their post/rank, qualification, experience and performance (Pu 2009). The performance-based salary consists of two portions, a fixed base salary and flexible institutional remuneration and fringe benefits (Mohrman, Geng, and Wang 2011; Ma and Wen 2012). The government and the university are the two key sources of funds.

A base salary is determined by a faculty member's given rank and given level within that rank on the 13-level faculty rank system mentioned above, and the faculty's level of seniority. In other words, the amount of base salary is fixed and the same across universities in the country, with regional adjustments for living expenses. The difference between different ranks—that is, assistant, associate, and full professor—can be significant, but relatively small differences are found between the different levels of faculty within one rank (Mohrman, Geng, and Wang 2011). The amount of postrelated and seniority pay is usually half of the total yearly remuneration.

The university and its school/department provide the institutional remuneration and fringe benefits. Each university has the autonomy to determine this second portion of salary, depending on the resources available and faculty performance. Further remuneration consists of pay based on an individual faculty's teaching and research productivity, including teaching load, research grants, and number of publications. Schools and departments usually provide faculty members with additional bonuses based on the revenue generated from entrepreneurial activities, such as consulting and services to local governments, research projects, and continuing education. Other fringe benefits and stipends include housing, support for health care, and other compensation.

A wide range of factors causes variations in faculty salary in public universities (Ma and Wen 2012). At the level of the individual faculty member, these factors include the number of years worked, discipline and academic field, professional rank, teaching load, seniority, teaching and research productivity. At the institutional level, salary variations may be the result of institutional, regional, discipline, and academic field variables, as well as entrepreneurial behavior. Although base pay is largely the same across the country, institutional remuneration is likely greater in big cities and in top universities. A more diversified revenue stream allows top universities, such as the universities selected by the 985 and 211 Projects, to provide higher pay for faculty (Mohrman, Geng, and Wang 2011).

In general, this equity-based, competitive, and incentive-oriented compensation system aims to encourage university faculty development (Yuan 2011). According to data from various university websites, the average monthly basic salary (including stipend) for an assistant professor is around RMB 5,000 to RMB 5,833 (about US$794 to US$926 based on a flat currency exchange rate, or about US$1,157 to US$1,350 based on a PPP conversion); RMB 6,667 (about US$1,058 based on a straight currency exchange rate, or about US$1,543 based on a PPP conversion) for an associate professor; and RMB 7,692 (about US$1,221 based on a standard currency exchange rate, or about US$1,780 using a PPP conversion) for a professor.

Young academics' salaries do not compare favorably with those of their peers working in industry and private enterprise, as academics are less likely to afford a middle-class lifestyle with the level of remuneration currently offered. To increase faculty income, faculty members are usually allowed to engage in a range of additional activities, including consulting, teaching night classes, or participating in consulting and cooperative research activities particularly for faculty in research universities (Ma and Wen 2012).

The Role of Social Networks in the Academic Career

Social networks are traditionally important in the academic life of young faculty in the Chinese higher education system. Social networks can be interpreted as young faculty's connection with and to their peers, senior professors, and department heads. Such relationships may be seen as a form of membership or access to an academic group, which is called *guanxi* in Chinese. However, it can be argued that—in comparison to past practice—the importance of social networks may have been altered in the current context of employment reform and performance-based evaluation.

An individual faculty can increase the volume of social networks by possessing membership in a certain academic group, which can be a university, a department, and a particular research team. The membership in such an academic group can assure acquisition of academic resources, such as funding information and the latest research developments. These opportunities will provide young academics with insightful information and additional resource to improve their teaching and research performance. Within this academic group itself, researchers may have more possibilities for inspired ideas and more chances for research collaboration, which may in turn enhance the group members' research productivity. Thus, it is important for young faculty to build connections with senior professors, researchers, and their peer researchers. It is also critical for postgraduate students to choose the "right" advisors, so that they can gain access to rich research resources and build their social ties early enough in their career journey. However, how to become a member in an academic group is another issue. It depends on the open or closed nature of the social networks (Coleman 1988). For example, research shows that, when they first come back to China, young overseas returnees are less likely to possess high-volume social networks with existing research groups in China and thus tend to have more difficulties in developing collaborative research than their peers who received their postgraduate studies in Mainland China, in particular those who have studied and worked in the same institution or research team (Xie, Xu, and Wu 2012). Meanwhile, competitive approaches, including peer review processes, have been widely adopted in all sorts of research grant applications at both national and institutional levels, which to some extent have weakened the role of this group membership in terms of resource allocation.

Another important form of social network is related to successful promotion and contract extension. Prior to the employment reform, having informal support from influential senior professors and department heads was fairly important for young faculty members. However, as mentioned in the previous sections, the employment reform—emphasizing transparency, competition, and performance—has further weakened the role of social ties in young faculty's employment and promotion procedures. Objective requirements have been set up in the employment guidelines to judge faculty's teaching quality and research productivity. Faculty members' annual evaluation, salary level, and promotion are judged based on specific quantified criteria. For example, a doctoral degree is a prerequisite for applying for a faculty position. To be promoted to an associate professorship, a young faculty member must have a certain number of papers published in high-quality journals (such as Science Citation Index journals and Social Sciences Citation Index journals), and conduct a number of funded research projects at a national level. In addition, universities work transparently on employment and promotion activities, so that the decision-making processes can be reviewed by the public. Under these circumstances, senior professors and department leaders are unlikely to mobilize their social connections and exert their influence on the decision making about the professional advancement of young faculty, particularly if the candidate is unable to meet the basic requirements.

Though these quantified criteria have been often criticized as rigid numbers and have put great strain on young faculty's professional development, this performance-based evaluation system to some extent guarantees equal opportunity and open competition to all applicants. Therefore, the role of social networks has been weakened, and individual faculty needs to be more responsible for their own performance so as to enhance their job security.

The Current State of Young Faculty

This discussion has shown that young faculty have become a major force in developing higher education in China. This subgroup within the academic profession has been growing in terms of its size, and strengthening both its qualifications and overall quality. Increasing numbers of young faculty hold a doctoral degree. With research universities' policies favoring the hiring of overseas returnees, the percentage of young faculty holding an overseas doctoral degree has risen. For example, 498 out of 2,979 full-time faculty members at Shanghai Jiao Tong University earned their doctorates abroad (Shanghai Jiao Tong University 2012). Due to diversified educational opportunities available to young people since the 1980s, more young faculty members have obtained overseas degrees than their senior peers. At the same time, both the government and universities have promoted policies and provided funding to encourage faculty to conduct research for a certain period of time at elite universities abroad, to actively engage in international academic networks, to participate in international conferences, to publish their work in English, and in turn to raise their visibility in the international academic world. Those policies ultimately intend to enhance teaching and research excellence in Chinese universities. There are few statistics yet available on young faculty's productivity and their engagement in international academic networks; however, we can surmise that, with international learning and research experience, young faculty at Chinese universities can be competitive at both national and international levels.

Young faculty's loyalty to their academic profession can be discussed through the lens of young academics' job satisfaction, which has become an important research topic in China. Research shows that young faculty are in general satisfied with their current work and position (Zhu and Zhuo 2005; Li 2008; Liu 2009; Yan 2011; Guo 2012). Academic posts are regarded as being of higher status in comparison to other occupations, in terms of reputation and social respect. Academics also feel positive about working conditions, including school infrastructure, laboratories, and equipment (Shen 2008). In turn, young faculty have relatively high loyalty and commitment to their profession (Chen and Zhu 2003; Guo 2012). However, ongoing occupational stress is discernible in relation to teaching, research, promotion, and financial income. These issues and concerns are further analyzed in the next section.

Young Faculty and the Challenges of the Academic Profession

In spite of the growing quality of young faculty in Chinese universities, it has been argued that young faculty are embedded in a hierarchical academic system. Their status in academia is structured and decided by both bureaucratic controls and market forces (Zhang 2008). With limited cultural and social capital, young faculty members are in a relatively disadvantaged position in Chinese academia. Key challenges for young faculty's professional development can be analyzed from the perspective of teaching, research, and financial incomes. These issues and concerns also reflect the structural forces influencing their career development and career opportunities.

From the perspective of teaching, young faculty are likely to have a higher teaching load than their senior colleagues. As a natural result of the expansion of Chinese higher education, increasing student enrollment caused growing demand for expanding teaching responsibilities. A large percentage of young faculty tend to teach more undergraduate courses than senior staff, as they have few research projects to conduct and have to fill departments' workload gaps (Yang, Ma, and Zhuang 2010). This practice can potentially constrain a young academic's professional development. Though few official statistics are available, research conducted by Shen, Gu, and Liu (2011) surveyed 68 universities in 11 provinces in China and showed that faculty assistant professor and teaching assistant positions in both teaching-oriented and research universities tend to spend more time teaching than their senior colleagues. In addition, faculty members in teaching-oriented universities teach significantly more hours than their peers at research universities.

Also, young faculty are generally highly educated and hold doctoral degrees, particularly at China's top universities. They may have achieved a high level of knowledge and skills in their own subject areas through postgraduate studies. However, possible lack of systematic teacher training may cause low teaching quality and fail to provide creative teaching methods. Universities usually provide short-term teacher training courses to new faculty prior to their beginning to teach; however, the training course itself focuses more on theoretical perspectives of teaching, such as theories of higher education and educational psychology. It may help young faculty improve their teaching quality to a certain extent, but more practice connected to daily teaching is needed.

From the perspective of research, young faculty tend to have fewer research opportunities (Yang 2009). Many research and funding opportunities have emerged at both national, provincial, and university levels; however, research resources are not equally distributed (Qian 2005). In terms of applying for national research grants, young faculty under the age of 35 are at a disadvantage. With a limited research network, young faculty may not have a high research reputation or visibility, and thus cannot successfully compete with well-known and experienced professors. It is true that research grant opportunities targeted at early-career faculty have been set up at the national level and promoted to young academics. However, a close look at the application requirements shows that the age limit of such grants are between 40 and 45 and an associate professor post is required; otherwise, applicants who are assistant professors need two recommendations from full professors. Without adequate research support, young faculty may not be able to develop high-quality research; and without a solid research foundation, young faculty are unlikely to succeed in applying for future research grants.

The employment reform since 2006 may also impact on young faculty's professional development, in relation to performance evaluation and promotion. As mentioned in the previous section, the post- and contract-based employment system has proven effective in attracting competent people, motivating faculty to work hard, and encouraging excellence and quality assurance management (Chen 2003). However, recent research shows that faculty in general feel increasing pressure to publish. Though they believe that quantity does not reflect quality of research output, they ultimately feel they must conform to the new employment regime brought about by the reform. The tradition of "publish or perish" has become prevalent in Chinese academia. Such a practice has caused further stress for young faculty, in addition to the conflict they already experience between teaching and research.

Also, from the perspective of financial income, young faculty are less satisfied (Zhu and Zhuo 2005; Zhang 2008; Yan 2011). Various government policy documents state the intention to raise academic salaries to similar levels as those found in industry and companies in the public sector. Since the salary reform in 2006, academic remuneration has been increased to a certain extent, but it remains lower than what can be earned in other professional contexts. From a human capital perspective, the low salary for young academics cannot match their educational investment, that is, time, energy, and money expended. In addition to their interest in developing a respectable career, young faculty at the age of 30 to 35 also face practical issues in life, such as starting families. With the current salary structure, a young faculty member may not be able to afford such life events, let alone aspire to a middle-class lifestyle. Lack of competitive salaries may make the academic career less attractive and cause talent loss in the higher education sector (Zhu and Zhuo 2005). Realizing this issue, many universities have set up special financial support programs to encourage young faculty development, such as start-up research funding, and relocation fees (Li 2008).

It can be argued that young faculty are placed at a disadvantage in the academic labor market. They tend to have heavy workloads, access to limited research opportunities, and on top of this receive relatively low salaries. Their roles and responsibilities within the academic workplace are structured by factors well beyond their control, particularly different management mechanisms—including the academic hierarchy, employment reform, and differences across disciplines. Thus, their professional development faces real constraints.

To fully support and attract the best young faculty, the Chinese government and universities need to take the following issues and concerns into consideration. First, the government and universities need to improve working conditions for young faculty and provide adequate financial support. Beyond salaries, nonmonetary benefits can also play a positive role in attracting talent. Second, the government and universities should further improve the existing employment reform. A performance-based evaluation system adopting both quantitative and qualitative measurement may be helpful to encourage and motivate academics. Third, an on-the-job training system should be provided to improve young faculty's teaching and research capabilities. Young faculty need to be trained with both professional knowledge and teaching skills before entering the classroom. Systematic professional training needs to be offered to young faculty throughout their academic development, to ensure they are equipped with up-to-date knowledge and skills. For example, centers for teaching and learning development have been set up to promote teaching excellence in leading universities, such as Tsing Hua University and Shanghai Jiao Tong University. These centers aim to provide fundamental training for new faculty and to conduct evaluation and research to analyze teaching and learning. Such professional training concepts need to be adopted on a wider scale across the Chinese higher education system.

Conclusion

The number of young faculty has increased significantly during the higher education expansion in China in recent years. The capacity and professional development of young faculty determines the overall competitiveness of Chinese higher education. This chapter focuses on young faculty under the age of 35 at public universities in China. It provides an overview of the Chinese academic market and the role of young faculty in the national higher education system; it also analyzes the ways young academics enter the academic profession and their common career pathways. Through the discussion of career concerns and conditions for promotion, we argue that the transition of Chinese higher education to a competitive corporate culture has brought both opportunities and challenges to young academics. To attract the best young academics, the Chinese government and universities need to improve working conditions and provide adequate financial support, to further improve the employment reform and performance evaluation system, and to provide well-developed on-the-job training services.

References

Altbach, Philip G. 2011. "The Academic Profession: The Realities of Developing Countries." In *The Decline of the Guru: The Academic Profession in Developing and Middle-Income Countries*, edited by P.G. Altbach, 205–223. New York: Routledge.

Austin, A.E., M.D. Sorcinelli, and M. McDaniels. 2007. "Understanding New Faculty: Background, Aspirations, Challenges and Growth." In *The Scholarship of Teaching and Learning in Higher Education an Evidence Based Perspective*, edited by R.P. Perry and J.C. Smart, 39–92. Dordrecht, Netherlands: Springer.

Chen, W.W., and H.Y. Zhu, 2003. "A Study of Young Teachers' Occupational Stability in Universities" (in Chinese). *Journal of Zhenjiang Education Institute* (5): 91–101.

Chen, X.M. 2003. "The Academic Profession in China." In *The Decline of the Guru: The Academic Profession in Developing and Middle-Income Countries*, edited by P.G. Altbach, 107–134. New York: Palgrave Macmillan.

China Post-Doctoral Researchers Committee. 2012. *Statistics for Post-Doctoral Training System* (in Chinese). http://res.chinapostdoctor.org.cn/Program/623ebe76-9731-46b7-a94c-011187683367/623ebe76-9731-46b7-a94c-011187683367_0.html.

Coleman, J. 1988. "Social Capital in the Creation of Human Capital." *American Journal of Sociology* 94(Supplement): 95–120. Reprinted in *Education, Culture, Economy and Society*, edited by A.H., Halsey, H. Lauder, P. Brown, and A.S. Wells. Oxford: Oxford University Press.

"Doctoral Education Quality in China" Research Group. 2010. *Report on Doctoral Education Quality in China* (in Chinese). Beijing: Peking University Press.

Goastellec, G., E. Park, G. Ates, and K. Toffel. 2013. "Academic Markets, Academic Careers: Where Do We Stand?" In *The Academic Profession in Europe: New Tasks and New Challenges*, edited by B. Kehm and U. Teichler, 93–120. Dordrecht, Netherlands: Springer.

Gu, H.B., and F. Cao. 2006. "The Weakness of University 'Academic Inbreeding' " (in Chinese). *21st Century Economic Report*, July 31.

Guo, Y.M. 2012. "A Satisfaction Study of University Young Faculty: A Case Study of Xia Men University" (in Chinese). *Reform and Opening* (4): 125–126.

Hong, Y., B.L. Zhong, Y.S. Zhao, and X.X. Zhang. 2012. "The History, Current Issues and Reform Orientation of China's Graduate Education" (in Chinese). *China Higher Education Research* (7): 41–46.

Jiang, X.M., and J. Shi. 2008. "An Analysis on Academic Inbreeding in China" (in Chinese). *Contemporary Education Forum* (1): 11–12.

Lai, M.H. 2012. "The Changing Work Life of Academics: A Comparative Study of a Renowned and a Regional University in the Chinese Mainland." *Australian Education Research.*

Li, F., J. Morgan, and X. Ding. 2008. "The Expansion of Higher Education, Employment and Over-Education in China." *International Journal of Educational Development* 28: 687–697.

Li, S. 2008. "An Analysis on University Faculty and the Economic Factors" (in Chinese). *Entrepreneur* (11): 106.

Li, Y., and X.F. Chen. 2006. "Reflection on the Scale Expansion of Graduate Education in China" (in Chinese). *Journal of Higher Education* 27(1): 70–75.

Lin, J. 2009. "Comparison of Faculty Inbreeding Between American and Chinese Higher Education Institutions" (in Chinese). *Journal of Higher Education* 30(12): 39–51.

Liu, Y. 2009. "Research on University Young Teachers' Career Development Planning" (in Chinese). *Higher Education Research and Evaluation* (7/8): 54–56.

Ma, W.H., and J.B. Wen. 2012. "A Study on Academic Salary and Remunerations in China." In *Paying the Professoriate: A Global Comparison of Compensation and* Contracts, edited by P. Altbach, L. Reisberg, M. Yudkevich, G. Androushchak, and I.F. Pacheco. London: Routledge.

Ministry of Education, China. 2012a. *Statistics for 2010.* http://www.moe.gov.cn/publicfiles/business/htmlfiles/moe/s6200/201201/129605.html.

Ministry of Education, China. 2012b. *Educational Statistics Yearbook of China 2010.* Beijing: People's Education Press.

Mohrman, Kathryn, Y. Geng, and Y. Wang. 2011. "Faculty Life in China." *The NEA 2011 ALMANAC of Higher Education.* Washington, DC: National Education Association.

Ni, M., S.D. Xiong, X.L. Zhang, C.Y. Cao, and K.Y. Yang. 2005. "About the Graduate Education in China Science Academy" (in Chinese). *Journal of Hunan University of Science and Engineering* 26(11): 296–298.

Pu, S.Z. 2009. "From Title to Post: Higher Education Salary System Reform" (in Chinese). *China Economic Guide* (16): 91.

Qian, H.L. 2005. *A Study of the Impact Factors on the Stability of Young Teachers in Higher Education* (in Chinese). MA dissertation. Wuhan: Huazhong University of Science and Technology.

Shanghai Jiao Tong University. 2012. *Shanghai Jiao Tong University Statistics 2011.* Strategic Planning Office, Shanghai Jiao Tong University.

Shen, H. 2008. "Progress of the Academic Profession in Mainland China. The Changing Academic Profession in International Comparative and

Quantitative Perspectives." Report of the International Conference on the Changing Academic Profession Project, 2008, *RIHE International Seminar Reports* 12 (September): 251–264. Research Institute for Higher Education, Hiroshima University, Japan.

Shen, H., Z.Y. Gu, and Q. Liu. 2011. "An Empirical Study on the Influencing Factors of Faculty Working Time" (in Chinese). *Journal of Higher Education* 32(9): 55–63.

Stith, A.L., L. Liu, and Y.B. Xu. 2011. "The Shaping of China's Postdoctoral Community" (in Chinese). *Chinese Education Society* 44(1): 58–92.

Sun, C., and Z.J. Wang. 2010. "Faculty Structure and Development in Chinese Higher Education Institutions" (in Chinese). *University* 8: 69–75.

The 985 Project Research Team. 2009. *The 985 Project: Ten-Year Summary Report* (in Chinese). Unpublished report.

Wang, Q., and J. Lowe. 2010. "Young People's Management of the Transition from Education to Employment in the Knowledge-Based Sector in Shanghai." *Journal of Education and Work* 24(1): 119–140.

Wong, S. 2009. "In China, An Easy Route to Academic Glory." *Asia Times Online*, November 25, http://www.atimes.com/atimes/China/KK25Ad01.html.

Xie, H.M., X.J. Xu, and D.Q. Wu. 2012. "Career Development of Returned Chinese Overseas Scholars in Universities" (in Chinese). *Contemporary Youth Research* 319(10): 19–24.

Yan, G.C. 2011. "The Situation of Academic Profession in China and Its Analysis" (in Chinese). *Journal of Higher Education* 32(11): 1–9.

Yang, B., Z.J. Ma, and S. Zhuang. 2010. "University Faculty Professional Development" (in Chinese). *Hei Long Jiang Higher Education (Higher Education Research and Evaluation)* (5): 53–54.

Yang, R. 2005. "The Chinese Professoriate in Comparative Perspective: Self-Perceptions, Academic Life, Gender Differences and Internal Differentiation." In *The Professoriate: Profile of a Profession*, edited by A. Welch, 179–192. Dordrecht: Springer.

Yang, X.P. 2009. *The Research of Impetus of the Growth of Young Faculty in Research Universities: Take Dalian University of Technology for Example* (in Chinese). MA dissertation, Dalian University of Technology.

Yu, K., A. Stith, L. Liu, and H.Z. Chen. 2010. *Tertiary Education at a Glance: China*. Shanghai: Shanghai Jiao Tong University Press.

Yuan, B.F. 2011. "Higher Education Performance-Based Salary System Reform" (in Chinese). *Journal of Huazhong Normal University* 50(6): 22–28.

Zhang, J.C. 2008. *The Floating Tribe in University Field: The Status Quo and Coping Strategies of Development of Young Teachers in Research University* (in Chinese). PhD thesis. Wuhan: Huazhong University of Science and Technology.

Zhang, Z.H., and L.H. Jiang. 2010. "Building Teams of Teachers Is Important to Assure the Quality of Higher Education: Analysis of Teachers' Employment" (in Chinese). *Academy* (1): 80–84.

Zhao, R. 2007. "Graduate Education in Chinese Research Institutions in the Context of Internationalization" (in Chinese). *Management and Review of Social Sciences* (1): 44–54.

Zhao, Y.D., D.S. Deng, Y. Ma, and Y.B. Hong. 2010. "Doctoral Graduates Employment Orientation." *Chinese Talent* (in Chinese) (4): 73–74.

Zhu, X.P., and Y.Z. Zhuo. 2005. "Research on Satisfaction of College Young Teachers: Analysis and Strategy" (in Chinese). *Journal of Higher Education* 26(5): 56–61.

Chapter 4

France

Long Waiting Lists Despite Minimally Attractive Academic Positions

Christine Musselin

As in many other countries, the situation of French PhDs is not flourishing. In contrast with many other countries, permanent positions are accessible just after completing a dissertation. However, the number of openings is decreasing while the number of applicants is not. With the development of project-based research, the number of temporary positions increased and doing a postdoc before getting a permanent position has become more frequent, when not compulsory in some disciplines. As a result, many PhD holders are going from one postdoc to another and are still waiting to become permanent faculty members.

This lack of available positions and the rather low salary offered to the lucky ones able to enter the permanent faculty staff of French universities lead many observers[1] to even more pessimistic views. They question the future capacity of French academia to attract the best graduates into doctoral programs.

In order to examine more thoroughly the French situation, the issues at stake, and the future trends, this chapter is organized as follows. First, some information is provided on the French higher education system and its main characteristics. In the second section, hiring procedures and their recent evolutions are described. In the third section, the French labor market for young academics is discussed: prospects for jobs in academia and outside academia are described, as well as the profiles of the newly recruited candidates and their evolution, and the underlying dynamics of this labor market. The next section is dedicated to the insertion of the newcomers into their departments and focuses on material, institutional, and relational conditions, while the following section provides some insights about what French young researchers themselves think about their prospects and experiences. Finally, reflections on the main issues at hand and future trends are identified.

General Characteristics of the French Higher Education System

This chapter focuses on universities but one must first acknowledge that France is probably the only country where universities are not the most prestigious institutions and generally do not train the elites. For historical reasons (Musselin 2004 [2001]; Verger and Charle 2012), vocational higher education institutions, called *grandes écoles*, train the industrial, commercial, and administrative elites. Until recently, many of the permanent faculty members of these schools were former students of these same schools, in some cases holding no PhD degree, not committed to research, and focused on providing vocational knowledge. Moreover, and also for historical reasons, French universities have for a long time not been the main sources for scientific production. The Napoleonic university, created at the beginning of the nineteenth century, was primarily teaching-oriented. In the 1930s, the French government decided to create a national research institution called the CNRS (Centre National de la Recherche Scientifique) to create research capacity. The CNRS covers all disciplines and is mostly oriented toward fundamental research. In the 1950s and 1960s, more research institutions were introduced; they are not as large as the CNRS and are more topic-based. Today, this institutional divide between the grandes écoles, the universities, and the research institutions, stressed by all publications on the French system, is blurred. On the one hand, some of the grandes écoles are now situated within universities. At the same time, research units within universities are often affiliated both to their university and simultaneously to one or more national research institutions. As a result, the staff working in these units might be either an employee of a research institution or a faculty member of the university. Fewer and fewer employees of research institutions are working in units exclusively affiliated to the research institution. For instance, 80 percent of the CNRS permanent researchers are located in universities.

University faculty members are only one part—even if the larger one—of the French higher education and research system. There are approximately 60,000 permanent university faculty members, compared to 11,450 CNRS permanent researchers. In order to simplify and to make this chapter comparable with others, there is a focus on faculty members in universities, but the reader must be aware that all new PhD holders may apply for a university position, a position in a research institution or, if their discipline is taught in the grandes écoles, for a position in a grande école. The hiring procedures in institutional sectors are different and they may stress different competences—for instance, the quality of research is the main criteria for the CNRS, but research is one among several criteria of interest for universities (Musselin 2009 [2005]). The career development issues are also specific to each sector, and the mobility between the sectors remains rather low. The attractiveness of the different sectors also varies; in management, for instance, grandes écoles increasingly recruit PhD holders and offer them better salaries and conditions, leading many young doctors in management studies to go for positions at the grandes écoles rather than at the university. In biology, the INSERM or the CNRS is more attractive than universities or engineering schools for young doctors who are strongly research-oriented. The chance of getting a position is also different across the sectors, and generally higher at universities than at research institutions,[2] or at grandes écoles, where the ratio of permanent teachers to students is generally much lower than in universities because the grandes écoles more often employ part-time faculty or practitioners in their teaching programs.

Even if the share of university students in the overall student population tends to decline, it remains the largest share because access to undergraduate studies at universities is guaranteed to all *baccalauréat* holders, while access to grandes écoles—and among them to the most prestigious ones—remains very selective. Therefore, the first wave of massification (that occurred from the end of the 1950s to the end of the 1960s) and the second wave (from the second half of the 1980s to mid-1990s) were first of all confronted and absorbed by universities. To face this challenge, the number of university faculty members has increased substantially since the 1960s, but always with some delay and often less rapidly than the increase in student numbers.[3] It also stagnated each time the increase in students slowed down, thus adopting a stop-and-go dynamic. For this reason, French universities have seen periods of job opportunities followed by periods of scarcity, coinciding with the retirements of those who had the chance to enter the academic career or a new increase in the student population. For some years now, the main drivers for vacancies have been retirements (baby boomers are going into pension) and the last decade has been especially difficult for early career researchers. The stagnation in student numbers and the financial crisis led to a decrease in the number of open positions within the last five years (discussed later in this chapter), while the training of doctorates progressed both qualitatively—with the introduction of doctoral schools and doctoral programs—and quantitatively (up 9 percent from 2000 to 2009, according to the ministry[4]). Parallel to this evolution, the trend toward project-based funding favored the expansion of postdoctoral positions and the constitution of a population of casual research staff working on time-limited contracts. Unfortunately, there are no general figures about this population.

Another French characteristic worth noting is the composition of the university faculty staff and the specific career trajectory of French academics. As stated by Enders and Musselin (2008), the French approach is different from both the tenure track system of the United States (consisting of two time-limited contracts of three years followed by an extensive evaluation to decide whether an academic becomes tenured) and the "survivor" process that is typical in Germany, for instance (involving a long period of time-limited contracts that may finally culminate in securing a professor position, mostly after age 40). France is characterized by a pyramidal system in which access to a permanent position—with the title *maître de conferences*—is supposed to occur just after receipt of the PhD and happens rather young (at age 33, on average, in 2011).

After writing a second thesis (called the *habilitation à diriger des recherches* or HDR) or, for some disciplines (law, management, economics, political science), after successfully passing a national selective exam called the *agrégation du supérieur*, some maîtres de conférences enter the corps of the *professeurs* (equivalent to associate or full professors in the United States). However, some never make it to this level, either because they decide not to write an HDR or prepare the agrégation du supérieur, or because they try but fail. Because there is no "up or out" mechanism, those who do not achieve the level of *professeur* remain in a position of maître de conférences until they retire. The proportion between the two corps is about one-third professors (36 percent) and two-thirds (64 percent) maîtres de conferences. This means a heavy bottom and a rather narrow summit. The group formed by these two populations is collectively called the *enseignants-chercheurs* and they are civil servants. There exists other categories of permanent (civil servant) faculty members teaching at French universities, namely high school teachers assigned to universities[5] (*professeurs certifies* or *professeurs agrégés*). These individuals might have a PhD but most of them do not. They teach twice as much as maîtres de conferences and are not expected to do research. They mostly teach undergraduates.

All other members of the university faculty staff (a little more than 25 percent) are working on time-limited contracts. Some are "PAST" (*professeurs associés* or affiliated staff)—they work part time outside academia (within a firm, for instance) and the other half as maîtres de conférences or professors at the university. Another important group consists of the ATER (*attachés temporaires d'enseignement et de recherche*); most of the time, these positions consist of a two-year, nonrenewable contract for doctoral candidates close to the end of their PhD, or new PhD holders. The teaching duties are the same as for a maître de conférences. A final group consists of PhD candidates with a doctoral contract (which provides a salary paid for a three-year period in order to prepare a PhD).[6] These individuals get a higher wage if they teach 64 hours a year at their university. In terms of numbers for the different groups of faculty teaching at French universities, Table 4.1 provides the most recent figures.

In recent years, a new population has developed in French academia. They are called *postdocs*. This term designates all kinds of time-limited contracts for PhD holders. Two groups should be distinguished here: the postdocs working on a research project directed by one professor or a group of permanent staff, and the postdocs opened for one or two years where the position holders independently decide the topic on which they will work. In the former case, the content of the research led by the postdocs is determined by the research project of permanent members and might be quite different from what they did during their PhD or would like to work on. In the latter, which is rarer, the postdocs can better develop their own research agenda and spend time writing publications based on their doctoral work and enriching their resume. Both types of positions existed before (even from the early 1980s) but they were not all called postdocs and, more important, they were less numerous in the past. Since the creation of the ANR (*Agence Nationale de la Recherche*, a national research council) in 2005, project-based research has flourished and the number of postdoc positions has increased. It is nevertheless very difficult to say by how much and also how many there are today. There is no central tracking of this fluid population, so we do not know precisely their number, what they do, or what they go on to become. We just see their share growing in the yearly social report of the French national research institutions.[7]

Table 4.1. University academic staff, 2010–2011

	Professors	*Maîtres de conférences*	Affiliated staff	High school teachers	Specific staff	ATER	PhDs with fellowships	Total
Law*	2,697	5,991	1,252	1,658		1,545	3,293	15,184
Humanities	4,641	11,188	934	6,851	1,057**	2,051	4,372	30,160
Science	8,131	17,255	688	4,382		2,212	4,772	36,752
Medicine	5,002	3,342	233		4,249***	116	246	12,955
Total	21,084	38,266	3,110	12,891	5,306	5,948	12,683	96,178

Source: http://cache.media.enseignementsup-recherche.gouv.fr/file/2012/36/8/NI_MESR_12_082012_221368.pdf (accessed December 15, 2012)

Notes:

Gray = civil servants

*Law = law, economics, management and political science

**Lecturers in languages mostly

***Specific staff in medicine

Ways to Enter the University Job Market

The general description provided earlier sets the frame in which academic trajectories develop in France, so we now look at how one enters the university job market.

In the 1970s and 1980s, access to academic careers mainly relied on interpersonal relationships. Most of the people interviewed for a study on academic trajectories (Musselin, Pigeyre, and Sabatier 2011), who had been recruited to permanent positions at that time, explained that they had been asked "by chance" by one of their professors if they would like to become an assistant. This might still exist today, but most of the time more collective, competitive, and strategic processes are observed. As a matter of fact, the path leading from a master's to a PhD is more organized than before.

In the mid-1990s the Ministry pushed for the creation of doctoral schools[8] and this led to the introduction of procedures, rules, and criteria in decisions pertaining to PhD candidates. The idea was to create specific structures in charge of PhD programs, most of the time for a group of disciplines. With the Bologna Process, the idea that PhD candidates should be taught has spread and such candidates are now required to attend 90 hours of taught coursework in three years. Before, PhD candidates had no classes and their training only occurred through the relationship with their supervisor, which was sometimes very loose and intermittent. The main objective of the new doctoral schools is to reduce the number of years spent on PhDs, to diminish the dropout rates, to improve the quality of the PhDs produced and the quality of the supervision, and also to revise the master-disciple relationships prevailing between a PhD candidate and his *directeur de thèse* (PhD supervisor, only one person most of the time in France). Today, the allocation of PhD fellowships (now called *doctoral contracts*) is no more in the hands of the person in charge of a master's program as it was in the past, but is more and more collectively decided on by a committee.[9] In some cases, calls for proposals are issued in order to encourage candidates trained in master's programs from other universities to also apply, thus increasing the level of competition and the formalization of the process, as selection procedures are explicitly designed (including selection on dossiers and interviews) and criteria are detailed. The research units in which the PhD candidates will prepare their doctorate may also have introduced a selection process before pushing for their candidates at the level of the doctoral schools. The variety in the concrete practices developed by the graduate schools is high and all did not go as far in the formalization of these processes (Dahan 2011), but there is a general trend toward more rules and more competition. This is probably the reason why, in the interviews held with recently recruited faculty, these individuals showed more strategic behaviors than their predecessors in the way they handled their career. For example, in the 1970s, a professor might have suggested that a student apply for a PhD fellowship. But such a process no longer depends solely on the suggestion of one's professor. The interviewees also often say that they were aware of the problems of employment faced by PhD holders and tried, for some at least, to be strategic about the choice of where to complete the PhD with poststudy employment prospects specifically in mind.

With important variations among disciplines, and from institution to institution within the same discipline, there is also a global trend toward more attention paid to PhD training and more collective supervision. This includes preparing the future doctors to hiring norms, that is, making sure they will meet the minimum expectations (for instance, having some teaching experience or having a paper published or submitted for publication), and even in some cases, "coaching them"—some labs organize mock interviews in order to train their doctorates for the interview phases.

Once a doctor—and with the exception of some disciplines like life sciences, but also physics, where at least one postdoc (abroad, if possible) is required—the early career researcher can apply for vacant positions leading to permanent posts as maîtres de conférences in universities. The first step is to apply for what is called *qualification*; this step is required for university positions but not for the CNRS. A national body, the *Conseil National des Universités* (CNU), made of discipline-based commissions, examines once a year the dossiers sent by new doctorates[10] and decides whether they are qualified, that is, whether a person can apply for a position in a French university. What is required might vary from one discipline to another (as can be seen by reading the advice to applicants posted in recent years by most of the discipline-based commissions of the CNU on their websites). However, some general issues are common for all, such as: the quality of the PhD; the assessments collected in the report written by each PhD defense jury;[11] the teaching experience of the candidates (have they taught different levels of classes and a variety of topics?); any papers or books already published, and their quality.

Those who are qualified by the CNU can then apply to all vacant maîtres de conférences positions. The qualification policy of the various CNU commissions might be quite different. Some are very Malthusian and

Jacobin,[12] and they qualify the number of individuals that is quite close to the number of positions that will be opened, thus leaving little room to the recruiting universities; others qualify all the people they consider bright enough to compete for vacant positions. The rate of qualification[13] in 2011 ranged from 20 percent in public law to 95 percent in mathematics.[14] This qualification is granted for four years and is renewable.

Since the 2007 act, a *comité de sélection* (hiring committee) is set for each vacant position at the department level, and its composition must be approved by the university president. It can include between 8 to 16 academics, 50 percent of them being external, that is, coming from institutions other than the recruiting university. When they meet, at least 50 percent of the present members must be external.[15] They generally start by meeting once in order to sort out some of the dossiers and invite a short list of candidates (ten to fifteen) to come for an interview. Most of the time the candidates are invited on the same date and are submitted, one after another, to an interview lasting 20 to 30 minutes. This is a very short time to decide that someone will serve as a civil servant over the next thirty years, and although this standard is not compulsory but rather inherited, most universities still proceed in this way,[16] "as they always have." At the end of the day, the committee makes a decision and produces a ranking. If the top candidate accepts the position, the process is over. In most cases there is no negotiation with the candidates about the working conditions. The salary is fixed according to a national scale and therefore salaries are the same for all disciplines and all universities.

The Labor Market for Young Academics

After this description of the processes leading to the university job market, we look at how the latter is developing. In the first section we address this specific issue and then describe the job market outside academia.

The University Job Market

Although the quantitative growth in project-based research increased, the number of positions available for work on a research project for a limited period of time (sometimes up to four years), the number of maîtres de conférences positions opened each year tends to diminish. (See Table 4.2.)

One could expect that these two parallel dynamics would lead to an increase in the average age of access to a first permanent position and

Table 4.2. Number of first positions opened (2004 to 2011)

Year	2004	2005	2006	2007	2008	2009	2010	2011
Positions	1,975	1,967	**2,318**	2,135	2,060	1,977	1,797	**1,709**

Source: Figures were extracted from the statistics available on the website of the French ministry for Higher Education and Research (MESR): http://www.enseignement sup-recherche.gouv.fr/cid22708/bilans-statistiques.html (accessed December 15, 2012)

a longer delay between the end of the PhD and this first position. But this is not the case. A recent study (Musselin, Pigeyre, and Sabatier 2011) compared the profiles of those getting a first permanent position today with those in the 1990s, 1980s, and 1970s. The study looked at the average age, the delay between the PhD and access to a maître de conférences position, and the age of the academics when they obtained their PhD. Surprisingly, we observed that those who get such positions display the same profiles today as in the last several decades. They are young, quick, and early. In recent years, the average age of access has remained stable, between 32 and 33, with important variations across disciplines (six years of difference in average between humanities and sciences), see Table 4.3.

Most of the candidates getting a first maître de conférences position get it within two to three years following completion of their PhD (again, with variations according to disciplines) and received their PhD quite young, meaning that they had a rather standard scholar trajectory (no or few repeated years, no or few bifurcations from one trajectory to another, etc.). Between 2007 and 2011, for instance, almost 50 percent (although a little less in 2011) of those who got a maître de conférences position were "qualified"[17] the year they applied for this position. As most people apply for qualification just after getting their PhD,[18] the delay between the end of the PhD and their access to a position was very short for these candidates. Twenty-five percent of the newly recruited were qualified a year before, and around 16 percent two years before, so almost 90 percent of the new maîtres de conférences received their PhD within three years.[19] The differences among disciplines are quite interesting here. In 2011, 66 percent of the newly recruited were "qualified in the year" in law, almost 40 percent in humanities (however, this rate stood at 51 percent in 2007 and has decreased every year since), and 45 percent in science. The decrease in open positions mentioned above therefore leads to the fact that more and more candidates who are young, early, and rapid do

Table 4.3. Evolution of the average age of access to a position of *maître de conferences* (2001–2011)

Year	2001	2002	2003	2004	2005	2006	2007	2008	2009	2010	2011
Average age in years, months	33, 7	33, 10	33, 5	32, 8	32, 9	32, 8	32, 10	32, 9	33	33	33, 1

Source: Figures were extracted from the statistics available on the website of the French ministry for Higher Education and Research (MESR): http://www.enseignementsup-recherche.gouv.fr/cid22708/bilans-statistiques.html (accessed December 15, 2012) not get a position when they apply (while they would have gotten one if more positions were opened). Thus, demonstrating these characteristics (i.e., young, quick, and early) does not guarantee access to employment anymore. These characteristics are decisive factors, but not sufficient conditions to ensure employment success.

Two consequences can be drawn from the previous remarks. On the one hand, French hiring committees do not seem to modify their preferences despite the scarcity in positions. In other words—and too simplistically—they generally prefer a young candidate having just finished a PhD to a candidate who has not secured a position five years after completing a PhD. On the other hand, and as a result, it seems that the longer you work as a postdoc, the less chance you have to get a maître de conférences position. A kind of reverse seniority process seems to be in place.

These trends are not easy to document, as there are no complete data on French part-time staff. But a recent study led by the ANR about the postdocs employed on projects funded by the ANR seems to confirm this dynamic and adds another component to it. The ANR declared that "their" postdocs often get a position during the project (which is a problem for the project leaders who must recruit new staff) or just after this postdoc experience. ANR projects are rather prestigious because they result from a selective process. This means that project leaders can also be selective in the recruitment of their postdocs (and choose among those just finishing their PhD). Thus, being a postdoc on a ANR project becomes a quality signal for hiring committees when ANR postdocs apply for a job. This reveals the existence of segmentation among postdocs. Therefore, the problem is not so much to get a postdoc (with the general development of project-based research, the offer in postdocs has increased) but to get a "good" postdoc, that is, a postdoc with a reputable research team, leading to interesting publications, not too far from your own interests or field, that can be used as a signal for quality among prospective employers.

Beyond being young, early, and rapid, the newly recruited maîtres de conférences share further characteristics.[20] First, the percentage of females is rising. In the three disciplines studied by Musselin, Pigeyre and Sabatier (2011), they observed a clear trend in this direction, even if some disciplines like physics remain very male. (See Table 4.4.)

In some disciplines (life sciences or management, for instance) women are more numerous.[21] Nevertheless, in the sciences the share of females remains low among both candidates and those hired. Even if indi-

Table 4.4. Percentage of women recruited in the different cohorts and disciplines

	Cohort 1976–1977	Cohort 1986–1987	Cohort 1996–1997	Cohort 2006–2207
Management	40	16	48	54
History	32	26	41	42
Physics	22	27	23	17

Source: Musselin, Pigeyre and Sabatier (2011)

rect discrimination may happen and is still difficult to control (Musselin and Pigeyre 2009), it seems that hiring committees are not discriminatory at the entry level.

Because of the idiosyncratic character of the recruitments procedures (i.e., a PhD is not enough, and you must be qualified before applying for vacant positions, which, furthermore, are most of the time posted on university websites and in ministerial publications but not in newspapers), newly recruited maîtres de conférences are not very international. When there are international applications, they are also mostly emanating from internationals already familiar with the French system. The whole process being in French (and classes mostly given in French), applicants must be francophone. This reduces the scope of potential international candidates even if university faculty members are among the few civil servants allowed not to be French. Between 1998 and 2010 (a 13-year period), 2,697 non-French maîtres de conférences were recruited, so about 207 each year. For the 174 recruited in 2010, 85 came from Europe, 53 from Africa, 25 from Asia, 7 from South America, 3 from North America, and 1 from Australia.[22]

When it comes to the reverse situation, French young researchers are not often looking at the international job market.[23] Mobility primarily concerns postdocs and is first of all oriented to the United States. The number of French working abroad as academics seems rather low, except for some disciplines (such as economics, for instance). Nevertheless, as highlighted by the frequent declarations on the brain drain threat faced by France, it seems that French academics who apply abroad are successful. Further studies would be needed to more precisely know which disciplines are concerned, and the conditions to meet in order to get a position abroad (for example, in which language was the individual's PhD written, what kind of publications had been produced when he or she applied abroad, did he or she spend a postdoc period or was the individual visiting in the country where he or she was recruited). Research quality is at stake in international recruitments but networks are not completely irrelevant (Musselin 2009 [2005]).

A further characteristic of the French university job market, despite its national character, is that it is not uniform—each position is unique. As a result, the pressure ratio (number of candidates applying for a position) for each position depends on the discipline and on the post itself—whether it is "high-profile," whether the department is well-known, whether it is a department involved in vocational teaching (which means more time for pedagogical duties, less time for research, and more risk of not being able to do what is needed to become a professor), whether it is located in an attractive place (i.e., well served by public transportation, or sunny, or close to family), and so on. The national data provided each year by the French ministry on the yearly recruitments show that some positions easily find a candidate while others remain vacant. The 2011 report concludes that universities located in the Ile de France (i.e., Paris and its suburbs) and in large French metropolises received many applications and were successful in recruiting someone in close to 100 percent of the cases. But, the situation is more difficult and reveals important variations among universities located in small cities; in some cases, they were able to recruit for only 80 percent of the positions opened. In some cases all the candidates ranked by a committee declined the offer (32 of the 1,707 positions opened in 2011 remained vacant for that reason), because the candidates got another offer in a more attractive place.

In such situations, inbreeding may be a way out, but in recent years, this practice has been heavily criticized (see, for instance, Godechot and Louvet 2008), and the inbreeding rate has become one of the indicators institutions have to provide when they are evaluated by the National Agency for Evaluation (AERES, *Agence d'Evaluation de la Recherche et de l'Enseignement Supérieur*). This might explain why inbreeding tends to decrease, no matter how it is measured,[24] In 2010, only 25 percent of the new maîtres de conférences were recruited by the university that already employed them as a postdoc or ATER, and this number decreased over the previous ten years (it reached 43.2 percent in 2002 and 32.6 percent in 2005, for instance). Also in 2010, 79 percent of the new maîtres de conférences got their PhD from a university other than the one that recruited them (meaning that 21 percent were recruited by the same institution where they got their PhD). Many reasons can explain the resilience of inbreeding, even if it decreases. There is security provided by the fact that you already know the person and that he or she will be able to provide what is expected. There is less probability that this person will move rapidly to another place or refuse the offer. There is a higher chance that this person will feel committed to the hiring institution's location and not be a "prof TGV."[25] This is also a way to secure some positions for your own PhDs and still remain an attractive place for new PhDs.[26]

As a whole, the university job market in France has evolved in many respects (more women, less inbreeding), but in others it remains quite the same (still not very international, for instance). Despite the increase in postdoc positions and in opened positions, the average age of access to a permanent position remains stable and reveals a preference for young, early, and rapid candidates, leaving outside those pursuing postdocs for too long.

The Job Market Outside Academia

In the case of France, this situation of young doctors not getting a job in academia is all the more problematic given that firms and public administration are still reluctant to hire PhDs. As a result, positions traditionally held by doctors in other countries are occupied in France by graduates from master's programs. The case of engineers is typical and exemplary for this. The prestige of the French engineering grandes écoles leads research and development (R&D) departments in firms to recruit among the engineers (master's level) trained by these schools rather than among PhD holders trained by universities. As mentioned in the introduction, this is (slowly) evolving—in the past, the engineering grandes écoles were hardly research-oriented and had no or very limited doctoral programs, but today they are pushing some of their students to go for PhDs, or some of these schools deliver PhD programs themselves. The same reluctance for PhDs is nevertheless observable for high civil service positions in the French administration. The creation of a specific grande école to train civil servants (the *Ecole Nationale d'Administration*, created in 1945), and the quasi-absence of relations between this school and universities, has never facilitated the access of PhDs to such positions.

Reciprocally, because jobs for PhD holders were first of all for the academic profession, PhD candidates rarely engage in doctoral study with the aim of working outside academia. Not getting a job in the academic profession was long seen as a failure and not as an opportunity or a positive choice. Although many efforts have been undertaken—such as the development of joint PhD fellowships, linking a university and an employer—to change the situation on both sides (i.e., among employers and PhD candidates), PhDs are still not recognized as a level of qualification (as master's are for instance) by firms or public administration, and do not provide access to a higher position or a higher salary in the public and private sector.

This probably explains the decrease in numbers of students in research-oriented master's programs (as opposed to the professional master's degrees) created with the Bologna reform. Indeed, when choosing where to apply for master's-level study, bachelor's degree holders prefer a path possibly leading more directly to a job. As some nevertheless opt for a PhD after their professional master's, the number of PhD candidates remains high, but academics frequently express doubts about the attractiveness of their profession and the quality of those wanting to prepare a PhD. They often complain that they lose the best students, which is impossible to demonstrate.

Nevertheless, it seems reasonable to observe that the recurrent critiques written about French universities, the job insecurity of young researchers, and the low prestige of academic positions in French society, do not help attracting young people to academia. However, one might also argue that only the very motivated are entering the academic process and making it successfully through the whole process.

Contracts at Entry Level

But what is the situation of the happy few who get a permanent job? Let us now turn to what happens in terms of salary and working conditions once a maître de conférences is hired. We first address the financial conditions before looking at their professional integration.

As mentioned earlier, maîtres de conférences are permanent civil servants. After an 18-month period of probation, the newcomer is confirmed.[27] There is then no end to the position until retirement, except for extraordinary reasons (criminal activity, for instance). The access to the civil service comes with all the social benefits attached to it (permanent employment, social insurance, pensions, etc.)

How to Read Salaries in France

Except where noted in the text, the salaries presented in this part of the chapter are monthly and "brut," which means that what the employer pays for social insurance, pensions, etc. has already been deducted but not the compelling share the employee has to pay him/herself for the same welfare programs. This share reaches around 16 percent of the "brut" salary. This means that when you have a brut of 2,000 euros per month, you only get around 1,700 euros in your bank account. You then have to pay revenue taxes. It is impossible to give an idea of the percentage of the salary taken by these taxes, as it depends on whether one is married or not, the salary of the spouse, the number of children, etc.

The salary conditions for a candidate getting a maître de conférences position are set according to a national salary scale that takes into account the individual's past trajectory, his family situation, and the location of the university. The location of the university is relevant in the sense that France is divided in three zones; zones 1 and 2 allow access to a "territorial premium" (1 percent top up of the salary in zone 2 and a 3 percent top up in zone 1, where Paris is located) in order to take into account the differential cost of living in different places.

The first degree on the salary scale is 2,068.85 euros (*brut* [gross]). But often the individual's previous positions (for instance, as an ATER or as the holder of a three-year PhD fellowship), are taken into account in the calculation of seniority and this provides access to a higher salary group on the maîtres de conférences scale. Salary then increases according to seniority from echelon 1 (2,069 euros per month *brut*) to echelon 9 (3,800 euros per month brut). Some maîtres de conférences will be promoted (based on merit) to maîtres de conférences *hors classe*. This opens access to another seniority-based salary scale, from echelon 1 (3,046 euros brut) to echelon 8 (4,460 euros brut). This *classe* is mostly for those who will not try to, or never succeed in, becoming a professor.

With the exception of a few places, there is no negotiation about research conditions or specific housing options when an individual is offered a maître de conférences position. Getting one's own office, even one's own desk within a shared office, is not always guaranteed.

In recent years, some universities have tried to improve the conditions for new arrivals. Some organize a welcome party with all the newly recruited staff of the year; some reduce the teaching duty for newcomers in order for them to still have time to carry on their research while at the same time preparing their classes. But, this is still rare and the first years are often a period where one must teach classes that are new, which have to be developed from nothing, and are often those courses the other teaching staff do not want (i.e., not one's first choice); and where one is asked to take over the responsibility of a program (for instance, the third year of the bachelor program) or some administrative responsibility. Given these circumstances, it is not rare for some to quickly start disengaging from research.

The texts defining the duties of maîtres de conférences are national and not very precise. Maître de conferences are supposed to spend half of their time teaching and half researching. The teaching obligation is for 192 hours a year, including grading exams and other activities (for instance, being head of department), as specified in the 2009 reform.[28] This leaves room in the individual's schedule, and therefore the first years following the first permanent position are crucial for the development of individual career trajectories and, *in fine*, for access (or not) to professorship. Different factors may have an influence. The first is the place where one is recruited. Departments (or disciplines) that are student-heavy are less favorable in terms of teaching load. In a study focused on four disciplines, for instance, Musselin and Becquet (2008) observed that the demand for training in management was so high that it was difficult for newly recruited academics not to accept supplementary hours, particularly if they gave access to extra income. Even if this study observed that the preparation and the content of teaching in this discipline was rather specific and could be less time consuming, the young maîtres de conférences all had to spend many hours in class, while the physicists had a less heavy teaching load because of the heavy decrease in student numbers in these disciplines. The same study also observed that in large departments it is more frequent to teach one's own topic, while in small departments, more polyvalence is required. The existence and competence of some administrative support also makes a difference—in order to send applications to the young researcher program of the ANR or to the early career ERC (European Research Council) grants, places with dedicated staff provide an advantageous environment for their young faculty interested in research.

For some of the newly recruited, the first position might be a shock if they prepared their PhD in a rather protected research unit and developed an idealized representation of what academic life is, but then got a position in a department facing a heavy teaching load, where students are less well-prepared and where the newest hires are given the classes and responsibilities no other faculty member wants (a practice still rather frequent in French academia!). Some realize with fear that they will not be able to carry on their research ambitions, that their day-to-day life will be mostly dedicated to teaching and administrative tasks, despite the fact that they decided to prepare a PhD for the sake of "Science." As resignations by maîtres de conferences are rare, one might conclude that such individuals eventually learn to cope with this situation. Nevertheless, in interviews with academics recruited in 2006/2007, disappointment and criticism were rather frequent, even if these individuals were at the same time relieved to have a permanent position (Musselin, Pigeyre, and Sabatier 2011).

To these contextual constraints, one must add more relational ones. Within the same discipline, Becquet and Musselin (2008) studied places where the older staff was very supportive of young people, reminding them of the career requisites and encouraging them to meet such expectations, or even allocating tasks in a way that allowed those writing their *habilitation* or preparing the agrégation du supérieur to teach less or have less administrative burden. In other places, nobody cared about the newcomers or bothered to coach them. As quantitatively shown by previous work on the United States (Allison and Long 1990), the work environment also plays a role in France—belonging to a department where research is prioritized and where colleagues publish in good journals provides a push to publish and to do research. The discourses held by those recruited in very active places was clearly different from what was heard from others located in more "sleepy" departments (Musselin and Becquet 2008). Nevertheless, Musselin and Becquet (2008) also concluded that the management of careers in France is mostly dependent on individuals themselves, within the framework constructed by the opportunities and constraints mentioned earlier. Compared to the influence of the human resource management offices in the United Kingdom (Paye 2013), which have developed procedures, instruments, and devices, and followed the careers of individuals faculty members, French academics are left quite alone and free to construct their own route. This is, on the one hand, an opportunity, as this increases autonomy, but, on the other hand, it may be a danger if one follows a path to a dead end.

Finally, family situation and gender also play a role in this process. In a study of the access to professorships in management, Pigeyre and Sabatier (2012) observed that women with children were clearly discouraged when it came to preparing and applying for the agrégation du supérieur—the very time-consuming preparation it requires is difficult to achieve and tiring when you have young children and a husband working as an executive in a firm with no flexible schedule (which was frequently the case for the women interviewed for the study) (Pigeyre and Sabatier 2012). On top of that, success with the agrégation du supérieur may result in getting a position located quite far from one's residence, and many of the young women interviewed were less willing than men to become a "prof TGV" for at least three years (the minimum period before being allowed to apply for another position). As a result, while the application and hiring process is not discriminatory itself—female applicants are as successful as men (Pigeyre and Sabatier 2012)—the number of female applicants remains low compared to men.

Being in a department with a strong research tradition or a heavy teaching load, having supportive colleagues or, on the contrary, colleagues not caring about the younger staff or even leaving them the tasks they do not want to take on, makes a difference for newly recruited staff and might affect their career development and chances to become a professor. This might be accentuated by the publication of the evaluations of research labs by the Agency for the evaluation of research and teaching (AERES) since 2006.

Current State of Young Generation of University Faculty

Are young, French, academic staff satisfied? Do they think like their older colleagues? Do they have different expectations? Because no large survey on French academics has been undertaken, it is very difficult to know what French academics think and whether the young generation thinks differently from the older. This chapter, therefore, relies on rather heterogeneous sources in order to first provide information about the postdoc population and then offer an overview on some attitudes observed among the French university staff.

Not surprisingly, postdoctoral positions are not easy to cope with. This was one of the conclusions of previous but already quite old qualitative studies (Mouranche 1997; Dedieu 2002) on postdocs that showed that the living conditions of postdocs are difficult, not only because of job insecurity but also because of their work situation. Postdocs are expected to work hard for their employers and convince themselves that they have an interest in working hard in order to improve their CV. In science, especially, they are often working on topics whose results and processes are less certain than those of doctoral candidates, thus increasing the stress on results. Furthermore, most of the research units employing them indicate that they do not feel responsible for them; what happens to them after their contract is over is not an issue for their employers. Finally, when they are obliged to work on projects that are quite far from their own interests (a situation that is rather frequent in humanities and social sciences), they are also often torn between what they have to achieve for the project and their own aspirations for publication.

The recourse to temporary staff is not new in France but the situation of the current postdocs is rather different from the situation of young researchers in the mid-1970s and even mid-1980s (although vacant positions were also very scarce at that time). The temporary contracts on which the older generation relied before getting a job were one-year contracts, renewed within the same department until a permanent position was opened and most of the time allocated to the temporary teacher with the highest seniority. This waiting list system was not comfortable but was more secure than successive postdocs in different places, and the department (often) felt responsible for these individuals. As a result, biographical interviews with the older generation show that they were less mobile, often in their temporary positions by chance, waiting for their turn, and not under pressure for publication. By contrast, academics who recently succeeded in entering the academic profession say that the period before they got a job was characterized by time pressure, that they themselves were anxious, and that they developed rather strategic behaviors: looking for the right unit to prepare the right PhD, trying to choose the right place for their postdoc, applying for some places and not for others (at least the first time they applied).

If we now consider university permanent staff, whatever their seniority, two studies provide some information. The first one is a survey conducted in 2005 (Faure and Soulié 2006) on a population of academics who signed a petition against the Belloc report (2003), which suggested new rules for the academic profession. Despite this sampling bias, it is interesting to notice that there is a consensus among them on the increase in the variety of tasks they have to achieve as well as on the expansion in teaching and administrative activities (thus, less time for research). They were also very preoccupied by the change in norms and values academia was experiencing, according to them. A more recent survey (Chatelain et al. 2012), which again did not cover all academics[29] and aimed at studying the governance of French universities, suggests further conclusions because it included some questions on individual attitudes. It shows that the feeling of belonging to their university is rather high among French academics. Affiliation to the disciplines is somewhat higher, but the differences between the two are quite low. On a scale from 1 (low) to 7 (high), faculty members indicate a feeling of belonging of 6.13 to their discipline and 5.75 to their university.

Chatelian et al. (2012) also looked at their attachment to public values, their attitudes vis-à-vis performance-based funding, and increased differentiation among individuals, units, or institutions. They observed that, compared with administrative staff and the president and their team, French academics are attached to public values and rather against performance-based funding and increased differentiation, but much more so if they were maîtres de conférences rather than professors, and somewhat more so if they had seniority of more than ten years in academia. One may conclude that the attitudes and values of the young generation, despite having been trained in a more competitive setting, have not radically evolved.

Main Challenges and Future Trends

The new national government in place following the presidential elections in May 2012 is preparing some reforms that should be announced by spring 2013. Some orientations are already known, such as a decrease in project-based funding (an increase in lump-sum budgets), the creation of new positions (1,800 in 2013), the recognition of the PhD as a qualification, and so on. This could somewhat relax the tensions in the academic labor market. However, there is not much hope that it will strongly improve this labor market or that a dramatic expansion of the university system will occur and lead to more recruitment; most of the retirement wave is over and no strong increase in the student population is expected. Doors will not be largely opened in a near future, if ever.

Three main challenges are to be faced. The first one concerns the attractiveness of doctoral programs. There is a risk that fewer students will begin a PhD, or that the best students will not pursue advanced studies. This could change if PhD holders were better welcomed by the nonacademic market and better paid than master's degree holders. The recognition of the PhD is therefore a first important step to keep doctoral programs attractive, renew the population of faculty members in the future, but also to train highly qualified staff for the nonacademic sector.

Another challenge has to do with the competition between the salaries and working conditions offered by firms or even the top public administration and those offered by universities. Even with the recent investments in the higher education and research system, universities simply cannot offer the same material benefits as these other potential employers. The lack of prestige of French universities in the training of a highly qualified labor force has led to endemic underfunding and rather low investments in this sector for a long time. This cannot be radically modified in a few years.

The last challenge for French universities deals with their international attractiveness. If the best PhDs do not go for firms, they might go abroad where better conditions and salaries might be offered to them. This could be compensated by the hiring of international academics in France who might be attracted by the fact that access to permanence occurs early (earlier than in the United States and much earlier than in Germany) and that there has been no reduction in the number of permanent positions (again, in contrast with Germany and the United States). Nevertheless, this would require a profound change in hiring procedures, as they remain obscure to those not used to the French system and almost insurmountable for those not speaking French.

Notes

1. Brain drain is often a topic for newspapers or websites. See, for instance, among the more recent expressions and many others, what Saied Paivandi declared in November 2012 (http://www.atlantico.fr/decryptage/fuite-cerveaux-france-est-elle-en-train-faire-perdre-talents-saeed-paivandi-534157.html), or this dossier on the same issue: http://www.linternaute.com/science/science-et-nous/dossiers/06/recherche-francaise/0.shtml.

2. The number of positions opened at research institutions is much lower than at universities. In 2013, for instance, the three main research institutions (CNRS, INSERM, and INRA) opened a total of 463 positions while universities opened 3,600 positions in 2011 (2013 figures were not available at the time of writing).

3. Between 2000 and 2009, the number of professors and maîtres de conférences increased by almost 12 percent while the number of students increased by less than 4 percent (while student numbers grew by 31 percent between 1990 and 1995!).

4. See http://www.enseignementsup-recherche.gouv.fr/cid56113/doctorants.html.

5. In France, there are many ways to become a high school teacher. The more prestigious route is to pass a highly selective national exam (*concours*) called *agrégation du secondaire.* Those who pass it successfully generally teach in lycées (high schools for the three last years before the baccalauréat) or in postbaccalauréat classes preparing students for entry into the grandes écoles. However, some high school teachers are also assigned to universities and generally teach undergraduates. Because their teaching load is twice as heavy as the teaching load of the maîtres de conférences, the maîtres de conférences tend to be replaced by high school teachers, in order to deal with the high number of undergraduates.

6. Only those doctoral candidates are included in Table 4.1. Doctoral candidates with no fellowship—a situation still quite common in humanities and social sciences—are not considered here.

7. There are no national statistics on this increase and comparisons over time are made difficult because the terminology and ways of counting are changing. However, looking at the data published by the CNRS each year on its staff, it seems that the number of nontenured researchers multiplied by almost 3 from 2000 to 2010, reaching about 2,400 individuals today (*Bilan Social CNRS 2000*, http://bilansocial.dsi.cnrs.fr/pdf/bilan-social-2000.pdf, and *Bilan Social du CNRS 2010*, http://bilansocial.dsi.cnrs.fr/pdf/bilan-social-2010.pdf).

8. Before, everything relied on the interpersonal relationship between a PhD candidate and his or her supervisor.

9. The composition of this committee may vary a great deal.

10. These committees also look at the dossiers of doctors who received a qualification four years ago but in the intervening period have not gotten a job and are applying again for qualification.

11. Each PhD ends with a public defense in front of a jury made up of at least the supervisor, two reviewers (external to the university of the candidate), and a president. Members of the jury write a report with their review of the thesis; these reviews are assembled into one text signed by all of them.

12. They restrict the choice of universities by qualifying a restricted number of individuals and thus exercise a centralized and national control over their discipline. This is often the case in the field of law.

13. Information taken from http://cache.media.enseignementsup-recherche.gouv.fr/file/statistiques/74/8/bilan_recrutement_2011_etude_version_def_211748.pdf.

14. It reaches 95 percent in mathematics but in this discipline there is a cooling-off process designed to discourage doctors with a weak case from applying for qualification.

15. This means that if five internal and four external academics are present, one of the internal academics has to leave the room. This has led to tricky situations where none wanted to leave and a decision has to be made by the university president.

16. The composition of the committee and the compulsory participation of at least 50 percent of external members encourages universities to keep this "tradition." They generally manage to invite all the short-listed candidates over one day and thus the external academics do not have to spend many days sitting on the committee. Recently, some universities tried introducing more extensive job interviews, but this is very limited.

17. "Qualified" in this context means allowed to apply for vacant positions of maîtres de conférences by a national body called CNU (see previous section of this chapter).

18. This is true except in disciplines such as life sciences and physics where one or two postdoc experiences, preferably abroad, have become the norm before sending a first application for a position of maîtres de conférences.

19. See the reports posted on http://www.enseignementsup-recherche.gouv.fr/cid22708/bilans-statistiques.html.

20. Because collecting data about ethnicity or religion is not allowed in France, we have no information on these aspects. We also lack information about social background.

21. But they are, nevertheless, much rarer in the corps of the professors.

22. See http://cache.media.enseignementsup-recherche.gouv.fr/file/statistiques/89/0/orig2010_192890.pdf.

23. Language might be a first explanation for that, but also the fact that for many years the situation in France was not as difficult as in some other countries, given the early access to permanent positions, the new positions created each year until 2007, a rather large national market, the civil servant status of academic staff, and so on.

24. The data in this paragraph are drawn from http://cache.media.enseignementsup-recherche.gouv.fr/file/statistiques/89/0/orig2010_192890.pdf.

25. "Prof TGV" is the slang term for faculty members not living close to the university but commuting (with the high-speed train called the TGV) to give their classes and not spending time in the department or taking over service activities.

26. In France, unlike the United States, all universities have PhD programs. They therefore all have to care about their placements in a country where public administrations and firms are very reluctant to hire doctorates.

27. The cases where a decision is made not to confirm a maître de conférences are extremely rare.

28. After this reform, universities were asked to write a "teaching referential" specifying what activities will be included in the teaching duties and for how many hours. There is a national framework, but universities can adapt it to their specific cases.

29. It was sent in spring 2011 to university presidents and their teams of vice presidents, the directors of administrative services at the central level, the elected members of the various university bodies (*conseil d'administration*, *conseil scientifique* and *conseil des études et de la vie étudiante*), the deans, the heads of

department, the directors of research units and their administrators. About 2,600 interviews were conducted.

References

Allison, Paul D., and J. Scott Long. 1990. "Departmental Effects on Scientific Productivity." *American Sociological Review* 55 (4): 469–478.

Belloc Report. 2003. *Propositions Pour une Modification du Décret 84–431 Portant Statut des Enseignants Chercheurs.* Ministère de la Jeunesse, de l'Education Nationale et de la Recherche.

Charle, Christophe, and Jacques Verger. 2012. *Histoire des Universités.* Paris: PUF.

Chatelain, Stéphanie, Stéphanie Mignot-Gérard, Christine Musselin, and Samuel Sponem. 2012. *La Gouvernance des Universités Françaises: Pouvoir, Évaluation et Identité*, Monograph, CSO, CNAM, UPEC and HEC Montréal, http://cso.edu/upload/dossiers/Rapport_GouvernanceUniversitesFrance_2012.pdf.

Dahan, Aubépine. 2011. *Mettre en Oeuvre le Changement dans une Organisation Professionnelle Publique? Pratiques et Identité Professionnelles Face aux Réformes.* PhD in Sociology, University of Paris-Est Marne la Vallée.

Dedieu, François. 2002. *Les Chercheurs et Post-Doctorants Étrangers Travaillant dans les Institutions Publiques de Recherche et les Entreprises.* Report for the Direction de la Programmation et du Développement, Ministère de l'Education Nationale, France.

Enders, Jürgen, and Christine Musselin. 2008. "Back to the Future? The Academic Professions in the 21st Century." In *OECD Higher Education 2030*, vol 1: Demography, 125–150. Paris: OECD Editions.

Faure, Sylvia, and Charles Soulié. 2006. "La Recherche Universitaire à l'Épreuve de la Massification Scolaire." *Actes de la Recherche en Sciences Sociales* 164: 61–74.

Godechot, Olivier, and Alexandra Louvet. 2008. *Le Localisme dans le Monde Académique: Un Essai d'Évaluation.* La Vie des Idées.fr, http://www.laviedesidees.fr/Le-localisme-dans-le-monde.html.

Mouranche, Emmanuelle. 1997. *La Mobilité des Chercheurs Publics en Europe.* Rapport Comparatif sur les Enquêtes Qualitatives Menées en France, Allemagne et Grande Bretagne. Report for the Ministère de la Recherche, Paris.

Musselin, Christine. 2009 [2005]. *The Markets for Academics.* New York: Routledge. (Le Marché des Universitaires. France, Allemagne, Etats-Unis. Paris: Presses de Sciences Po.)

Musselin, Christine, and Frédérique Pigeyre. 2009. "How Mechanisms Implicated in the Collective Process of Academic Hiring in France Affect Discrimination." *Sociologie du Travail* in English, 51S: e81–e103

Musselin, Christine, Frédérique Pigeyre, and Mareva Sabatier. 2011. *Becoming an Academic Today and Yesterday: French Academia from 1976 to now (1976–2006).* Uppsala Business lectures, University of Uppsala, September 2011.

Musselin, Christine, and Valérie Becquet. 2008. "Academic Work and Academic Identities: A Comparison between Four Disciplines." In *Cultural Perspectives on Higher Education*, edited by Jussi Välimaa and Oili-Helena Ylijoki, 91–108. Dordrecht: Springer.

Paye, Simon. 2013. *L'Économie du Travail Universitaire. Allocation, Organisation et Régulation du Travail dans Deux Universités Britanniques (1970–2010).* PhD in sociology, Sciences Po Paris.

Pigeyre, Frédérique, and Mareva Sabatier. 2012. "Recruter les Professeurs d'Université: Le Cas du Concours d'Agrégation du Supérieur en Sciences de Gestion." *Revue Française D'administration Publique* 142(2): 399–418.

Chapter 5

Entering Academia

Realities for New Faculty in German Higher Education

Barbara M. Kehm

Introduction

Entering academia in Germany is both considerably diversified and riddled with hazards. It can be considered diversified in several ways. First, there are options in the university sector characterized by fundamental *functions*, that is, academic teaching and research. There is also diversification by virtue of *sector*, given that there are universities of applied sciences (*Fachhochschulen*) characterized by professional education and mostly teaching-only jobs, and there are extra-university research institutes characterized by basic and applied research, with no teaching obligations. Entering academia is also hazardous, however, because there are hardly any permanent positions below professorships, there is no proper and reliable career progression, and no tenure track. After a brief description of the basic principles of the German higher education system and the structure of academic careers, key issues for entering academia are considered. In particular, an emphasis is put on the status of doctoral candidates, the basic principles of the academic job market, contracts at entry level, as well as current challenges and future perspectives for young academic staff.

The German system of higher education is essentially a binary system with two main types of institutions: universities and universities of applied sciences. Only universities have the right to offer research training and to award doctoral degrees, the minimum entrance qualification for an academic career. Meanwhile, universities of applied sciences focus on a smaller spectrum of subjects and study programs, are more practice-oriented, and prepare their students mainly for professional careers outside academia. Despite the fact that universities of applied sciences originally were conceived to conduct no research—and accordingly afforded no proper research infrastructure—there are a number of universities of applied sciences active in research, which mainly carry out research and development projects in cooperation with industry. Young graduates of universities of applied sciences wanting to continue toward a PhD degree either must study for another year or two at the master's level of a university and then embark on a PhD degree, or make use of the possibilities offered by cooperation agreements between the university of applied sciences and a university with regard to joint supervision of PhD candidates and final award of the degree by the university. Such agreements are not the rule, however, their number is increasing.

Two other key aspects of the German structure of academic careers are that (1) as a rule, a master's degree is required in order to be accepted as a doctoral candidate, and (2) doctoral candidates are not regarded as students but as junior researchers. In fact, more than 60 percent of doctoral candidates in Germany are employed by their university, either as part of the staff infrastructure of a professorial chair or as research assistants in third-party funded projects. Thus, they are considered to be junior academic staff and not students. As a rule, they have part-time contracts for about 50 percent of the regular working hours per week, including all fringe benefits for employees in the civil service (e.g., paid vacation time, social security, payments into the pension fund, sick leave and parental leave), and they can be employed for up to six years after graduation. There are no tuition fees in Germany for doctoral candidates, regardless of whether they are Germans or from abroad. In fact, in a number of subjects foreign nationals are actively recruited as doctoral candidates and offered paid positions. The remaining 40 percent of doctoral candidates not getting their degree in the framework of a position as research or teaching assistants are either scholarship holders or have jobs and work on their degree in their spare time.

In the following sections of this chapter, the pathways for entering academia in Germany are analyzed. This entails a description of the road to the doctorate, a discussion of the neglected postdoc phase, and an analysis of opportunities and problems in getting a tenured professorship. As the pathways toward a professorship are quite distinct between universities and universities of applied sciences, each is presented separately. In addition, a brief overview is provided for academic careers in extra-university research institutions (e.g., the Max Planck Institutes or Fraunhofer Institutes). The road to academia is analyzed by focusing on basic principles of the academic job market and progression in it, contracts and income, and socialization into academic norms and values. The last two sections of this chapter discuss the current situation of junior academic staff and main challenges as well as future trends.

The Status of Doctoral Candidates in the German Higher Education System

There are currently 118 universities operating in Germany and having the right to award doctoral degrees. In relationship to the size of its higher education system, Germany is very strong in producing PhDs, amounting to more than 25,000 awarded annually. The proportion of women being awarded a PhD was around 44 percent in 2010 and the proportion of international doctoral candidates being awarded a PhD was around 15 percent in the same year (Statistisches Bundesamt 2011).

Doctoral education and training in Germany is currently undergoing a major reform shifting from being rather informal to introducing more formalized structures. However, until now there is no nationwide system of registering doctoral candidates and Germany has no official statistics yet about how many young people are actually embarking on a doctorate or are in the process of obtaining the degree. Accordingly there are also no statistics about the number of dropouts. A study by Wolters and Schmiedel (2012) is the first attempt to come up with some realistic figures, and politicians as well as university management are aware that some type of registration system for doctoral candidates is urgently needed.

In the earlier mentioned study carried out in 2010 and published in 2012, results of a representative survey among professors supervising doctoral candidates and among doctoral candidates in the process of getting their degree indicated that in 2010 there were more than 200,000 master's level graduates in the process of getting their doctoral degree. Half of these were officially registered at their university, while the other half had simply been accepted by a professor as doctoral candidates under an informal agreement to supervise. Of the overall group included in the study, 83 percent were employed inside or outside the higher education system (Wolters and Schmiedel 2012, 26).

There is no official part-time status for doctoral candidates. Those who are employed by the university as teaching and/or research assistants are typically on a 50 percent part-time contract and have a defined amount of time for their doctoral research and thesis writing in the framework of this contract (about one-third of their working time). But basically they are expected to do their doctoral work in the other 50 percent of their time, which is not paid. This is often different for those young research assistants being funded in the framework of a third-party funded research project. Their doctoral work and thesis topic is mostly linked to the project research and they gather their data in the framework of the project. The disadvantage here is that the doctoral candidates are frequently required to work more hours than they are paid for because they have to go with the flow of the project and the related time pressures. So they often do not have sufficient time to work on their theses.

Because the majority of doctoral candidates are employed by the university, they are registered as employees in the civil service. The others have no defined status vis-à-vis the university and a formal procedure of registering as doctoral candidates is started only once the thesis has been submitted. However, many universities are currently introducing some kind of registration for doctoral candidates at the beginning of this phase of qualification, and professors who act as supervisors are requested to inform the responsible administrative unit once they accept to supervise a person. All professors are free to accept as many appropriately qualified young people as doctoral candidates as they want to supervise. There are no restrictions on numbers, and the quality of the applicant is judged by the respective professor. Naturally, the relationship between a doctoral candidate and a supervisor is closer for those who work for the chair holder or in one of the third-party funded projects than it is for those with a scholarship and for external candidates. But with the shift in attention from product (dissertation) to process (doctoral education and training) and the introduction of doctoral programs and schools, a more formalized structure is currently being established.

The status of doctoral candidates as part of the academic staff of a given department varies. Strictly seen, only those doctoral candidates who have an employment contract with the university and work for and with a professor supporting him or her in their research and teaching obligations are regarded as faculty. Doctoral candidates being employed in the framework of third-party funded research projects are not regarded as faculty proper. Scholarship holders and external doctoral candidates have no formal relationship to the university at all.

According to Wolters and Schmiedel (2012), roughly 29 percent of the doctoral candidates pursue their research in mathematics and natural sciences, 22 percent in engineering, 19 percent in the humanities, and 18 percent in the social sciences (including law, economics, and business administration). In 2010, more than half of the doctoral candidates were between 26 and 30 years old, 11 percent were 25 years old or younger, and 30 percent were 30 years old or older. On average a German university professor supervises six doctoral candidates, again with large variations among the disciplines, reaching from one candidate in the arts to up to fifteen candidates per professor in engineering. This picture is clearly related to the different research cultures of the disciplines. The average duration of getting a PhD degree also varies considerably according to subject. On average it is about four years, but higher in engineering and computer science and considerably lower (1.5 to 3.0 years) in medicine and law, for example.

We can say that we have now roughly determined the pool of candidates for an academic career in Germany. In 2010 there were slightly more than 200,000 doctoral candidates in the process of getting their degree and German universities are producing about 25,000 to 26,000 completed doctoral degrees per year. Of these about 10 percent manage to stay in academia and eventually get a professorship. There are many more who are trying because it is possible to stay in academia for six years after the doctorate and possibly longer on research contracts with third-party funding. In addition, first recruitment to a professorship is increasingly tied to fixed-term contracts (of six years), as well. Thus, it is a personal decision at what point in time and at what age to give up trying to get a permanent contract in academia or a professorship. There is no regulated career ladder that would be open for anyone who tries and is deemed good enough. An old rule has it that within universities not more than 30 percent of academic staff below the professorship should be on permanent contracts and recent analyses have shown that more than 80 percent of the current academic staff in higher education institutions are on temporary contracts, many of them on contracts lasting a year or so. Getting tenure or a professorship is very much dependent on the politics behind the stage and underneath it. These dynamics cannot be influenced and are mostly nontransparent. Connections, mentors, reviewers, and "good fit" (Musselin 2010) play an important role in this, but also age and, increasingly, costs.

Basic Principles of the Academic Job Market

In this section three types of academic job markets are presented: the first one in universities, the second one in universities of applied sciences, and the third one in extra-university research institutes. A doctoral degree is a precondition when seriously considering an academic career in all three academic job markets.

The University Job Market

Traditionally, the high road to a university professorship or a chair was the *habilitation*, a second formal qualification after the doctorate, known informally as the *second doctorate*. For the habilitation a major piece of research and a book had to be produced and a trial lecture had to be given. For this qualification, an employment period of six to eight years as an assistant was typical. In international comparisons, this position is often characterized as a functional equivalent to the American assistant professor. Assistant positions were still tied to a professorial chair, thus there was some amount of dependence. Assistants had a teaching obligation of up to four hours per week, that is, half the teaching obligation of a professor.

After successfully completing the habilitation, the candidates were awarded the title of *Privatdozent* (private lecturer), which gave them the right to examine students and offer classes, but typically as an unpaid activity. Candidates then had to apply for professorial positions at universities other than their own. Other than assistant positions, there has never been a defined status at German universities that was called, or could be called, *postdoc*. Young academics with a doctoral degree who did not manage to get an assistant position either had to look for jobs outside academia or compete for fixed-term researcher contracts mostly in the framework of third-party funded projects.

Until the introduction of the junior professorship, the habilitation was a precondition to become eligible for a professorship at a German university. However, the search committees could also consider applicants without habilitation. In such cases they examined whether the applicant had provided proof of "habilitation adequate" performance. The call to a professorship or chair without habilitation was widespread in the fields of engineering and education. When academics who came from abroad or had been working abroad after their doctorate were being considered for a professorship the search committee would also look for "habilitation adequate" performance as the normal way to issue a call (Janson et al. 2007, 79).

Junior professorships were introduced in Germany in 2002 with the purpose to provide highly qualified young researchers with a shorter and more direct path to a professorship without habilitation and independent from a professor. For these positions the new salary category of W1 was created. At the same time the former assistant positions for purposes of getting a habilitation were considerably reduced in numbers.

Junior professorships are fixed-term (six years as a rule) and an evaluation of performance is carried out after three years. With four to five hours per week the teaching load is lower than that of a professor. Only a few junior professorships have a tenure track attached to them; the majority of junior professors will have to apply for a professorship at another university in order to progress. To increase their chances, many junior professors still do a habilitation during their six years in this position. By the end of 2010, altogether 1,200 junior professorships had been established and filled at German universities (the original goal was 6,000) while between 2005 and 2009 there were on average 1,900 habilitations annually. The introduction of a junior professorship was critically discussed in the beginning. However, in the meantime it is recognized in most disciplines as one possibility among several to become a professor and many junior professors are successful with their applications for a regular professorship. With 37 percent, the proportion of women holding junior professorships is clearly higher than it is among the two categories of professorships (i.e., the equivalents of associate professor and full professor or chair holder), where they stand at 22 percent, and among those persons who successfully completed a habilitation in the year 2009 (24 percent) (Statistisches Bundesamt 2011).

Overall, the number of professors at German higher education institutions (including junior professors) has increased by 10 percent between 2002 and 2010 (to 41,462) while the number of habilitations has decreased from 2,302 in 2002 to 1,563 in 2011 (Statistisches Bundesamt 2011). This can be interpreted as a success of the junior professorship, but is also an indicator of the dwindling importance of the habilitation. At the same time, the proportion of women successfully completing a habilitation has increased from 18.4 percent in 2002 to 25.5 percent in 2011 (Statistisches Bundesamt 2011). However, the number of professorships does not equal the number of professors because many professorships cannot be filled quickly. Furthermore, successfully completing a habilitation does not automatically mean getting a professorship, it only means being eligible for consideration. The number of persons with the habilitation who end up not being recruited as a professor is not known. Neither is the number of professorship positions newly created because this depends on structural decisions of a given university and internal negotiations between departments and the university leadership.

Basically, all academic positions at German universities below those of (associated) professorships (W2 salary category) and full professorships or chairs (W3 salary category) are fixed-term (six years as a rule). In addition, an increasing number of professorships (W2 and W3) are also filled for a period of six years in those cases in which the candidate who is chosen receives his or her first call. Only after that, and possibly an additional evaluation or once again a change of university, permanent or tenured contracts are made. All professors, including junior professors, are civil servants, except if they explicitly choose to become (or to remain) employees in the civil service. In cases of nontenured, fixed-term contracts, academic staff in the "W" categories will normally become civil servants for the duration of the contract. But once a person is a tenured civil servant nobody can take this privileged status away (except in cases of criminal activity) and the person cannot get sacked.

In light of these basic principles of the university job market, and the fact that there is no tenure system, it becomes clear that German universities are characterized by what Musselin called "external labor markets" (Musselin 2010). In contrast to the "internal" academic labor market that is typical for the tenure-track model of the United States, the "external" academic job market, typical for Germany, requires academics to apply for a job at another university if they want a promotion. Those who are already professors in the highest category (W3) will apply periodically (e.g., every three to five years) for a professorship at another university and—provided they receive an offer—they will negotiate at both universities for a higher salary and a better infrastructure (staff and resources) for their chair.

> German universities offer no opportunities of internal career advancement, and the universities themselves have virtually no possibility of intervening in academics' work once they have decided to hire them. [. . .] The more fully a professor fulfills her contract (that is, the more active and productive she is), the less able the university will be to keep her, because her chances of getting hired quickly for a . . . position at another university are particularly high. (Musselin 2010, 188)

To some extent, though not in principle, the situation that Musselin describes has evolved with the shift to a new salary scale in 2004/2005. Universities were given more possibilities to reward high-performing professors by introducing clearly reduced basic salaries (the shift from the former C-categories to the W-categories)[1] and adding a performance related component. In the meantime, it is estimated that only about 10 percent of all professors in the salary categories W2 (equivalent to associate professor) and W3 (equivalent to full professor/chair holder) do not receive a performance related salary component. In 2012, the Federal Court of Justice, responding to a complaint by some professors paid according to W2 scales about the inadequacy of the W2 salary in the face of their qualifications, agreed with the plaintiffs and thus forced all German States to increase the basic salary in the category W2. The States are currently developing proposals for how to deal with this situation and the trend is to add the performance-related components to the basic salaries for all W2 professors. In this way, the court decision is implemented by making it more or less a zero sum game (Hartmer and Möhlmann 2012).

However, it is still the case that professors cannot be promoted from a junior professorship (W1) to a regular professorship (W2) or from a regular professorship to a chair (W3) without having to change university. The situation is different for all academics below a professorship. Salaries are fixed and non-negotiable, positions are either half-time or full-time, and the length of contracts is fixed, as well, at six years before the doctoral degree is obtained and six years after the doctoral degree is awarded. A change of university will not change these contract conditions. After six years the individual must move either "up" (into a postdoc position as assistant or junior professor) or "out." The only possibility to remain inside academia is to accept a position as a contract researcher in the framework of third-party funded research projects, which means varying contract lengths and possibly shorter or longer times of unemployment in between.

Due to the external labor market for academics in German higher education, all positions have to be publicly advertised (in newspapers, on websites, in selected journals). It is by no means unusual that there are internal candidates for positions below a professorship, for example, if a professor wants to hire a particularly well-performing graduate as a junior researcher and teaching assistant. In such a case, the job advertisement will be on the university website only, and only for a short time. In addition, the job description can be formulated in such a way that it exactly fits the qualifications of the chosen candidate. But some kind of public advertisement must be done.

With regard to salaries, there are fixed salary scales complemented by seniority levels. That means, upon recruitment, a basic salary category is offered (e.g., W1 for junior professors, W2 for associate professors, and W3 for full professors). Depending on age, experience, and performance, a seniority level can be accorded (though not in W1), which adds to the basic salary. Finally, there are direct performance-related salary components that can be earned but about which each university leadership decides individually. A professorial salary (including those of assistant positions and junior professorships) will allow for a middle class lifestyle as will a full-time academic staff salary after obtaining the doctoral degree. The 50 percent positions, on which most junior academics in the process of getting their doctoral degree are employed, make for a salary somewhat higher than typical student incomes, but not sufficiently high to support a family (see Table 5.2).

The Job Market at Universities of Applied Sciences

Qualification requirements, forms of recruitment and career progression at universities of applied sciences are different from those at universities. As the universities of applied sciences prepare students for nonacademic careers, a proper research infrastructure was never developed within these institutions, and accordingly no junior academic staff were hired. The most common position is that of a W2-professorship (which is the functional equivalent of an associate professor). In order to get a professorship at a university of applied sciences, potential candidates will normally have a doctoral degree and at least five years of practical experience in industry or the private sector. Often high-level and experienced engineers working in the private sector have an additional part-time job teaching at universities of applied sciences, though with a reduced teaching load. Compared to the eight hours per week teaching load of a university professor, professors at universities of applied sciences typically have a teaching load of 14 to 16 hours per week and no research obligations.

Over the years—universities of applied sciences were established from 1972 onward—some academic drift has occurred and many professors at universities of applied sciences use their good connections to industry in order to carry out applied research projects in cooperation with their former employers. In this context, there might be doctoral candidates carrying out their research in the framework of such projects, but then a cooperation agreement with a university has to exist in order to award the degree. There are a few research-active universities of applied sciences demanding the right to award doctoral degrees, however, the monopoly of universities is still strong in this regard.

Professorship positions at universities of applied sciences have to be publicly advertised and there will be a regular selection and recruitment process among eligible candidates. However, once recruited, no promotion or career progression is possible apart from salary increases due to seniority. Unlike universities, universities of applied sciences have no junior academic staff that could support a professor in his or her teaching duties. At the same time the percentage of nontenured positions is considerably lower than at universities.

The Job Market in Extra-University Research Institutes

Research careers are also possible at extra-university research institutes. Germany has a rather elaborate research infrastructure outside academia dominated by the multiple institutes of four large research organizations: the Max-Planck Society, the Fraunhofer Society, the Helmholtz Association, and the Leibniz Association. Except for the Fraunhofer Society, the other three organizations are mostly publicly funded but also compete for third-party funding. All of these organizations have research schools in which doctoral candidates are supervised. There are postdoc positions, positions for young research group leaders, and positions for directors of institutes or units. Each organization has its own website where job advertisements are published. Leadership positions might also be advertised in newspapers.

In contrast to the job market at universities, the extra-university research institutes have a higher percentage of permanent positions, especially researcher positions below the level of a professorship, which would be equivalent to the position of a director of a research institute.

Similar to some of the universities of applied sciences, the extra-university research institutes have also clamored for the right to award doctoral degrees, in particular the Max Planck Institutes, which have well-developed research training in place. Again, the universities have successfully resisted so far sharing their monopoly, but whether they will be able to continue to do so remains to be seen.

Young academics can apply for doctoral or researcher positions in these institutes, but such positions will be fixed-term at first. Moving up the career ladder and getting tenure depends on performance and available positions in the budget. Positions in the framework of third-party funded projects are fixed-term as a rule.

In the following sections the focus shifts to the university job market.

The Labor Market for Young Academics

It is extremely difficult to define the academic labor market for young academics in Germany in quantitative terms. All positions below a professorship can be either part of the regular budget for personnel of a given university—and then they are typically part of a given professor's staff infrastructure—or they can be financed through third-party funded research projects. In addition, there is a considerable variety of staff categories and there are both regular and contract staff. Official numbers from the Federal Office of Statistics provide information either pertaining to academic staff over a period of time for all higher education institutions (including universities of applied sciences and teacher training institutions), or for a particular year only and then divided according to type of institution. There are no statistics available providing information about how many positions in each staff category are filled annually.

In order to provide an overview of the number of academic staff over time, Table 5.1 is included. However, the staff numbers and staff categories include all higher education institutions in Germany and are not focused on universities exclusively.

Table 5.1 shows that much of Germany's higher education expansion—and with it the necessary increase in teaching provision—has been dealt with by increasing the number of low-paid, often precarious, often part-time, and mostly fixed-term contracts. In roughly ten years, the number of professors increased by only 10 percent and the assistant and lecturer positions (i.e., those positions in the framework of which a

Table 5.1. Regular academic staff according to staff categories at German higher education institutions (2001–2010)

Staff Categories	2001	2005	2010	Change in percent (2001 to 2010)
Professors	37,661	37,865	41,462	+ 10 percent
Assistants/Lecturers	14,602	9,874	4,038	- 72 percent
Junior research/teaching staff	101,524	111,343	156,497	+ 54 percent
Teaching staff for special tasks	6,602	6,655	8,552	+ 30 percent
Total	160,389	165,737	210,549	+ 31 percent

Source: Destatis (2011, 24). Personal an Hochschulen.

habilitation was traditionally done), have been reduced by more than 70 percent. However, the new category of junior professors is included in this table in the category of professors, although their proportion among all professors is only about 2 percent. The major reduction in assistantships is related to the fact that there are strong policy forces wanting to abolish the habilitation, while there are almost equally strong forces, especially in the learned societies of the more conservative subjects (e.g., law, economics) insisting on keeping the habilitation requirement. This leads to the fact that many aspiring young academics do their habilitation in the framework of other positions. These can be junior professorships but, given their low numbers, most are fixed-term, full-time or half-time positions, or positions as contract researchers.

The category "junior research and teaching staff" refers to those junior academic staff in the process of getting their doctoral degree and being employed on part-time (50 percent) contracts.

There is a considerable increase in the staff category "teaching staff for special tasks" that used to be a rare and rather exceptional position. These teaching-only positions have up to twice the teaching load of a professor (14 to 16 hours per week). Academics in these positions are mostly of a younger generation, almost always have a doctoral degree, and mostly do undergraduate teaching. If they have research ambitions they need to find their own funding for it and have to do it in their spare time.

As in most European countries, the competition for jobs opening up an academic career has shifted from the doctoral to the postdoctoral phase. Getting a junior professorship or taking over the leadership of a research group provide a good starting position. However, there are many more highly qualified young academics with a doctoral degree aiming for a traditional assistant position in the framework of which they have to do their habilitation. All three types of positions (junior professorships, research group leaderships, and assistant positions) have to be advertised and applicants have to compete against each other. But, in the end, many doctoral degree holders either have to leave the university and look for a job on the nonacademic labor market—which is common and easy in subjects like engineering, chemistry, or physics, and less common as well as more difficult in most of the humanities and social sciences—or they try to stay inside academia by working as contract researchers. The German Research Association (the German Research Funding Council) offers the opportunity for individuals up to age 36 to apply for research funding that includes the applicant's own salary. In the application, proof must be provided that the applicant has been accepted by a host university.

Staying in academia and trying to get a permanent contract or a professorship through age 40 or 45 requires a lot of intrinsic motivation. Universities still believe that they are only recruiting "the best," but this is by far no longer the case in all respects. Salaries in the private sector for highly qualified young people are considerably higher and often "the best" are recruited into the private sector. This is very much dependent on the discipline. Natural scientists, engineers, and medical doctors can have very attractive jobs outside academia. Scholars in the fields of social sciences and humanities find it harder to get appropriate jobs outside academia. Exceptions might be lawyers and economists. Thus, universities sometimes have difficulties recruiting professors in certain subjects while competition for few permanent jobs or professorships is very high in the social sciences and humanities.

This notwithstanding, working in academia still tends to be attractive for many. Not because of job security or high salaries but because of the freedom of teaching and research. In particular, the professoriate continues to have a high social status and many privileges in terms of social benefits and work autonomy.

Contracts at Entry Level

A doctoral candidate employed as a junior research and/or teaching assistant will always get a contract for 50 percent of the regular working hours per week (referred to as a *50 percent contract*). He or she thus becomes an employee of the university as well as (almost always) an employee in the civil service, with all relevant fringe benefits. The contract will include a clause that the candidate will be given the opportunity to acquire a doctoral degree. If the employment contract is connected to the work of a professor or chair holder, this means that, for most of the paid work time, the doctoral candidate has to provide services in support of the teaching and research tasks of the professor. At least 33 percent of the paid working time should be allowed for direct research and thesis work, however, working overtime is expected. The professor will be the individual's supervisor and main examiner for the doctoral degree. This arrangement has always been much criticized, given the extent to which doctoral candidates must depend on their supervisors. This was one of the reasons for the introduction of doctoral programs and graduate schools with multiple opportunities for supervision and advice, as well as the possibility to change supervisors. If the employment contract is in the framework of a third-party funded research project, the candidate has to dedicate all the paid working hours to the project. In this case, the thesis topic is often closely related to the project and much of the information, knowledge and data gathered can be used for the thesis.

The level of payment varies. After the reform of German federalism in 2006, in the framework of which the 16 German states reappropriated almost exclusive responsibility for higher education, each individual state passed its own laws concerning salary levels and scales. Salary levels were lowered and a performance-related component was introduced, though this performance-related salary component was soon restricted to professorial salaries only. Junior academic staff had to live with the fact that salaries were lower than before. In addition, each category on the salary scale has up to five levels, according to seniority.

As a rule, junior academic staff without a doctoral degree receive 50 percent of a full-time salary in the category E13. Table 5.2 from April 2011 provides an aggregate average overview of level 1 salaries in North Rhine Westphalia for young academic staff in half-time (50 percent) and full-time (100 percent) positions, the latter requiring a doctoral degree.

Table 5.2. Average income for junior academic staff at German higher education institutions, in Euros (2011)*

Income	50 percent Positions	100 percent Positions
Annual basic income	18,663	37,326
Supplementary payments	778	1,555
Annual gross income	19,441	38,881
Monthly gross income (average)	1,620	3,240
Basic monthly salary (gross)	1,555	3,111
Basic monthly salary (net)	1,111	1,937
Taxation and social security contributions	29.3 percent	38.2 percent

Source: http://mosworld.worldpress.com/2011/06/15/gehalt-wissenschaftliche-mitarbeiter-nach-tv-l-13-und-lehrer-nach-a13-in-nrw/

**Note:* Supplementary payments are automatic fringe benefits covering additional money for Christmas and holidays as well as compensations for the location of the work place in terms of different costs of living. Taxation varies according to marital status, income of spouse, and number of children. Social security contributions consist of payments for pension, unemployment benefits, health insurance, old age care needs, and a so-called solidarity contribution to support East German economic growth, productivity and development.

Level 1 is the lowest level, meaning first employment and no previous professional experience. After one year, there is an increase to level 2 and after two additional years there is an increase to level 3, and so on. To reach the highest level (level 5), ten years of experience on the job are required. The difference between the levels (in category E13) is about 11 percent more (plus 350 euros) when moving from level 1 to level 2; 5.3 percent more (plus 189 euros) when moving from level 2 to level 3; 9.8 percent more (plus 366 euros) when moving from level 3 to level 4; and 12.4 percent more (plus 507 euros) when moving from level 4 to level 5. However, it is necessary to point out that a junior academic will typically never reach a higher level than perhaps level 3 because of the fixed-terms contracts. The upper levels will be applied, if at all, to academically qualified administrators and middle management staff.

Because there is a considerable proportion of doctoral candidates who finance themselves with a scholarship, it is worthwhile to take a look at those scholarship averages. A doctoral scholarship will provide a monthly basic income of 1,050 euros plus 100 euros for books or special research-related expenditures. If the person is married, the scholarship will be raised by 150 euros per month and by another 155 euros per month for the first child (followed by 50 euros per month for each additional child). Thus, for an unmarried doctoral candidate with a scholarship the monthly income would be at least 1,150 euros compared to 1,111 euros for a doctoral candidate who is employed as a junior research and teaching assistant and has to work 50 percent of the regular weekly working time. Because no taxes and social security contributions have to be paid for scholarships, they can be a disadvantage in the long term, despite the higher income. There will be no unemployment benefits, health insurance has to be taken care of privately, and no pension funds will be built up. In addition, there is no paid vacation time and no additional salary supplement at the end of the year (the so-called Christmas money). Furthermore, if a doctoral candidate or a postdoc is employed by the university, this means that the employing institution will cover 50 percent of the social security contributions (i.e., pension, unemployment dues, and health insurance). Neither scholarships nor 50 percent part-time positions enable a middle-class life style. These levels of income are a bit more than most university students have at their disposal but not enough to have, for example, a reasonably spacious apartment, a car, or the ability to go on vacation.

Looking at the salaries of junior professors the picture is somewhat different because they are (temporary) civil servants. Civil servants in

Germany do not have to pay for unemployment benefits and pensions and they get better deals on their health insurance because all or part of these are paid for by the state. The gross monthly salary for junior professors also varies by state. Taking the example of North Rhine Westphalia again, it is 3,816 euros per month. After three years and a positive evaluation, this salary is raised by 260 euros per month. There are no levels reflecting seniority. This level of income gets closer to middle-class living. It is approximately the level of school teachers' income and it is possible to finance the costs of living of a small family.

Concerning contracts for junior teaching and research assistants (doctoral candidates and postdocs) who are associated to a professor or a chair holder, they simply have to do whatever the professor tells them to do although there is normally a job description. But basically they provide services and support in teaching and research, apart from following up on their own activities. The majority of these individuals also take over teaching functions. The rule is that they can teach one or two classes per week (one class equals 90 minutes of face-to-face teaching). It is deemed increasingly important that junior academic staff hone their teaching skills and, if possible, participate in didactics seminars. In contrast to this, junior professors have full academic freedom in teaching and research. As a rule they teach two classes per week but recent surveys and evaluations have criticized an increase in the teaching load (three to four classes) in the second half of their contract period of six years, which seriously impacts their research output. Postdocs often have a 100 percent position and a reasonable middle-class life style is possible on that salary. In addition, they will receive regular increases in salary on the basis of seniority. However, due to the decrease in assistant positions (Table 5.1) there are more and more postdocs trying to increase their qualifications in precarious jobs or in 50 percent part-time doctoral positions.

These salaries by far cannot compete with what a well-qualified higher education graduate can earn in the private sector. Income varies highly according to field, but the average gross monthly salary of a higher education graduate in his or her first year of employment averaged 3,400 euros in 2012. West Germans earn about 20 percent more than East Germans and women earn about 23 percent less than men. If we consider that a higher education graduate in Germany embarking on a PhD will receive a gross monthly income of slightly more than 1,600 euros (in a 50 percent position) and after four or five years a postdoc in a full-time (100 percent) position will then receive slightly more than 3,100 euros gross income per month, we can calculate that entrance level salaries in academia are less than half of those in the private sector—and that even after four to five years academic salaries have not caught up with entrance level salaries in the private sector.

Generally, the salaries offered in the German higher education system cannot compete with salaries in the private sector. This is normal, and widely acknowledged and understood. However, scholarship and science are still considered more a vocation than a mere job for money. Doing research and teaching, and doing it well, very much continues to require intrinsic motivation. But there are also a number of privileges and positive features attached to working in academia. First of all, academic work carries with it rather high social prestige. Furthermore, there are ample opportunities to freely arrange one's working times, as well as enjoy considerable freedom in what one teaches and does research on. Finally, there are a good number of fringe benefits attached to working in academia and being a civil servant or an employee in the civil service. For example, civil servants do not have to pay any contributions for their later pension, which is taken over wholly by the state, nor must they pay for unemployment insurance because they do not run the danger of becoming unemployed once they have achieved tenure. Additionally, the state provides extra support for their health insurance. Employees in the civil service do not have all these privileges but are still well taken care of in terms of health insurance. They also enjoy between 29 and 35 days of paid vacation per year, sickness and maternity leave, and so on. In return, and despite fierce competition for jobs in academia, there is—if at all—only a quasi-market. Most academic staff positions are embedded in fixed salary categories, which are basically non-negotiable in all positions below a professorship. Professors can increase their salaries through performance and through applying elsewhere and then negotiating if they get an offer from another university. In rare cases when a university wants to hire a "star," the salary can be more freely negotiated, but it is normally capped at a certain level. Still, working in academia means being part of a highly state-regulated profession, which is traditionally not subject to real market conditions. The situation created by the increased competition has therefore been called *quasi-market*.

Socialization into Academic Norms and Values

Bourdieu (1982, 1988, 1997) has proven repeatedly in his works on academic habitus that socialization into academic norms and values starts with the beginning of studies or even earlier within the family. Students learn from their professors in various ways including, for example, dress code. In Germany, this is by far not a uniform experience, but varies according to subject. Typically, law and business administration professors are dressed in a more conservative and formal manner than, for example, social science and humanities professors.

Students also learn early on that plagiarism is taboo. After several public scandals in recent years with respect to high-level German politicians being found to have plagiarized parts of their doctoral theses, checks for plagiarism have become more frequent and departments have developed policies for how to deal with it. Typically, undergraduate students are taught about academic writing, correct bibliographies, and ways to quote and reference properly. Naturally, there is more emphasis on this in the social sciences and in the humanities than in the natural sciences and in engineering, where mathematical formulas are more important. Increasingly, though, the employability debate in the framework of establishing a tiered structure of study programs and degrees (central to the Bologna Process reforms) has led to a series of new focus areas for teaching, aiming to convey generic skills and competences, which are deemed important for both the labor markets inside and outside academia. These efforts can encompass a broad range of topics starting from presentation and information technology (IT) skills to better knowledge of foreign languages (especially English), time management, teamwork, and other themes.

Once students have graduated and are working on their doctoral dissertations, they will have additional opportunities to acquire knowledge about academic norms and values. If they are employed and work for a professor, they acquire such knowledge through observation and learning by doing. If they are members of a doctoral program or graduate school, the approach might be more structured and systematic through course work.

There are two ways to develop social networks and personal ties for young academics. The first one is with the professor or chair holder when employed as a young teaching and research assistant. Typically, a young staff member will be integrated into the research team of the chair. The size of such teams varies according to subject and level of third-party funding. They will be bigger in engineering and the natural sciences and smaller in the humanities and social sciences. The professor or chair holder has several roles to play in this constellation: He or she will be the direct boss in the working relationship; he or she will also be the doctoral thesis supervisor, the main mentor, and later on the main examiner. This dynamic has been criticized as fostering too much dependence on supervisors; the establishment of doctoral programs and schools is currently leading to multiple supervisors for doctoral candidates and less direct dependence. However, in the traditional relationship, the professors would also take care to integrate the young academics into their scientific networks and groom the young staff persons for a future professorship. In doctoral schools or programs, the social networks develop more strongly among the doctoral candidates themselves. And while there are increasingly more formalized career stages and definitions of the particular skills a young academic should acquire in order to be able to compete on the academic labor market, the model of the close personal relationship with professors who might use their contacts and networks informally to promote their own candidate has become less prevalent.

The second way for a young aspiring academic to develop social networks and personal ties is in the framework of doctoral programs and schools. As mentioned before, personal ties in these frameworks develop more strongly among peers, that is, with other doctoral candidates in the program or school. Skills acquisition is more formalized through course work and doctoral candidates are typically provided with opportunities to publish and go to national or international conferences or even spend some time abroad. Ties with supervisors become more formal, as well, and young candidates are more strongly groomed to manage anticipated competition for academic jobs without being able to count on the informal telephone call.

However, this is not a complete either/or situation. The higher degree of transparency and the reduction of high dependency levels that are to be achieved through doctoral programs and schools can still be complemented by informal support. Such support is never made public and never openly discussed but will be able to topple ranking lists of candidates established by search commissions. In addition, there is mostly no official recruitment commission for young academic staff or doctoral candidates. Their selection is the choice of the professors who will offer the employment contract. They might draw in somebody from the research team, and there are certain regulations concerning the presence of a union representative and a female representative to assure equal opportunities in recruitment processes. Furthermore, minutes have to be taken and an argument has to be delivered for why a certain candidate has been chosen over another one, but that particular language is easy to learn and provides only superficial accountability. But again, all this is very much dependent on the question of whether a known or possibly internal candidate already exists, or whether a job advertisement is truly open and there is no real preference for a certain candidate. Candidates applying from outside who try to inquire as to whether a preferred candidate already exists will in most cases not be given a true answer, but instead will be encouraged to apply to enlarge the pool of potential candidates, even if a decision has more or less already been taken. The duty to recruit outside candidates comes into force only from the professorial level onward. Interestingly, the recruitment of internal candidates to junior academic positions is not regarded as "inbreeding." It is seen as part of the selection of talent. There might be an undergraduate student attracting the attention of the professor because of his or her active and intelligent participation. So the professor might offer a student assistant position to this person and groom him or her until the award of the doctoral degree. After that, it becomes normal to start changing universities with every step in the career ladder.

The work of doctoral candidates being employed as junior research and teaching assistants is only assessed informally. There are no rules and regulations requiring periodic formal assessment. As they are employed by and working for a professor, this supervising professor typically forms an opinion about the performance of these young academics. The most important part of any assessment is the submission of the doctoral thesis and its defense. The only group of academics who are officially and formally evaluated are junior professors. As a rule they are evaluated after three years in order to determine whether the contract will be renewed for another three years.

Current Situation of Junior Academics

As has been indicated before, German universities produce a very high number of doctoral degree holders. But although it is normal in some subjects (e.g., chemistry and medicine) to get a PhD and then move on to the nonacademic labor market, and although in general the nonacademic labor market in Germany is particularly open for doctoral degree holders, many young people holding a doctoral degree aim for an academic career. This is particularly the case in the humanities and social sciences, that is, in those subjects that do not have well-defined and clear professional options in the nonacademic sectors of the labor market.

The few junior professorships and the greatly reduced number of positions for assistants and lecturers (see Table 5.1), which are the typical entry positions for an academic career, have contributed to fierce competition during the postdoc phase. This situation is aggravated by openings that are increasingly advertised internationally, so that competitors from abroad make the situation even more difficult. In recent years, an increasing number of well-qualified young academics from abroad have applied for jobs in the German university system and the extra-university research institutes. There are two main reasons for this. First, there is a widely supported policy in place to further internationalize the German higher education and research system in order to demonstrate its international attractiveness and competitiveness. Second, information is spreading that there continue to be good, even increased, opportunities for research funding, which is no longer the case in a number of other European countries. In addition, the German Excellence Initiative (Kehm and Pasternack 2008), with its considerable extra funding for clusters of research excellence, has encouraged German universities to advertise academic job openings internationally and to make additional efforts to recruit top talent from abroad.

In 2010, 15 percent of all doctoral candidates in Germany (25,630 in total) who completed their dissertations successfully and were awarded the degree were from abroad. The proportion of international academic staff is currently about 10 percent, more than half of them from Europe. Among the professors in German higher education the proportion of persons with a foreign nationality is 5.7 percent. Many of the young international doctoral degree holders will try to stay in Germany, especially if they come from developing countries. However, they will mostly have an opportunity for an academic career in Germany if they are qualified in subjects (or disciplines) in which universities have problems recruiting talent, especially because such talent is highly attractive for the private sector as well (for example, in the fields of engineering or computer sciences). In other subjects, non-German doctoral degree holders will have to compete with a relatively high number of German candidates. Good knowledge of the German language is almost a must in these situations.

Despite this, career management has become very difficult for junior academics in Germany. Many doctoral degree holders who want to stay in academia but do not manage to get an assistant position or a junior professorship stay on for a while as contract researchers in third-party funded research projects. During this time they try to raise their profiles by publishing, going to conferences, and building up their networks. However, it is important to identify the right point in time for giving up, and many miss this point because it is not really fixed. Beyond 52 years of age, there is basically no opportunity any longer to get a first call.

In 2009 Enders and Kottmann presented a major study looking into the careers of doctoral degree holders and comparing those who had earned their degree in the framework of a graduate school funded by the German Research Association (DFG) (n = 480) and a control group (n = 817) of doctoral degree holders having earned their degree in another way. Table 5.3 provides an overview of the respective career paths of these groups.

The table shows that about two-fifths of doctoral degree holders end up in jobs within the higher education sector and another 15 percent to 17 percent in research and development (R&D). However, the authors of the study also point out that there are considerable differences according to subject. More than half (57 percent) of the doctoral degree holders in humanities and social sciences took up jobs in teaching and research at a higher education institution. However, humanities and social sciences were also those subjects in which the highest proportion of young academics is on fixed-term and discontinuous contracts. In life sciences, the authors found the highest proportion of continuous and permanent jobs at a higher education institution or a research institute. About half of the doctoral degree holders in the natural sciences go into the private sector after completing their degree and doctoral degree holders in engineering mostly go into the private sector, especially into R&D.

These results indicate that well-defined and clearly demarcated professional options outside academia—be these in the private or in the public sector—provide interesting alternatives for the job search of highly

Table 5.3. Careers of doctoral degree holders in Germany, according to sector, by percentage (2008)

Sector	Former DFG Graduate School Members	Other Doctoral Degree Holders
Private sector, permanent	21	20
Private sector, not permanent	5	5
Research and teaching, permanent	40	36
Research and teaching, not permanent	9	10
Public service sector	9	13
Research and development	15	17

Source: Enders, Kottmann (2009, 121)

qualified doctoral degree holders. In many cases, these career options are better paid, as well, and often universities have difficulties recruiting appropriate candidates for professorships. In some subjects (e.g., medicine or chemistry) the nonacademic labor market even expects potential candidates for higher-level jobs to have a doctoral degree. In the humanities and in some of social science subjects, though, competition for academic jobs is fierce. However, this does not mean that doctoral degree holders will not find jobs. Search times might be longer in some subjects and sometimes entry-level employment is inadequate for the individual's qualifications. Eventually, though, the overwhelming majority of doctoral degree holders find appropriate employment.

But what is the situation of the young generation of academic staff? Staying in academia requires in most cases a high level of intrinsic motivation and a willingness to accept precarious employment and insecurity, at least for some years (on average until the age of 40 or 41). Grooming for an academic career starts nowadays during the doctoral phase. Course work in doctoral programs and schools frequently includes provisions like presenting at national or international conferences, time management, academic writing and publication experience, project proposals and project management, and didactic seminars to hone teaching skills. In the postdoc phase, when young academics seriously start to look for jobs in academia, they will continue to increase those qualifications that will make them more competitive—for example, via research stays abroad, publishing and editing, didactic skill-building and teaching experience, presentations at international conferences, successfully acquiring third-party research funds, and supervising master's level students. They will also seek to extend their networks in a more strategic manner, be it during conferences or in international or European Union–funded research projects that require cooperation with partners from abroad. In that phase, it is also important to make oneself known in the respective learned societies by becoming a member, presenting at the annual conferences, or becoming involved in one of the many working groups.

Despite the fact that all of these opportunities are available to young academics, salaries, contracts, and systematic career development opportunities or support are not necessarily attractive, nor do they provide a great deal of security. There are a number of nontransparent and informal elements in most recruitment processes that prevent clear-cut career progress. Even if a potential candidate has fulfilled all conditions and requirements and is appropriately qualified to be eligible for a professorship there is no guarantee that he or she will make it in the end. The main issue is to behave strategically and try again and again until one gets lucky. If this "getting lucky" does not occur, it is the young academic's own decision at what point in time and at what age to give up. If that happens too late the proverbial saying is that "the system has produced another dead duck."

Main Challenges and Future Trends

In 2008, the very first comprehensive overview and analysis was published (Burkhardt 2008) looking into academic careers in Germany and the related scholarship and support system for junior academics (i.e., doctoral candidates and postdocs). At that point in time, one of the major recommendations was to create some kind of system for registering doctoral candidates and to improve empirical research in this field. In 2013, a follow-up study was published, involving essentially the same team of researchers, looking more closely into the postdoc phase (Konsortium Bundesbericht Wissenschaftlicher Nachwuchs 2013). Among policy makers, the postdoc phase has also become an issue of concern. On the one hand, there are demands to provide more structured and systematic pathways into an academic career and, in particular, to create permanent positions beneath the level of a professorship (Kreckel 2013). Kreckel (2013) has compared the core (full-time) academic staff categories at German and U.S. universities in 2010 and presented the following overview:

Table 5.4. Academic core staff at German and American universities according to status, by percentage (2010)

Staff Category	Germany	USA
Independent professors/chair holders (Germany: W3; USA: Full professor)	11	34
Independent professors (Germany: W2; USA: Assoc. prof.)	6	26
Junior faculty (Germany: Junior prof.; USA: Assist. Prof.)	1	24
Dependent academic staff (tenured)	18	1
Dependent academic staff (Germany: fixed-term; USA: non-tenure track)	64	1

Source: Kreckel (2013, 11)

Table 5.4 clearly demonstrates that teaching and research at German universities falls heavily on the shoulders of younger, nontenured academic staff.

Thus, the current situation is more or less characterized by "you either get lucky or you don't" and many doctoral degree holders with aspirations to embark on an academic career do not get lucky, although this varies considerably according to field. However, increasing degrees of university autonomy—and, for some institutions, a change in legal status (from being a corporation under public law to becoming a foundation)—have also led to more independence in recruitment. Rather than professors being civil servants of the state they become employees of the university and can freely negotiate their salary. But they also lose some of the typical fringe benefits that have been traditionally associated with professorial positions as civil servants tenured for life.

Another major study published in 2008 (Kreckel) analyzed academic careers between award of the doctoral degree and obtaining a professorship in Germany, and compared the respective pathways of German academics with those in six other European countries and the United States. The authors suggested introducing a reform of academic careers in Germany by establishing three parallel academic career tracks in the future: one via junior professorship or habilitation into a career (through a call or tenure track) combining teaching and research in equal parts; a second track for the same group and with the same mechanisms, but leading to a teaching career, with limited time for research; and a third pathway also for the same group and with the same mechanisms, but focused on a research-intensive career with only half the teaching load as is currently the norm. Young academic staff with a doctoral degree should have the opportunity to become independent teachers and members of the junior staff (Kreckel 2008, 370).

Ultimately, the basic challenges for the future of (junior) academic staff in Germany are:

- The creation of tenured positions in teaching and research below those of a professor.
- The establishment of regular career pathways for doctoral degree holders in academia, including evaluation of performance and indication (as early as possible) whether there are real chances for an academic career.

- Abolishing *de facto* the prohibition to give a call to a professorship to somebody from the same university.

In particular, the latter regulation forces young academic staff again and again to change jobs and move to a different city or start commuting. In a phase of life where young academics are starting families and where they often have small children, this becomes a problem, especially for the academic careers of women. Furthermore, the typical procedure of recruiting someone for a professorship or junior professorship guarantees that external reviewers are part of the assessment and members of the search committees. This should be sufficient independent expertise to prevent inbreeding or favoritism.

As this chapter has demonstrated, the German higher education system has to deal with a high level of turnover among academic staff. In fact, professors having stayed at the same university for twenty or more years often have an implicit reputation as being research inactive. The times an academic has successfully been on the list of potential candidates for a professorship at another university, or even has received a call (regardless of whether the call is accepted), are mentioned in the CV as a rule and serve as proof of the attractiveness of a given candidate. This fluctuation is a normal way of life in German universities and is not seen as impacting on educational quality or research development. Accepting a call to a professorship elsewhere will normally mean that the professor moves his or her research funding plus his or her best doctoral candidates to the new place of work. The university that is left then has to recruit another appropriate candidate. Important research clusters that are part of the institution's profile will typically be big enough so that the loss of one professor does not lead to a total breakdown of the cluster. And teaching obligations can be continued because every professor is expected to be able to teach the full breadth of topics in his or her field. The field for which expertise and teaching experience are required is already clearly defined in the job advertisement.

However, the fluctuation impacts on the social and private lives of the individual academics and on the organization of the department. Due to the fact that recruitment to a professorship often takes up to two years and empty professorships are not in all cases temporarily filled with substitutes, the department has to organize temporary teaching staff to take over the teaching duties of the professor who left or retired until the position has been filled again. This group of teaching-only positions is typically inhabited by teaching staff for special tasks.

Note

1. The C-salary scale was valid in all of Germany and applied to academic staff in higher education institutions. It consisted of four levels (from C1 as postdoc position for the purpose of getting a habilitation to C4 as full professor or chair holder position) with each level having several increases according to seniority. After the reform of federalism, a new salary scale was introduced in 2005 called the W-salary scale. This consisted of three levels (W1 as junior professorship to W3 as full professor position) with a considerably reduced basic salary compared to the C-scale but the possibility to be awarded performance-related salary components. In addition, the basic salary levels in each category vary according to state. It is unknown to the author what the C stands for. In the new salary scale the W stands for Wissenschaft (science and scholarship).

References

Bourdieu, Pierre. 1982. *Die feinen Unterschiede. Kritik der gesellschaftlichen Urteilskraft*. Frankfurt/M.: Suhrkamp.

Bourdieu, Pierre. 1988. *Homo academicus*. Frankfurt/M.: Suhrkamp.

Bourdieu, Pierre. 1997. "Zur Genese der Begriffe Habitus und Feld." In *Der Tote packt den Lebenden Schriften zu Politik & Kultur 2*, edited by P. Bourdieu. Hamburg: VSA Verlag, 59–78.

Burkhardt, Anke, ed. 2008. *Wagnis Wissenschaft. Akademische Karrierewege und das Fördersystem in Deutschland*. Leipzig: Akademische Verlagsanstalt.

Enders, Jürgen, and Andrea Kottmann. 2009. *Neue Ausbildungsformen—andere Werdegänge? Ausbildungs- und Berufsverläufe von Absolventinnen und Absolventen der Graduiertenkollegs der DFG*. Edited by Deutsche Forschungsgemeinschaft. Weinheim: Wiley-VCH.

Hartmer, Michael, and Sandra Möhlmann. 2012. "Peinliche Verrechnung. Zur Kürzung von Leistungsbezügen durch die Reform der W-Besoldung." *Forschung & Lehre* 19(12): 980–983.

Janson, Kerstin, Harald Schomburg, and Ulrich Teichler. 2007. *Wege zur Professur. Qualifizierung und Beschäftigung an Hochschulen in Deutschland und den USA*. Münster: Waxmann.

Kehm, Barbara M., and Peer Pasternack. 2008. "The German 'Excellence Initiative' and Its Role in Restructuring the National Higher Education Landscape." In *Structuring Mass Higher Education. The Role of Elite Institutions*, edited by D. Palfreyman and T. Tapper. New York, London: Routledge, 113–127.

Konsortium Bundesbericht Wissenschaftlicher Nachwuchs. 2013. *Bundesbericht Wissenschaftlicher Nachwuchs 2013. Statistische Daten und Forschungsbefunde zu Promovierenden und Promovierten in Deutschland*. Bielefeld: Bertelsmann Verlag GmbH & Co. KG.

Kreckel, Reinhard, ed. 2008. *Zwischen Promotion und Professur. Das wissenschaftliche Personal in Deutschland im Vergleich mit Frankreich, Großbritannien, USA, Schweden, den Niederlanden, Österreich und der Schweiz.* Leipzig: Akademische Verlagsanstalt.

Kreckel, Reinhard. 2013. "'It Would Be a Good Idea.' Der US-amerikanische Tenure Track als Importmodell." *Forschung & Lehre* 20(1): 10–12.

Musselin, Christine. 2010. *The Market for Academics.* New York, London: Routledge.

Statistisches Bundesamt. 2010. Prüfungen an Hochschulen. Fachserie 11, Reihe 4.2. https://www.destatis.de.

Statistisches Bundesamt. 2011. Personal an Hochschulen. Fachserie 11, Reihe 4.4. https://www.destatis.de.

Wolters, Miriam, and Sven Schmiedel. 2012. *Promovierende in Deutschland 2010.* Edited by *Statistisches Bundesamt Wiesbaden.* https://www.destatis.de/DE/Publikationen/Thematisch/BildungForschungKultur/HochschulenPromovierende5213104109004.pdf?_blob=publicationFile.

Chapter 6

Entering an Expanding Academia

The New Generation of Faculty in India

N. Jayaram

Introduction

Analyses of the academic profession in India at the turn of the century showed that the hallowed position of the guru was in jeopardy (Jayaram 2003). This fall from grace was a reflection of the crisis confronting higher education in the country (Jayaram 2009). The situation reached a crisis point, with the knowledge economy (occasioned by globalization) making competing demands for talent and the best talent turning away from the academic profession. At last, the government of India realized that the country was losing out on the demographic dividend that had come its way because of the nature of the age-structure transition in its population (Altbach and Jayaram 2010). Several initiatives were hurriedly set in motion: the salaries of the professoriate were revised steeply upwards, effect retroactively from January 1, 2006 (University Grants Commission [UGC] 2010), the National Knowledge Commission (NKC 2007) was established, and the university system was allowed to expand with little or no preparation (Altbach and Jayaram 2009). What does this turn of events now mean to the academic profession, in general, and to the new generation of teachers entering it in particular?

Simple as this question appears, there is no easy answer. As Pawan Agarwal (2009) has observed, "India's large size, long history and diverse culture and the complicated nature of Indian polity and policy process make Indian higher education a very complex enterprise" (Agarwal 2009, xxx). There has been no consistent long-term higher education policy for the country as a whole—both federal and state governments make policies, and policy making largely consists of ad hoc responses to contingent situations (Tilak 2004).

It is in this context of an expanding university system and irresoluteness of policy about it that this chapter reviews the academic profession in India today, with special reference to the new generation of teachers entering it, a generation on which rests the future of academia and higher education in the country. This chapter begins with an analysis of the growth of, and diversity in, Indian higher education. The diversity is reflected in the variety of teaching positions, which is outlined next, followed by an elucidation of the streamlining of qualifications for entry into the professoriate post-2006. The policy and practice of protective discrimination (a form of affirmative action) in appointments to teaching positions is discussed next. The procedures of recruitment, terms of appointment and prospects of career advancement of young faculty are explained. The salary and nonsalary benefits form the theme of a separate section. The chapter concludes with some reflections on the emerging scenario in higher education and the academic profession.

Growth and Diversity in Indian Higher Education

In India, higher education has expanded rapidly during the last six decades: from 30 universities and 695 colleges in 1950/1951 to 634 universities and university-level (degree-awarding) institutions and 33,023 colleges by the end of 2011. As many as 100 (15.78 percent) of the 634 universities are private and, de facto, mostly for-profit institutions, a phenomenon that is new in the history of higher education in India. Correspondingly, the number of teachers has increased from 23,549 in 1950/1951 to 816,966 in 2010/2011, and that of students, from 397,000 to 16,975,000 during the same period. Much of this expansion has taken place since 2000/2001 (see Table 6.1) (UGC 2012a).

This massive system of higher education—the third largest in the world, behind China and the United States—is also diversified: the institutions vary in terms of their degree-granting authority, legislative origin, functions, and funding (see Table 6.2). Broadly, we can delineate five types of educational institutions, forming an informal hierarchy: (1) institutions of national importance, (2) central universities, (3) state universities,

Table 6.1. Growth of Higher Education in India, 1950/1951 to 2010/2011, selected years

	1950/1951	1960/1961	1970/1971	1980/1981	1990/1991	2000/2001	2010/2011
Universities	30	55	103	133	190	256	564
		(83.33)	(87.27)	(29.13)	(42.86)	(34.74)	(120.21)
Colleges	695	1,542	3,604	4,722	7,346	12,806	33,023
		(121.87)	(133.72)	(31.02)	(55.57)	(74.33)	(157.87)
Teachers	23,549	59,673	128,876	193,341	263,125	411,628	816,966@
		(153.39)	(115.97)	(50.02)	(36.09)	(56.44)	(157.87)
Students#	397	1,050	1,954	2,752	4,925	8,399	16,975
		(823.25)	(86.10)	(40.84)	(78.96)	(70.54)	(102.11)

Note: *634 as of December 2011; @ includes all categories of teachers including part-time, ad hoc, contract and visiting teachers; # enrolment in '000s; figures in parentheses refer to decadal percentage increase

Source: Computed from UGC charts (UGC 2012a)

Table 6.2. Typology of Indian Higher Education Institutions

Defining characteristics	Types of institutions
Degree-granting powers	1. Institutions of national importance 2. University—unitary 3. University—affiliating 4. College
Legislative origin	1. Central 2. State 3. 'Deemed-to-be university'
Funding	1. Public—government 2. Public—grant-in-aid 3. Private—unaided (*de jure* not-for-profit, *de facto* for-profit)

Source: Adapted from Agarwal (2009, 2)

(4) grant-in-aid colleges that are constituents of or affiliated to a university, and (5) unaided (purely private) universities/colleges. The differences across institutions are reflected in various aspects of academic employment, including their recruitment and remuneration systems as well as working conditions; thus, there are huge differences between university teachers and college teachers.

Institutions of national importance include the sixteen Indian Institutes of Technology (IITs), three institutions specializing in medical sciences, and one each specializing in statistical techniques and the Hindi language.[1] All these institutions are pan-India in their orientation, lay greater emphasis on research in addition to teaching, spend more per student, and offer better remuneration and working conditions as compared to all other universities.

Central universities (43), founded by the government of India (GoI), are multidisciplinary in their spread, combining postgraduate teaching (mainly) with research (secondarily). Besides these, the government of India has recognized 129 institutions as "deemed-to-be universities" and some of these institutions also receive governmental funds. They, like the institutions of national importance, are pan-India in their orientation, have better academic reputations, greater research orientation, better remuneration and working conditions, and spend more per student as compared to state universities.

State universities (297 in all) receive funding from the governments of the respective states constituting the Indian federation. They have a central campus housing schools and departments of study that offer instruction largely at the postgraduate level and undertake research. Most state universities have colleges affiliated to them, whose academic work they regulate and oversee.

Grant-in-aid colleges are funded to the tune of 85 percent to 90 percent by the state governments concerned—a practice going back to colonial times. The academic standards of these colleges are determined and overseen by the state university to which they are affiliated, which also conducts centralized examinations for the students enrolled in them.

Unaided (purely private) universities [100] *and colleges* are privately run institutions; they do not receive any financial support from the government, excepting perhaps land at concessional rates. They rely almost entirely on funding from tuition fees and donations (often as a consideration for enrollment into the institution). Private colleges are established and managed by private trusts; although trust laws govern their administration and finance, their academic programs are determined and overseen by the university to which they are affiliated. Because they raise their own funds, the purely private universities and colleges mostly offer programs—like computer science, biotechnology, management studies—which are in high demand and financially lucrative.

The bulk of the expansion in student enrollments in higher education has taken place in affiliated colleges in state universities and in first degree courses (about 86 percent) (UGC 2010/2011, 301), and in general education (arts, science, and commerce) (about 72 percent) (UGC 2012a).[2] Most (83.5 percent) of the teachers are also working in these institutions (UGC 2010/2011, 4), and their work almost exclusively entails teaching and examining candidates at the undergraduate level. Among degree-awarding higher education institutions, only in the institutions of national importance, central universities, and selected departments in state universities is research a priority. That is, the university system has largely concentrated on "retailing knowledge" rather than creating and refining knowledge—a function assigned to specialist institutes and laboratories outside the university system. This peculiar disjunction between universities and research institutes explains the paradox that the large and experienced system of higher education in India is hardly known for its excellence in research (Jayaram 2007).

Official documents often emphasize the phenomenal expansion in higher education over six decades since planned development began in

1950/1951: university numbers have grown by 1,780 percent (18.8-fold), college numbers by 4,651.51 percent (47.52-fold), teacher numbers by 3,369.22 percent (34.69-fold), and student numbers by 4,175.82 percent (41.76-fold) (UGC 2012a). An analysis of the decadal increase in these areas reveals interesting facts (see Table 6.3).

The growth in the number of teachers has not kept pace with the increase in the number of universities and colleges and the expansion of student enrollment. Partly, the faculty shortage was caused by the hiring moratorium imposed by the central and the state governments in the 1980s to curtail public spending. The rapid expansion of universities and colleges since 2000/2001 has only made this shortage more acute. According to the Indian Ministry of Human Resources Development's (MHRD) task force report, the faculty shortage is estimated to be around 54 percent (Times News Network 2011b); the Delhi University Teachers Association reports that as many as 4,000 permanent teaching positions are lying vacant in the premier University of Delhi and its constituent colleges (*Daily Pioneer* 2012); and the Standing Committee on Human Resource Development has revealed that in eight newly established IITs the faculty shortage is as high as 60 percent (Anand 2012).

For this reason, causing discomfort to the MHRD, the Planning Commission has decided against including the establishment of new universities and colleges in the Twelfth Five-Year Plan period (2012–2017) except under "exceptional circumstances." The Commission has advised the MHRD to focus on "consolidation and not expansion" during the next five years, as there is already a "huge liability" from the proactive expansion in the Eleventh Five-Year Plan period (2007–2012) (*Economic Times* 2012).

Thus, the current acute shortage of teachers in a rapidly expanding system of higher education creates opportunities for the younger generation of master's and doctoral degree holders, as well as challenges for policy makers and administrators. On the one hand, the number of aspirants who are "formally qualified" for teaching positions is growing and, with the steep upward revision of salaries, the academic profession is now an attractive option in the job market. On the other hand, the universities and colleges have been finding it difficult to recruit "suitable" candidates for the vacant positions, either because such candidates are hard to come by or because of impedimental statutory/regulatory requirements. Meanwhile, institutions have to ensure that teaching work goes on with ad hoc arrangements. In what follows, we examine the implications of this for the academic profession and those who seek to enter it.

Table 6.3. Teaching Staff Relative to Universities, Colleges and Students in India, 1950/1951 to 2010/2011, selected years

	Year						
Average number	1950/1951	1960/1961	1970/1971	1980/1981	1990/1991	2000/2001	2010/2011
Teachers per university	784.97	1084.97	1251.22	1453.69	1384.87	1607.92	1448.52
Teachers per college	33.88	38.70	35.76	40.94	35.82	32.14	24.74
Students per teacher	16.86	17.60	15.16	14.23	18.71	20.40	20.78

Source: Computed from UGC charts (UGC 2012)

Varieties of Teaching Positions

In India, the professoriate is not a homogenous category. This is due to the diversity of the system of higher education, on the one hand, and the arrangements that have evolved to address the shortage of teachers, on the other. There are different types of teaching positions in terms of the duration of employment and the privileges that go with them. The most coveted is the *permanent* (tenured) teaching position in a publicly funded university or college. Appointees to these positions are placed on *probation* for a period of two years. Probation provides an opportunity for the university/college to evaluate the appointee's strengths and weaknesses as teacher, colleague, and employee, just as it provides an opportunity for the teacher to ascertain the prospect of a suitable academic career. During probation, the institution can terminate the appointment of a teacher by giving one month's notice (or instantly by giving one month salary) without giving any reason for termination. Similarly, a teacher on probation can resign from service by giving one month's notice (or instantly by paying back one month salary). In most universities and colleges, probation is viewed as a formality, and rarely does one come across a teacher whose appointment has been terminated while on probation.

The appointees who successfully complete the period of probation are *confirmed* in the *post*, and they remain in the employment of the institution until they reach the age of superannuation, which varies from 60 to 62 years (in state universities and grant-in-aid colleges) to 65 years (in central universities and centrally funded institutions). Thereafter, these individuals receive about 50 percent of their last drawn salary as a pension, which is ample to live comfortably. Once confirmed, it is rare for a teacher's services to be terminated, unless she or he is found guilty of moral turpitude. The procedure for termination is long and cumbersome, and courts often favor the teacher against the institution. Teachers holding a permanent position can voluntarily retire from their post with full pension benefits after completing twenty years of uninterrupted service. They can also be compulsorily retired (as a penalty) or prematurely retired (in "public interest") or retired on medical grounds (after fifty years of age or thirty years of service). Thus, a candidate taking up an academic position in a college with only a master's degree around twenty-four years of age, or in a university with a doctorate around twenty-seven years of age, can theoretically work for anywhere between thirty-six to thirty-eight years, depending on whether the institution is a state university/affiliated college or a centrally funded one.

Permanent positions are nonexistent in purely private universities and unaided colleges affiliated to universities. Appointment to teaching positions in such institutions is *contractual* in nature. The duration of the contract may vary from about five months (one semester) to five years. The *terms of contract* may vary from case to case and they are specifically spelled out in each case, unlike the *terms of appointment* to permanent positions that are uniform and stipulated in the statutes and ordinances governing the publicly funded institutions. Given the shortage of well-qualified and experienced teachers, retired teachers often find opportunities for contractual appointments in purely private institutions. Because contractual appointments offer greater flexibility in human resource management and involve limited long-run financial commitments, even publicly funded institutions are now turning to such appointments.

Both permanent and contractual teaching positions involve full-time engagement in teaching in the institution. Different from this is the part-time teaching position. In India, the concepts of *part-time teachers* (who teach for a specified number of teaching hours in a week) and *guest faculty* (who help the college/department to round out portions of the syllabus) originated as a result of the unmet demand for teachers in particular disciplines. For some positions, full-time teachers were either not available (in narrow fields or specializations) or it was not viable to appoint full-time teachers (as they would not have sufficient work load, defined as number of classroom teaching hours). Typically, the part-time teachers and the guest faculty are paid a consolidated sum by way of remuneration for the number of hours of teaching work they are assigned. Their monthly remuneration is nowhere near what a permanent teacher gets. Furthermore, they are not entitled to any statutory employment benefits—leave, medical insurance, pension, gratuity, and so on. Obviously, they are looked down on in the system as "daily wage workers." Guest lecturers, if they are professionals (medical doctors, lawyers, chartered accountants, etc.), enjoy better emoluments and status than those who are underemployed master's degree holders.

What was introduced as an interim solution to a practical problem in academic administration has gradually become a modality of appointment of teachers, especially in private colleges, which do not receive governmental support.[3] State universities, too, depend on part-time teachers; however, the central universities rarely do so. From the college or university's point of view, it is obviously more economical to employ part-time teachers than permanent teachers. There is greater flexibility in hiring and firing of part-time teachers, more so considering the large number of unemployed or underemployed master's degree holders.

From the prospective candidates' perspective, part-time teaching offers *some* employment opportunity, and the possibility of gaining experience, which may be useful if and when opportunities for more stable or full-time permanent/contractual employment arise. Periodically, part-time teachers with ten or more years of service have brought political pressure to bear on the state governments to "regularize" their appointments on humanitarian grounds. Courts of law have also been sympathetic to their cause. To overcome the administrative and financial problems resulting from such "backdoor entry" into the academic profession encouraged by grant-in-aid private colleges, some governments have abolished the post of part-time teachers and suggested the reappointment of retired teachers on a contract or hourly basis (Jayaram 2003).

To address the faculty shortage in specific subjects in a limited way and for short duration, some universities are assigning teaching work to *PhD scholars* receiving research fellowships awarded by the UGC. Some state universities, which have few or no such awardees, have instituted their own fellowships for PhD scholars who are assigned teaching work (*India Education Review* 2012). Similarly, some institutions have introduced the informal position of *teaching assistants* who, in fact, function as teachers.

Thus, the diversity of higher education and the shortage of teachers have resulted in heterogeneity of the Indian professoriate precluding any blanket generalization about either the academic profession or those entering it. Difficult as the task is, while revising the salary and service conditions of teachers in higher education in 2006, the UGC attempted to standardize the qualifications of various categories of teachers, the procedures for recruiting them, the requirements and process of their career advancement, and the salaries and nonsalary benefits to which they are entitled. The following sections present this standardization and examine what this means to those entering the academic profession today.

Qualifications for Entry into the Professoriate

Since January 2006 a three-tier academic hierarchy—namely, professor, associate professor, and assistant professor—has been standardized in publicly funded higher education institutions across the country. In most cases, entry into the academic profession is at the assistant professor's level, both in the university departments and in the colleges.[4] For appointment to the post of assistant professor in arts, commerce, education, humanities, journalism and mass communication, languages, law, sciences and social sciences, in a college or university or university-level institution, a candidate must have obtained a score of 5.5 on a 10-point scale on the master's level examination in the relevant subject.[5] Furthermore, the candidates must have qualified via the National Eligibility Test (NET), or an accredited State Eligibility Test (SET).

The NET as an eligibility criterion for entry into the academic profession is perhaps unique to India. In order to ensure minimum standards for entry into the teaching profession (since 1989) and research (since 1984) the UGC introduced an "eligibility test." Those qualifying on the basis of this test become eligible for an entry level teaching position (assistant professorship) in universities or colleges; in addition, those with "higher merit" become eligible for a Junior Research Fellowship (JRF) to pursue research in any UGC-recognized institution for a period of five years (UGC 2010–2011, 180). The UGC conducts this test twice a year (in June and December) in 78 subjects at 74 centers spread across the country (UGC 2012b). The eligibility test for five core science subjects—chemical sciences, life sciences, physical sciences, mathematical sciences and earth/atmospheric/ocean/planetary sciences—is also conducted twice a year by the Council of Scientific and Industrial Research (CSIR) under the Joint CSIR–UGC NET. The eligibility certificates issued by the UGC do not expire.

In the two tests conducted in 2010, of the 604,951 candidates who registered, 417,407 (or 69 percent) appeared for the test (189,863 in June and 227,544 in December). Of the 417,407 who appeared for the test, 6,480 (1.55 percent) qualified for both assistant professorship and JRF and 13,680 (3.28 percent) qualified for assistant professorship only. That is, in all, 20,160 (4.83 percent) qualified to enter the academic profession (UGC 2010–2011, 181). In addition, under the two Joint CSIR–UGC tests conducted in the same year, 4,889 candidates qualified for both assistant professorship and JRF and 4,389, for assistant professorship only (ibid., 186). However, eligibility is only a precondition for consideration—the qualified candidates must go through the process of recruitment and prove their suitability before they formally enter the academic profession.

As is clear, the percentage of candidates successfully qualifying via the NET to enter the academic profession is very small. This partly reflects on the poor quality of education and the liberal standards of evaluation at the master's level in Indian universities. To increase the number of candidates qualifying through the NET, the UGC abolished negative marking for wrong answers to test questions from June 2010 onward. As a consequence of this retrogressive step, the number of NET-qualifying candidates jumped from 3,190 in December 2009 to 7,233 (by 126.74 percent) in June 2010, and to 12,927 (a further 78.72 percent) in December 2010 (ibid.).

To address regional specificities, many state governments have been permitted by the UGC to conduct a State Eligibility Test (SET), which was treated as equivalent to the NET, for assistant professorship eligibility. In some states, to cope with various demands, the standards of the SET were so appallingly diluted and the norms so brazenly flouted that the UGC had to withdraw the permission granted them to conduct the SET (Jayaram 2003). The UGC has since introduced a system of accrediting the SETs conducted by the state governments to ensure that the patterns and standards of the SETs are the same as that of the NET. The accreditation is renewed periodically based on a review by an expert committee. Moreover, since June 2002, the candidates qualifying via the SET are eligible to apply for assistant professorships only in the universities and colleges in the respective states.

Considering that many candidates who had obtained the PhD degree had not cleared the NET/SET, in 2009 the UGC exempted such candidates from the requirement of NET/SET qualification for recruitment to assistant professorships. (A similar exemption exists for applicants with master's degrees in disciplines for which the NET is not conducted.) This has not only sparked a debate in the academy, but has also resulted in litigation. Those critical of this exemption are of the opinion that it will pave the way for backdoor entry into the academic profession and adversely affect the quality of higher education. Those supportive of it argue that it will ease the problem of the faculty shortage (Anand 2010).

Unlike for higher-level teaching positions, such as professor or associate professor, for assistant professorships, no additional qualification in the form of research publications or work experience is prescribed as essential. However, candidates with such qualifications are preferred compared to those without, especially for appointments in the university departments. For this reason, many candidates accept contract appointments or appointments as part time, ad hoc, or guest lecturers, even if they are paid on an hourly basis, given that they can cash in on such work experience when vacancies arise.

A majority of assistant professors in the universities now possess doctoral degrees. In colleges, the percentage of assistant professors with doctorates is very low; those with a doctorate seek upward mobility as an associate professor (or even as an assistant professor) in a university. Insistence on the doctorate as a qualification for entry into the academic profession increased the demand for enrollment in PhD programs and diluted the quality of doctorates (Jayaram 2008, 230–241). Thus, as a rule of thumb, if not as a formal guideline, a doctorate from an internationally renowned university is valued more as compared to the doctorate from state universities or unknown foreign universities.

In publicly funded institutions, the regulations governing minimum qualifications can hardly be flouted. There are far too many applicants vis-à-vis the number of posts available, and the slightest doubt that an appointment is made by flouting a regulation is challenged in a court of law, and such appointments are struck down by the courts. The institutions have also become more careful after the enactment of the Right to Information Act in 2005, whose provisions will invariably be invoked by unselected applicants.

The purely private universities and colleges have greater flexibility in the matter of qualifications of teachers. However, they, too, would like to ensure the minimum as regards the academic qualification of the faculty, such as the grade in the master's level and the doctorate. As for unaided private colleges, the university to which they are affiliated acts as the watchdog.

Studies on Indian college teachers in the 1980s and early 1990s invariably underlined the sad deficiency of academic preparation of those entering the academic profession and their declining commitment to it (Jayaram 2003, 207–208). The National Commission on Teachers (NCT 1985) also bemoaned the fact that most teachers were merely making a living and not following a vocation. In addition to the poor quality of postgraduate education, this unsatisfactory situation was attributed to the absence of training or orientation to teaching on the part of the new entrants. To rectify this, the UGC, following the National Policy on Education, 1986 (GoI 1986), introduced the NET as an eligibility criterion for entry into the academic profession and established Academic Staff Colleges (ASC) to groom the new entrants to the profession and keep those already in it abreast of the latest developments in their field.

Starting in 1987, the UGC established at least one ASC in each state with the mandate to improve standards of teaching through "orientation courses" (focusing on pedagogy and the social relevance of education) for the new entrants to the profession and "refresher courses" (providing up-do-date information on the contents of various disciplines) for those already in it. In 2010/2011, there were 66 ASCs spread across the country. The duration of the "orientation course" is 24 working days, involving 144 contact hours, and that of the "refresher course" is 18 working days and involves 108 contact hours. Attending an "orientation course" is mandatory for confirmation of an assistant professor, and attending two "refresher courses" is a requisite before an assistant professor becomes eligible for promotion to the next stage in the academic career. To build an element of seriousness, an end-course assessment has been introduced.

As with all such well-intentioned innovations by the UGC, the orientation and refresher courses are now ritualized at the ASCs (Jayaram 2003, 209–211). As early as 1993, a review of the ASCs revealed that "while some of them are functioning well, mainly due to the competence and enthusiasm of the director, about a third have been observed to be decidedly poor" (Indiresan 1993, 317). Recognizing that the institution of the ASC has been ritualized, in a recent report, the National Assessment and Accreditation Council (NAAC) has advised that the ASCs should be renamed Human Resource Development Centers, which should make "induction training" mandatory for all entrants into the academic profession, including those appointed in private institutions and on temporary basis (*Times of India* 2012). It is doubtful if the NAAC's advice will be heeded and, if heeded, that it, too, will not be ritualized.

The Policy of Protective Discrimination

Although merit is emphasized in direct recruitment to academic positions in publicly funded higher education institutions, these institutions are also required to reserve a certain percentage of such positions for candidates hailing from indigent sections of the population. As per the constitutional mandate, 49.5 percent of the posts in all public institutions are reserved under the policy of protective discrimination: 15 percent for the Scheduled Castes, 7.5 percent for the Scheduled Tribes, and 27 percent for the Other Backward Classes.[6] Selection for the reserved positions is also based on the merit of the candidates from among these castes, tribes and classes. Besides this so-called vertical reservation, there is horizontal reservation to the extent of 3 percent (across categories) for People with Disabilities, 1 percent each for candidates with auditory, visual, and orthopedic disabilities.

Reserving positions in public institutions is a form of affirmative action that is special to India. This provision, mandated by the Constitution of India in conformity with its avowed principles of equality and social justice, is intended to rectify the centuries-old inequalities resulting from the Hindu caste system and to ameliorate the general backwardness of the population. The Constitution has identified three categories of the population for protective discrimination: the Scheduled Castes and Scheduled Tribes (so called because of the Schedules in which these castes and tribes are listed) and Other Backward Classes. This provision has since been extended to "People with Disabilities."

Although initially intended for a period of ten years, the provision of reservation has been extended every ten years through an Act of Parliament, and it is now widely regarded as a permanent part of state policy. In public parlance, it is a sensitive issue, and it has been frequently challenged in courts of law, including the Supreme Court of India. Generally, the legal position has been in its favor. However, opinion on its practice in the sphere of higher education is divided: some view this as debilitating the quality of education, while others uphold it as an instrument of social justice and dub its critics as retrograde and elitist.

For many a reserved position, no doubt, it is difficult to find suitable candidates; it is against the law to fill such positions with candidates who do not belong to the specified categories. This is often cited as one of the reasons for the acute faculty shortage. For instance, in the 43 central universities around the country, 341 (46.08 percent) of the 740 positions reserved for the Scheduled Castes and 197 (53.39 percent) of 369 positions reserved for the Scheduled Tribes at the entry level (assistant professor) were vacant in 2010/2011. For both these categories together, the percentage of vacant positions was higher at the posts of associate professor (over 84 percent) and professor (92 percent) (*Hindu* 2012). There is no provision of reservation in purely private universities and unaided colleges; the demand for reservation in the private sector has not gained political momentum yet.

Recruitment Procedures

All vacancies in publicly funded higher education institutions have to be compulsorily advertised in the government's weekly *Employment News* (brought out in both English and Hindi) and at least in one national level newspaper (and also in a vernacular newspaper, in the case of a state university). Vacancy advertisements are also posted on the websites of the institutions and in *University News*, a monthly magazine of the Association of Indian Universities. The advertisement should specify the posts that are reserved for specific categories of candidates. Although purely private institutions are not obliged to advertise their vacancies, they do so in leading newspapers and magazines.

All appointments in publicly funded institutions are made on the recommendations of duly constituted selection committees as prescribed by the UGC/MHRD and incorporated under the statutes/ordinances of the universities and institutes. Because the number of applicants far exceeds the number of vacancies, some institutions set up a screening committee to shortlist the candidates to be called for interview. To avoid applicants stalling the selection process by invoking legal intervention on the ground that they have not been called for interview, in state universities, all applicants fulfilling the minimum qualification for the post are called for an interview. The interviews in such universities go on for several days, and most often the process is carried out as a ritual to satisfy the judicial requirements.

In order to make the system more credible and efficient, some central universities and institutes and all institutions of national importance assess the candidates' teaching ability and/or research aptitude through a seminar or classroom lecture. Institutions vary widely in terms of the procedures adopted, but such test seminars/lectures are held outside the purview of the selection committee. The faculty present may give their feedback to the selection committee on the suitability of the candidates and rank them in order of their performance.

Although the elaborate guidelines suggested by the UGC underline the importance of transparency and credibility of recruitment to teaching positions, in actual practice rules are bent and appointments are often manipulated and fixed. Not infrequently, complaints of favoritism, nepotism, and corruption are heard, even as most institutions go through the process of recruitment with a veneer of legality and fairness. In many institutions there is backdoor entry into the academic profession for candidates who cannot face competition. Such candidates are first appointed as ad hoc/temporary assistant professors and given an opportunity to gain "experience." At the interview, the chairperson of the selection committee (the vice chancellor, director, or the president of the governing body) pleads their case, and generally the external experts are very obliging. Selection of candidates on extraneous considerations or through dubious methods often results in charges of nepotism and corruption in publicly funded institutions. On this, however, data are hard to come by.

Data are also hard to come by on the role of social networks in recruitment to the academic profession. Teachers, especially doctoral supervisors, and class-fellows or friends bring to the attention of the prospective candidates the availability of teaching positions and give tips on how to go about applying for the positions. Teachers and supervisors write letters of recommendation for the candidates and often "put in a word" in their favor, if they know the members of the selection committee. Websites managed by the bighearted among those in the academic profession and, Facebook, too, are used by prospective candidates.

By law, appointment to teaching positions in publicly funded institutions is open to all citizens of the country. Although there is provision for inclusion through reservation of posts, no candidate can be excluded on sociocultural or regional considerations. However, in most state universities and colleges affiliated to them, candidates from the state are privileged in the hiring process by making knowledge of the regional language a desirable qualification. This has had the inadvertent consequence of limiting mobility among teachers and perpetuating a deleterious inbreeding within the institutions.

The private universities and unaided private colleges are not bound by any formal guidelines for recruitment to teaching positions. They are not obliged to advertise their vacancies, and their advertisements are frugal on details. Their recruitment procedures are not transparent. Since most are de facto (though not de jure) for-profit institutions, the financial interest of the institution outweighs quality considerations. Even so, some of the private universities such as Amity University, Azim Premji University, and Symbiosis University have proclaimed their commitment to quality in higher education. Given the type of resources that some of the private universities have been able to mobilize, they seem to have greater elbow room in the matter of scouting for talent and selecting high-quality teaching faculty. Incidentally, as private enterprises, they are not encumbered by the policy of protective discrimination.

Terms of Appointment: Service and Working Conditions

In publicly funded institutions, once the recommendations of the selection committee are approved by the executive body of the university/institute, a letter offering the appointment and terms thereof is sent to the selected candidate. In case the selected candidate does not accept the offer or does not report for duty within the stipulated period, the first candidate on the "wait list" is offered the post. The list of selected candidates is valid for six months, after which the post has to be re-advertised.

In some state universities, the recommendations of the selection committee as approved by the executive body have to be ratified by the chancellor, who is the governor of the state. The appointments in grant-in-aid private colleges have to be approved by the state government's department of education. Appointments to teaching positions in the government-run colleges are made by a statutory authority called the state public service commission.

The terms of appointment are specified in *the appointment order*, and they are enforceable in a court of law. Among other things the order specifies the pay in the "pay band" (salary scale) and other admissible allowances and benefits. Generally, in the universities, there is no negotiation on salary or other benefits. But, during the interview, the candidate can make out a case for a higher starting pay, and if convinced, the selection committee may recommend, with reason, up to five increments, that is, a maximum of a 15 percent higher basic pay.

In private universities, theoretically, the terms of appointment are negotiable. In reality, however, such negotiations take place only in the case of faculty of very high caliber or faculty in narrow fields of specialization. That is, private institutions have the autonomy to compete for faculty and can use better salaries, fringe benefits, reduced teaching obligations, research subsidies, and so on to make an offer that is more attractive than an offer by other similar institutions or publicly funded institutions. Apparently, the publicly funded institutions are, on occasion, at a disadvantage. However, the private institutions can hardly match the employment security, career advancement, and graduated increase in salary and other statutory benefits that are on offer in publicly funded institutions. Not surprisingly, publicly funded institutions, especially those funded directly by the MHRD/UGC, are the best bet for aspirants to the academic profession.

While announcing the revised pay scales in 2008, the UGC (ibid., 60) prescribed for teachers with full-time appointments a workload of 40 hours a week, for 30 working weeks (180 teaching days) in an academic year. Moreover, teachers are required to be available in the university department/center or college, as the case may be, for at least five hours daily. The number of contact ("teaching-learning process") hours per week for assistant professor is sixteen. This heavy workload hardly leaves any time for research by teachers, especially those in colleges.

Since the grant-in-aid colleges are dependent on government funds, they enforce workload norms strictly; teachers with inadequate workloads are required to teach in another college in order to meet these obligations. If in any subject the workload falls well below the prescribed sixteen hours, it is farmed out to part-time teachers. For paucity of financial resources, especially since the introduction of new pay scales, many state governments across the country have imposed an embargo on recruitment to teaching positions in the universities. The state universities are permitted to recruit teachers only if they justify the need in terms of the unmet workload. Central universities, centrally funded deemed-to-be universities and the institutions of national importance, however, do not observe the UGC prescriptions. There is no standardized workload in private universities, and workload in private colleges is exploitatively higher than in grant-in-aid colleges.

The main responsibility of college teachers is to teach the prescribed curriculum to the students and prepare them for examinations conducted by the university. Besides teaching, university teachers are also required to be engaged in research. Only in a few university departments/centers and institutions of national importance is the primary emphasis on research. As such, publication as an academic activity is more characteristic of university teachers than college teachers; and a college teacher being engaged in research and publication is commendable indeed. Often this enables the college teachers to move to a university, pursue their research interests, and improve career prospects. In private universities, the emphasis is almost exclusively on teaching. In all universities and colleges, teachers are expected to assist the university/college in such administrative activities as processing applications for admission, counseling students, assisting with the conduct of examinations (supervision, invigilation or "proctoring," and evaluation), and participating in extension, co-curricular and extracurricular activities. Some teachers perform nonteaching work as a matter of duty; most teachers avoid it, if they can.

Career Advancement

For several decades, the job performance of teachers in higher education institutions remained unevaluated, and any attempt at evaluation was either resisted or done perfunctorily. Only in government-run colleges were "confidential reports" of teachers written by their principals and filed in their service registers. In universities and institutes, teachers on probation were confirmed generally on the basis of confidential reports by the head/chairperson of the department, or the dean if the teacher was the head/chairperson of the department. However, as part of the package of pay revision and increases, performance evaluation of teachers in all publicly funded universities and colleges has been introduced.

The UGC (2010, 103–107) has listed three categories of teacher's contributions for appraisal, namely, (1) teaching, learning, and evaluation related activities, (2) curricular, extension, and professional development related activities, and (3) research and academic contributions. For each category indicators and weights are specified. To suit their specific requirements, the institutions have been advised to adapt the template provided by the UGC or devise their own self-assessment-cum-performance-appraisal forms for teachers in compliance with the UGC prescriptions. Purely private institutions do not have a mandatory or standardized self-appraisal system. This performance appraisal system has just been introduced in the university system, so it is too early to judge on its efficacy. But past experience with the UGC's mandatory measures (Jayaram 2003) does not permit optimism, as the UGC, being a small organization, lacks resources to oversee hundreds of universities and thousands of colleges.

The Indian professoriate is pyramidal in structure: there are fewer positions of professor than that of associate professor, and fewer positions of associate professor than that of assistant professor; and this is more so in the affiliated colleges (see Table 6.4). To improve the opportunities of teachers for moving up the career ladder, and as an incentive to performance, a six-stage Career Advancement Scheme (CAS) has been introduced. How soon entry-level assistant professors can move to stage 2 depends on whether they possess a PhD degree (four years), an MPhil degree (five years), or only a master's degree in the subject (six years). Assistant professors who have completed five years of service in stage 2 are eligible to move to stage 3. After completing three years of service in stage 3, they will be eligible to move to stage 4 and be designated as associate professor; and after three years of service in stage 4, associate professors can move up to stage 5 and become a professor. After ten years of service in stage 5, one can become eligible for promotion to stage 6. Promotion under the CAS will be based on the performance appraisal of teachers referred to earlier. It is not possible for a teacher to jump stages under the CAS, but a candidate who is eligible for associate professorship can compete for that position under direct recruitment.

Promotions from stage 1 to 2 and from 2 to 3 are conducted by a "screening-cum-evaluation committee," and promotions from stage 3

Table 6.4. Distribution of Teachers by Position in Indian Higher Education, 2010/2011

Position	Universities and university-run colleges		Affiliated colleges	
	Number	Percentage	Number	Percentage
Professor	25,106	(18.71)	48,694	(7.13)
Associate Professor	31,26	(23.30)	137,415	(20.13)
Assistant Professor	72,085	(53.72)	476,536	(69.79)
Tutors/Demonstrators*	5,720	(4.27)	20,142	(2.95)
Total	134,179	(100)	682,787	(100)

Notes: *These positions have since been abolished

Source: Computed from Appendixes VIII and IX in UGC (2010/2011, 305 and 306)

to successive higher stages will be made by a duly constituted "selection committee." The process of promotion has to be initiated by the teacher through an application. Candidates who fail the selection process can be reassessed only after one year. The promotion will be effective from the minimum period of eligibility in the case of candidates being successful on the first attempt, and, in other cases, from the date on which a teacher is successfully reassessed. Promotion under the CAS being personal to the incumbent teacher, the substantive sanctioned post will be restored on that teacher's superannuation.

The newly introduced CAS is well-defined and more rigorous than the erstwhile Merit Promotion Scheme (MPS), which had almost been reduced to be a time-bound promotion scheme under which teachers were indiscriminately promoted to higher levels based only on the number of years of service they had put in. But India is a land of great rituals; only time will tell if the CAS will live up to its expectations or if it will also be diluted, like its predecessor MPS (Jayaram 2003). Incidentally, seldom does one come across a case of a teacher in a publicly funded higher education institution who has been dismissed from service for poor performance. Thus, the university system in India is a haven for mediocrity.

Incidentally, student feedback is not taken into consideration in the performance appraisal of teachers for the CAS (nor was it considered under the MPS). Some centrally funded deemed-to-be-universities and institutions of national importance obtain student feedback on curriculum and teaching, but such feedback is not a formal part of the performance appraisal of teachers. Private universities are new in India, so very little is known about their performance appraisal practices. However, student feedback apparently influences the renewal of teachers' contracts in those universities.

Salaries and Nonsalary Benefits

The implementation of the new pay bands by the UGC since January 2006 has made teaching an extraordinarily attractive career option for master's and doctoral degree holders on the job market. The gross monthly salary of a new entrant now consists of five components: (1) pay in the pay band, (2) academic grade pay, (3) transport allowance, (4) dearness allowance,[7] and (5) house rent allowance. The gross salary drawn by assistant professors at the bottom, middle, and top of the pay band is shown in Table 6.5. Being in higher ranges of income, all assistant professors now pay graduated income tax (10 percent or 20 percent) depending on the range in which their gross income falls after availing themselves of tax concessions and incentives for saving. In publicly funded institutions, payment of income tax can hardly be evaded, as it is the employer's responsibility to deduct income tax from the employees' salaries.

In publicly funded institutions, irrespective of the academic field, all assistant professors are paid similarly. However, in private institutions, teacher salaries vary depending on the demand and supply of teachers in particular disciplines. Assistant professors in the institutions of national

Table 6.5. Salaries of Assistant Professors as of 1 September 2012

Salary Details	Bottom of Pay Band	Middle of Pay Band	Top of Pay Band
Pay	15,600	27,350	39,100
Grade Pay	6,000	7,000	8,000
Transport Allowance	3,200	3,200	3,200
Dearness Allowance	14,040	22,328	30,615
House Rent Allowance	6,480	10,005	11,910
Gross Salary	45,320	69,883	92,825

Note: All figures in Indian Rupees; approximately, $1 = Rs 55.

Source: Adapted from UGC (2010)

importance (like the IITs and IIMs) are paid marginally better salaries. Even among publicly funded institutions, those in centrally funded institutions get relatively higher gross salaries than those in state-funded institutions, as in many states transport allowance is not paid and the house rent allowance is fixed as per state government rates, which are invariably lower than the central government rates.

Over the decades, the gap in salaries at the entry level between academic and other professions has narrowed considerably. Nevertheless, those entering in the management, ICT (information and communication technology) and biotechnology sectors earn considerably more than teachers. However, in India, as regards teachers' salary, the general comparison is with that of bureaucrats, and the salaries of these two are now more or less comparable, though the bureaucrats get better perquisites.

It must be noted that the minimum gross salary of assistant professors varies marginally between centrally funded institutions and state-funded institutions, and between universities in general and the institutions of national importance. In fact, the UGC has fixed the remuneration even for part-time teachers and guest faculty. To ensure transparency and avoid cheating by grant-in-aid private institutions, the salary of teachers is credited to their bank accounts. In contrast, there is no minimum pay in purely private universities and colleges. Seldom are their salary scales and allowances advertised. Most of them are evasive on pay matters; many of them pay their teachers in cash.

In all publicly funded institutions, all teachers, including assistant professors, are entitled to get an annual increase of 3 percent in their basic pay (that is, pay in the pay band plus academic grade pay). Stoppage or deferment of increments is viewed as a punishment and it must be justified through appropriate disciplinary procedures. Apart from this, teachers get a bigger hike in salary if they are promoted under the CAS. There is, however, no negotiation on salary size or service conditions. In purely private institutions, negotiation is possible; most often such negotiations are to the advantage of the management.

Overall, those entering the academic profession in publicly funded universities and colleges now lead a comfortable middle-class lifestyle based on the salaries they are paid. Housing and conveyance are additional components of the salary. Inflation in the economy, that is, the rise in cost of living, is also addressed through biannual revision of the "dearness allowance," as noted earlier. And, there is no difference in pay scales among academics in different faculties: those teaching English or mathematics get paid the same as their counterparts teaching Urdu or history. Because the pay scales are now uniform across the country, though with minor interstate differences, the quality of life of academics living in small towns has also improved. For teachers in purely private universities and colleges, the story is different; market conditions rule here, and there are large salary differentials across the disciplines and depending on the qualifications of the teachers. In some private institutions, the salaries are exploitative. In all institutions, the part-time teachers are invariably worse off.

For those seeking entry into the professoriate, security of service and statutorily guaranteed salary are the key attractions. Location of the university/college, reputation of the institution, availability of facilities for research, and so on, could also be influential for the few who have a choice. The nonsalary benefits that teachers receive are all based on government provisions, and they have no bearing on the choice of teaching as a career or of a particular institution.

Those appointed to permanent teaching positions in publicly funded institutions after January 2004 have to contribute 10 percent of their basic pay to the pension fund, and the government makes a matching contribution. They are eligible for a variety of paid leave benefits, but none of them can be availed as a matter of right. Every academic year, teachers can take eight days of *casual leave* (to meet exigencies) and this leave cannot be accumulated. They can get one day of *earned/privilege leave* for 11 days of work and this leave can be accumulated to a maximum of 300 days. This leave can be exchanged for additional pay at the time of superannuation. The most attractive part of the academic profession is the fully paid *vacation leave* for eight weeks in a year.

Female teachers get a maximum of one year of fully paid *maternity leave* during their career and their spouses get a maximum of fifteen days of fully paid *paternity leave* for each child born (and for not more than two children). Besides maternity leave, female teachers are entitled to two years of fully paid *childcare leave* provided they have exhausted all other leaves to their credit. This leave can be availed anytime until the child attains 18 years of age; it can be split between two children.

Teachers are also eligible for the benefit of "leave travel concession" (return fare for self and dependents) once in two years by using their vacation or applying for leave to go on a holiday in India. In lieu of this, teachers hailing from outside their place of work can avail "home travel concession" to visit their "hometown" (as declared at the time of joining the service). The amount paid by the university or college toward such travel is taxable.

Teachers are eligible for medical leave and medical assistance both for themselves and for their dependents. They are entitled to the use of central or state government health service facilities. In lieu of this, some institutions have extended medical insurance coverage to teachers or they reimburse medical expenses up to a particular amount. To check misuse of this facility (by the hospitals, insurance companies, and teachers alike), there are elaborate norms governing medical assistance.

As part of their salary, teachers are given a percentage of their basic pay (pay in the pay band, the grade pay, and transport allowance) as house rent allowance depending on the location of the university/college. According to the government of India's classification, those in Category A cities (e.g., Bangalore, Chennai, Delhi, Hyderabad, Mumbai, and Kolkata) get 30 percent; those in Category B cities (e.g., Ahmedabad, Chandigarh, Jaipur, Lucknow, and Patna), 20 percent; and those in others, 10 percent. In case the university provides housing (no college does that), teachers will not get the house rent allowance; they will have to pay a small sum as "license fees" and maintenance charges, and the electricity and water charges are payable based on consumption.

Housing provided by the university is in great demand, as it provides residential security and obviates commuting to work. However, some teachers prefer to stay away from campus, especially if they can get cheaper accommodation, as they would save some money from their house rent allowance. Furthermore, with income tax rebates given to those who build houses or buy apartments, it is doubly advantageous to live off-campus. This choice is exercised particularly by those teachers who decide to settle down in the city in which they work. Besides house rent allowance, there are special categories of allowances like tribal area allowance, hardship area allowance, and island special pay, but this is applicable to very few institutions. Before the liberalization of lending by banks, until the mid-1990s, universities that had surplus funds advanced loans at concessional rates to teachers for buying or building houses and buying cars.

As an incentive for promoting the small family norm, male teachers undergoing vasectomy or female teachers undergoing hysterectomy are given one increment in pay on production of certificate from a medical authority. Such teachers must have one surviving child and not more than two children. To be eligible for this incentive, the male teacher must not be over 50 years of age and his wife must be between 20 and 45 years of age. Similarly, the female teacher must not be over 45 years of age and her husband must not be over 50 years of age.

The foregoing nonsalary and service benefits are statutory entitlements in publicly funded institutions. That is why, once in a permanent job, generally no teacher would voluntarily retire. These benefits are, however, a matter of contractual agreement in purely private educational institutions; in very rare cases they will offer more attractive packages than publicly funded educational institutions.

There are few opportunities for supplementary employment for new entrants into the academic profession. Those occupying a permanent position in a publicly funded university or college are prohibited from taking up supplementary employment. However, with the permission of the institution, they can undertake teaching assignments in another university/college as a visiting/guest faculty for a brief period (by availing themselves of up to thirty days of "duty leave" to which they are entitled in a year). The remuneration received for this work is called an *honorarium* (not salary) and is liable to be taxed. Generally, teachers collect the honorarium in cash and do not disclose this in tax returns. The restriction on working in more than one institution does not apply to part-time teachers. In purely private institutions, the relative provision may be part of the contract. Incidentally, young faculty doing consultancy or moonlighting is very rare. But some of them (mostly college teachers and rarely university teachers) earn additional income by giving private tuition or writing guidebooks (in question-answer format) for students preparing for university examinations.

Conclusion

Overall, the academic profession in India today is an attractive option for those graduating from universities. Many of those completing their master's degree, who would not have thought of teaching as a career a decade or so ago, are now appearing for the UGC-NET with the intention of gaining employment in a college or university. This also explains the steady increase in the enrollment of candidates in doctoral programs. This generalization, however, needs to be qualified, as the system of higher education in the country is diverse.

The institutions of national importance (like the IITs and the IIMs) pay higher gross salaries and offer better service conditions. Closely following them are the well-established central universities and centrally funded university-level institutes, which come under the umbrella of the UGC. But the vast majority of teaching positions are in the state universities and grant-in-aid colleges affiliated to them. For teachers working in these universities and colleges, the salary and allied benefits could not be better.

As regards the purely private universities and colleges, the vagaries of the market for higher education will continue to mediate their recruitment practices and remuneration packages. But, if the private universities hope to carve out a niche for themselves in higher education, they will have to improve on what is already on offer in centrally funded institutions. Only then will they be able to attract the best teaching and research talent. This is what some private institutions backed by leading industrial houses and committed academic administrators aim to achieve. But it will take some time before their efforts will bear fruit.

Paradoxically, however, at a time when the university system is undergoing rapid expansion and when the salary and working conditions of the professoriate have improved remarkably, the system is facing an acute shortage of faculty. With the imminent entry of foreign educational establishments into the country, the competition for well qualified and experienced faculty is sure to increase. Only institutions offering the best remuneration and service conditions can expect to attract the best teaching talent. Viewed in this light, the prospects for state universities and grant-in-aid colleges, which constitute the largest segment of higher education system in the country, do not appear to be bright.

For the MHRD, the faculty shortage is a serious challenge. It wants to triple enrollment in higher education from around 13 million to 40 million to reach the ambitious target of a 30 percent gross enrollment ratio by 2020. This it wants to achieve by expanding the university system even if it means throwing caution to the wind. But the Planning Commission, which appears to understand the problem better, wants the MHRD to consolidate the expansion that has already taken place before expanding further. In this context, many options have come up for addressing the faculty shortage.

The MHRD has now permitted the centrally funded institutions to reemploy superannuated teachers for one year at a time for up to five years. Such reemployment is subject to evaluation of the teacher and the teaching requirements of the institution. Reemployment is entirely at the discretion of the institution and it cannot be claimed as a matter of right by the superannuating teacher. Reemployed teachers continue to get all the benefits that they got before superannuating. In some universities, the retired teachers are invited as visiting faculty.

Some vice chancellors and educational managers feel that the retirement age should be uniformly raised to 65 years, as the faculty shortage will soon become acute with retirements at 60 to 62 years of age already occurring in some state universities and colleges. Others argue that this is only a makeshift arrangement and it will affect the prospect of young people wanting to enter the teaching profession (Anand 2011). The available vacancies are high, so the argument against raising the age of retirement does not seem to hold water. But, it must be conceded that raising the retirement age by itself will not serve the purpose, as the faculty should also be competent to hold their positions.

Making the academic profession an attractive option for those moving successfully through the university system is no more a problem; but filling staff vacancies with competent young faculty is. This calls for fresh thinking and quick action, or else the faculty shortage may become the Achilles' heel of higher education in India, and the dream of making the country's higher education system "world class" will remain just that.

Notes

1. Although the Indian Institutes of Management (IIMs) (13 in all) have established a niche for themselves in graduate business education, and assist industry through research and consultancy, they are not granted the status of "institutions of national importance." The IIMs are not authorized to award degrees as universities do, although they do award diplomas and fellowships that are considered equal to degrees and doctorates awarded by the universities. a recommendation for enacting legislation to allow the IIMs to award degrees without any erosion of their existing autonomy, made by a committee headed by Professor Madhava N. Menon (Seshagiri 2011), is under the active consideration of the MHRD (Mukul 2012, 6).

2. In 2010/2011, those enrolled in first degree courses constituted 86.11 percent of all enrollments; the rest were enrolled in postgraduate (12.07 percent), doctoral (0.81 percent), and diploma/certificate (1.01 percent) courses (UGC 2010/2011, 301). In terms of fields and disciplines, arts (36.39 percent), science (18.42 percent), and commerce/management (17.11 percent) accounted for 71.92 percent of all enrollments; the rest were enrolled in engineering/technology (16.86 percent), medicine (3.85 percent), education (3.36 percent), and other (4.01 percent) courses (UGC 2012).

3. Reliable data on part-time teachers are hard to come by. As early as 1983, the National Commission on Teachers (NCT 1985) had found that only 70.7 percent of the university teachers and 68.5 percent of the college teachers had permanent employment with all statutory benefits. Since then the percentage of part-time teachers has evidently increased considerably.

4. In institutions of national importance, such as the Indian Institute of Science (IISc, Bangalore) and the IITs, a fourth level, namely, "assistant professor (to be recruited on contractual basis)" was introduced in September 2009. This position is not part of the regular faculty cadres in these institutes and appointment to this position is made on a contractual basis to enable bright young doctorate degree holders to teach and gain experience in premier institutions. It is stipulated that at least 10 percent of the total faculty strength should be recruited at this level.

5. In academic fields such as engineering and technology, medicine and pharmacy, management/business administration, occupational therapy and physiotherapy, physical education, music and performing arts, special qualifications are prescribed for different levels of teaching staff (UGC 2010, 4–36).

6. This odd percentage is explained by the fact that the Supreme Court of India has ruled that reservation shall not exceed 50 percent of the total posts. In states like Karnataka and Tamil Nadu, populist politics has pushed reservations beyond this limit, and the matter is now before the Supreme Court.

7. The "dearness [high cost, in British English] allowance" is intended to compensate for inflation, and it is revised twice a year (on the first of January and July respectively) based on the price index (100 points as of January 1, 2006). As of July 1, 2012, it was 65 percent of pay (that is, pay in the pay band plus academic grade pay plus transport allowance).

References

Agarwal, Pawan. 2009. *Indian Higher Education: Envisioning the Future.* New Delhi: Sage.

Altbach, Philip. G., and N. Jayaram. 2009. "India's Effort to Join 21st-Century Higher Education." *International Higher Education* (The Boston College Center for International Higher Education) 54 (Winter): 17–19.

Altbach, Philip. G., and N. Jayaram. 2010. "Can India Garner the Demographic Dividend?" *The Hindu* (Delhi), December 1: 12.

Anand, A. 2010. "UGC Announces Net Exemption Cut-Off Date for Mphil Holders." *Indian Education Review,* November 9, http://www.indiaeducation-review.com/features/impact-ugc-regulation-exempting-net-mphil-holders.

Anand, A. 2011. "Increasing Retirement Age: A Long Term Solution or Just a Make Shift Arrangement." *Indian Education Review*, March 1, http://www.indiaeducationreview.com/features/increasing-retirement-age-long-term-solution-or-just-make-shift-arrangement.

Anand, A. 2012. "Why Are the 8 New IITs in India Facing Faculty Crunch?" *Indian Education Review,* May 18, http://www.indiaeducationreview.com/features/faculty-shortage-8-new-iits-directors'-viewpoint.

Daily Pioneer. 2012. "4,000 UGC Approved Teaching Posts Lying Vacant in DU" (July 24), http://www.indiaeducationreview.com/news/4000-ugc-approved-teaching-posts-lying-vacant-du.

Economic Times. 2012. "No New Universities in 12th Plan, Says Planning Commission" (July 31), http://www.indiaeducationreview.com/news/no-new-universities-12th-plan-says-planning-commission.

Government of India (GoI). 1986. *Programme of Action: National Policy on Education.* New Delhi: Ministry of Human Resource Development.

The Hindu. 2012. "Half of SC/ST Teaching Posts in Central Universities Unfilled" (July 4), http://www.indiaeducationreview.com/news/half-scst-teaching-posts-central-universities-unfilled.

India Education Review. 2012. "On Shortage of Faculty at Universities" (Comments). http://www.indiaeducationreview.com/vc-desk/shortage-faculty-universities-0.

Jayaram, N. 2003. "The Fall of the Guru: The Decline of the Academic Profession in India." In *The Decline of the Guru: The Academic Profession in Developing and Middle-Income Countries*, edited by P.G. Altbach, 199–230. New York: Palgrave Macmillan.

Jayaram, N. 2007. "Beyond Retailing Knowledge: Prospect of Research-Oriented Universities in India." In *World Class Worldwide: Transforming Research Universities in Asia and Latin America*, edited by P.G. Altbach and J. Balán, 70–94. Baltimore: Johns Hopkins University Press.

Jayaram, N. 2008. "India." In *Toward a Global PhD?: Force and Forms in Doctoral Education Worldwide*, edited by M. Nerad and M. Heggelund, 221–245. Seattle: Center for Innovation and Research in Graduate Education, University of Washington and University of Washington Press.

Jayaram, N. 2009. "Higher Education in India: The Challenge of Change." In *Structuring Mass Higher Education: The Role of Elite Institutions*, edited by D. Palfreyman and T. Tapper, 95–112. New York and London: Routledge.

Jayaram, N. 2011. "Toward World-Class Status? The IIT System and IIT Bombay." In *The Road to Academic Excellence*, edited by P.G. Altbach and J. Salmi, 167–193. Washington, DC: World Bank.

Mukul, A. 2012. "IIMs May Get Legislative Cover, Award Degrees." *Times of India* (New Delhi/Chandigarh), September 5: 6.

National Commission on Teachers (NCT). 1985. *Report of the National Commission on Teachers, II, 1983–85.* New Delhi: Controller of Publications, Government of India.

National Knowledge Commission (NKC). 2007. *Report to the Nation—2006.* New Delhi: National Knowledge Commission, Government of India.

Seshagiri, Mathang. 2011. "It's Time IIMs Give Degree, Not Diploma: Panel." *Sunday Times of India* (Bangalore), May 1, http://articles.timesofindia.indiatimes.com/2011-05-01/india/29492823_1_iim-directors-iim-b-indian-institutes.

Tilak, J.B.G. 2004. "Absence of Policy and Perspective in Higher Education." *Economic and Political Weekly*, 39: 2159–2164.

The Times of India. 2012. "Induction Training Must of College Teachers: NAAC" (August 29), http://www.indiaeducationreview.com/news/induction-training-must-college teachers-naac.

Times News Network. 2011a. "Core Engineering Jobs Rule IIT–B Placements This Year." *Times of India* (Mumbai), July 29: 4.

Times News Network. 2011b. "Higher Edu Short of 54% Teachers." *Times of India* (Mumbai), August 10: 15.

University Grants Commission (UGC). 2010. *UGC Regulations on Minimum Qualifications for Appointment of Teachers and Other Academic Staff in Universities and Colleges and Measures for the Maintenance of Standards in Higher Education*. New Delhi: UGC.

University Grants Commission (UGC). 2010–11. *Annual Report, 2010–2011*. New Delhi: UGC.

University Grants Commission (UGC). 2011. *Inclusive and Qualitative Expansion of Higher Education: Compilation Based on the Deliberations of the Working Group for Higher Education In the 12th Five-Year Plan (2012–17)*. New Delhi: UGC.

University Grants Commission (UGC). 2012a. *Higher Education in India at a Glance*. New Delhi: UGC, available on www.ugc.ac.in.

University Grants Commission (UGC). 2012b. *Notification for NET (National Eligibility Test)*. New Delhi: National Educational Testing Bureau, UGC, www.ugcnetonline.in/notification.php.

Chapter 7

The Academic Career System in Norway

Svein Kyvik

Introduction

Entrance to the academic profession can be regarded from different angles: from the perspective of state authorities responsible for the development of the national system of higher education and research; from the perspective of the higher education institutions that train and employ academics; and, from the perspective of the young researcher recruits who aim for a career in academia. From the perspective of the state, the main issues are related to the scale, quality, relevance, and efficiency of doctoral and postdoctoral training. From the point of view of the institutions, it is important to have a pool of highly qualified young academics from which to pick the best applicants for an academic position. And for PhD candidates and postdocs aiming for an academic career, it is important to be able to plan a predictable future as a permanent member of the academic profession, and to create stable conditions for themselves and their families. To understand the various issues related to the entrance to the academic profession, it is useful to keep these three perspectives in mind, as well as recognizing that the interests of the state, the institutions, and young academics do not always coincide.

The problematic issues are first of all related to the scale of the research training system and the career prospects for young academics. How many PhD candidates and postdocs should be trained beyond the needs of the higher education institutions? On the one hand, PhD candidates play an important role in research production. It is estimated that, in Norwegian research universities, PhD candidates undertake 60 percent more person-years of research work than academic staff in permanent positions (Thune et al. 2012). On the other hand, no more than 40 percent of the PhD candidates can expect to have a lifetime career in academia. Is there really sufficient need and demand for people with research skills in industry and the public sector, or does the state overeducate people and waste money on research training? A more recent issue involves the large influx of non-Norwegian citizens into doctoral and postdoctoral training. Although it is in the interest of the state and the institutions to attract a large number of well-qualified young academics from abroad, questions have been asked as to whether Norway educates too many foreign PhD candidates and postdocs, many of whom will leave the country for an academic career abroad.

What should the career structure in universities and colleges look like, and at what stage and age should young academics achieve a permanent position? For young academics undergoing research training or in a postdoctoral qualification phase, career prospects and their wish for permanent employment are the main issues. In these respects, Norway does not seem to differ from other countries (McAlpine and Åkerlind 2010). However, because the average age of Norwegian PhD candidates and postdocs is relatively high, and because it is common to take up temporary assignments or positions after finishing the PhD and postdoc periods, most academics are relatively old when they get a permanent post.

For those who manage to obtain a permanent academic position, the main issues are related to working conditions. The scholarly literature on higher education reports a relative decrease in the status and salaries of academic staff (Welch 2005; Altbach et al. 2012), and increasing differentiation of academic career paths, which affects working conditions and status relations in the academic profession (Gappa, Austin, and Trice 2007; Enders and Musselin 2008). These accounts are largely, but not entirely, applicable to the Norwegian academic profession.

On the one hand, an academic career is still attractive for many young people. Interest in positions as a PhD fellow or postdoc is generally high, despite the fact that it will not guarantee permanent employment as an academic staff member. Traditionally, being a full professor has been a high status position. According to a 1985 opinion poll ranking Norwegian occupations, full professor ranked as number 6 out of 66 various occupations, surpassed only by prime minister, supreme court president, president of parliament, ambassador, and head surgeon; it was placed ahead of member of parliament, bishop and bank manager (Økonomisk rapport 1985). There is, however, reason to believe that the status of professors in society has declined since that time, partly due to various reforms that have led to a considerably larger number of full professors. Despite this, the drive to become a full professor is strong among junior staff, because opportunities to achieve this status are now possible through promotion, and not only based on the successful outcome of competition for vacant professorships. In addition, achievements in research now have a stronger effect on individual salaries due to a reform of the pay structure (Kyvik 2012a). This career system was introduced in the mid-1990s, resulting in high numbers of full professors in the universities. On the other hand, professors have experienced a relative decrease in their status and salaries, and there seems to be a common perception among academic staff that working conditions have deteriorated (Kyvik 2012b).

Furthermore, the international trend towards greater "diversification of career paths and the restructuring of contractual arrangements" (Enders and Musselin 2008) does not fit very well with developments in Norway. Although different career tracks have been formalized and further developed, homogenization tendencies are in many ways stronger than differentiation efforts. The academic profession has become more homogeneous over time both with regard to career structure and general working conditions, but individual salary differences have increased, due to a stronger emphasis on market value and research performance (Kyvik 2012b). From a comparative perspective, the Norwegian academic profession is characterized by minor differences in work duties between ranks. The egalitarian aspects of the Norwegian higher education system have clearly counteracted state initiatives to differentiate working conditions and rewards between groups of academic staff.

In the following section, this chapter provides a brief introduction to the Norwegian higher education system, followed by an overview of the academic career structure. Thereafter, the chapter provides data on the labor market for young academics, before giving an account of the appointment system and entry-level contracts for academic staff. Finally, the chapter discusses some of the main challenges from the perspectives of young academics, the higher education institutions, and the state authorities.

The Higher Education System

Norway has a binary higher education system, divided into a university and a college sector. The latter predominantly provides professional programs at a bachelor's level in teacher training, nursing, engineering, social work, business administration, and so on, but also offers some master's programs and a few doctoral programs. However, this system has come under pressure from colleges with university ambitions, and in recent years it has been discussed whether the binary divide should be abolished (Kyvik 2009a). In 2004, the government decided that colleges that fulfill certain minimum standards could apply for accreditation to receive university status, and three colleges have now attained this status.

As of 2012, Norwegian higher education is provided by eight state universities (with 91,500 students), four of which are traditional research universities; nine specialized university institutions (with 7,500 students), three of which are private institutions; 21 state university colleges (with 75,000 students); and about 20 small private colleges (with 10,000 students). There is a fairly high level of student mobility across the two sectors, due to the establishment of a flexible transition system, which is rather unique in an international context.

Since the mid-1990s, Norway has had a common career structure across universities and colleges, implying that professors in the two sectors have the same salaries, enabling mobility of staff between colleges and universities and vice versa. Moreover, since 2003 public and private higher education institutions have been regulated by a joint act, which provides a common framework for the organization and governance of these institutions.

In 2011, the public universities and colleges had close to 20,000 academic staff in full-time positions, of which 7,000 were on short-term contracts (four years or less) primarily involving PhD candidates with a fellowship and postdocs. Private institutions had fewer than 1,000 staff members in full-time positions.

In most higher education systems, there is now a sense of competition to attract talented academics from abroad. In Norway, it is a political goal to increase the number of well-qualified foreign PhD students, postdocs, and academic staff in order to enhance the quality of academic research, and to establish networks with foreign research environments. In 2010, a new immigration act and new immigration regulations came into force, making it simpler for foreign researchers from outside the European Union to stay in Norway. Researchers are entitled to a residence permit as a skilled worker or as a specialist. However, there are still many barriers related to inbound mobility; getting a residence permit is still a time-consuming process for applicants from a country with a visa requirement for Norway, especially if they want to bring their family (DAMVAD 2012).

Nevertheless, since the millennium the academic profession in Norway has become increasingly internationalized, partly because there is a general lack of Norwegian applicants in some subjects, and partly because foreign applicants are better qualified. This trend applies in particular to postdocs, but also to PhD candidates and permanent academic staff members. In 2009, approximately 25 percent of the total number of PhD candidates, postdocs, and permanent academic staff were immigrants, among which 5.5 percent were from other Nordic countries, 10.5 percent were from other European countries, 4.8 percent were from Asia, and 2.2 percent were from North America (Børing and Gunnes 2012).

The Academic Career Structure

Norwegian higher education institutions have a common academic career structure including two different career tracks: a research-oriented and a teaching-oriented track, and a range of permanent and temporary positions. The latter includes positions as a PhD candidate, postdoc, and research assistant, although very few are now engaged as assistants. Over the last two decades, most of the research assistant positions (two- to four-year fixed-term contracts) have been transformed into fellowships for PhD candidates. Thus, in order to fully understand the academic career structure in Norway, it is necessary to include postdocs as well as PhD candidates with a contract from a higher education institution.

PhD Candidates

It is important to note that (contrary to most other countries) PhD candidates in Norway holding a fellowship are temporarily employed as academic staff. They have a regular salary (see Table 7.5), competitive with the entry-level salary for master's degree holders in the public sector; they are entitled to the same benefits as permanent academic staff, including the right to salary during sickness, maternity/paternity leave, and pension rights; and, they are provided with office space.

In 2011, twenty-three higher education institutions were authorized to offer PhD programs: eight universities, nine specialized university institutions (six state institutions and three private), and six university colleges. Although the universities have a general authorization to provide PhD training, the university colleges have to apply for accreditation of specific programs.

Doctoral studies are funded in various ways, the most important of which is PhD fellowships. The Ministry of Education and Research funds about 40 percent of all PhD candidates through its annual budget allocations to the individual institutions, and the Research Council of Norway funds another 20 percent through competitive contracts. In addition, the health trusts, medical funds, and research institutes are important funding sources.

PhD fellowship holders are appointed to temporary posts in universities and other research institutions for three years, or four years including a 25 percent teaching obligation alongside their studies. In addition to writing a thesis, PhD candidates have a taught-course element, normally requiring half a year of work, although these requirements vary between disciplines and institutions.

Approximately two-thirds of PhD candidates hold a PhD fellowship position. The remaining candidates are enrolled in doctoral programs on a part-time basis, and work in research institutes, university colleges, hospitals or private enterprises. Their PhD studies are likely to be funded by their employers, or more commonly by conducting contract research. Thus, many Norwegian PhD candidates spend their research training period mainly outside of the universities, partly doing ordinary work and partly working on their theses.

In 2011, there were about 9,000 PhD candidates in Norway; twice as many as in 2003 (Table 7.1). This strong growth has, however, not been equally distributed across fields of learning. The increase in the number of PhD candidates has been particularly strong in medicine and the health sciences, while a more modest growth has taken place in the humanities. Women currently account for about 50 percent of doctoral candidates; varying between 60 percent in the social sciences, medicine and health sciences, 50 percent in the humanities, 45 percent in the natural sciences, and 25 percent in technology.

From an international perspective, Norway is attractive for PhD candidates, because they are appointed to temporary posts and receive salaries commensurate with a first appointment in the public sector for candidates holding a master's degree. Due to these circumstances, in 2007, 23 percent of PhD candidates were non-Norwegian citizens, varying between 13 percent in the humanities and 41 percent in technology (Olsen and Sarpebakken 2011). Of the non-Norwegian PhD candidates who graduated in the years 2008 to 2010, 13 percent came from the other Nordic countries, 39 percent from the rest of Europe, 25 percent from Asia, 15 percent from Africa, 4 percent from North America, and 3 percent from Latin America (Olsen and Sarpebakken 2011).

Table 7.1. Norwegian doctoral candidates 2003–2011, by field

	Years				
Field	2003	2005	2007	2009	2011
Humanities	657	726	751	826	950
Social sciences	934	1330	1652	1877	1963
Natural sciences	1213	1572	1785	2203	2300
Technology	896	1093	1234	1417	1444
Medicine and health sciences	776	1313	1669	2054	2384
Total	4476	6034	7091	8377	9041

Source: Database for Statistics on Higher Education (DBH).

In 2011, about 1,300 PhD candidates were awarded a PhD. A steadily increasing share of PhD candidates holding a fellowship completes their degree (close to 80 percent). However, completion rates and time-to-degree differs considerably between fields. In the 2002 to 2003 cohorts of fellowship holders, 60 percent of those in the natural sciences graduated within four years, in contrast to 30 percent in the social sciences. Within eight years, completion rates had increased to 84 percent in the natural sciences and to 67 percent in the social sciences (Kyvik and Olsen 2013). Women complete at the same rate as men, and in 2011, women accounted for nearly 50 percent of those completing a PhD.

Postdocs

The use of postdoc positions has a relatively short history in Norway (Kyvik and Smeby 2004). The introduction of organized research training in the 1980s and the subsequent increase in the number of doctoral awards led to a need for temporary postdoc positions to retain talented doctoral graduates in the universities, to further prepare them for an academic career, and to widen the recruitment base for permanent academic positions. In addition, the postdoc position has been regarded as an appropriate means to enhance the quality and internationalization of Norwegian research (through sojourns at foreign universities during the postdoctoral period), to increase the proportion of female academic staff in permanent positions, and to increase mobility between universities. The research councils introduced fellowships for postdocs in the late 1980s, while the universities were not allowed to establish such positions until 1997. Positions as a postdoc have durations of two, three, or four years.

When the period of employment is three years or more, the university can require the postdoc to perform teaching or similar tasks. At the University of Oslo, this is limited to a maximum of 10 percent of the position in terms of time. As an exception, up to 25 percent of clinical work can be assigned in cases where there is a need to maintain clinical competence in the postdoctoral post, with a view to subsequent work positions. Postdocs are better paid than PhD fellows (see Table 7.5), but have a lower salary than their counterparts in the public sector.

Over the last decade, there has been a sharp increase in the number of post-doc positions (Table 7.2), providing good opportunities for PhD graduates to further develop their research competence and to qualify for a permanent academic position. The down side of the introduction of these postdoc positions is that it has extended the period of temporary employment. Although young academics might previously have entered the academic profession on completion of their PhD, in many disciplines the completion of a successful postdoc period has now become a common requirement.

In 2011, 48 percent of the postdocs were women, varying between 61 percent in medicine and health sciences, 57 percent in the humanities, 52 percent in the social sciences, 36 percent in the natural sciences, and 30 percent in technology.

An increasing number of postdocs come from abroad; partly because salaries for postdocs in Norway are competitive on the international academic market, and partly because many of the foreign PhD candidates who graduated in Norway continue in a postdoc position at a Norwegian university. In 2007, a total of 42 percent of postdocs were non-Norwegian

Table 7.2. Post-docs in Norwegian higher education institutions 2003–2011, by field

	2003	2005	2007	2009	2011
Humanities	77	74	82	109	114
Social sciences	73	119	127	173	200
Natural sciences	222	314	397	331	336
Technology	82	109	135	185	211
Medicine and health sciences	248	288	348	377	414
Total	702	904	1089	1175	1275

Source: NIFU. Research Personnel Register.

citizens, varying between 27 percent in the social sciences and 65 percent in technology (Olsen and Sarpebakken 2011). On the one hand, this development indicates that the competition for a postdoc position has increased, but on the other hand that there is a relatively weak interest in an academic career among Norwegian master's and PhD graduates in technology and the natural sciences.

Permanent Academic Positions

As mentioned, Norwegian universities and colleges have two different career tracks; a research-oriented and a teaching-oriented track. The research-oriented permanent academic positions are *associate professor* and *professor*, while *lecturer, senior lecturer*, and *docent* are teaching-oriented positions, but with the possibility of doing research (Table 7.3). The docent position is a newly established top position for senior lecturers. The post of *assistant professor* was removed in 1995, and after this date no new appointments for assistant professors have taken place, but those that already had this title are still entitled to use it. Lecturer and senior lecturer are positions that are not widely used in the university sector. The position of *college teacher* is used in practice-related professional programs, mainly in teacher training and health education, and the holders of this position do not have a master's degree. People appointed to any of these positions will immediately get permanent employment status. In addition, the universities (and to a limited extent the university colleges) have positions for full-time *researchers*, some of which have permanent employment, while most are on fixed-term contracts.

As in most other higher education systems, the relative number of women is smaller the higher the rank. Women account for 23 percent of full professors, 39 percent of associate professors, 47 percent of senior lecturers, and 60 percent of lecturers.

The criteria for appointment and promotion to teaching and research posts are laid down by the Ministry of Education and Research. For appointment as an associate professor, the normal requirement is a Norwegian doctoral degree in the subject area concerned, or a corresponding foreign doctoral degree. However, competence at a corresponding level as documented by academic work of the same scope and quality as a doctoral degree may also be accepted. For appointments to lecturer and senior lecturer positions, a master's degree is the minimum requirement.

As shown in Table 7.3, the percentage of permanent academic staff in the universities and specialized university institutions in full professor positions is very high (40 percent). This is due to a reform of the academic career system two decades ago. Since 1993, associate professors in both universities and colleges have been able to apply for promotion to full professor on the basis of their research competence (Olsen, Kyvik, and Hovdhaugen 2005). This reform made it possible to become a full professor in three different ways: (1) by applying for a vacant professorship in open competition and being appointed as the best qualified applicant, (2) by applying for a vacant professorship in open competition, being found competent but not the best qualified by the evaluation committee and then being promoted to full professor at his or her department, and (3), by applying for promotion to full professor on the basis of their research competence and being found competent by a unanimous peer review committee. The latter strategy has now become the most common way of becoming a full professor, while substantially fewer people are appointed to an ordinary professorship, due to there being relatively few vacant positions.

The Age Distribution of Academic Staff

The extended research training period leads to a relatively high average age among PhD graduates holding a fellowship. In 2011, the average age of these graduates was 36.4 years, while the median age was 34.0 years. The median age of PhD graduates varied between 31.2 years in the natural sciences and 37.0 years in the social sciences.

The average age of PhD graduates has not declined over the last decade, and the relatively high age of new PhD holders is regarded as a problem. A recent evaluation of Norwegian research training states that the time available for developing an academic career is inevitably shortened, as such careers usually consist of further training during the postdoc period. A high age at completion might also be regarded as a disadvantage for a career in the private sector (Thune et al. 2012).

Table 7.4 provides an overview of the age distribution of academic staff including PhD fellows and postdocs. Because PhD candidates have a temporary post and a salary, many middle-aged people are attracted to these fellowships. In 2011, one-third of the PhD fellows were above 35 years of age. In turn, the age structure of PhD fellows affects the age of postdocs, of which nearly 50 percent were between 35 and 44 years of age. The average age of postdocs was 36.4 years. The bulk of permanently

Table 7.3. Academic staff in permanent positions in Norwegian public universities (including specialized university institutions) and university colleges in 2011, by rank.

	Universities		University colleges		Total	
Rank	Number	Percent	Number	Percent	Number	Percent
Professor	2,938	40	354	7	3,292	27
Associate professor	2,201	30	979	21	3,180	26
Assistant professor	151	2	46	1	197	2
Docent	31	—	54	1	85	1
Senior lecturer	304	4	533	11	837	7
Lecturer	1,295	18	2,285	48	3,580	30
Other permanent staff	324	4	148	4	472	4
College teacher	111	2	332	7	443	4
Total	7,355	100	4,731	100	12,086	100

Source: NIFU. Research Personnel Register.

Table 7.4. The age distribution (by percentage) of academic staff in Norwegian public universities (including specialized university institutions) and university colleges in 2011, by rank

Age	PhD fellow	Post-doc	Lecturer	Senior lecturer	Associate professor	Professor
–35	67	43	8	1	4	—
35–44	25	48	23	7	29	9
45–54	7	7	29	23	31	30
55–64	1	2	34	55	27	41
65 +	—	—	6	14	9	20
Total	100	100	100	100	100	100
N	5,925	1,224	3,580	837	3,180	3,292

Source: NIFU. Research Personnel Register.

employed academic staff are also relatively old; in 2011, 36 percent of associate professors, 40 percent of lecturers, 61 percent of full professors, and 69 percent of the senior lecturers were more than 55 years of age. The required retirement age is 70 years of age.

The Labor Market for Young Academics

From an international perspective, the labor market for young academics in Norway must be characterized as good, in spite of frequent complaints by PhD graduates and postdocs about too few vacant positions in the higher education sector. The large majority find relevant employment before or on completion of their training periods (Kyvik and Olsen 2012). Furthermore, the international Changing Academic Profession survey undertaken in 2008 revealed that 55 percent of the permanent academic staff in the universities disagreed with the proposition that "this is a poor time for any young person to begin an academic career in my field," while 25 percent agreed. In this respect, Norwegian academics were more optimistic than their counterparts in most of the other countries included in this study (Bentley et al. 2010).

An academic career seems to be most attractive in those subjects where a position in the public sector would be an alternative. In these subjects, the number of applicants for PhD fellowships is much larger than those appointed. Exceptions are the field of technology, some subjects in the natural sciences, and professional subjects such as medicine, economics, and law, where job alternatives in the private sector offer notably higher remuneration. In these disciplines it is therefore a problem that some of the most talented graduates are not interested in a university career.

The Labor Market for PhD Graduates

Slightly more than 40 percent of doctorate recipients from the period 1970 to 2008 work in a higher education institution. Another 20 percent have a research career outside universities and colleges—in research institutes, hospitals, industry and so on—while slightly less than 40 percent have found other employment (see Figure 7.1). This means that the traditional purpose of research training—to qualify for an academic career—applies to only four in ten doctoral candidates. Compared to the employment situation for doctoral degree holders a decade ago (and

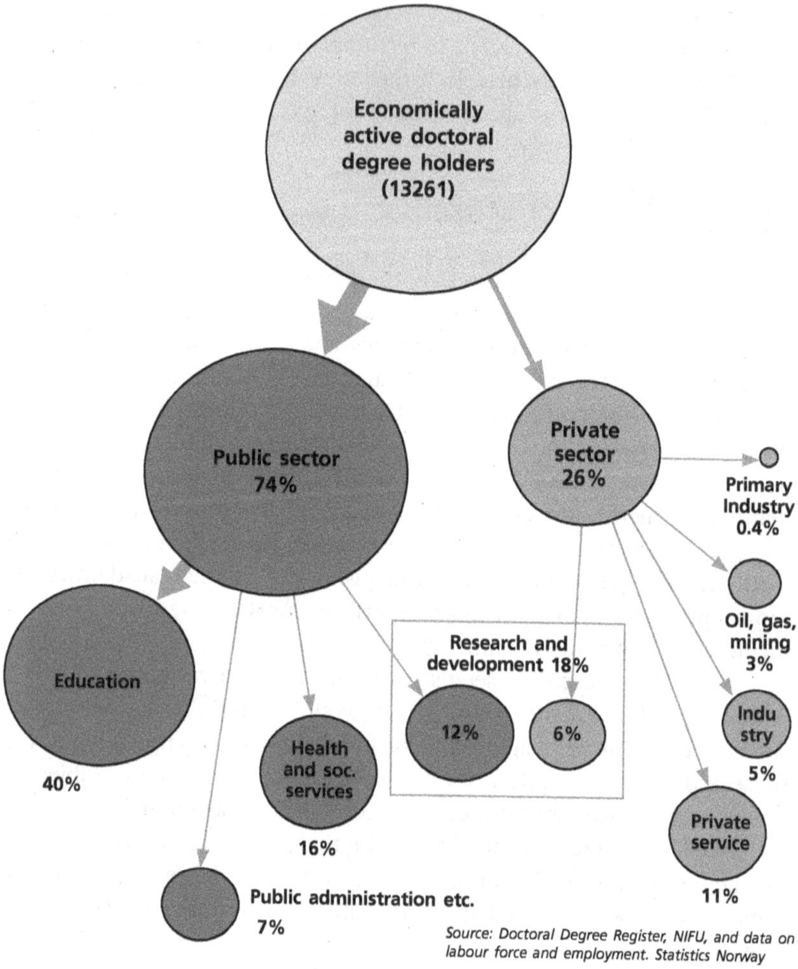

Figure 7.1. Sectors of employment for PhD holders in Norway in 2009.

before the implementation of the PhD degree in 2003), there have only been very moderate changes in sectors of employment for doctoral degree holders, although the number of doctoral degree holders has increased significantly in each sector (Thune et al. 2012). This "surplus" of PhD candidates in relation to the number of available posts in higher education is the result of a planned policy to increase the number of doctoral candidates in industry, public administration, hospitals, nongovernmental agencies, and so on.

A survey undertaken in 2007 among all PhD recipients in Norway in 2002 and 2005 provides some relevant information about career plans and employment (Kyvik and Olsen 2007). The doctorate holders were asked about their initial career plans on commencement of their doctoral training period. In total, 43 percent answered that they planned an academic career in a higher education institution, 21 percent planned another research career, 15 percent planned a career outside the research system, while 21 percent had no clear vision of what they wanted to do. There were, however, large differences between fields. In the humanities, about 75 percent hoped for an academic career, in contrast to 55 percent in the social sciences, 45 percent in medicine, about 35 percent in the natural sciences, and only 20 percent in technology.

In 2007, 43 percent of this group of PhD holders were still employed in a higher education institution (of which nearly half were postdocs), 25 percent worked in research institutes or industrial laboratories, and 31 percent had other employment. Again, large differences between fields are apparent. In the humanities and social sciences, about 60 percent had employment in higher education institutions; in the natural, medical and health sciences this share was approximately 40 percent, and in technology about 25 percent.

The job market for PhD holders seems to be good. In all fields, 90 percent responded that they had obtained a relevant job (including postdoc positions) within six months after graduation. In fact, two-thirds already held a relevant job, and more than 40 percent had permanent employment. Of those who were still in a higher education institution, one-third reported that they had obtained a permanent job before graduation, varying between more than 50 percent in the social sciences and less than 20 percent in the natural sciences. The major explanation for this difference is that postdoc positions are much more common in the latter field than in the social sciences.

Finally, the survey indicates that there is a relatively good match between career plans and employment. Of those who planned an academic career, more than 60 percent were employed in a university or a university college, either in a permanent or temporary (postdoc) position, while about 25 percent had found a nonresearcher job. Of those who initially wanted to continue as, or become a researcher outside academia, more than 50 percent had fulfilled their plans, and of those who planned a career other than research, 60 percent had found such employment. Still, a large share of the PhDs seems to end up in a different job than planned. This picture applies more or less to all fields, but there is some variation; in the social sciences about 75 percent of those who planned an academic career succeeded, in contrast to 50 percent in technology. These field differences reflect the fact that there is a planned "surplus" of PhD candidates in technology in relation to the number of available jobs in academia, due to the anticipated demand for doctoral candidates in industry and applied research institutes. Technology is the only field in which the main purpose of doctoral training is to educate people for the nonacademic labor market. Hence, the competition for permanent academic posts might be strongest in the field of technology, although technology faculties frequently complain of too few applicants for academic positions due to much better paid jobs in industry.

For the universities, this surplus of PhD candidates aiming for an academic career is important, because competition for vacant posts is a quality assurance mechanism. For the candidates themselves, this situation may create frustration, but many are also aware that they may not achieve their preferred career. A 2008 survey of PhD candidates revealed that only one third of the respondents were optimistic about realizing their career ambitions (Thune et al. 2012).

The Labor Market for Postdocs

The achievement of a postdoc position in a Norwegian university does not guarantee an academic career, although the majority evidently end up in a university—in Norway or abroad. A study of the careers of those who held a postdoc position in 2001 reports that, as of 2009, 50 percent had obtained a permanent position in the higher education sector in Norway, while 15 percent still had temporary employment in a university or college. There were, however, large differences between fields. Of the 2001 postdocs in the humanities and social sciences, more than 75 percent were employed in the higher education sector eight years later, compared to around 60 percent in medicine, around 40 percent in the natural sciences, and 25 percent in technology (Vabø et al. 2012). There were also differences according to national origin; 75 percent of the native Norwegian postdocs and 60 percent of the foreign-born postdocs were employed in the higher education sector in Norway eight years after their postdoc period (Børing and Gunnes 2012). The reason for this difference is that many non-Norwegian postdocs return to their country of origin after completing their postdoc period. This applies in particular to postdocs in technology, where 65 percent of the postdocs in 2007 were foreigners. But technology is also the field where there is a sizeable nonacademic job market for postdocs, based in applied research institutes and industry. Still, there is a "surplus" of postdocs who do not continue in research, either because they do not manage to find a job, or because they want to shift to another career in public administration, in industry, or in nongovernmental organizations.

The Appointment System in Higher Education

In public higher education institutions, hiring procedures for academic staff are strictly regulated by the Ministry of Education and Research and the individual institutions. Vacant posts at all levels should normally be advertised internationally, unless the content, subject, or the tasks involved in the vacant position are oriented toward Norwegian conditions.

In accordance with the act on universities and university colleges, a committee comprised of three to five persons will be appointed to assess the academic qualifications and personal suitability of candidates for a given position. The committee shall conduct an interview, solicit references, and reach a consensus for recommendation to the faculty. These requirements may, however, be adjusted for positions that are not professorships.

PhD Fellowships and Postdoc Positions

In the evaluation of applicants for PhD fellowship and postdoctoral positions, weight shall be given to their aptitude and ability to complete the research training program. The evaluation is based primarily on academic qualifications, the project description (whenever this is required in the call for applicants), the quality of the project and personal suitability of the candidate. As a general rule, an interview shall be conducted during the appointment process.

In 2010, 1,685 new PhD candidates were admitted into PhD programs, but less than half of the candidates were recruited through openly announced PhD fellowship positions (Thune et al. 2012). This means that more than half of the new candidates were recruited without applying for an openly announced position, either by being employees in research institutes, hospitals, or other institutions conducting research, or via less formal recruitment processes.

About half of the new PhD candidates employed as research fellows in 2010 had a master's degree from the same higher education institution, and 30 percent had a master's degree from a university outside Norway (Thune et al. 2012). Only 17 percent of new PhD candidates in

2010 had a master's degree from another Norwegian higher education institution.

There has been a strong increase in the number of PhD candidates coming from outside Norway. This is reflected in the growing share of doctoral degrees awarded to non-Norwegians; up from 13 percent in 2000, to 33 percent in 2011 (Thune et al 2012). It is common for international applicants for PhD positions to be brought to Norway for interviews, but due to the complexity, workload, and costs related to international recruitment, as well as the large number of unqualified applicants responding to open calls, some programs have stopped announcing new PhD positions through open channels.

Permanent Academic Positions

Hiring procedures for applicants for permanent academic positions are cumbersome; in many instances more than a year can pass before a vacant position is filled. A review committee is set up to make a recommendation about who should be appointed. In addition, the highest ranked applicants should be assessed with a view to certifying their personal suitability for the post, for example, in relation to collaboration with colleagues and their abilities as teachers and supervisors of students. Therefore, as a general rule the applicants are called for an interview, and the faculty may further determine that trial lectures will be conducted. Normally, private higher education institutions now follow these hiring procedures, because they are included in the common act on higher education and receive state subsidies.

Temporary Appointments

After completing appointments as a PhD fellow and postdoc, it is common to have temporary appointments as a lecturer, associate professor, or researcher while applying for a permanent position. Due to the sabbatical leave system (every five to six years in universities, but not in university colleges), as well as the many vacant positions due to a cumbersome appointment system, and because externally funded research projects often need temporary researchers, the higher education institutions have some flexibility to offer short-term contracts to young academics. In 2009, almost 40 percent of university lecturers and more than 80 percent of researchers were temporarily employed. The trade unions are very dissatisfied with this practice, and in 2010 the government set up a committee to assess the use of temporary appointments in the higher education sector. In its report (Rindal Committee 2010), the committee claimed that too many academic staff (about 20 percent) are temporarily employed in universities and colleges. This figure is twice as high as the average rate for temporary employment in Norway (less than 9 percent), and the committee suggested a number of measures to reduce this percentage. The government agrees that the number of temporarily employed academics is too high, and has instructed the higher education institutions to change their employment practices.

Entry-Level Contracts for Permanent Academic Staff

According to Norwegian law, professors, associate professors, docents, senior lecturers, and lecturers are to be permanently appointed by their institution unless there is statutory authority for a temporary appointment. Appointments of temporary staff to permanent positions are permissible if no qualified applicants are available during a period of 3.5 years following an appointment. The contract with individual institutions must last for a full 12 months.

Working Conditions

According to governmental regulations, undertaking research is neither an individual duty nor right, but an institutional responsibility. It is the institution that must determine the distribution of research time among staff, when determining the annual work program for each individual. In the universities, the practice seems to be that staff should use as much time for research as for teaching, irrespective of their age and academic position. As a rule of thumb, professors and associate professors in the universities should teach five hours a week (supervision not included) and use as much time for research as for teaching. A survey about the use of academic staff time in 2007 indicates that university staff spend, on average, exactly the same number of weekly hours on research (17.5) as on teaching (Bentley and Kyvik 2012).

Younger staff in universities use 30 percent of their total, average working time for research; the same percentage as their older peers (Kyvik and Olsen 2008). As expected, academic staff below the age of 35 report slightly fewer publications than their older peers, but staff aged 35 to 39 publish at the same level as their older peers (Kyvik and Olsen 2008).

In a 2008 survey, a clear majority of academic staff (55 percent) responded that working conditions had deteriorated since they started their university career, while a minority (15 percent) maintained that conditions had improved (Vabø 2011). Many academic staff have a sense that expectations of their work and task performance have increased, and that they therefore must work longer hours. However, various surveys undertaken over more than two decades indicate that the number of self-reported working hours has been relatively stable over time, and has even declined among young staff. The latter trend is partly due to a larger share of women staff members, and partly due to a change in attitudes and values among young men, who seem to be less willing to sacrifice family life and leisure time to long working hours. Hence, it seems that academics have intensified, rather than extended their working time, to cope with increased workloads (Kyvik 2012b).

In the university colleges, a survey undertaken in 2006 reports that university college staff use an average of 20 percent of their time for research and development and 55 percent for teaching. However, time available for research differs considerably between individual staff members (Kyvik and Larsen 2009). The main criterion for allocating time for research seems to be status; the higher the rank, the more research time people have, but the criteria and principles applied in these processes vary considerably between colleges and also between faculties within the same institution (Kyvik 2009b). In most cases, full professors in the university colleges seem to have similar working conditions to professors in research universities, while young doctorate-level college staff seem to have less time available for research than their counterparts in universities.

Salaries

By international standards, differences in salaries according to rank are relatively small within the Norwegian higher education sector (Kyvik 2012a). Lecturers, senior lecturers, and associate professors are paid according to a scale based on seniority, but other criteria may also be applied. For professors and docents, individual salaries are negotiated between the trade unions and institutions, within the limits of a pay scale. Individual salaries are determined according to a set of different criteria, the most important of which are the applicant's productivity in research and market value. Most salaries for these positions tend to be at the lowest level within the scale, or close to this, but in recent years universities and colleges have increasingly applied the span of the pay scale to reward staff members. Rewards have largely been allocated on the basis of achievements in research, but have also been used to attract professors from abroad.

The bottom of the pay scale, which constitutes the entry salary for most academics, is shown in Table 7.5. Although the pay scale is similar across all institutions and disciplines, professors have higher salaries in some disciplines than in others, but these differences are relatively small.

In general, academic staff in public higher education institutions have salaries that are slightly lower than those of civil servants with comparable competence and seniority, and considerably lower than their counterparts in industry and the business sector. Moreover, these differences have increased over time (Kyvik 2012b).

Socialization into the Academic Profession

In Norway, research training has historically started at the master's level with courses in theory and research methodology, followed by the writing of a research thesis under the supervision of an academic staff member. Master's theses have traditionally been regarded as important contributions to the research produced by various departments (Bleiklie, Høstaker and Vabø 2000, 177–183). The master's degree is stipulated as being a two-year process, with the thesis playing an important part, in particular for those students who aim at a research career. Although the government has enforced regulations to reduce the thesis workload to half a year to enhance the likelihood that master's students complete their degree on

Table 7.5. Monthly entry salary for academic staff in Norwegian public higher education institutions, as of December 2012

Rank	NOK	US$
PhD fellow	34,690	6,250
Post-doc	39,010	7,030
Lecturer	39,690	7,150
Senior lecturer	46,840	8,440
Associate professor	46,840	8,440
Docent	57,270	10,320
Professor	57,270	10,320

Source: Norwegian Association of Researchers.

time, students who aim for a research career put a lot of work into their thesis. In fact, the quality of the thesis is the main criterion for selection of students for PhD fellowships, and those candidates who are selected thus have a solid research platform to build on.

All new PhD candidates are enrolled in a PhD program or a research school, which provides courses in theory and methodology, and an administrative and scholarly environment for the candidates. According to the regulations, each PhD candidate should have two supervisors, but this recommendation is not followed in all cases. A recent evaluation of Norwegian research training (Thune et al. 2012) shows most PhD candidates are satisfied with the supervision they receive, and indicates a high degree of satisfaction among PhD candidates with the frequency of contact and competencies of their supervisors. However, a considerable minority reports that they receive too little supervision. Another important rationale for establishing PhD programs and research schools was to integrate PhD candidates into research groups and networks, to make sure that they become part of active research communities. The evaluation reports that all institutions pay a lot of attention to integrating PhD candidates into research groups or research projects. In reality, this is only common in the STEM subjects, while the majority of social science and humanities candidates work independently. Not unexpectedly, candidates who belong to a research group are generally more satisfied with their research training than those who work independently (Thune et al. 2012).

There is a long tradition in Norway that research training should be undertaken in close contact with international research: through encouraging PhD candidates to attend international conferences, through shorter or longer stays at foreign universities (Kyvik et al. 1999), or through participation in international research projects. Participation in international conferences and workshops is common among PhD candidates across all fields, and about one-fifth of candidates have a study period at a foreign university. In addition, surveys indicate that half of the candidates participate in international networks (Thune et al. 2012). A previous study also showed that permanent academic staff aged 35 to 39 years were significantly more active in international research collaboration than their older peers. The most likely explanation is that younger academics are more cosmopolitan in their behavior than their older colleagues, due to generational differences in sociocultural influences and socialization processes at different points in time (Kyvik and Olsen 2008).

There is ample reason to believe that the academic quality of new entrants to permanent academic positions in universities and colleges is higher than ever. Their doctoral training is more thorough than before and is increasingly succeeded by a postdoctoral period. The recent evaluation of Norwegian PhD education indicates that PhD dissertations are of a high international level (Thune et al. 2012). In Norway, the thesis is evaluated by a committee constituted of three members, of which at least one should come from a foreign university. For a small scientific community like Norway, this procedure is regarded as an important quality assurance mechanism. In a mail survey, the foreign members of these committees were asked for their opinion about the quality of PhD dissertations. When asked to rate the most recent Norwegian thesis they had evaluated, about 15 percent rated it as being "excellent," about 45 percent answered "very good," 30 percent said it was "good," and approximately 10 percent thought it was "acceptable;" only 1 percent characterized the thesis as "poor."

Because most PhD candidates have been employed in university positions where they have traditionally been treated as members of the academic staff, and increasingly continue in a postdoc position, young academics who achieve a permanent university position have gone through a long period of socialization into the academic profession, though usually more as researchers than teachers. Hence, those who are appointed to permanent positions have to take a course in pedagogy of up to four weeks duration within the first two years of appointment.

Conclusion

From a national point of view, Norway must be said to have a well-functioning system for the recruitment of people to the academic profession: PhD candidates have a regular salary, and postdocs have salaries that are competitive on the international market; the quality of training seems to be good; and young academics that do not attain a permanent post in the higher education sector seem to find employment relevant to their training. Still, there remain several challenges related to the structure of research training and careers for young academics, of which the following should be mentioned: (1) whether the scale of research training is appropriate, (2) whether the influx of foreign PhD candidates and postdocs has become too large, and (3) whether Norway should introduce a tenure track system.

Over the last few years, the scale of the research training system has been publicly debated. The Ministry of Education and Research (2012) has estimated that there will be an increasing need for PhDs in Norwegian society; thus it can be expected that state funding of PhD fellowship positions (and also postdoc positions) will increase. From an institutional point of view, such positions are to be welcomed, as doctoral candidates and postdocs are the most important research resources. But the institutions also argue that they will need more permanent academic positions to handle the increased number of research recruits in need of supervision. Over the last decade there has only been a modest increase in the number of permanent academic staff in public universities and colleges (20 percent between 2003 and 2011), while the number of postdocs increased by 75 percent, and the number of doctoral candidates holding a fellowship position increased by 100 percent. This imbalance in growth rates will most likely lead to stronger competition for permanent academic positions—to the advantage of the higher education institutions and the disadvantage of young academics. Hence, many PhD candidates have questioned whether Norway really needs to expand research training, because they cannot see the point in educating a large number of researchers who will end up in other types of jobs.

A second issue is the large influx of non-Norwegian citizens in doctoral and postdoctoral training. The recent evaluation of Norwegian research training found that 40 percent of the managers of PhD programs agree that they see too few applicants with a degree from Norwegian universities, and 25 percent report that they have a majority of international PhD candidates in their programs (Thune et al. 2012). This group accounts for an increasing share of new PhDs, up from 13 percent in 2000 to 33 percent in 2011. The share of foreign postdocs is even higher, at more than 40 percent in 2011. In some doctoral programs within the STEM field, the clear majority of PhD candidates are non-Norwegian citizens, and in many research groups all postdocs come from abroad. The challenge is to retain these candidates after graduation, but so far, 40 percent of foreign born PhD candidates (including immigrants) have left Norway (Olsen and Sarpebakken 2012).

A third dilemma that has been on the public agenda is to find a balance between the need of the higher education institutions to appoint the best candidates to permanent academic positions, through a thorough selection process stretching over the PhD and postdoc periods, and the need of young academics for a predictable career trajectory and stable work environment. Because of the discontent with the present situation, alternative career structures have been suggested.

The Norwegian Association of Researchers (NAR) has pointed out that the percentage of academic staff employed on temporary assignments other than PhD fellows and postdocs has increased over the last decade: "On average, one out of five academic staff members at state universities and university colleges is on a fixed-term contract (not including recruitment positions). This is more than twice as many as in working life otherwise. Extensive use of temporary academic positions makes jobs less attractive to those seeking a career in research" (NAR 2009, 8). The Association further argues that this situation should lead to changes in the career structure:

> Academic career paths are characterized by long periods of temporary employment. For that reason, a new type of academic position should be explored, e.g. tenure track or an entry-level position. This position should provide greater predictability than is the case with short-term temporary positions, since an entry-level position may ultimately lead to a longer term of employment and to being considered for tenure. (NAR 2009, 8)

The introduction of a tenure track system has been discussed, but counterarguments have, until recently, proven stronger. Firstly, both the EU Fixed-Term Contract Directive (which was introduced to prevent employers from using successive temporary contracts to avoid permanent employment) and Norwegian law have been regarded as obstacles to the introduction of a tenure track system on top of temporary appointments as PhD fellow and postdoc. Second, it has been argued that a tenure track system might in fact prolong the period of temporary employment, and eventually increase the age at which young staff can obtain a permanent post. Today, a major challenge is that academics competing for a permanent position in universities and colleges are relatively old. The main reason is that PhD candidates are 31 years of age, on average, at appointment to a fellowship position, varying between 28 years of age in the STEM subjects, 33 years in the humanities and social sciences, and 34 years in medicine and health sciences. Due to the excessive research training period, the estimated average age at appointment to a postdoc position is 35. This means that a large number of postdocs are in their forties when they finish their postdoctoral training.

Third, it has been argued that a tenure track system might lead to a situation where the de facto selection of new members of the academic profession takes place at too early a stage of the academic career, eventually leading to less competition for permanent academic positions.

Nevertheless, the universities have for some time wanted to introduce tenure track positions to make an academic career more predictable and attractive for talented young researchers, and in 2013 the Ministry of Education and Research suggested that 300 tenure track positions could be established for a trial period in the fields of technology, natural sciences and medicine.

In conclusion, it is a paradox that the development of the PhD and postdoc systems over the last decade has strongly improved the research training of young academics, while at the same time academic career prospects for PhD candidates and postdocs have become less certain, due to increased competition for permanent positions, and because the average age for obtaining a permanent position has increased. On the other hand, young academics who have obtained a permanent position as an associate professor have good career prospects, due to changes in the academic career structure which give them the opportunity to apply for promotion to full professor irrespective of vacant professorships. This situation also applies to lecturers, who may apply for promotion to senior lecturer and docent on the basis of their qualifications. Employment conditions for the group of permanently employed young staff have thus been improved. To sum up, while the career structure for permanent academic staff has changed from a *competition* model to a *promotion* model, the competition model has been further extended for academics in recruitment positions through the expansion of the postdoc system.

References

Altbach, Philip, Liz Reisberg, Maria Yudkevich, Gregory Androushchak, and Ivan Pacheco, eds. 2012. *Paying the Professoriate. A Global Comparison of Compensation and Contracts*. New York: Routledge.

Bentley, Peter J., and Svein Kyvik. 2012. "Academic Work from a Comparative Perspective: A Survey of Faculty Working Time Across 13 Countries." *Higher Education* 63: 529–547.

Bentley, Peter James, Svein Kyvik, Agnete Vabø, and Erica Waagene (2010). *Forskningsvilkår Ved Norske Universiteter I Et Internasjonalt Perspektiv. En Undersøkelse Av 7 Land*. Oslo: NIFU.

Bleiklie, Ivar, Roar Høstaker, and Agnete Vabø. 2000. *Policy and Practice in Higher Education. Reforming Norwegian Universities*. London: Jessica Kingsley.

Børing, Pål, and Hebe Gunnes. 2012. *Internasjonal Rekruttering Til Norsk Forskning*. Oslo: NIFU.

DAMVAD. (2012). *Integrating Global Talent in Norway—What Do We Know?* Oslo: DAMvAD.

Enders, Jürgen, and Christine Musselin. 2008. "Back to the Future? The Academic Professions in the 21st Century." In *Higher Education to 2030. Volume 1: Demography*, 125–150. Paris: OECD.

Gappa, Judith M., Ann E. Austin, and Andrea G. Trice. 2007. *Rethinking Faculty Work*. San Francisco: Wiley.

Kyvik, Svein. 2009a. *The Dynamics of Change in Higher Education. Expansion and Contraction in an Organisational Field*. Dordrecht, Netherlands: Springer.

Kyvik, Svein. 2009b. "Allocating Time Resources for Research Between Academic Staff: The Case of Norwegian University Colleges." *Higher Education Management and Policy* 21: 109–122.

Kyvik, Svein. 2012a. "Academic Salaries in Norway: Increasing Emphasis on Research Achievement." In *Paying the Professoriate. A Global Comparison of Compensation and Contracts*, edited by Philip Altbach, Liz Reisberg, Maria Yudkevich, Gregory Androushchak, and Ivan Pacheco, 255–264. New York: Routledge.

Kyvik, Svein. 2012b. "Academic Workload and Working Time: Retrospective Perceptions Versus Time Series Data." *Higher Education Quarterly* 67: 2–14.

Kyvik, Svein, Berit Karseth, Jan A. Remme, and Stuart Blume. 1999. "International Mobility Among Nordic Doctoral Students." *Higher Education* 38: 379–400.

Kyvik, Svein, and Ingvild M. Larsen. 2010. "Norway: Strong State Support of Research in University Colleges." In *The Research Mission of Higher Education Institutions Outside the University Sector*, edited by Svein Kyvik and Benedetto Lepori, 219–236. Dordrecht, Netherlands: Springer.

Kyvik, Svein, and Jens-Christian Smeby. 2004. "The Academic Workplace. Country Report Norway." In *The International Attractiveness of the Academic Workplace in Europe*, edited by Jürgen Enders and Egbert de Weert, 310–331. Frankfurt/Main: Gewerkschaft Erziehung und Wissenschaft.

Kyvik, Svein, and Terje B. Olsen. 2008. "Does the Aging of Tenured Academic Staff Affect the Research Performance of Universities?" *Scientometrics* 76: 439–455.

Kyvik, Svein, and Terje B. Olsen. 2012. "The Relevance of Doctoral Training in Different Labour Markets." *Journal of Education and Work* 25: 205–224.

Kyvik, Svein, and Terje B. Olsen. 2013. "Increasing Completion Rates in Norwegian Doctoral Training: Multiple Causes for Efficiency Improvements." *Studies in Higher Education*. (Published online June 3, 2013)

McAlpine, Lynn, and Gerlese Akerlind. 2010. *Becoming an Academic. International Perspectives*. New York: Palgrave Macmillan.

Ministry of Education and Research. 2012. *Etterspørsel Etter Og Tilbud Av Stipendiatstillinger I Norge Frem Mot 2020*. Rapport Fra En Arbeidsgruppe Nedsatt Av Kunnskapsdepartementet Og Universitets—Og Høgskolerådet.

The Norwegian Association of Researchers: Work Program 2010–2012.

Olsen, Terje B., and Bo Sarpebakken. 2011. *Utlendinger i Norsk Forskning*. Oslo: NIFU.

Olsen, Terje B., Svein Kyvik, and Elisabeth Hovdhaugen. 2005. "The Promotion to Full Professor—Through Competition or by Individual Competence?" *Tertiary Education and Management* 11: 299–316.

Rindal Committee. 2010. *Bruk av Midlertidig Tilsetting I Universitets- Og Høyskolesektoren. Rapport Fra Arbeidsgruppe*. Oslo: Ministry of Education and Research.

Thune, Taran, Svein Kyvik, Sverker Sörlin, Terje B. Olsen, Agnete Vabø, and Cathrine Tømte. 2012. *PhD Education in a Knowledge Society. An Evaluation of PhD Education in Norway*. Oslo: NIFU.

Vabø, Agnete. 2011. "Norway: Between Humboldtian Values and Strategic Management." In *Changing Governance and Management in Higher Education. The Perspectives of the academy*, edited by William Locke, William K. Cummings, and Donald Fisher, 263–280. Dordrecht, Netherlands: Springer.

Vabø, Agnete, Hebe Gunnes, Cathrine Tømte, Ann C. Bergene, and Cathrine Egeland. 2012. *Kvinners og Menns Karriereløp i Norsk Forskning*. Oslo: NIFU.

Welch, Anthony, ed. 2005. *The Professoriate. Profile of a Profession*. Dordrecht, Netherlands: Springer.

Chapter 8

Young Doctorates in a Fast-Changing Higher Education System

The Case of Portugal

Hugo Horta and Sandra Hasanefendic

Introduction

The Portuguese higher education system has been changing at an accelerated rate in the last decade. The system has been recently reformed, and science policies associated with a strong public investment have led to an unprecedented number of new doctorates being awarded in all disciplinary fields by Portuguese universities. These have been integrated within a higher education system that has so far been able to absorb them. This absorption, though, is becoming less traditional, more focused on fixed-term contracts and dependent on research project funding. Moreover, recent salary cuts and public budget constrains derived from the financial crisis are raising concerns about the employability and career prospects of young doctorates. These developments are making the entry of young doctorates into the university's traditional academic careers difficult.

The present situation is raising uncertainty for young doctorate's careers. It is also pointing toward more flexible and transient career paths (more typically seen in nontraditional academic careers) and less to "one job for life" positions typical of the traditional academic careers. Nonetheless, it is expected that the higher education system in Portugal will continue to employ new doctorates, remaining as the main employer of doctorates in the country. It is also expected that some of the young doctorates will continue to be gradually employed by universities in the traditional academic careers, because the qualifications of the academic staff at Portuguese universities are still relatively low when compared internationally.

In this chapter we analyze the current employment challenges and salary situation of young doctorates by articulating the evolution of the higher education system, relevant public policies, and present and future employment challenges. We particularly distinguish the employment situation of those doctorates that are in traditional academic careers, that is, the ones that are tenured or in a tenure-track situation, from those that are in nonacademic careers—in other words, postdoctoral fellows, those on fixed-term contracts, and individuals in nontenured situations. In order to do this, we start by contextualizing the Portuguese higher education system and the role of public policies on increasing qualifications, in particular, of doctorates. We then analytically describe the career paths of young doctorates in academia, as well as public policies fostering the employment of doctorates, and the existing challenges to these dynamics, including how the current financial crisis is augmenting these challenges. In this context, we briefly refer to doctorate employment outside academia and the role that universities have in fostering it, by helping their doctorates to start science base firms. Finally, we present the conclusions where we highlight our main findings.

The Portuguese Higher Education System

In this section, the Portuguese higher education system is outlined in terms of its growth, structure, recent key reforms, and the evolution of the student population in terms of total enrollment, the cycles of studies of this enrollment, gender, and percentage of international students.

Structure and Recent Key Reforms in the Portuguese Higher Education System

Higher education in Portugal is organized as a binary system. The university sector aims at providing solid academic training, combining the efforts and responsibilities of both teaching and research. The polytechnic system is more professionally oriented, based on vocational and advanced technical training. Students can attain bachelor (*licenciatura*) and master's (*mestrado*) degrees in both the university and polytechnic higher education sectors, but the PhD degree is only conferred by universities (EURYDICE 2010). The current system is comprised of fourteen public universities and one public university education institute, fifteen public polytechnic institutes, several nonintegrated polytechnic schools and higher education schools, which are dependent on the Ministry of Education and Science (OECD 2007). The private sector is represented by thirteen universities (mostly concentrated around Lisbon and Porto), two polytechnics, some nonintegrated higher education schools, and nonintegrated polytechnic higher education schools.

The legal regime of higher education institutions of 2007 (Law no. 62/2007) is a recent reform that mainly altered the way higher education institutions are organized, opening them further to society (by bringing civil society into the governing bodies of the universities) and granting them greater levels of—and opportunities for—institutional autonomy (for a detailed and extensive description and analysis of the reform see Magalhães et al. 2013, and Heitor and Horta 2012). This new legal regime establishes the organizational principles of the higher education system, defining autonomy and accountability parameters, instituting governing boards with external participation, and promoting organizational diversity. It also allows for the establishment of consortia, and recognizes research centers as part of the university management framework (ECFIN 2010). An important feature of the Law no. 62/2007 is the possibility for the creation of public foundations operating under private law (Hasan 2007; MCTES 2011). A university foundation is a public university in its essence, but operates as a public foundation governed by private law in such aspects as finance, assets, and personnel management (Hasan 2007; MCTES 2011). It gives greater autonomy to universities in terms of the ownership of assets, greater independence from the state financial system, and a management of human resources delinked from the civil service system.

This is important because it allows the universities that opt to become public foundations operating under private law to hire academics with a much higher degree of autonomy. So far, three public universities (University of Porto, University of Aveiro, and ISCTE-IUL) have been granted this status, while the University of Minho is waiting for approval. The effects of hiring new academics outside the civil servant career rules at these universities, however, are still to be assessed due to the short time period since this change took place. In the meantime, it is likely that these effects have been disrupted by the impact of the financial crisis on university budgets.

Also, a new Legal Framework for the Evaluation of Higher Education was introduced in 2007 (Law no. 38/2007) and, along with it, a new Higher Education Evaluation and Accreditation Agency (A3ES) was created in 2007. The Agency, A3ES, has been fully operational since July 2009 as a private and independent foundation established for an indeterminate period of time. It is responsible for the assessment and accreditation of Portuguese higher education institutions and their study cycles, as well as the integration of Portugal into the European system of quality assurance for higher education.

By June 2010, A3ES had already contributed to the universities' efforts to reorganize their educational portfolio, including the improvement of doctoral program quality. Of the 697 PhD programs registered with the Directorate General of Higher Education in 2010/2011, only 568 were submitted for accreditation, meaning that Portuguese universities voluntarily discontinued 129 PhD programs in one year. This illustrates that these reforms had an effect on the drive for quality of the PhD programs that Portuguese universities were already undertaking, partly related to the forthcoming assessment and accreditation process. It is expected that additional PhD programs will be discontinued during the ongoing accreditation process.

Student Enrollment: Cycles of Study, Gender, and Internationalization

The number of students in higher education in Portugal has been increasing slightly in recent years, although with fluctuations. This trend is expected to stagnate or decline in the coming years due to the effects of the financial crisis, and the increasing difficulty of students and their families to support educational costs. Still, in 2010/2011, there were 403,445 students in higher education, of which 193,633 students were enrolled at public universities, 120,399 at public polytechnics, 61,336 at private universities, and 28,077 at private polytechnics (GPEARI/MCTES 2011c). This represents a growth of 6 percent since 2004/2005, when 381,231 students were enrolled in higher education. Of these 174,114 students were enrolled at public universities, 108,436 at public polytechnics, 66,478 at private universities, and 32,203 at private polytechnics. From 2004/2005 to 2010/2011 the percentage of students enrolled in public higher education grew from 74 percent to 78 percent.

Throughout this period, in public and private universities, the number of students enrolled in the first cycle of studies decreased by

23 percent, while the number of students enrolled in the second cycle more than quadrupled, and the number of students enrolled in doctoral programs more than doubled (MCTES 2011). The same trend can be observed at public and private polytechnics, where the number of students enrolled in the first cycle of studies decreased by 10 percent while those enrolled in the second cycle increased by a factor of 36 (MCTES 2011). This is related to several issues, including the growing importance of education for the knowledge society, the high private benefits derived from having a higher education degree, and changes that have occurred in the Portuguese higher education system as a result of its adaptation to the Bologna process and reform. The participation of women in higher education continues to be a feature of the Portuguese higher education system, as 53 percent of the total enrolled students in 2010/2011 were women.

The international students enrolled in the Portuguese higher education system represent 6 percent of the total number of students enrolled in 2010/2011, evolving from 3 percent in 2000/2001. Students from the Community of Portuguese Speaking Countries (CPLP) represent the majority of international students (64 percent) in Portugal. Brazilian students alone represent 24 percent of the total international students, followed by students from Cape Verde (15 percent) and Angola (14 percent). The second major group of international students in the Portuguese higher education system originates from European Union member states (22 percent), where Spanish is the most represented nationality. These figures suggest that language and geographical proximity play a key role in the internationalization of the Portuguese higher education system as a whole, when measured in terms of incoming student mobility.

Investing in Highly Qualified Human Resources: Increasing Qualifications in Higher Education

In this section we describe first the evolution of the number of academics in the higher education system in recent years and the doctoral degrees completed or recognized by Portuguese universities in the last four decades. Then we examine the accelerated growth of the number of academics in Portugal, their qualifications, and the proliferation of new PhDs in the first decade of the twenty-first century as a result of public policies fostering the advanced training of human resources specifically in support of academia.

Unprecedented Numbers

For the past decade, the number of people in higher education involved in research, but also in teaching and service related activities, almost tripled in Portugal. These numbers—including those representing individuals in traditional academic careers (full, associate, and assistant professors) as well as those in nontraditional careers (e.g., postdoctoral fellows)—increased from more than 17,000 in 2001 to about 47,000 in 2008 (Heitor and Horta 2013). During the same period, the numbers only for those in traditional academic careers at Portuguese public and private universities increased from about 10,000 up to about 13,500, a growth of 37 percent. These figures suggest a growth that was mainly driven by the increase of people in the nontraditional careers in higher education. Perhaps more important is that the pool of people engaged in scholarly activities in Portuguese higher education institutions increased to levels never seen before. This is an outcome of a broad range of public policies to modernize higher education institutions, increase qualifications in academic and research settings, and foster better quality research and teaching activities.

In this regard, of particular importance for the new generation of academics are science policies (encompassing all disciplinary fields and sectors of research performance including higher education), focused on institution-building and advanced training and professional development. Policies concerning institution-building, including the reinforcement of the assessment and evaluation culture at Portuguese universities, are of relevance to the development of the Portuguese higher education system, but are discussed in detail elsewhere (see Heitor and Horta 2012). We concentrate on those policies focused on the advanced training and development of human resources for academia, as they are more pertinent for the purposes of this book.

Breaking with Tradition: A Fast-Growing Number of New Doctorates in Recent Years

The considerable public investment in advanced training and professional development clearly boosted doctoral education and the development of research and postgraduate activities in Portuguese higher education. When this is articulated with changes in the enrollment of students in higher education, two related trends are observed. The first is that the highest educational levels are being sought by students and, due to public policies, funding opportunities (in the form of publicly funded doctoral fellowships) exist at the third cycle of studies[1] to support students' further education. The second observable trend is that for universities to offer second and third cycles of studies, that is, master's and PhD degrees, that are accredited by the Evaluation and Assessment Agency (A3ES), better qualified academic staff, with strong research training, is needed. For that purpose there are public policies and funding aimed at supporting academics already in the traditional academic careers to undertake a PhD. They also support a younger generation to pursue doctoral studies, and potentially enter academia on completion of the doctorate.

As Figure 8.1 shows, Portuguese universities awarded or recognized more new doctorates over the last decade than over the three previous decades combined. The percentage of PhDs obtained by women also increased significantly from 16 percent in the 1970s to 50 percent in the 2000s, and with 54 percent of students enrolled in doctoral programs at Portuguese universities now female, this share is expected to increase in coming years. This parallels a strong increase in the participation of women in the upper levels of higher education (Pinto 2012), even if the proportion of women in the traditional academic career decreases as the

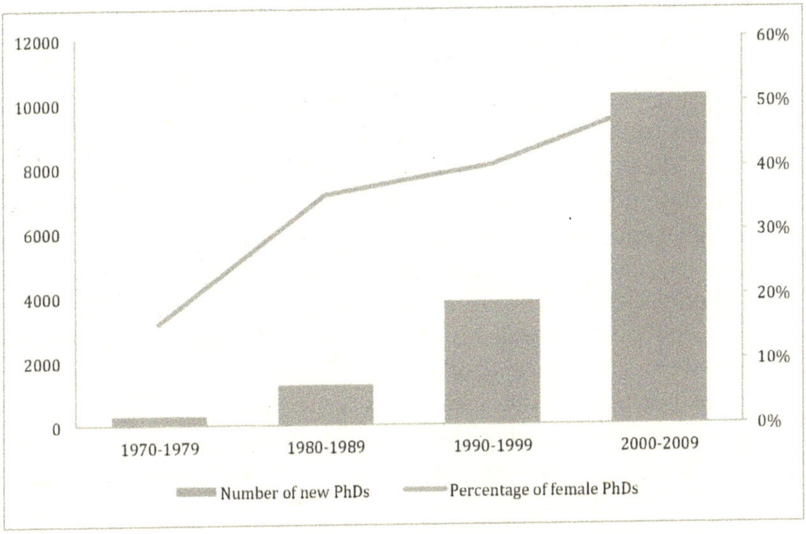

Source: Direção-Geral de Estatísticas da Educação e Ciência (DGEEC), Ministry of Science and Education

Figure 8.1. Number of new PhDs and percentage of those obtained by women, 1970–2009.

academic rank increases. By 2009, 42 percent of the assistant professors, 32 percent of the associate professors, and 22 percent of the full professors were women at Portuguese public universities.

In the 2000s, 29 percent of the PhDs were obtained in natural and exact sciences, 22 percent in engineering and technology, 22 percent in the social sciences, 13 percent in the humanities, 11 percent in the health sciences, and 4 percent in agriculture. This does not present a large variation when comparing with the previous decade, except for the growing proportion of PhDs undertaken in the social sciences (15 percent in the 1990s) and the decreasing proportion of PhDs in the health sciences (17 percent in the 1990s). The median age for obtaining the PhD degree, according to the data from the Careers of Doctoral Holders study (CDH09), is 35 across all fields (Auriol 2010). However, there are strong variations by disciplinary field in terms of the median age to obtain the PhD. The median age for obtaining a PhD degree in the natural and exact sciences is 32, sciences of engineering and technology 34, health sciences 37, social sciences and agriculture 38, and humanities 39.

Public Policies Promoting Doctoral Studies and New Doctorates

Public policies in Portugal have focused to a large extent on the advanced training of people, independent of nationality. Such policies led to a considerable increase in the number of doctoral students and new doctorates in the first decade of the twenty-first century (see Figure 8.1). They were largely supported by the Portuguese Foundation for Science and Technology (FCT). The FCT is the Portuguese governmental institution responsible for financing and evaluating science in Portugal, including that performed in the higher education sector. Its mission is mainly accomplished through the funding, subsequent to the evaluation of merit, of proposals presented by institutions, research teams or individuals in open public calls. It also funds institutions, research teams and individuals through cooperation agreements and other forms of support in partnership with universities and other public or private institutions, in Portugal and abroad.

The FCT support for the advanced training of people is done through doctoral fellowships. The public support for doctorate studies through the FCT is important because doctoral students are not considered as members of the academic staff, and do not have a working contract with the universities. Doctoral students in Portugal are students, and the fellowship stipend guarantees the financial sustainability of the doctoral work for four years (recently reduced to three years). The fellowships are granted under a framework of exclusivity, preventing doctoral students who benefit from the fellowships to accumulate the stipend with other revenue, including contracted work. The rationale is that the fellowship stipend provides for financial stability throughout the doctorate, allowing for the student to concentrate exclusively on the doctoral work.

Fellowships stipends vary according to the location of the doctoral work so that adequate stipends are available to cover variable costs of living both at home in Portugal and abroad. In this context, fellowships are organized around a typology based on where they are undertaken: "national fellowships" are granted to doctoral students enrolled at Portuguese universities, supporting short term visits abroad; "abroad fellowships" are granted to doctoral students enrolled in doctoral programs abroad; and "mixed fellowships" are granted to doctoral students based at Portuguese universities, but support relatively long spells abroad in the context of the doctoral work. The monthly tax free stipend paid in Portugal for a doctoral fellowship is 980€, while the monthly tax free stipend paid abroad rises to 1,710€ (see FCT, 2012a, 2012b). The stipends come with other associated subsidies, such as a subsidy to support traveling abroad to present articles at international conferences, and covering fully or partly the tuition fees (this subsidy has a threshold).

From 1994 to 2010, about 19,000 doctoral fellowships were awarded by FCT. The growth of doctoral fellowships awarded accelerated in recent years, as 55 percent of the 19,000 doctoral fellowships were awarded between 2005 and 2010 (FCT website). These figures do not include those performing the PhD supported by funded research projects, but the stipends for these doctoral students are the same. Of the total doctoral fellowships awarded between 1994 and 2010, about 11,000 were "national fellowships," more than 4,000 were "abroad fellowships," and about 4,000 were "mixed fellowships."

The fact that these fellowships allow for periods abroad is critical during the doctoral socialization period, because spending a certain period abroad permits the assimilation of new knowledge and integration into academic and scientific networks (Van de Sande et al. 2005). This has been having a positive impact on the internationalization of Portuguese academics and universities and their integration into global academic networks (Horta 2010). The impact of this mobility on diminishing academic inbreeding's detrimental effects has also been evident in the Portuguese context (Horta 2012). However, the impact of these policies has been broader. Besides creating a pool of new doctorates, many with substantial international experience for the higher education institutions to hire, they triggered a mentality change in Portuguese academia, leading many academics in the traditional academic career to pursue a doctoral degree. The result is an increasingly qualified academic staff in the traditional academic careers. The percentage of academic staff holding a PhD reached 68 percent in public universities, 39 percent in private universities, and 19 percent in both public and private polytechnics by 2009. In 2001, this figure stood at 48 percent at public universities, 21 percent at private universities, and roughly 8 percent in both public and private polytechnics (GPEARI/MCTES 2011b).

Career Paths for Recent Doctorates in Academia

In this section, we focus first on nontraditional academic career paths, by referring to the role of postdoctoral positions and their increasing prevalence in Portuguese academia, followed by the attempts to foster scientific careers in higher education through research working contracts. Then, the traditional academic careers are analyzed in terms of their career structure, salary levels, entry and progression. The traditional careers are analyzed for the public sector only. This is because the possibility to obtain a stable academic job in the sense of a traditional career happens mostly in the sphere of public higher education. The predominantly teaching-oriented private higher education institutions in Portugal are dealing with a decreasing number of enrollments (tuition being their main source of revenue), thus showing a lesser ability to hire academics on a permanent basis. In this context, some postdoctoral fellows tend to lecture at private universities on an "as needed" basis. In this way, the postdoctoral fellows accumulate teaching experience and extra earnings, while private universities have access to highly qualified staff to teach students mainly at undergraduate and master's levels, under relatively flexible and low-cost contractual arrangements.

Postdoctoral Positions: A Nontraditional Path and Increasingly the Norm

Recent doctorates entering academia through the traditional career path is not as usual as it was two or three decades ago. Holding a postdoctoral position after concluding the doctorate is becoming increasingly common in all disciplinary fields. FCT, in this case as well, is the main funder of postdoctoral fellowships in Portugal. The doctoral fellowships' rules of exclusivity, associated subsidies (except tuition fee coverage), and stipend variation according to the location of work are the same. The difference is that the value of the stipends is higher for postdoctoral fellowships. The monthly stipend paid in Portugal for a postdoctoral fellowship is 1,495€. The monthly stipend paid abroad rises to 2,245€ (see FCT 2012a).

From 1994 to 2010, almost 6,000 postdoctoral fellowships were funded, of which 88 percent were based in Portuguese universities with shorter or longer periods of research abroad (FCT 2012b). This percentage is understandable because the postdoctoral fellowship policy intended to promote brain-gain: a substantial share of postdoctoral holders has a foreign nationality or are Portuguese that did the PhD outside Portugal. But the policy also intended to help rejuvenate the academic staff in the traditional academic careers, and reinforce the knowledge base of Portuguese universities. In this context, it was important that the new doctorates had a postdoctoral period at a Portuguese university to be better acquainted with Portuguese institutional academic culture and working behaviors. This is expected to facilitate their integration into Portuguese academia in general, helping them to familiarize themselves with institutional cultural and social dynamics, norms, and taken-for-granted attitudes and working behaviors at Portuguese higher education institutions. At the same time, during the period of further learning and experience in research and teaching that the postdoc position represents, the recent doctorates contribute to the overall academic activities of the higher education institutions hosting them. This they do, and their role in that is becoming more visible and pronounced than ever (Araújo 2009).

As happens with doctoral students who benefit from a doctoral fellowship, postdocs holding a fellowship (either paid for directly by FCT or a research project) do not have a working contract with the university, and are not part of the university staff. Postdoc fellows are part of an increasing nontraditional academic career at Portuguese universities, contributing with increasing intensity to the research, teaching, and service functions at these universities. Postdoctoral fellows at Portuguese universities hope that these activities will enhance their employability opportunities and the entrance into traditional academic careers and a permanent academic position, as happens in other parts of the world (Stephan and Ma 2005).

As opportunities for traditional academic careers are becoming scarcer in Portuguese academia (even more since the start of the financial crisis), situations where one postdoctoral position is followed by another postdoctoral position—or a three-year postdoctoral position is extended for another three years—are increasingly common. In this regard, Araújo (2009), in her analysis of postdocs in Portugal, stated that postdoctoral fellows increasingly "live in an enduring state of waiting, whereby their lives are suspended until they secure another fellowship or a stable working contract" (2009, 232). Further analyses of how postdoctoral fellows are viewed in Portugal show that they are perceived as a cheap workforce, dependent, and vulnerable to intellectual exploitation (Araújo and Sousa 2007).

However, the consecutive rounds of postdoc and the increasing numbers of nonpermanent positions may not be a characteristic exclusive to a constrained Portuguese academic job market. Rather, it can be related to an overall shift in the world of professions: the "one job for life" model is changing to professional paths that demand flexibility, adaptability, and the ability to cope with uncertain employment conditions (Bridges 1996). An example of this is that even with situations of multiple postdoc positions and scarcer openings for traditional academic careers, Portugal is an attractive country for PhD holders worldwide, as evidenced by a situation of brain-gain of doctorates in the country in 2009 (GPEARI/MCTES 2011a).

Attempts to Foster Scientific Employment

In the mid-2000s, Portuguese public policy fostered the employment of doctorates through several programs, the "Compromisso com a Ciência" (Compromise with Science) program being the most prominent. It was launched in 2006/2007 to support, initially, contractual arrangements for 1,000 doctorates with some research experience, through university-based research centers, universities, and associate laboratories. The Compromisso com a Ciência aimed to stimulate major changes in the academic community and facilitate the renewal of teaching and research staff by bringing to the Portuguese universities relatively young but experienced doctorates who could develop scholarly activities and potentially be hired by the hosting universities. This is particularly important as the average age of those in the traditional academic careers has been increasing consistently. In 2009, the average age of those in the traditional academic careers in the Portuguese public universities was 46 years old.

The Compromisso com a Ciência also aimed at promoting a greater internationalization of the Portuguese higher education system by attracting promising young foreign scholars to be hired by Portuguese universities. By 2009, about 1,200 new doctorates were hired, of whom 41 percent were foreigners. However, unlike the internationalization of the student population in the higher education system, only 4 percent of the new doctorates hired originated from the Community of Portuguese Speaking Countries. Rather, 19 percent of the new doctorates hired were from non–European Union countries, and 18 percent were from European Union countries, with Spanish, Italians, and Germans figuring as the most represented nationalities. In terms of disciplinary fields, 43 percent of the newly hired doctorates were from the natural and exact sciences, 24 percent from the sciences of engineering and technology, 12 percent from the social sciences, 10 percent from the health sciences, 7 percent from the humanities, and 5 percent from agriculture sciences.

In 2012, this program was renamed "Investigador FCT" (FCT Researcher) and substantially downsized in terms of the number of contracts offered. A total of 80 vacancies were available to which a total of 1,187 applications were submitted by May 2012 (FCT Newsletter, FCT website 2012). This downsized number of vacancies raises concerns about scientific and academic employment in the near future, and the ability to integrate young doctorates with some years of postdoctoral experience into Portuguese research and academic institutions, even if the academic staff qualifications at universities requires further growth.

The gross salary paid by this program is 3,192€ per month for 14 months up to 2010 (in 2012, it was reduced to 2,931€ for 12 months due to public budget restrictions and cuts). The Investigador FCT program offered two possibilities for young doctorates. One option, focused more on those starting a scientific career, maintained the same salary level as the Compromisso com a Ciência program, 2,931€ for twelve months. This option was for those doctorates who could not be considered as scientifically independent and who concluded the doctorate within the last six years. The other option still relatively applicable for young doctorates with more experience—specifically for those doctoral degree holders who concluded the PhD within the last six to twelve years, but who are considered to have been scientifically independent for at least six years—would lead to a higher salary of 3,275€ for twelve months. There was a third option, but was for researchers at a more advanced stage of their career.

Academic Careers in the Public University Sector

When entering a traditional academic career in the public higher education sector, young doctorates can join universities or polytechnics. For the purposes of this chapter, the focus is on the Decree-Laws that regulate the traditional academic profession at Portuguese public universities.

The differences between university careers and those in the polytechnic sector are not overly substantial, and the differences that do exist relate to the different denomination of ranks and to features that are mainly associated with the unique institutional mission of these higher education institutions.

The norms guiding the academic profession in Portuguese universities are laid out in the Statutes of University Teaching Careers of Decree-Law 448/79, of November 13, 1979, which has changed several times since its creation. The most recent version is the Decree-Law no. 205/2009, of August 31, 2009. The Statutes of University Teaching Careers define the ranks, functions, recruitment, appointment, duties and rights of, as well as the regimes governing the provision of services by, academics in higher education. It states, for example, that a full-time contract requires 35 working hours per week, divided between teaching (on average six to nine hours/week), research, administrative tasks and services rendered to external organizations and society, or that the retirement age for academics is 65, but it is possible to work until age 70.

This legislation also regulates salaries. In Portugal, academic salaries do not vary by discipline, institution, region, or any urban-rural divide. They are also not negotiated with the public universities. Remunerations are centrally and nationally stipulated by the state for public universities varying by academic rank and by "escalões" (associated to tenure seniority) as shown on Table 8.1.

A full professor in "escalão 1" earns exactly the same salary as anyone else in the same rank and escalão, independent of the academic commitment and productivity of the individuals in question. Other characteristics, such as gender, do not play a role. Everyone in the same rank and escalão receives the same salary. The only circumstances for salary differences among academics in the same rank are when academics are in a regime of exclusivity, and where there are full-time versus part-time employment arrangements. The salary of those academics that are not in a regime of exclusivity is defined by law as corresponding to two-thirds of the salary that academics on the exclusivity regime earn. Therefore, a full professor in escalão 1 in the exclusivity regime earned 4,198.47€ per month in 2011, while in the same year a full-time professor in escalão 1 not in the exclusivity regime earned 2,770.99€ per month.

The academics that opt for a regime of nonexclusivity tend to do so because they obtain extra earnings by teaching at private universities, by being managers of firms and spin-offs, by engaging in consultancy, or by being engaged in any other practices that allow them to earn greater

Table 8.1. Public universities: Salary table for 2010 and 2011 (full time exclusive regime)

		"Escalões" (associated with tenure seniority)			
Academic Ranks		1	2	3	4
Full Professor	Salary 2010	4,664.97	4,910.49	5,074.17	5,401.54
	Salary 2011	4,198.47	4,419.44	4,566.76	4,861.39
Associate Professor with "agregação"	Salary 2010	4,010.23	4,173.92	4,337.60	4,664.97
	Salary 2011	3,618.60	3,756.52	3,903.84	4,198.47
Associate Professor without "agregação"	Salary 2010	3,601.03	3,764.71	4,092.08	4,255.76
	Salary 2011	3,274.86	3,412.36	3,687.34	3,830.18
Assistant Professor	Salary 2010	3,191.82	3,437.34	3,764.71	4,010.23
	Salary 2011	2,931.13	3,137.37	3,412.36	3,618.60

Note: Gross values in Euros and reductions following the budget cut of 2011 (Article no. 19 of the Law no. 55-A/2010 of the 31st of December).

Source: Sindicato Nacional do Ensino Superior http://www.snesup.pt/htmls/_dlds/CopiadeVencimentos2011_site.pdf

revenue than if they were on the exclusivity regime. The salaries of the academics in part-time employment correspond to the percentage of commitment in relation to full-time employment with a nonexclusivity regime. Taking the same example of the full professor in escalão 1 in the nonexclusivity regime: if his or her commitment is only 50 percent, then the salary would be reduced to 1,385.49€ per month (50 percent of 2,770.99€ per month).

There is also no differentiation in the remuneration of academics within the same rank based on merit or performance. However, academic performance is evaluated according to a set of regulations adopted by each university. A good performance in terms of scientific publications in particular can have an impact on remuneration, because it is critical for promotion and progression in the career. A positive performance evaluation is also one of the preconditions for the signing of tenured contracts with *Assistant Professors*, who start the career as nontenured faculty but are on the "tenure-track." Similarly, a positive performance is needed for the renewal of fixed-term contracts with academics who are not integrated in the traditional academic careers.

The universities that opted to become public foundations operating under private law are allowed to offer different salaries because they have greater autonomy in human resource management. However, assessing the impact of this autonomy on academic salaries is still difficult for two reasons. The first reason has to do with the embryonic stage of this process, as the three existing universities under this regime have only been operating as such since 2009. The second reason is that this is still a stage of transition, and for now such salary issues are only impacting the newly recruited academics, because the existing academics at these universities retained the status of public servants.

An important feature of Table 8.1 is the impact that the public financial cuts have had on the salaries of academics. Salaries were considerably reduced for all academic ranks from 2010 to 2012, and in 2013 further direct and indirect salary cuts are predicted as the country struggles with the financial crisis. Interviews conducted by the authors with deans of schools and department chairs of Portuguese universities revealed their growing concern that the most internationally recognized academics may leave the country and the difficulty in replacing them. In addition, they are concerned with the inability to fill vacant positions with new doctorates, because constraints to hire new academics are becoming increasingly prevalent. This, in combination with deteriorating economic prospects—possibly affecting negatively the enrollment of students in higher education—further limits the opening of vacancies and will negatively affect the hiring of young doctorates to the traditional academic careers in future years.

This situation is problematic in the sense that 86 percent of the doctorates in Portugal work in the higher education system, either in traditional or nontraditional academic careers, making this sector the main employer of doctorate holders up to now. If this sector is unable to hire academics to traditional academic careers, the difficulties for young doctorates in obtaining permanent and more stable work contracts increases. The most likely situation is that they will continue to remain as grant/fellowship holders for long periods of time (Perista and Silva 2004). For the universities, this will also be problematic because one of the major challenges in future years is to increase the share of doctorates in the traditional academic careers. The impact that a highly qualified academic staff has on teaching quality at higher education institutions has been evidenced by various studies (e.g., Rehman et al. 2009), and it is particularly needed in Portugal, a country where the formal qualifications of the labor force are still low when compared internationally.

Entry and Career Progression in the Public University Sector

The traditional academic career progression tends to start from the *Professor Auxiliar* (Assistant Professor) position. Then, one progresses to become *Professor Associado* (Associate Professor), and finally, *Professor Catedrático* (Full Professor). To become a full professor, some cumulative conditions are needed: specifically, one must have attained the rank of associate professor and have been successful at obtaining the "agregação" (Article 40, Decree Law 205/2009 of August 31, 2009). The agregação can be obtained by a doctoral degree holder if he or she undertakes a successful evaluation by peers based on scientific and pedagogical curriculum and merits. The agregação demands some years of experience as well as contributions to teaching and research, and this achievement impacts on the academics' salaries (see Table 8.1). The agregação is similar to the habilitation in Germany. It represents the greatest proof of academic and scientific maturity, and thus is a necessary requirement for attaining the position of full professor.

Young academics usually start their careers in the public university sector as assistant professors for which they need to hold a PhD, and preferentially have prior research experience and a relevant number of publications. Five years into the position, they can be offered a tenured position. For that purpose, their activities and output are evaluated by a scientific council, which makes the decision to grant tenure, depending on the evaluation of the postulant's academic performance. Some argue that during this stage of their career, young academics at Portuguese universities continue to be in a precarious professional condition (Santiago and Carvalho 2008). They argue that these young academics are overworked, overly tasked with teaching and administrative responsibilities, and highly dependent on tenured academics for several reasons, including those associated with future prospects of academic employment. This creates a fragmented academic profession at Portuguese universities. However, the diligent work that these early-stage Portuguese academics undertake is also recognized internationally, and there is a widespread assumption that young Portuguese scholars are internationally competitive. This is evidenced by several examples, such as the highly reputed Howard Hughes Medical Institute considering that five Portuguese researchers out of a group of 28 (from about 800 applications) are "people who, 10 years from now (. . .) will be the scientific leaders in their countries" (HHMI 2012).

Young academics can also apply directly for an associate professor position when a vacancy opens. However, to have a chance to accede directly to such a position, these young academics should have an outstanding academic record. Should this be the case and they are granted the position, the new associate professor needs to have a positive assessment after a one-year probation period before becoming tenured. It is rarer for young doctorates to enter academia directly to a full professorship position, although the possibility exists.

In terms of recruitment, when a university decides to fill a vacant post, a formal procedure is initiated through the publication of announcements in nationally circulated newspapers and in the *Legal Official Journal* (Soares and Trindade 2004). Recently, these announcements are increasingly being placed internationally, as well, to attract a wider range of candidates.

The candidates who fulfill the required application conditions must submit substantial documentation to be evaluated by an academic jury nominated for this purpose. The jury must include members from other university institutions and the jury's composition is published in the *Legal Official Journal* (Soares and Trindade 2004). The documents that the candidate usually needs to submit for the application consist of a detailed curriculum vitae; two copies of every scientific, technical, or pedagogical document mentioned therein; and a report detailing the general framework, contents, learning methods, and organizational information related to a course or group of courses that the candidate proposes to teach. Many feel it is too burdensome to document an entire academic and scientific career in the (generally) short application period allowed (Delicado 2010). This overly bureaucratic recruitment process is also known to undermine the attractiveness of Portuguese universities to the international workforce (Horta 2009).

Also, in Portuguese academia, the practice of academic inbreeding endures. This is a typical feature of inward looking universities where academic mobility is not the rule (OECD 2007). Recent analyses show that inbreeding rates are steady or even diminishing in recent years but that it will take some years for this practice to be further reduced (Heitor et al. 2012). Inbreeding's diminishing trends in Portugal can be explained by three main factors. The first reason is related to the effect of the advanced training public policies that fostered a greater internationalization of the doctorates during the PhD socialization years, but also of their mentors through co-mentoring PhD theses with peers based abroad. The second reason is the change of mentality of the academic staff that comes from institution-building policies, mostly from the ones associated with the country's evolving evaluation and assessment practices (Horta 2008). Finally, the broader advertisement of the vacancies nationally and internationally is bringing in more candidates with greater quality, making it much more difficult for universities to choose their own PhD graduates.

However, other issues persist in the traditional academic careers at Portuguese universities, not so much in relation to recruitment, but rather to progression. Career progression in the traditional academic careers is based on available vacancies, which for the posts of associate professor and full professor is defined according to student/staff ratios and fixed by the Ministry of Education and Science (but ultimately allowed—or not—by the Ministry of Finance). Even if merit is shown, a vacancy needs to be made available for progression to take place. The fact that promotions are based on vacancies rather than merit is considered as one of the biggest disincentives for young academics, as the possibilities to remain an assistant professor for many years is real, independently of how much merit an individual demonstrates (Athans 2001). This makes the traditional academic career structure at Portuguese universities pyramidal in shape, with few full professors at the top and a large base formed by assistant professors. A historical analysis (undertaken for this chapter) of the career structure in the public university sector from 2001 to 2009 shows a reinforcement of the traditional academic careers' pyramid shape. During this period, the number of full professors increased by 12 percent, associate professors by 18 percent and assistant professors by 56 percent.

What about the Employment of Young Doctorates outside of Higher Education?

The employability of doctorates in Portugal is very high (around 98 percent). Only 0.4 percent are unemployed, which is the lowest unemployment rate of doctorates in the countries assessed by the OECD's survey on the careers of doctoral holders (1.6 percent are inactive). The majority of doctorates (around 86 percent) work in the higher education system, 8.4 percent in the government sector (mostly in state laboratories), whereas employment in the business sector for doctorates is negligible. The number of doctoral holders working in companies represents 4.5 percent of the total number of working PhDs in Portugal (GPEARI/MCTES 2011a), a low percentage when compared to other European countries. In the United Kingdom this figure rises to 50 percent, France 46 percent, Spain 27 percent, and Italy 12 percent (Lafont and Obrador 2010).

Low employability of doctoral holders in the business sector in Portugal stems from several factors. One refers to the underdeveloped scientific and technological capacity and activities performed in firms, which do not feel the need to hire highly qualified personnel (Fontes 2004). Firms also have concerns about the real added-value brought by doctorates, associated with an unawareness of the range and level of skills that doctorates bring to firms (Lafont and Obrador 2010; Melin and Janson 2006). Small and medium enterprises (SME), especially, see doctorates as too theoretical, lacking flexibility and business drive. Large companies with in-house research and development (R&D) departments are more likely than SMEs to target doctorates as employees (Kaipainen et al. 2000; Silva and Leitão 2007). However, the Portuguese economic structure is based on SMEs and only recently has the R&D intensity in Portuguese firms started to develop

In this framework, what has become a new option for young doctorates is to establish their own start-ups (Kolvereid and Moen 1997). The number of such undertakings is not yet high, but it seems to be increasing over time. For example, at the University of Porto, the number of start-ups expanded from 5 in 2007 to 106 in 2012. Similarly, at the University of Minho there were 6 start-ups in 2005, whereas in 2011 there were 43 (CRUP 2012). Other universities reported similar trends. These start-ups represent 362 million euros worth of business in Portugal, and employ 2,226 highly qualified people. Recent analyses in Portugal have shown the strong impact of universities on technology firm creation through university-based start-ups and the fostering of regional social and economic development (Baptista et al. 2011). However, young doctorates feel that their training at the doctoral level does not prepare them with the needed skills to tackle everyday business and administrative matters (Fontes 2004; Gerry, Marques, and Nogueira 2009; Marques, Caraça, and Diz 2010). In this context, universities and university-based R&D units have been invaluable in providing support; for example, they have established incubators benefiting these young doctorate entrepreneurs and their start-up firms (Marques et al. 2010).

Conclusion

In this chapter, we show a country where the higher education system has undergone several reforms, growth, and change, associated with a strong public investment that led to an increasing qualification of academics in both the traditional and nontraditional academic careers. Portuguese universities are increasingly able to offer doctorate programs, award more doctorates per year, produce more scientific outputs, and become more integrated in international scholarly and research networks. Yet, the qualification of the academic and research staff at Portuguese higher education institutions is still relatively low when compared internationally, and requires further effort so that the universities can enhance not only their knowledge base in terms of producing research outputs, but also train, with greater levels of quality, the future workforce that will face the growing complexities of the labor market in globalized learning economies and societies. This is particularly important for the development of the Portuguese economy, and its integration into a global economy, where low levels of formal training and qualifications of business owners and workforce still persist (Baptista et al. 2012).

In this context, the role of young doctorates can be of utmost importance, and their contribution to the development of Portuguese higher education institutions needs to be nurtured and fostered. So far, the higher education system, as the main employer of doctorates, has been able to absorb and integrate the new doctorates into academic and research activities, and the potential problem of unemployment for young doctorate holders is not observed. To the contrary, evidence indicates that Portugal had a doctorate brain-gain situation until at least 2010 (GPEARI/MCTES 2011a).

Still, there is a growing uncertainty in terms of the possibility for young doctorates to enter a stable academic career, and a greater perpetuation of fixed-term positions as "knowledge workers" within universities seems to be occurring. The careers based on moving from research project to research project, and from grant to grant, as analyzed by Araújo (2009), are increasingly regular for the Portuguese scientific system, underlining severe levels of uncertainty, duress, and lack of stability both for present and future careers and family prospects. This limits the future prospects of young PhDs who are intent on pursuing the path of a traditional academic career. Due to the financial crisis, and the enforcement of measures to curtail public expenditure, the recruitment of academic staff for the traditional academic careers at public universities is "frozen" and it is expected to remain as such for years to come. This raises concerns not only for these younger PhDs but also for the universities, as constrained academic job markets tend to lead to the entrenchment of nefarious practices such as academic inbreeding, which still endures despite the growing internationalization and openness of Portuguese academia.

Concurrently, the decreasing number of students entering private higher education—associated with the lower reputation of private institutions, their nearly exclusive focus on teaching, and limited offerings in terms of disciplinary areas—limits the ability of these institutions to provide options for the pursuit of a traditional academic career. The private higher education institutions in Portugal have always constituted a smaller sector in terms of academic staff when compared with the public sector institutions, relying much more on part-time lecturers, fixed-term contract-based arrangements, and lesser-qualified academics to support their scholarship activities.

From an institutional perspective, there is an inability to hire young doctorates on a more regular basis due to institutional budget cuts, salary reductions, and a stagnation of research resources derived from government policies to meet the financial crisis. The decreasing of public funds to foster scientific employment at universities reinforces this trend. It also raises concerns for the future, because the need for further reinforcement of the qualifications of academic staff and promotion of scientific employment to support the growth and quality of the scientific and higher education system is evident. This suggests that it is likely that, despite the need for the academic staff in Portuguese universities to attain higher qualifications, the periods of waiting (in the postdoctoral phase) and the number of recent PhDs in nontraditional academic careers are both likely to increase in the near future.

However, in the larger picture of the evolution of employment in knowledge societies, this trend follows a larger trend of greater uncertainty in the professions in general. It is not exclusive to higher education but seen broadly in the erosion of the "one job for life" career in all professional fields (Bridges 1996).

Note

1. Following the Bologna terminology, the third cycle of study refers to doctoral education.

References

Araújo, E.R. 2009. "With a Rope Around Their Neck: Grant Researchers Living in Suspended Time." *New Technology, Work and Employment* 24(3): 230–242.

Araújo, E., and P. Sousa. 2007. *Ser bolseiro em Portugal: Breves retratos*. Porto: Ecopy.

Athans, M. 2001. *Portuguese Research Universities: Why Not the Best?* Working paper, Lisbon, Instituto Superior Técnico.

Auriol, L. 2010. "Careers of Doctoral Holders: Employment and Mobility Patterns." In *Working Papers, OECD*. Paris: OECD.

Baptista, R., F. Lima, and J. Mendonça. 2011. "Establishment of Higher Education Institutions and New Firm Entry." *Research Policy* 40(5): 751–760.

Baptista, R., F. Lima, and M.T. Preto. 2012. "How Former Business Owners Fare in the Labor Market? Job Assignment and Earnings." *European Economic Review* 56: 263–276.

Bridges, W. 1996. *How to Prosper in a Workplace Without Jobs*. London: Nicholas Brealey.

CRUP. 2012. *Start Ups: Universidades Gerem Cada Vez Mais Empresas*. http://www.crup.pt/pt/imprensa-e-comunicacao/recortes-de-imprensa/831-start-ups-universidades-geram-cada-vez-mais-empresas.

Delicado, Ana. 2010. "International Mobility of Researchers: Policies, Trends and Impacts." In *Portugal in the era of the knowledge society*, edited by D. Belyaev and Z. Roca, 155–188. Lisbon: Edições Universitárias Lusófonas.

ECFIN. 2010. "Efficiency and Effectiveness of Public Expenditure on Tertiary Education in the EU." In *European Economy: Occasional Papers, ed. European Commission*. Brussels: EC.

EURYDICE. 2010. *National System Overviews on Education Systems in Europe and On-Going Reforms*. Brussels: European Commission.

FCT. 2012a. *Regulations for Advanced Training and Qualification of Human Resources 2012*. http://www.fct.pt/apoios/bolsas/regulamento.phtml.en.

FCT. 2012b. *Advanced Fellowships and Grants*. http://www.fct.pt/apoios/bolsas/index.phtml.en.

FCT Newsletter (2012). http://newsletter.fct.pt/.

Fontes, M. 2004. "Emprego Científico Ou Emprego Para Cientistas? Situação E Perspectivas Do Mercado De Trabalho Para Doutorados em Portugal." Paper presented at the conference *Emprego Científico em Portugal.Que Futuro?* Lisbon.

Gerry, C., C.S. Marques and F. Nogueira. (2009). "Graduates and Business Start-Ups: An Assessment of Entrepreneurial Propensity in a Portuguese University." In *From the University Environment to Academic Entrepreneurs*, edited by Tonis Mets, 35–53. Turku: European Council for Small Business and Entrepreneurship.

GPEARI/MCTES. 2011a. *Fluxos e Situação Profissional Dos Doutorados em Portugal*. Lisbon: MCTES.

GPEARI/MCTES. 2011b. *Docentes Do Ensino Superior: 2001–2009*. Lisbon: MCTES.

GPEARI/MEC. 2011c. *Inscritos No Ensino Superior (2000/01–2010/11)*. Lisbon: MEC.

Hasan, Abrar. 2007. *Independent Legal Status and Universities As Foundations*. Paris: UNICEF.

Heitor, M., and H. Horta. 2012. "Science and Technology in Portugal: From Late Awakening to the Challenge of Knowledge Integrated Communities." In *Higher Education in Portugal 1974–2009: A Nation, a Generation*, edited by Guy Neave and A. Amaral. Dordrecht: Springer.

Heitor, M., and H. Horta. 2013. "Democratizing Higher Education and Access to Science: The Portuguese Reform, 2006–2010," *Higher Education Policy*, doi:10.1057/hep.2013.21

Heitor, M., H. Horta, and J. Mendonça. 2013. "Developing Human Capital and Research Capacity: Science Policies Promoting Brain Gain." *Technological Forecasting and Social Change*. doi:10.1016/j.techfore.2013.07.008

Horta, H. 2008. "On Improving the University Research Base: The Technical University of Lisbon Case in Perspective." *Higher Education Policy* 21: 123–146.

Horta, H. 2012. "Deepening Our Understanding of Academic Inbreeding Effects on Research Information Exchange and Scientific Output: New Insights for Academic Based Research." *Higher Education* 65(4): 487–510.

Horta, Hugo. 2009. "Global and National Prominent Universities: Internationalization, Competitiveness and the Role of the State." *Higher Education* (58): 387–405.

Horta, Hugo. 2010. "The Role of the State in the Internationalization of Universities in Catching-Up Countries: An Analysis of the Portuguese Higher Education System." *Higher Education Policy* (23): 63–81.

Howard Hughes Medical Institute. 2012. "World-class Scientists Chosen for HHMI's First International Early Career Award." *Research News*, January 24, http://www.hhmi.org/news/pdf/iecs20120124.pdf.

Kaipainen, P.O., and S. Ahola. 2000. "Finland." In *Academic Careers: A Comparative Perspective*, edited by Jeroen Huisman and Jeroen Bartelse, 51–58. Enchede: University of Twente: CHEPS.

Kolvereid, L., and O. Moen. 1997. "Entrepreneurship Among Business Graduates: Does a Major in Entrepreneurship Make a Difference?" *Journal of European Industrial Training* 21(4): 154.

Lafont, R., and I. Obrador. 2010. "High-Level Skills Needs of Employers." In *Transferable Skills and Employability for Doctoral Graduates: Survey of the Current Landscape*, edited by Jane Sugars and Ellen Pierce, 29–39. Brussels: European Commission, Directorate General for Education and Culture.

Magalhães, A., A. Veiga, F. Ribeiro, and A. Amaral. 2013. "Governance and Institutional Autonomy: Governing and Governance in Portuguese Higher Education." *Higher Education Policy* 26: 243–262.

Marques, J.P.C., J.M.G. Caraça, and H. Diz. 2010. "Do Business Incubators Function as a Transfer Technology Mechanism from University to Industry? Evidence from Portugal." *Open Business Journal* 3: 15–29.

MCTES. 2011. "Science, Technology and Tertiary Education in Portugal 2011." Paper presented at the *OECD's Seminar on Science, Technology, Innovation and Higher Education Policy Developments in Portugal*, Paris.

Melin, G., and K. Janson. 2006. "What Skills and Knowledge Should a PhD Have? Changing Preconditions for Phd Education and Postdoc Work." in *Formative Years of Scholars*, edited by Ulrich Teichler, 105–118. London: Portland Press.

OECD. 2007. *Tertiary Education in Portugal*. Paris: OECD.

OECD. 2011. *Science, Technology and Industry Scoreboard 2011: Innovation and Growth in Knowledge Economies*. Paris: OECD.

OECD. 2012. *Main Science and Technology Indicators (MSTI): 2011/2 Edition*. Paris: OECD.

Perista H., and A. Silva. 2004. *Science Careers in Portugal*. Lisbon: CESIS, Vicente Mosquete, T. & Trejo.

Pinto, J. 2012. "Cultural and Educational Heritage, Social Structure and Quality of Life." In *Higher education in Portugal 1974–2009*, edited by Guy Neave and Alberto Amaral. Dordrecht: Springer.

Rehman, S., A.A. Gujjar, S.A. Khan, and J. Iqbal. 2009. "Quality of Teaching Faculty in Public Sector Universities in Pakistan as Viewed by Teachers Themselves." *International Online Journal of Educational Sciences* 1(1): 48–63.

Santiago, R., and T. Carvalho. 2008. "Academics in a New Work Environment: The Impact of NPM on Work Conditions." *Higher Education Quarterly* 62(3): 204–223.

Silva, M.J., and J. Leitão. 2007. *What Determines the Entrepreneurial Innovative Capability of Portuguese Industrial Firms?* http://mpra.ub.uni-muenchen.de/5216/.

SNESup. 2011. *Tabela de Vencimentos Para 2011*. http://www.snesup.pt/cgi-bin/getinfos.pl?EEVVEuklZkURspRUwQ.

Soares V.M., and A.R. Trindade. 2004. "The Attractiveness of the Academic Career: Country Report Portugal." In *The International Attractiveness of the Academic Workplace in Europe*, edited by J. Enders and Egbert de Weert, 349–372. Frankfurt/Main: GEW (Gewerkschaft Erziehung und Wissenschaft).

Stephan, P., and J. Ma. 2005. "The Increased Frequency and Duration of the Postdoctorate Career Stage." *American Economic Review* 95(2): 71–75.

Van de Sande, D., L. Ackers, and B. Gill. 2005. *Impact Assessment of the Marie Curie Fellowships under the 4th and 5th Framework Programs of Research and Technological Development of the EU (1994–2002)*. Brussels: European Commission.

Chapter 9

The University Sector in Russia

Young Romantics and Losers Welcome?

Maria Yudkevich

Introduction

The current state of the academic profession in Russia is a subject of great concern for people in academia as well as for policy makers and the general public. During the last several decades, Russian universities have gradually lost their position as an attractive employer and an enterprise of knowledge production on a competitive level with the international academic market. As a consequence, they no longer attract the best and brightest through their doors, as those individuals prefer either further training and an academic career in U.S. or European universities, or a career in the nonacademic labor market.

The distinctive features of the current situation are aging of the faculty, and weak and inadequate training of the new faculty that come to universities. In this chapter we discuss how these features are related to financial, institutional, and infrastructural problems in the Russian university system. In particular, we consider the negative impact of low salaries, the low funding and support for research conducted by universities, inbreeding, counterproductive academic norms, and the adverse selection of faculty. We also discuss the role of low mobility due to lack of infrastructure, social security, and the Moscow-centered organization of the labor market. In conclusion, we describe recent government initiatives to improve the situation with university faculty and to attract recent graduates to academia.

General Characteristics of the Russian Higher Education System

The academic profession in Russia is traditionally divided between the university sector and the nonuniversity sector, the latter represented by the research institutions of the Russian Academy of Sciences. In this chapter we focus on the university sector only.

Currently, the university sector in Russia is not as financially or socially attractive as it used to be during the Soviet period. On average, senior faculty salaries do not provide for a middle-class standard of living. The average salaries for senior faculty are just slightly higher than the average wages of people with a university diploma. For young faculty, the situation is even worse: their salaries are less than the average in the economy (including workers without higher education), and to support themselves they need to either teach in several universities, give private lessons, or have some employment outside academia.

Because the option to apply for a master's or PhD program abroad is becoming more and more common, and political perspectives look more uncertain and unattractive for educated young people in Russia, a smaller number of bright graduates than in the past is choosing to enter a PhD program at their home university or elsewhere in Russia. In general, this contributes to brain-drain, though this is not as significant an issue as it was one or two decades ago.

Russian Higher Education Institutions

At the moment, there are 1,115 institutions in the Russian system of higher education, with 7,049,800 students in total. In the public sector there are 653 institutions (with 2,859,500 students in full-time programs and 2,989,200 students in distance programs). On average, private institutions are smaller and there are 1,201,100 students in that sector now, with only 214,200 students studying full time. While in the public sector, full-time programs capture the larger proportion of enrollments (around 75 percent of students), in the private sector only 25 percent of students are enrolled in full-time programs.

The private sector of the higher education system is associated in general with education of low quality. This is reflected in at least three aspects. First, the student quality is low (Unified State Examination scores for students admitted to privates are significantly lower than for public institutions). Second, infrastructure and material support are quite poor, and expenditures per student are quite low. Finally, the faculty body at these institutions is rather weak—most teachers work part time or are on hourly based contracts while working full time at public higher education institutions.

The aggregate faculty body consists of 324,800 people in public institutions of higher education and 32,000 in the private sector. Because most private institutions do not have their own full-time faculty and attract faculty from public universities on a part-time or hourly contract basis, in this chapter we mainly focus on faculty at public universities.

For a better understanding of the current situation for faculty (in particular, young ones) in Russian higher education institutions, two general features of the Russian academic labor market should be mentioned at the beginning.

First, there is *a deep and centuries-old university academic tradition.* Some universities in different regional centers across Russia are still rather strong despite geographical and labor market disadvantages. In these universities, "scientific schools" could be quite productive, with generations of capable researchers serving as heads of these stable research teams. With almost no competitive pressure from outside (during the Soviet period, universities were not financially able to compete with each other for faculty), universities were able to support and nurture these groups, which consisted at times of several generations of researchers working simultaneously.

The second key feature of the academic labor market worth noting is its *capitals-centered structure.* The majority of universities (especially high-quality research institutions) are situated in Moscow and Saint Petersburg. There are also a number of university centers in different parts of Russia (the most famous and important ones being in Siberia, Krasnoyarsk, and Novosibirsk, founded in the 1950s and 1960s). In addition, there are quite few high-quality educational institutions. As employers, regional universities are also significantly less attractive than those in Moscow and Saint Petersburg—in terms of quality of academic conditions, salaries, access to information, cultural rigidity, and career opportunities for young faculty.

In general there are few economic or social incentives to move from Moscow and Saint Petersburg to accept an entry-rank position at a regional university: people would prefer to find a job outside the academic sector rather than move from these urban centers. On the contrary, able graduates from the regions would be happy (generally) to move to the urban centers, which are associated with better job opportunities. In the Soviet period, there was a mechanism of obligatory work placement for all graduates, which gave the regional academic sector an opportunity to attract many young bright researchers and retain them until they became research leaders themselves. Now, that generation of academics is not young anymore (more precisely, they have reached the third tier of their careers) and soon will no longer serve as the core of their research groups.

During the last two decades, the academic profession within the university sector has experienced significant feminization. While in 1992 (Levin-Stankevich and Saveliev 1996) the majority of faculty members in Russia were men, now men comprise less than half of the faculty body (see Table 9.1). That may be explained, among other reasons, by lower remuneration and the decreasing social status of the academic profession in comparison with the situation two decades ago. However, at higher academic ranks and for administrative posts, men still occupy the clear majority of positions.

Young faculty members (under 30 years of age) only represent about 12 percent of the whole faculty body (see Table 9.2). However, the share of senior faculty is rather large and grew substantially during the last twenty

Table 9.1. Faculty (academic and administrative positions) at Russian public higher education institutions (2009/2010)

			Gender distribution (percentage)	
	Female	Male	Female	Male
Faculty[1]—total				
Thousands	189.2	153.5		
Percent	100	100	55	45
including:				
Rectors	0	0.4	9	91
Vice-rectors, branch directors	0.8	2.3	29	71
Deans	1.1	2.4	37	63
Chair heads	5.2	10.7	37	63
Professors	5.5	17.2	28	72
Associate professors	40.3	41.9	54	46
Senior lecturers	27.7	13.8	71	29
Lecturers, assistants	19.5	11.2	68	32

[1]Full-time faculty, 2009/2010 academic year

Source: "Men and Women in Russia," 2010, Federal State Statistics Service (Rosstat)

Table 9.2. Faculty by age at public higher education institutions (2011)[1]

Age	Number	Percentage
Under 30	35,239	11
From 30 to 39	78,625	25
From 40 to 49	56,839	18
From 50 to 59	65,795	21
60 and over	82,459	26

[1]Full-time faculty, beginning of 2011/2012 academic year

Source: Rosstat (2012)

years (see Sivak and Yudkevich 2013 for comparison). Such a change in the relative size of the different age cohorts could be explained in two ways: on the one hand, incentives for young people to enter the university sector, as we demonstrate later, are quite low today. On the other hand, incentives for senior academics to retire are few, if any. Indeed, even after the age of official retirement most senior faculty prefer to keep their positions and to benefit from getting both pension money and salary.

Doctoral Schools in Russia

In the Russian higher education system, graduate education consists of two separate levels—master's education (*magistratura*, which constitutes two years of coursework and the defense of a master's thesis at the end) and doctoral education (*aspirantura*, which includes work toward a PhD dissertation). The master's level only recently emerged as a separate stage; before Russia joined the Bologna process, the first level of university education included five years of study with the conferring of a specialist diploma on successful completion. So, in many universities, the master's level is considered a "natural way" to continue studies, and universities accept their own baccalaureate program graduates into corresponding master's programs without any admission exams. Most young people now consider master's studies as a necessary part of general higher education, not as a part of academic training, specifically; this is a belief shared by employers, as well. To the contrary, doctoral programs have a long tradition of separate entry exams and separate intakes, and always considered (at least formally) applications from candidates with diplomas from other universities. Now, to enter a PhD program, an applicant should possess either a master's degree or a specialist diploma (which corresponds to five years of study).

More than half of higher education institutions run their own doctoral programs. The share of universities and nonteaching research institutions that run PhD programs is rather stable. In 2011, PhD programs existed in 1,570 institutions—among them, 805 research organizations (mainly institutions of the Academy of Science) and 750 higher education institutions. Each year, the aggregate intake of new PhD candidates is about 50,000 (with 50,582 in 2011 and 54,558 in 2010), while only about 33,000 graduate each year. Only one-third of graduates undertake a dissertation defense (see Table 9.3). So, dropout rates are rather high while defense rates are quite low. How can that be explained?

Although universities are interested in large PhD programs, many PhD candidates do not consider their PhD study as a step toward an academic career. Male students often consider doctoral study as a relatively cheap and safe way to escape obligatory army service. These male students do not even need to defend a PhD thesis to accomplish their goal of getting military service exemption for a few more years of study. Once this study program is completed, most students are already beyond the age of obligatory service. Some other candidates are attracted by the benefits of higher social prestige with which, for many employers, PhD status is associated, and the rather low effort needed to achieve this.

Doctoral schools are crucial in terms of producing both research and new researchers. To understand how the academic system functions and performs one needs to understand how doctoral education is organized. The concept of doctoral education has been imported to Russia from Germany, and has two important features.

First, it does not assume any extra rigorous training in the narrow research field or in broader aspects of the discipline. Doctoral programs

Table 9.3. Graduation rates (with dissertation defense) from Russian doctoral programs (selected years, 2005–2010)

Fields	2000	2005	2006	2007	2008	2009	2010
Natural sciences	330	29.2	27.5	29.4	30.4	31.8	30.8
Engineering	18.7	17.6	17.8	18.2	18.7	18.1	19.8
Social sciences	48.2	53.2	54.7	52.5	50.9	50.1	49.4

Source: Rosstat (Russian Statistical Yearbook, 2011, Federal State Statistics Service)

normally last for three years (four years for the part-time option). Doctoral students are obliged to pass a comprehensive exam in their field after two years.

Second, doctoral training assumes one-on-one work with a scientific adviser on a dissertation. So, the quality of the dissertation and the training in general for each particular candidate is, to a large extent, determined (at least in disciplines that do not require collaboration in groups, like experimental physics or field geology) by the quality of the academic adviser. In those cases when the advisers are deeply integrated into academic networks, their students get full advantage from this situation. On the contrary, weak advisers do not provide their students with adequate training and connections to people in their field.

The situation, however, is starting to change. From the end of 2013, according to the new Law on Education, PhD programs are considered as part of university education (not postuniversity education, as before). PhD candidates will now be considered as students (which was not so until recently) and state educational standards are to be elaborated and approved by the Ministry in the near future. Although some experts believe that an introduction of such standards may improve the quality of education within PhD programs, others are rather skeptical.

Universities get government funding per PhD candidate. However, in many disciplines that do not require any expensive equipment (like social sciences or math), the actual monetary cost of running such a PhD program is substantially lower than for master's and bachelor programs. Universities, therefore, have strong incentives to have large intakes for doctoral programs. At the same time, they do not have substantial external incentives for maintaining quality. Indeed, PhD degrees are granted not by the particular university where the dissertation is defended, but instead by a special State Attestation Committee. Under these circumstances, "adverse selection" may occur (i.e., poor doctoral candidates may easily pass their dissertation defense), because there is huge pressure from the Ministry of Education and Science to keep defense rates at a high level, and there is no individual university reputation associated with any PhD degree (see Akerlof 1970 for more on the phenomenon of "adverse selection").

The situation is also worsened by the fact that there is no national academic market for PhD graduates and the majority among those PhD graduates who choose an academic career will stay at their home university. There is no external validation of quality and no need for graduates to compete with each other on the national level. Therefore, at the university level there is a clear trade-off between quality and quantity, and the choice is quite often made at the expense of quality.

Summing up this discussion of the doctoral education system in Russia, we should stress several key contemporary features. There are extremely large intakes—many people who are enrolled in full-time doctoral programs know from the beginning that they do not want to stay in academia in the future. Substantial portions of those who enter PhD programs just need a PhD degree for use in the future as a signal of quality in the nonacademic labor market. This is easily illustrated by the fact that the flow of people who enter doctoral programs has been growing constantly during the last decade, despite the poor conditions within academia (see Table 9.4). Many experts now are very concerned about the inflation of PhD degrees and by the fact that dissertations and degrees have become a market commodity (a special commission created at the end of 2012 by the Ministry of Education and Science suggested withdrawing some PhD degrees issued by one public university due to revelations of fake dissertation production).

Ways to Enter the University Job Market

One of the features that is important for understanding how entry into academia is organized in Russia is the fact that the academic career for most young people starts not with getting a PhD degree but with entering a PhD program.

Normally, when the head of a chair or department needs a person to teach classes, one of the professors of this chair/department offers this position to one of his or her students. Usually, at the same time (at the beginning of academic year) this student starts a PhD program, with the professor who has nominated the student to teach in the role of scientific adviser. So, such PhD candidates undertake both teaching (in the role of teaching assistant) and research toward the dissertation. Such inbreeding is rather widespread in Russian universities.

The low academic mobility is supported by rather low geographical mobility for highly skilled people between the regions of Russia, in general (which, in turn, is due to infrastructural and social obstacles that make moves from region to region complicated). Inbreeding makes impossible the existence of an open academic market, with consequences in line with the main findings on the impact of inbreeding on academic productivity (Wyer and Conrad 1984; Soler 2011; Eisenberg and Wells 2000). Young people are usually hired from within and there is little or no competition between these newcomers, but rather competition between their research

Table 9.4. Enrollment rates in Russian doctoral programs (selected years, 2005–2010)

	2000	2005	2006	2007	2008	2009	2010	Growth (percentage)
Intakes	**43,100**	**46,896**	**50,462**	**51,633**	**49,638**	**55,540**	**54,558**	1.27
Math and Physics	2,671	2,559	2,490	2,625	2,615	2,998	3,126	1.17
Chemistry	1,009	1,019	1,038	1,114	1,088	1,359	1,185	1.17
Biology	1,913	2,107	2,238	2,266	2,314	2,303	2,398	1.25
Techinical	11,059	11,567	12,583	12,786	11,799	14,244	14,500	1.31
Cultural studies	249	295	375	433	323	391	366	1.47
Psychology	871	1,061	1,202	1,355	1,254	1,374	1,343	1.54
Economics	8,160	8,632	9,211	9,514	9,186	9,975	9,179	1.12
Pedagogy	2,612	2,766	3,409	3,400	3,223	3,642	3,385	1.30
Law	2,123	3,640	3,874	4,020	3,860	4,244	3,914	1.84
Political science	356	645	704	729	645	691	796	2.24
Medicine	2,831	3,052	3,332	3,343	3,300	3,269	3,771	1.33

Source: Rosstat (Russian Statistical Yearbook, 2011, Federal State Statistics Service) advisers or mentors. For a university, there is no way to check the quality of external candidates by relying on various market signals because there are no such market indicators. Although competitive procedures for hiring do exist formally, nobody (neither universities nor candidates) relies on them in reality.

Contracts at Entry Level

There is no tenure or tenure-like (permanent) contracts in the Russian university system. Contracts, in terms of their structure and basic conditions, are identical at all steps of the career ladder. All faculty employment contracts have a finite duration, which can be one, three, or five years.

Thus for entry-level academics there are several contract possibilities. First, a person can have a full-time position at a university with a contract for several years. Normally, a one-year contract is signed first, followed by a three-year contract, and then a five-year contract. If a person is promoted to another rank, the contract duration sequence often starts over again—first one, then three, then five years. The second standard option is a part-time contract. Finally, a person can work at a university department on an hourly teaching contract (which is not a labor contract but rather a service contract that is often related to some particular course). People who work on part-time and hourly contracts are not considered part of the faculty body.

In any case, positions (full time and part time) are attached to the chair (organized around one or several leading professors teaching related disciplines) and assume a certain amount of annual teaching loads. In most universities, only full-time faculty are eligible for grant programs, academic bonuses, and other incentive mechanisms and monetary rewards.

Some general features of university faculty contracts are important. For example, contracts for all academic ranks are presented in the same framework, although the contract conditions may be different for different ranks. Formally, all contracts specify the same rights and obligations for the faculty in quite general terms (Andrushchak and Yudkevich 2012).

All contracts are focused primarily on teaching, not on research. Although there are some that (in rather vague wording) include an explicit requirement for research output, research inputs are not contractually regulated, and time for research is not spelled out in working hours (in contrast to teaching).

Teaching loads for each university rank are regulated by the Ministry of Education and Science, which defines some upper and lower limits. Universities, therefore, fix teaching requirements within these limits. In particular, they determine teaching loads that are the same for the same rank within each university. So, average annual loads for an entry position may vary from 750 to 1,000 hours (including time for grading and other teaching-related activities), while more senior ranks assume 600 to 800 hours of annual teaching. In weekly terms, this means that at least three days are fully packed with teaching plus grading student homework.

The main activities that are counted in this load are: (1) giving lectures; (2) teaching classes, tutorials, lab work; (3) grading different written assignments (including exams and term papers); (4) supervising PhD students.

So, one can see that young faculty are in a somewhat disadvantaged position. Indeed, lectures contribute to the teaching load with a coefficient of 2, so each hour of lecturing adds two hours to the calculated annual load. Young faculty members without a degree are usually teaching classes and seminars, while lectures are given by more senior faculty. So to fulfill the formal teaching load requirement, young people have to teach more.

Senior faculty members supervise PhD students while young faculty (with rare exceptions) do not. Because each PhD student contributes about 50 hours toward the annual teaching load, having three students allows senior professors to cover 25 percent of their teaching responsibilities through this function. Young faculty cannot do that.

Grading exams and term papers are also calculated relatively generously toward the teaching load, so senior faculty prefer to conduct oral examinations, which is a simple way to gain hours. More inefficient work (in term of earning hours toward the annual teaching load), such as seminars and tutorials, is left for young peers. Young faculty, therefore, have to spend significantly more time on teaching than relatively senior faculty members. At the contract level, there are no exemptions from teaching loads. Generally, it is not possible to diminish teaching loads on the basis of research or other obligations.

The choice between full-time and part-time employment can be made by either side. Sometimes (which is often the case for young faculty) there is not enough of a teaching load to justify a full-time position at a given department, so the department head offers a young person a temporary solution to start with a part-time contract while waiting for another position at the department to become vacant. In other cases, a person is employed full time at one university and signs a part-time contract elsewhere. Often, low remuneration at one university pushes a person toward moonlighting.

Salaries at the entry academic rank are substantially lower than at the senior ranks and do not provide enough resources for a basic standard of living. No more than one-third of young academics get regular income from their research activity. Administrative positions and duties do provide good rewards, however, young people seem to be involved in these activities less often than their senior colleagues. Many young faculty have to work as private tutors, take extra teaching loads, and also teach at other universities. A substantial share of "faculty" in private universities is composed of faculty from public universities who must moonlight to achieve an appropriate level of income.

In general, a basic salary within a university is the same for all faculty of the same rank. There is no opportunity (with rare exceptions) for an entry-level faculty member to bargain over the level of salary. Normally, universities also have few resources to pay bonuses, in addition to basic salaries. It is often the student fees that serve as the main (though indirect) source for such payments. So, more than half of faculty do not get any extra bonuses at their main workplace (see Table 9.5).

Table 9.5. Extra payments and internal grants available from universities (percentage)

Extra payments and internal grants within university	Young faculty	Others
	N=206	**N=802**
Extra teaching loads	10	13
High evaluation of teaching by administration	3	10
Bonuses based on research productivity	7	11
Administration duties	6	16
Methodological work (preparing new courses, teaching materials etc.)	6	15
Good student evaluations	2	4
Miscellaneous bonuses	14	26
No extra payments and internal grants	58	38
Grants and bonuses for research	9	13

Source: Monitoring of Education Markets and Organizations, 2011

Note: The yearly "Monitoring of Education Markets and Organizations" study consists of representative surveys of students and their families, school teachers and faculty of colleges and universities, heads of colleges and universities, and employers. It is designed and administered by the Higher School of Economics, with financial support form the Ministry of Education and Science of the Russian Federation.

Even if there are such bonuses, only in 20 percent of cases do they constitute 30 percent to 60 percent of the basic salary. In 40 percent of cases, their amount is 10 percent to 30 percent of the basic salary; in all other cases, bonuses provide the equivalent of less than 10 percent of basic salary. Universities often provide their faculty with some extra benefits (see Table 9.6). It is important to stress, however, that what the university really provides and the level at which people use these opportunities are different for different age cohorts.

When a contract period comes to an end, the university is obliged to make an open call (with announcements published in the general press and on the university website) for the vacant position. To get his or her contract extended, the faculty member must apply for this position. If there are alternative candidates (either from the same university or elsewhere) the candidates compete with each other. Formally, a "sitting" faculty member does not have any advantages over potential external candidates. The academic committee that makes the decision on extension (and compares candidates, if there are any alternatives) is usually an internal body and consists of people from the very same chair. This committee

Table 9.6. University resources and usage (last 3 years, percentage)

	Young faculty		Others	
Resources	Used	Exists, never used	Used	Exists, never used
Free copy services	59.2	19.9	69.7	12.1
Financial support for on-job training	41.3	39.3	48.9	28.7
Grants for conference travel	18.4	39.3	23.4	27.1
Access to electronic libraries	46.1	28.6	51.9	24.2
Support for publishing teaching books, lecture notes or other teaching-related materials within university	34.5	44.7	49.0	29.9
Support for publishing working papers and other scholar papers	23.8	48.5	38.2	33.5
Free of subsidized medical insurance	7.8	22.3	12.5	15.6
Apartments in university, subsidized apartments	4.4	29.6	6.1	18.5

Source: Monitoring of Education Markets and Organizations, 2011

passes its decision to the Faculty Senate (which normally approves this decision if there is no conflict associated with a particular person); the decision is then approved by the University Academic Council. In reality, people do not apply for calls for positions, because nobody believes that an external candidate would be chosen over an internal one. So, if there is at least minimal publishing output (including lecture notes and other teaching materials) and there are no social tensions within the chair, the contract is extended. To some extent, such a practice is similar to what occurs in Argentine universities, where strict formal rules of contract extension and faculty promotion coexist with relaxed implementation in reality (Garcia de Fanelli 2012).

There are basically two types of part-timers in public universities—those who teach at other universities full time and those who would like to work full time but there is not enough of a teaching load. In the latter case, a person is working part time waiting for a moment when new opportunities in terms of extra hours will emerge. Because each position is attributed to a specific chair and specific courses to be filled, chairs are interested in putting more courses into the curriculum to assure the current size of the chair and to encourage the opening of new positions. In the case of senior faculty, some new courses might be introduced in the curriculum just to be able to employ a certain person, while for entry-level faculty, this it is not the case. Part-timers generally receive no special incentives, and are usually discriminated against in terms of salaries and extra benefits.

Contracts in private universities are normally reviewed each year. Often, young people find such jobs via recommendations of their chair head or senior colleagues. These contracts do not assume any research activities or outputs. It is also expected that people teaching in private institutions will not spend extra time there beyond their teaching obligations.

The Role of Social Ties in University Life

Although social ties are important in any organization, they are especially important in Russian academia. There are at least several reasons for this. First, due to extremely low mobility between universities—mobility is more often due to problems experienced at the current workplace than a result of promotion and career growth—many people have a single university career. People associate themselves more with their particular institution than with their discipline as a whole. This means that ties with different people from other universities are rather weak. At the same time, ties within the employing university become more important, and seniority starts playing a major role in access to extra benefits, which often creates a discriminatory atmosphere for the younger generation.

Further, an academic supervisor who is both a mentor in teaching and an adviser in research matters becomes (together with department chair) one of the most important people for the young faculty member. This means that it is important for the young academic to maintain good relationships with them. Young faculty members learn from more senior people within the same department. People value greatly the idea of the "scientific school," that is, a stable research group working for a particular university for a long period and hosting several generations of researchers (that is professors, their former PhD students, and their PhD students in turn) at the same time. For the stability of such schools, personal ties and loyalty are critically important.

Third, there is obviously a lack of transparent information about different outside opportunities. Information about competitive opportunities comes from above, so quite often the faculty administration or chairs are the only possible source of information. In many cases, to apply for external grants, fellowships, or summer school, faculty members need approval or a reference letter from their department.

Last but not least, there is no peer-review culture. All expertise and review processes are, in general, extremely personalized. It is therefore important to maintain good relations with colleagues in order to secure support for one's projects and publication in local journals. Thus, young people often mention the role of personal connections in getting their papers published. Whether this role is really important or not, young people often believe that it is. Young faculty members often use the help of a research adviser, department head, or other colleagues to find a proper journal for publication (Kozmina et al. 2007). Moreover, inbred faculty use this strategy more often than noninbred ones (Sivak and Yudkevich 2009).

Social ties may also be important for young faculty members for promotion and contract extension. Indeed, because in reality all "open" competitive procedures for hiring are often reduced to hiring from within and promoting from within, it is very important for a young person to have someone influential to support his or her candidacy. Such informal support often complements other existing grounds for decision making about the professional advancement of young faculty (such as teaching quality and research results). One of the reasons for this is that each open entry position is attached to a chair and is normally associated with a certain discipline to be taught, and often a certain professor who give lectures within this discipline. Those professors often prefer to choose people to work with on personal grounds, favoring those whom they have previously known as students.

External ties in many cases are less influential. There are no national grant programs in Russia that support institutional cooperation, so such ties are not associated with direct benefits or important resources. Both in teaching and research, faculty (especially inbred ones) rely on the practices and experiences of their "inner circle," considering students and chair colleagues as main reference groups (see Table 9.7).

Ties with the *international community* should also be considered. The degree to which these ties are strong depends greatly on the network connectivity of senior people within the department or chair. In general, one can say that social ties are formed around administrative networks and that administrative governance is more influential than academic influence (see Gouldner 1957, 1958 for definitions, and Grimes and Berger 1970 for further discussion).

In terms of loyalty to the profession, all age cohorts in Russia are rather attached to the university system in general; however, a larger share of young people is ready to consider competitive offers from the nonacademic sector (see Table 9.8).

Table 9.7. Reference groups for teaching (percentage)

What groups are relevant for you in the aspect of your teaching?	Strong	Weak	No impact	Do not know
Students	61	32	6	7
Administration	29	33	17	22
Chair colleagues	62	25	6	7
Colleagues from your university within the same discipline	29	37	17	17
Colleagues from your university	12	34	32	23
Colleagues from other universities	18	33	26	23

N=722

Source: Kozmina et al. (2007)

Table 9.8. Loyalty to profession (*Would you change your job to retain one outside university?* (percentage)

	Young faculty	Other faculty
Yes. However, hard to say an exact salary level	43.7	33.9
No. Regardless the salary level	25.2	36.0

Source: Monitoring of Education Markets and Organizations, 2011.

It is important to stress that salaries, being quite low, obviously are not considered as an important factor that keeps people at their university (see Table 9.9). Indeed, if a person works for the university for low remuneration, it is not a salary, or other direct monetary rewards, that keeps him or her there. The research quality of the team is of little importance for a large share of faculty, who are more attracted by the stable positions offered, the good atmosphere at the workplace, and the good relationships with university administration. Most people (both young and senior) do not see any career perspectives in the short run.

Table 9.9. Factors you find attractive at your work place (percentage)

	Young faculty (N=206)	Senior faculty (N=802)
Good atmosphere at the workplace	57	59
Good working schedule	51	42
High university reputation	24	39
Modern curriculum	10	16
Good relationships with university administration	23	26
Good working conditions at the workplace	10	19
University is not far from the living place	25	17
Good career perspectives	14	8
Research quality of the team	17	21
Moderate teaching loads	5	5
Good students	17	21
Good infrastructure (library, databases, computers etc.)	8	12
High salary	2	4

Source: Monitoring of Education Markets and Organizations, 2011.

Current State of the Young Generation of University Faculty

In most Russian universities, faculty members hold positions that are focused on teaching not on research. In the case of young faculty, in many disciplines the quality of their doctoral education does not allow them to compete at the international level, and there are almost no competitive mechanisms at the national level. Even in research universities teaching loads are such that young people have little time for research.

Just a tiny share of young faculty has international experience during their studies. Although this share has been growing in recent years, it is still too small to have a nonzero systemic impact on the academic environment and norms within Russian universities. The research productivity of faculty, in general (see Table 9.10), is rather low. People tend to publish in local journals, which (in many cases) are not peer-reviewed and are quite often of poor quality. Among inbred faculty, the tendency to publish locally is even more widespread. That is also the case for conference presentations—the entire presentation experience of some faculty often consists of presentations at local conferences organized by the home university with little or no competition for being selected to present a paper.

Table 9.10. Research productivity (*Please indicate whether you had publications and presentations during the last year—2011*) (percentage)

	Young faculty ("Yes" response)	Others ("Yes" response)
Academic papers in Russian-wide (national) journals	23.3	35.0
Academic papers in your university journals	42.2	42.8
Academic papers in other universities journals	20.9	25.1
Working papers published in your university series	4.4	7.7
Working papers published in other university series	2.4	5.0
Book chapters etc.	3.9	12.3
Books	2.9	10.6
Lecture books, teaching notes	12.6	25.6
Other teaching materials (local publishing)	20.9	37.9
Presentation at research conferences within this university	33.5	43.9
Presentation at research conferences outside this university	20.4	34.5

Source: Monitoring of Education Markets and Organizations, 2011.

The level of English proficiency among Russian faculty is, on average, low and does not allow an absolute majority of people to take active part in professional communication with international colleagues. Younger faculty, as a group, have better English skills, however their reading skills are better than their speaking ability, and many have had little professional experience associated with international communication. It also makes it extremely difficult (if not impossible) to attract international students by offering courses in English.

Russian academics' publication activity in English is low, on average, and varies by discipline; it is higher in mathematics, physics, and the natural sciences, while extremely low in the social sciences.

According to faculty surveys (for example, ECS 2011), no more than 15 percent of the entire faculty body took part in summer schools, workshops, faculty exchanges, and research visits during the last three years. This share is the same for junior and senior faculty—both for events in Russia and abroad. As a consequence, people often stay at the periphery of academic networks outside university.

A significant minority of faculty believes that it is ethically possible to accept monetary rewards or gifts directly from their students or their parents. This share (about 15 percent) is the same for different age cohorts. So, there are no age dynamics here: one cannot say that norms are different in different age cohorts. Rather, a new generation is reproducing a common norm of tolerance toward such practices.

According to a survey of university faculty at Russian universities, conducted by the National Research University–Higher School of Economics in November 2011, a substantial proportion of faculty pay for their texts (research papers and conference proceedings) to be published (Yudkevich 2012). In particular, about 40 percent of the 2,800 respondents reported that they had made payments in the range of USD30 to USD800 related to the publication process within the last year, and about a third among those who paid spent more than USD150. One might say that these numbers are not big. However, compared to Russia's relatively low faculty salaries, these expenditures are not that small. There is also no difference between junior (younger) and senior academics in this regard (Yudkevich 2012).

One can say that there are no clear career pathways for young faculty in Russian universities. People do not see clear perspectives for real changes (at least in the short term) in their professional situations (see Table 9.11). For most of them, there is no plan for mobility (either within Russia or abroad), and no plans to find a job outside the university sector.

Table 9.11. Career expectations (*What changes might you expect in next 3 years?*) (percentage)

	Young faculty (N=206)	Others (N=802)
To get next academic rank	43	20
To achieve (higher) administrative status	8	8
To move to better university	3	4
To move to non-academic job	11	4
Take part in on-job training	27	26
Take job in another city within Russia	2	2
Take job abroad	7	5
Nothing mentioned	17	33

Source: Monitoring of Education Markets and Organizations, 2011.

Many young people expect to move up to a higher academic rank (often associated with obtaining a PhD degree or spending a sufficient number of years within one university). There is not much ambition associated with an academic career, and many people do not see any career opportunities associated with their academic talents and skills. Rather, they see opportunities to "get ahead" as a function primarily of seniority and administrative status within their institution.

Main Challenges and Future Trends

In recent years, some positive shifts can be seen in government policy concerning support for the university sector and the attraction of the best young people to academia. It is worth mentioning the most important of these efforts: establishment of international research centers and changes in international validation procedures.

In the year 2010 a new national competition was launched by the government to establish a number of research centers headed by international scholars (about fifty such centers exist across the country at the moment). The idea behind these centers is to bring international scholars into the Russian university sector and to attract young people into strong research environments, cultivating centers for positive academic growth.

The strict requirements for such centers include a long stay in Russia for the international leader of the team (not less than four months during two consecutive years), and the involvement of several students and PhD candidates as core members of the team. The Russian government provided generous financial support for these centers (each annual center's budget is about USD2 million), which allows for competitive salaries both for Russian and international scholars, travel support, and necessary infrastructure and equipment for proper functioning of these centers. In universities that are poorly equipped and always suffering from low budgets, the creation of such a lab also provides broader institutional benefits, in terms of subscriptions to databases, electronic libraries, and access to modern computer equipment.

The changes in international validation procedures are also important. Validation of international degrees in Russia is a very complicated procedure. In fact, to get a non-Russian PhD degree validated in Russia, applicants must translate their thesis into Russian in the appropriate format and complete copious paperwork before submitting all documentation to a special State Committee. This creates few incentives for Russians educated abroad to come back after getting a PhD degree outside Russia. Without a validated degree, otherwise qualified individuals inevitably experience problems securing an associate professor position and supervising PhD students. Recently, there was a positive shift: a presidential decree determined a list of 300 universities across the world whose degrees will be accepted without this special validation procedure. To be included on the list, the university should appear sufficiently high on the *Times Higher Education*, QS, and Shanghai rankings conducted in recent years.

There are two lingering concerns about these new developments. First, although these conditions about ranking position sound rather reasonable, they are related to overall quality of institutions, and may have nothing to do with the quality of a particular program completed by the PhD degree holder. Second, the list of official documents that need to be presented as a proof of the PhD degree has not been announced (half a year after the decree was signed). Some administrative problems are anticipated here, as well, given that Russian legal tradition assumes that all official documents with legal status (such as diplomas) should have an official institution stamp (seal), which does not exist at all in some countries.

Despite the encouraging developments noted earlier, there are many challenges for universities in Russia with respect to attracting the best young people to academia. For example, there are more negative than positive incentives today for young people to start academic careers in Russia. The most important of these is that salaries at the entry level do not provide enough money for a basic standard of living. This means that people entering academia even at their most productive period still have to spend considerable time and effort on other activities to secure extra income. Career concerns are also important: low mobility and the importance of seniority make the academic sector relatively less attractive than other parts of the labor market.

In many fields (e.g., social sciences) Russian universities cannot deliver education at the graduate level that is competitive on the international academic market. So, an important challenge is to send people to other universities (in United States and Europe) and also bring (back) to Russia young people with good PhD training.

The measures mentioned earlier concern mostly the best research universities in the country (with many of them located in the two Russian metropoles—Moscow and Saint Petersburg). However, improving the conditions for young faculty in the majority of Russian universities is a big challenge. In addition to many other issues, the social factor plays a critical role here. Although the best research universities in Russia are able to provide support for academic mobility and further research training (sending young people abroad for conferences, summer schools, or research visits), the majority of universities and other higher education institutions are not able to provide the financial, academic, and infrastructural conditions to foster competitive research careers. Those young people who start working in these "lower tier" institutions, in most cases, have little chance for career mobility or doing anything apart from teaching. Although they are formally supposed to do research, in reality they are overloaded by teaching and have no opportunities to build a competitive research career.

Legal limitations play an important role in this situation. According to Russian labor law, there is no such thing as tenure contracts (with long-term guarantees). So, universities that might attract top-level people (particularly from abroad) for tenure-track positions cannot legally offer them such arrangements. They can only rely on their international academic market reputation as good employers. This is still a weak proposition, however, given, for example, the Russian pension system does not allow international scholars working in Russia to contribute toward their pensions. This makes the future prospects of non-Russian academics uncertain. For now, there are about five universities across Russia that recently started international recruitment efforts. However, for this number to grow, these limitations must be overcome.

The absence of a national academic market and extremely low academic and geographic mobility reproduce inbreeding, which is harmful for the academic environment within universities and detrimental to research productivity. Inbreeding may cause positive results in the best universities, but in the case of weak academic environments it has clear negative consequences.

Systemic improvement should be targeted in several directions. First, there is a need for doctoral education reform. The quality of doctoral education will not be improved without several measures that are unpopular in the university sector. In particular, only high-quality universities should have a right to run graduate programs; intakes should be reduced, and the practice of working full time outside academia during graduate studies should be abolished. Certainly the abolition of this external employment cannot occur without extra funds being provided for stipends and fellowships. This means that improved quality standards for PhD theses should also be introduced. As one of the obvious means for this, many experts consider it crucial to introduce university PhD diplomas in place of the single state PhD diploma, which does not allow reputational mechanisms to function effectively. Such a reform is currently under discussion in the Ministry of Education and Science.

The system of academic salaries should be also changed. Until academic salaries provide a comfortable standard of living and eliminate the need for people to seek outside employment that encroaches on their academic activities, there is no chance to bring the "best and brightest" to the university sector and provide them the proper conditions for professional growth. Salary policy should reward research and teaching excellence, and provide incentives for people to learn. It should also make universities capable of attracting qualified professionals for part-time teaching as experts (who are able to share their work experience).

Finally, certain steps should be taken to build a national academic market with the transparent and competitive mechanisms for recruitment that are associated with much lower levels of inbreeding. This academic market should be viewed as an integral part of the international academic labor market. Barriers for international recruitment should be abolished, or at least significantly diminished. This implies both administrative and legal changes.

Although part-time and contract appointments are also important for university sustainability, they should not be relied on at the expense of proper academic contracts for the core faculty body. Being an important part of the higher education system in many countries, part-time arrangements should only support a healthy system of full-time academic contracts.

Our analysis shows that young faculty in Russian universities, in general, reproduce academic norms and share the patterns of teaching and research activities and standards maintained by their more senior colleagues. To open the university system toward the global academic market and to secure Russia's competitive position in the global academic university race, a new generation of academics should be provided with different incentives and working conditions.

Acknowledgment

The author thanks Gregory Androushchak for fruitful discussions and Alexander Novikov for assistance with data collection.

References

Akerlof, George A. 1970. "The market for 'Lemons': Quality Uncertainty and the Market Mechanism." *Quarterly Journal of Economics* 84(3): 488–500.

Altbach, Philip G., ed. 2013. *The Global Future of Higher Education and the Academic Profession: The BRICs and the United States*. New York: Palgrave Macmillan.

Andrushchak, Gregory, and Maria Yudkevich. 2012. "Russian Higher Education: Salaries and Contracts." In *Paying the Professoriate. A Global Comparison of Compensations and Contracts*, edited by Philip G. Altbach, Liz Reisberg, Maria Yudkevich, Gregory Androushchak, and Iván F. Pacheco, 265–279. New York and London: Routledge.

Eisenberg, Theodore, and Martin T. Wells. 2000. "Inbreeding in Law School Hiring: Assessing the Performance of Faculty Hired from Within." *Journal of Legal Studies* 29(1): 369–388.

Fanelli, de Garcia A. 2012. "Labor Contracts and Economic Incentives for Argentine University Faculty." In *Paying the Professoriate: A Global Comparison of Compensations and Contracts*, edited by Philip G. Altbach, Liz Reisberg, Maria Yudkevich, Gregory Androushchak, and Iván F. Pacheco, 37–49. New York and London: Routledge.

Gouldner, Alvin W. 1957. "Cosmopolitans and Locals: Toward an Analysis of Latent Social Roles—I." *Administrative Science Quarterly* 2: 281–306.

Gouldner, Alvin W. 1958. "Cosmopolitans and Locals: Toward an Analysis of Latent Social Roles—II." *Administrative Science Quarterly* 2: 444–480.

Grimes, Andrew J., and Philip K. Berger. 1970. "Cosmopolitan-Local: Evaluation of the Construct." *Administrative Science Quarterly* 15: 407–416.

Kozmina, Yana Y., Anna A. Panova, and Maria M. Yudkevich. 2007. *Survey of Economics Departments at St. Petersburg Higher Education Institutions.* Moscow: Vershina (in Russian).

Levin-Stankevich, Brian L., and Alexander Savelyev. 1996. "The Academic Profession in Russia." In *The International Academic Profession: Portraits of Fourteen Countries*, edited by Philip.G. Altbach. Princeton, NJ: Carnegie Foundation.

Sivak, Elizaveta, and Maria Yudkevich. 2009. "Academic Inbreeding: Pro and Contra." *Voprosy Obrazovania* 1(36): 170–187 (in Russian).

Sivak, Elizaveta, and Maria Yudkevich. 2013 "Academic Profession in a Comparative Perspective: 1992–2012." *Foresight-Russia* 7(3): 38–47 (in Russian).

Soler, Manuel. 2001. "How Inbreeding Affects Productivity in Europe." *Nature* 411: 132.

Wyer, Jean C., and Clifton F. Conrad. 1984. "Institutional Inbreeding Reexamined." *American Educational Research Journal* 21(1): 213–225.

Yudkevich, Maria. 2012. "Publication for Money: What Creates the Market for Paid Academic Journals?" *Inside Higher Education*. http://www.insidehighered.com/blogs/world-view/publications-money-what-creates-market-paid-academic-journals#ixzz28WHlsIdM.

Zakharova, Alexandra, and Grigory Shabanov. 2012. "More Female Bosses Worldwide." *Voice of Russia*. http://english.ruvr.ru/2012_03_08/67888878/.

Chapter 10

Challenges and Opportunities for New Faculty in South African Higher Education

Chika Sehoole and Emmanuel Oluseun Ojo

Introduction

A strong, well-educated, and committed professoriate is a necessary requisite to guarantee the future of academia. Given the fact that by its nature the academic profession is finite in the supply of labor, and that labor laws that govern recruitment of academics in each country have to be followed, there is often a constant need to replace the aging and retiring professors. Invariably, the future of the university lies in the younger generation of faculty and how they are treated has both professional and administrative resonance. Universities are also faced with the challenge of attracting and retaining the best minds. It is against this background that this chapter on the future of South African universities based on the current status of young academics is presented. This chapter analyzes and discusses the situation of young faculty by drawing from general faculty profile trends, the academic labor market, as well as institutional realities and challenges with particular focus on young faculty.

Some of the key findings and observations concerning the status of young faculty in South Africa include the fact that in 2011 there were about 49,983 academics employed in South African universities, of which 19,144 or 38 percent are considered young faculty, that is, 35 years of age and below. About 9,476 (49.5 percent) of the young faculty were Black (these include three racial groups other than White, namely African,

Indian and Colored[1]). Only 1,059 (5.5 percent) of these young faculty have PhDs, with the majority (696 or 65.7 percent) being White. Similarly, women constituted a majority 10,240 (52 percent) of young faculty. A sizable number representing 78 percent (829) of the young faculty with PhDs work in traditional universities in South Africa, of which the majority are in the top five research universities.

In general, the majority of young faculty start their university careers without the PhD in hand and this weakens their bargaining power for better salaries. Two main strategies are used in recruiting young academics in South Africa. The first uses an internal "grow your own timber" strategy of established academics identifying and giving outstanding postgraduate students some teaching/research assistantship as a litmus test to ascertain their interest and subsequent assimilation into the faculty. The second strategy is external advertisement of vacancies and by attracting postdoctoral fellows into the universities. Mentorship initiatives are currently being employed by many South African universities as a way of inducting and settling new faculty into the profession.

This study used qualitative and quantitative methods of data collection, and included a literature review and documentary analysis of official university documents from various institutions as well as government policy documents. Though the analysis of the statistics of the entire faculty in higher education in South Africa is based on 2010 data, that of the young faculty (35 years of age and below) is based on 2011 data. This is due to nonavailability of reliable data for analytical purposes for both years.

Features of the South African Higher Education System

South African higher education was, until the mergers that started in 2002, characterized as a binary system comprised of fifteen technikons (polytechnics) and twenty-one universities. Technikons were vocationally oriented institutions that had evolved out of colleges of advanced technical education (CATES), which historically specialized in offering diploma and certificate courses that were geared to the needs of industry. It was only in 1993 that technikons were allowed to offer degree programs including doctoral programs (Sehoole 2005). As a result of their emphasis on nondegree programs, it was never a requirement for staff employed in technikons to have degrees or postgraduate qualifications. However, having a degree or a postgraduate qualification was an added advantage. This phenomenon later had an impact on the profile of staff in higher education after the mergers, as the "underqualified" staff from the technikons became part of the university system when technikons were merged and became universities of technology (UoTs).

On the other hand, universities always had degree-granting status up to the doctoral level. Universities in South Africa under apartheid and in the premerger period were differentiated according to their history and their mission. Under apartheid, universities were classified into what came to be known as historically white universities (HWUs) and historically black universities (HBUs) based on their purpose and the racial groups they were created to serve. Historically black universities were created as teaching institutions with an emphasis on undergraduate programs. As a result, the majority of faculty employed in these institutions never had doctoral qualifications. On the other hand, the majority of historically white institutions had both teaching and research mandates, and where a research mandate did not exist at inception this became embraced with time. Given the postgraduate mandate that many historically white institutions carried, including the offering of master's and doctoral programs, it was a common practice to have faculty members employed with master's or doctoral qualifications. Where these did not exist at the time of employment, it was expected that this would become a priority for staff to ensure that they attain them. As a result, faculty in historically white universities would be more qualified than their counterparts in historically black universities.

The outcome of the mergers of higher education institutions after 2002 was the creation of a single coordinated higher education system that was made of twenty-three universities, which are differentiated into eleven traditional universities, six comprehensive universities, and six universities of technology. Traditional universities are those that were not affected by mergers, although some of them incorporated some entities of higher education institutions during the merger process, without this having any impact on their identities. Universities of technology were established out of a merger of two or three technikons, whereas comprehensive universities were established out of a merger of a university and a technikon (DOE 2001). The mergers brought to an end the existence of technikons.

The structure of the academic profession in South Africa is comprised of five ranks: junior lecturer, lecturer, senior lecturer, associate professor, and professor. Those who are appointed at the junior lecturer rank would either be busy working on their master's degrees or beginning their doctoral degrees. Some traditional universities such as the University of

Pretoria have as from 2013 abolished the junior lecturer rank in line with their mission of becoming research-intensive universities. Given the low number of people with PhDs, most universities do not demand a PhD at entry level. An appointment at the lecturer level would normally require a minimum of a master's qualification. Appointment as a senior lecturer requires a PhD and proven track record of research outputs in the form of peer-reviewed journal articles or book publications and evidence of involvement in postgraduate supervision. The minimum qualification for appointment as an associate professor and full professor is a PhD plus teaching and research experience beyond the requirement of a senior lecturer rank. In 2011, about 26 young faculty were appointed to the level of full professor and another 126 young faculty were appointed to the level of associate professor; the majority of young faculty were therefore employed at lecturer and junior lecturer levels. These entry requirements to faculty appointments apply to academics irrespective of age.

The South African postgraduate education system consists of three phases: a one-year honors degree (premaster's, offered between a bachelor and master's degree); a master's degree, normally offered over a two-year period; and a PhD. The master's degree provides the option of a "taught" master's or a research master's, At the pinnacle of the postgraduate education system in South Africa is the PhD degree, which as a rule is offered over a four-year period for full-time students, or over a five- to six-year period if pursued part time.

Table 10.1 shows that there are many staff members working in universities without master's and doctoral degrees. This depicts a phenomenon where the majority of academic staff is in university employment even as they upgrade their qualifications. This phenomenon, as explained by Koen (2007), is a peculiar characteristic of academic staff in South Africa, which until recently did not require the possession of a PhD as the minimum requirement for an academic job.

Table 10.2 also shows that 22.4 percent of academic and research staff were 30 years old and younger. This constitutes a 3 percent decrease from the 2005 count. On the other hand, the number of academic and research staff over the age of 50 grew from 16.7 percent to 18.2 percent, whereas those 60 years and older grew from 6.1 percent in 2005 to 9.1 percent in 2010. This shows that the profile of South African academics is aging and there will be a need to grow a new generation of young faculty to replace the aging and retiring faculty.

A study by the Council on Higher Education (2012) shows there is a decrease in the number of permanent positions being made available in

Table 10.1. Headcount of instructional and research staff qualifications level by race and across all age groups 2010

	UG Dip/Cert	UG Degree	PG up to Honors	Masters	Doctoral	Other*	Total
African	529	2,096	1,739	2,903	1,721	4,605	13,593
Colored	154	393	317	587	377	570	2,398
Indian	43	696	412	812	587	1,383	3,933
White	560	3, 144	2, 867	5, 326	6, 394	7, 780	26,071
Total	1,286	6,329	5,335	9,628	9,079	14,338	**45,995**

(*Note:* Data sourced from CHE 2012)

*Other includes all unknown and qualifications labelled as other,

Table 10.2. Headcount instruction and research staff members by age grouping between from 2005 and 2010

Age	2005	%	2010	%
<30	11,004	25.7	10,912	22.4
30–39	10,080	21.0	11,364	23.3
40–49	9,722	22.7	10,950	22.5
50–59	7,225	16.9	8,890	18.2
>=60	2624	6.1	4463	9.1
Total	33,430	100	46,579	100

M (*Note:* Data sourced from CHE 2012)

universities. Of all positions, the proportion of temporary appointments increased from 62 percent in 2005 to 64 percent in 2010 (CHE 2012, 40). Similarly, the proportion of women faculty increased from 44 percent in 2005 to 46 percent in 2010. Of the 19,144 young faculty employed in South African universities, the majority (12,856 or 67 percent) are employed on a temporary, part-time basis, while a meager 3,746 (19.6 percent) are employed on a permanent full-time basis. These data indicate that the South African higher education system not only relies on part-time faculty, but that young faculty below the age of 35 are disproportionately hired into part-time positions.

The Profile and Status of Young Faculty in South African Higher Education

In 2011 there were about 49,983 academics employed in South African universities, of whom 19,144 or 38 percent are considered young faculty, that is, 35 years of age and younger. Of this total number, 1,059 (5.5 percent) had doctoral qualifications, with about 4,287 (22.4 percent) having bachelor's degree and below as their highest qualifications. The prevalence of such low qualifications may be the legacy of the technikons, which historically never required a degree or postgraduate qualification as a prerequisite for employment. Tables 10.3 to 10.5 present the profile and status of young academics across institutional types, academic rank, and qualifications, respectively.

Table 10.3. Headcount of young faculty in South African universities according to type of institution

Type of Institution	PHD	Master's	Honors	Bachelors	Diploma	Certificate	Other	Total / (%)
Traditional University	829	1,956	1,578	2,286	202	354	6,279	13,484 (70.4)
Comprehensive University	163	543	677	482	78	3	1,733	3,679 (19.2)
University of Technology (UoT)	67	383	166	657	194	30	484	1,981 (10.3)
Total/Percent (%)	1,059 (5.5)	2,882 (15.1)	2,421 (12.6)	3,425 (17.9)	474 (2.5)	387 (2)	8,496 (44.4)	19,144 (100)

(*Note:* Data sourced from the Department of Higher Education and Training, HEMIS system, 2012).

According to Table 10.3 above, of the 19,144 young faculty employed in these institutions, 70.4 percent (13,484) were employed in traditional universities, 19.2 percent (3,679) in comprehensive universities, and 10.3 percent (1981) in universities of technology (UOTs). This suggests that traditional universities (which include the top five research universities, namely the Universities of Pretoria, Cape Town, Witwatersrand, KwaZulu-Natal, and Stellenbosch University) employ more young faculty than other institutional types. Given the fact that many of these offer a number of master's and doctoral programs, these young faculty could also be graduate students who have been appointed on part-time or temporary bases as they work through their studies. As Table 10.4 shows, about 12,952 (67.7 percent) of all young faculty were employed on a part-time basis.

In terms of their academic qualifications, Table 10.4 further depicts that 1,059 (5.5 percent) of these young faculty had PhDs, 2,882 (15 percent) master's degrees, 2,421 (12.6 percent) honors, and 3,425 (17.9 percent) had bachelor's degrees as their highest qualifications. What is of concern is that about 6,707 (or 35 percent) have qualifications below the master's degree, and some working in universities have only diplomas and certificates. Many of these are more likely to have been employed in the former technikons, which have evolved into universities of technology (UoTs) as a result of mergers. Of the entire group of 19,144 young academics, only 26 (0.1 percent) and 122 (0.6 percent) have already attained the status of full professor and associate professor, respectively (see Table 10.5). The qualifications of

Table 10.4. Headcount of young faculty in South African universities according to academic qualifications and type of employment

Qualifications	Full-Time	Part-Time	%	Total
PhD	786	273	5.5	1,059
Master's	1,742	1,140	15.1	2,882
Honors	922	1,499	12.6	2,421
Bachelors	1,302	2,123	17.9	3,425
Diploma	182	292	2.5	474
Certificate	15	372	2	387
Other/Unknown Qualifications	1,243	7,253	44.4	8,496
Total	**6,192 (32.3%)**	**12,952 (67.7%)**	**100%**	**19,144**

(*Note:* Data sourced from the Department of Higher Education and Training, HEMIS system, 2012).

Table 10.5. Headcount of young faculty in South African universities according to rank

Ranks	Full-Time	Part-Time	%	Total
Professor	20	6	0.1	26
Associate Professor	94	28	0.6	122
Senior Lecturer	781	103	4.6	884
Lecturer	2,827	1,983	25.1	4,810
Junior Lecturer	1,696	881	13.5	2,577
Below Junior Lecturer	145	2,220	12.4	2,365
Others	629	7,731	43.7	8,360
Total	**6,192**	**12,952**	**100%**	**19,144**

(*Note:* Data sourced from the Department of Higher Education and Training, HEMIS system, 2012).

8,496 (44 percent) fall under other categories, whose qualifications or rank (as indicated below) could not be confirmed. These could be individuals who are employed as researchers and research assistants and their qualifications may not be relevant to the traditional academic ranks used by universities. Attempts to get an account of the qualifications for this category of staff were unsuccessful.

Comparing Tables 10.4 and 10.5, one sees that many of the under-35 faculty were employed at lecturer (4,810) and junior lecturer (2,577) levels, representing 38.6 percent of the entire young faculty population. These are the main entry levels into academia in South Africa. The concentration of employment at these levels could be related to the levels of the qualifications of young faculty, as presented in Table 10.4. These statistics point to the fact that the lower the level of qualifications, the more concentrated the numbers of junior lecturers. Junior lecturers are normally recruited for teaching purposes and many of them still ultimately have to obtain postgraduate qualifications toward a PhD. Because they do not have relevant research or publication experience at the time of their recruitment, they would be offered some of the lowest salaries available. This is a problem for the academic profession in South Africa and interventions to increase the PhD pool and to attract PhD graduates to academia, which is discussed later, are important to address this problem. The implications of having such a large number of staff at such low post levels and qualifications, who at the same time are busy with postgraduate studies, are that these faculty cannot effectively participate in two fundamental activities of the academic profession, namely, research production and postgraduate supervision. This statistic further indicates the extent to which universities in South Africa rely on academics with qualifications below a PhD. This has an impact on the capacity of these institutions to deliver high-impact research and postgraduate output, as these require staff with qualifications at the doctoral level as a minimum requirement.

The Academy of Science for South Africa (ASSAf, 2009) report indicates that the supervisory capacity—explained in terms of (1) the share of permanent academic staff in possession of doctoral degrees, and (2) the ratio of enrolled doctoral students to permanent academic staff with a doctoral qualification—in universities is thinly stretched. According to the study, in 2007 41 percent of permanent academics among traditional universities' staff had doctoral degrees. In the universities of technology, 12 percent of permanent academics held doctoral degrees, and 27 percent of permanent staff in comprehensive universities held this terminal degree. In total, only 33 percent of academics across the sector had PhDs. (See Figure 10.1.)

The low qualification level of many academics in general—and those under the age of 35, in particular—has a huge impact on remuneration levels, and the importance of competitive remuneration cannot be overlooked. In a previous study on the "future of the professoriate," Sehoole (2012) noted that the minimum qualification for a lecturer in a research intensive university is a master's or PhD qualification. As for an associate professor and full professor, the necessary requirement is a PhD plus teaching and research experience. Multiple indicators—such as qualifications, experience, and skill levels; requirements for internal equity and fairness; strategic priorities; market profiles of individual staff; employment equity; and benchmarks—are used in the recruitment and hiring of academics. The combinations of these critical factors are considered in determining the starting salary of academics. Given that many would generally not have a PhD qualification, research publications, or research networks (which carry weight in the negotiation of a competitive salary package), many applicants would not have a strong bargaining position and, as such, start at a lower salary. The 2010 salary data across institutions show that average salaries for lecturers and junior lecturers, which are ranks at which the majority of academics under the age of 35 are employed, are very low.

The lack of a PhD, combined with the need to possess other relevant skills—such as research experience and a record of postgraduate

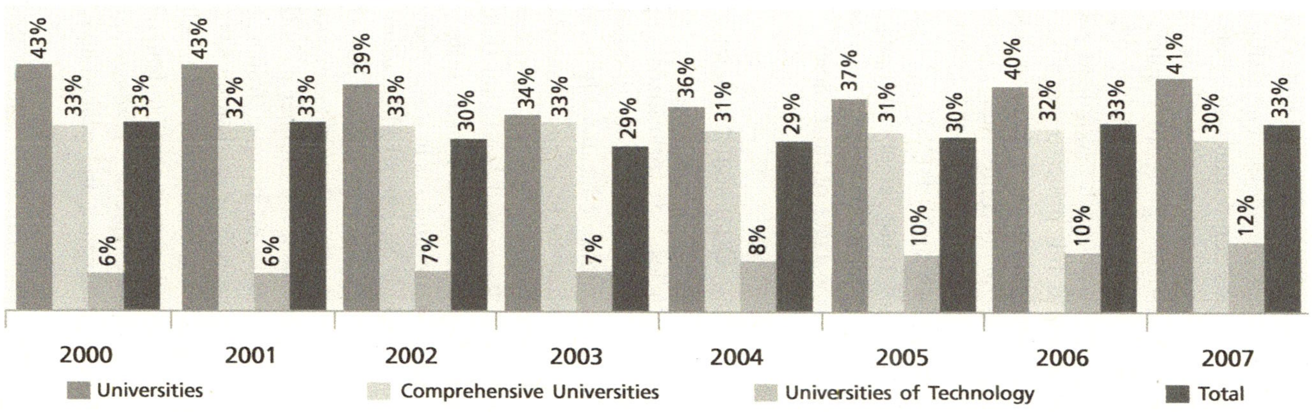

Note: Data sourced from ASSAF. "The Phd Study: Consensus Report." Pretoria: Academy of Science of South Africa, 2010.

Figure 10.1. Share of permanent academic staff at public higher education institutions in South Africa with a doctoral qualification, by university classification, 2000–2007 supervision—impact greatly on opportunities for promotion. For example, in many institutions, especially research-intensive universities, promotion from a lecturer to senior lecturer position requires completion of a PhD, evidence of teaching outputs, and supervision of graduate students. Promotion from senior lecturer to associate professor requires evidence of supervision of master's and doctoral students through to degree completion, book publications, and publications in accredited journals. Promotion from associate professor to full professor requires evidence of sustained teaching and research outputs in the form of successful supervision of master's and doctoral students to completion, sustained publication record as evidenced by books and journal articles, and outstanding research recognition as demonstrated by NRF (National Research Foundation) rating. The combination of these factors indicates the adverse circumstances young faculty face, in terms of opportunities for promotion and career advancement in the early stages of their career.

Initiatives to Address the Low Qualification Base of Faculty

Universities and government agencies have prioritized improving the pool of doctoral candidates and graduates in order to address this low qualification level of academics in higher education. In recent years the government has launched two initiatives to improve the production of PhD graduates. In 2005, the government, through its research support and funding agency, the National Research Foundation (NRF), initiated the South African PhD Project, which was a postgraduate student support program aimed at attracting more students to the world of academia. Other activities of the project include an annual PhD recruitment drive, creation of PhD peer-support groups, and allocation of bursaries for local and international PhD study opportunities. According to Moodie (2010), when the project was launched in 2005, the number of NRF-supported PhD students increased by more than 60 percent, from 1,360 in 2004 to 2,186 in 2005. The project set a target of graduating 6,000 doctorates annually by 2025 and 3,000 in science, engineering, and technology disciplines by 2018, which seems an almost impossible feat when looking at the current numbers. The number of doctoral graduates grew to 1,274 in 2007 when this initial cohort graduated, and peaked at 1,576 in 2011 (DHET 2012).

Universities also have their own initiatives to increase the pool of PhD graduates among their staff members. These include opportunities for staff members with master's degrees to apply for study leave or time off from their teaching responsibilities to enable them to concentrate on their doctoral studies, with a view to accelerating the completion time. Some of the strategies proposed are to use overseas study opportunities to supplement local capacity. Presenting the extracts of an interview with Michael Cherry, professor of zoology at the University of Stellenbosch and editor-in-chief of the *South African Journal of Science* (SAJS), Moodie (2010) noted Cherry's opinion that the suggestion to send many South Africans abroad to obtain their doctorates is "impractical" for three reasons: (1) funding constraints make studying overseas an unlikely option for most candidates; (2) the cost analysis for extending such a scheme on a large scale is not clearly presented; and (3) it is difficult to imagine how it could be more cost-effective for government than if such students were funded locally (Moodie 2010). Moreover, the ASSAf (2009) report found that 18 percent of South Africa's PhD cohort is made up of students from other African countries, mostly because studying in South Africa is cheaper than studying at overseas institutions. Cherry argues that it is unlikely that foreign governments would fund the training of South African doctoral students abroad, therefore getting a domestic PhD remains the most reasonable choice for young faculty.

As a result of a small pool of academics with PhD qualifications in South African universities, there is a strain on supervisory capacity resulting in some students taking longer to complete their postgraduate qualifications. The ASSAf (2009) study on doctoral education shows the average time to degree completion standing at around 4.8 years in 2007. According to the report, South African students take longer to complete, at 4.9 years, compared to international students, who take 4.5 years on average to complete their degrees. The study observes that students spend (on average) about five years on their degrees, and they are about 33 years old (in the natural and agricultural sciences) and 41 years old (in the social sciences and humanities) when first enrolling for a doctoral degree. This explains why most South African graduates are relatively mature when they eventually obtain their PhDs. The average age of doctoral students at graduation was 40 in 2007. This varied across disciplines and fields—for example, 35.3 years of age in engineering sciences, materials and technologies, and 44.5 years of age in the social sciences, broadly speaking. This differentiation in age at completion is also visible depending on the classification of university—that is, 39.5 years at traditional and comprehensive universities and 45 years at the universities of technology. The older age profile of graduates at universities of technology

(UOTs) may suggest that the majority of these individuals are staff members who were working in the former technikons, which never required a doctoral qualification. With the merger of technikons and the creation of universities of technology, pressure was put on academics in UOTs to have a PhD as a necessary requirement for working at a South African university. The ASSAf (2009) study shows that the share of permanent academic staff with doctoral qualification at universities of technology increased from 5 percent in 2005 to 12 percent in 2010. This increase could either be a result of staff at these universities enrolling for and obtaining doctoral qualifications or these universities recruiting staff who already have doctoral qualifications.

South Africa's Academic Labor Market

This section describes the general characteristics of the South African higher education system in order to provide the context for the significance of young faculty. The nature of the academic labor market cannot be dissociated from the broader characteristics of the South African labor market linked to the former apartheid political economy. Higher education, just like any other sector under apartheid, was used to promote apartheid's ideology and policy of racial segregation based on white supremacy. Race became the criteria on which access to better life opportunities was based. The higher education landscape in South Africa evolved along racial lines whereby, as late as 1990, there were institutions that were still the preserve of the Whites and those which were exclusively Black. Under apartheid, the Black majority were destined for unskilled jobs that require no formal training and only a privileged few had access to higher education training.

The outcome of these practices was that, with the dawn of democracy in 1994, the academic labor market reflected features of the "first economy," in terms of racial division of labor, which, according to former President Mbeki, produces the bulk of the country's wealth. Academic and senior administrative staff were predominantly White men—including in higher education institutions (HEIs) that were reserved for Blacks—and lower service levels were filled by Blacks and women. According to a 2004 report by the Council on Higher Education (CHE) on the profile of higher education workforce as of 1994,

> Of a total of some 45,000 staff across the public higher education sector, 80 percent of staff were Whites, 12 percent Africans,

> 4 percent Coloreds and 4 percent Indians. 34 percent of staff were women, and their status was generally lower than that of male staff.

It is against this background that higher educational policies and labor regulations since 1994 have been developed to redress these inequities. Staff equity has become a focus of institutional planning, not only of higher education policy requirements, but also of labor laws and legislation.

The statistics referenced earlier, which indicate the prevalence of low qualifications among faculty in South African higher education, also shed light on the characteristics of the academic labor market in South Africa. This includes the fact that future academics are already working in this labor market, as the majority of master's and doctoral candidates are already working for these institutions. These individuals are employed mainly as part-time or temporary faculty as they work toward their postgraduate qualifications. On completion of their studies, this group of part-time or temporary faculty stands the chance of being offered permanent positions. But, as the CHE (2012) study shows, and as indicated earlier, permanent positions in higher education are on the decline.

There are five factors that characterize, and impact negatively on, the South African labor market. The first are the high levels of unemployment in the economy at large, which, according to the International Monetary Fund (IMF), averaged 23.7 percent during the 2008 to 2011 period and stood at 24.5 percent in 2011. This is considered the highest unemployment rate among emerging economies (Patel 2011). The second is skills shortage, which is considered "the enemy of the state" (NPC 2011). The third is HIV/AIDS whose prevalence rate is estimated at about 10.6 percent, while the total number of people living with HIV/AIDS has risen from 4.21 million in 2001 to an estimated 5.4 million in 2011. The highest levels are among the youth: an estimated 16.6 percent of those aged between 16 and 49 are HIV positive. By way of comparison, the Higher Education AIDS (HEAIDS) sero-prevalence study that was conducted in 21 of the 22 contact higher education institutions in South Africa, shows a prevalence of almost 10 percent among service staff (9.9 percent), 4.4 percent among administrative staff, 1.5 percent among academic staff, and 3.4 percent among students in the higher education sector (Colvin et al. 2010). This clearly shows that academic staff are not unaffected by this pandemic, and highlights the risks and challenges of building a pool of educated young people from which to recruit young faculty.

The fourth key factor is brain-drain, which is a phenomenon that predates the dawn of democracy in South Africa. According to the Human

Sciences Research Council (2004) the loss of highly skilled citizens to other countries through emigration has been a cause for concern in South Africa for many years. Contrary to popular perception, brain-drain in South Africa started long before the inception of the new government in 1994, and the figures suggest that the flow of professionals from this country continues to increase rapidly. A study by Fourie (2006) shows that most professionals prefer to emigrate to developed countries, with Europe being the most popular destination. Another study indicated that in 2010, at least 588,388 individuals in OECD countries were recorded as having been born in South Africa. The countries with the highest numbers of individuals born in South Africa are the United Kingdom (227,000), Australia (155,690), the United States of America (78,616), New Zealand (41,676), and Canada (38,310). The major push factors, particularly for White South African emigrants, have traditionally been put down to high levels of violent crime (often personally experienced) and the affirmative action employment policies of the government. Fourie's 2006 study further shows that almost 10 percent of South African professionals emigrate to other African countries. The Middle East came in as the fifth most popular destination attracting 2.6 percent of all emigrating South African professionals.

The fifth factor worth noting is the decline in government funding of higher education, which we argue has contributed to the decrease in the number of permanent positions in universities in favor of part-time and temporary appointments. The Report of the Ministerial Committee on the Review of the National Student Financial Aid Scheme, released in 2010, highlighted the fact that in both real and student per capita terms, funding of higher education has declined. An analysis of expenditure between 2000 and 2004 shows that government funding of higher education declined by 3.1 percent in real terms. After peaking at 3 percent of the government budget in 2000, government funding of higher education has consistently declined, reaching 2.4 percent in 2008 (DHET 2010). One of the effects of coping with the decline in higher education funding is that universities are now filling permanent positions with part-time or temporary appointments, as these forms of appointment can be funded at a lower cost.

South African universities have prioritized knowledge production and self-advancement in their pursuit to become competitive universities in a globalized higher education landscape. To facilitate this competitive and comparative advantage of South African universities, a breed of promising local and international young faculty who have distinguished themselves through sustained journal publications, teaching, and research records, are recruited as postdoctoral fellows, PhD/research fellows, and teaching staff attached to research projects or research centers. So, in the same way that the number of U.S. faculty has increased and the faculty has become more diverse since 1969 (Altbach 1996), South African higher education in the postapartheid era has become increasingly diverse, with faculty (including young scholars) recruited from all regions of the world.

Linked to this recruitment drive is the desire for universities to attract top scholars from across the globe. There are key national and institutional strategies to enable and enhance this process of recruitment and retention of foreign skills in South Africa, through an enabling and conducive policy environment. In this regard, the Department of Home Affairs currently offers skills and work permit quotas to attract much needed scarce skills, and aims to ease the process of obtaining permanent residence status, which is useful in settling international young faculty. The National Development Plan (2011) acknowledges the role of foreign skilled labor in meeting the skills gap in South Africa. It argues that, if properly managed, migration will serve as an important instrument to fill gaps in the labor market and will contribute positively to South Africa's development. South Africa's immigration policy has sought to respond to the need for skilled immigrants (for example, the 2004 amendments to the Immigration Act), which facilitates the arrival of skilled labor from abroad into the country. This is done out of an appreciation on the part of the government that "resourceful migrant communities can contribute to local and national development, and diverse cosmopolitan populations are often the focus of cultural, economic and intellectual innovation." With these policy interventions, the government also attempts to counter the scourge of xenophobia, which can serve as a deterrent to the recruitment of foreign skilled labor.

Unlike the West, with fiscal constraints as a result of the current gloomy economic situation, South Africa has great potential for growth especially with respect to attracting young faculty to breed a new generation of academic leaders. This is also necessary because of the aging academic workforce in South African universities, which is considered to be a "looming staff crisis as nearly half of [the] most senior academics retire in the coming decade" (MacGregor 2008, 1). Badat (2008) warned that, "a failure to invest in and cultivate a new generation of high quality academics will have far-reaching consequence" (p. 28). In light of this situation, prospective young academics (local and international) must carefully decide on the universities to which they will apply. Potential recruits must take into consideration not just the financial benefits of making such decisions, but also the possibility of career and professional development by affiliating with universities with a proven culture of teaching and research, to further enhance their competitiveness in the future.

The recruitment of young faculty is strategically accomplished by different universities through the recruitment of national and international doctoral students. This is in response to the 2001 National Plan for Higher Education's (NPHE) call and recommendation for higher education institutions to recruit postgraduate students from the rest of the African continent in order to meet equity targets. The plan noted the concern that, by 2001, seven years into democracy, the staff in higher education had not changed in line with the changes in the student body. It observed that Blacks remained underrepresented in professional positions, especially at senior levels. It proposed two strategies to address this problem. First, but not necessarily in order of priority, was the recruitment of students from the African continent into postgraduate programs, as these individuals could serve as potential recruits into staff positions. The 2001 NPHE Plan argued that,

> The Ministry would also like to encourage higher education institutions to develop strategies to recruit postgraduate students from the rest of Africa, in particular, the Southern African Development Community, as well as other developing countries. This would contribute to building research capacity both locally and in the rest of the Continent especially as South Africa has a more developed infrastructure than many other countries. In this regard the Ministry would like to indicate that postgraduate students, irrespective of their country of origin, would be treated as South African students for subsidy purposes. (p. 72)

The second strategy is to recruit qualified staff from the rest of the Continent of Africa. In response to the poor representation of Blacks and women in staff composition of higher education institutions, the Plan recommended that,

> Institutions will therefore be expected to develop equity plans with clear targets for rectifying race and gender inequalities. The National Plan recognizes the difficulties in the short to medium term for achieving employment equity given the paucity

> of postgraduates and consequently, the small pool of potential recruits. It therefore encourages institutions to recruit black and women staff from the rest of the African Continent. (p. 6)

In addition to the above strategies, many South African scholars who have studied in the West are currently attracted back to the country, with offers of competitive remuneration and research incentives. Irrespective of the type of offer, the prospect of growth in academia depends on young faculty's performance during the probationary period in terms of research outputs, teaching, and university service.

Ways to Enter the University Job Market in South Africa

Within the South African context, there are broadly two strategies employed for recruiting academic staff: internal and external recruitment drives. For the former, a number of universities use the "grow your own timber" approach, in which outstanding postgraduate students, especially from the honors level (which is comparable to the premaster's stage in the North American system), are strongly encouraged by established professors to pursue an academic trajectory, by involving them as research/teaching assistants. By virtue of their academic record, many such students automatically qualify for postgraduate merit awards—a funding opportunity to pursue and complete postgraduate studies. As long as they maintain outstanding academic records, they have the prospect of being recruited as junior lecturers under the tutelage of their "sponsoring" professors. This leads to an inbreeding phenomenon, which is prevalent in many universities in South Africa.

A peculiar feature of the South African case, considering this internal approach, is that many of these outstanding students are international students from the Southern African Development Community (SADC) region[2] (predominantly Zimbabwe) and the rest of Africa. Few South Africans choose to come back to study for postgraduate programs after their first degree because of the appeal of private sector employment following completion of the three-year undergraduate studies. The opportunity cost for local students to continue with their postgraduate studies also mitigates against further education, as these first-degree holders are eager to assist family who may have sacrificed for them, and to pay back student loans.

On the other hand, the "external recruitment strategy" uses advertisements to attract willing and able young academics, who may want an African experience, especially at the doctoral and postdoctoral level. International postgraduate students who complete their studies and opt for postdoctoral fellowships, and who distinguish themselves through research outputs, have been offered academic positions by some South African universities.

The hiring of new staff entails public advertisement of positions in the media (and via the Internet) and through employment interviews. Depending on the post level, the candidate may be invited to give a seminar as a requirement of the recruitment process. For appointments of strategic value to academia, some universities use search committees to attract the right candidates. Universities offer various types of contracts that may be permanent (full time and part time) or temporary (full time and part time). Only permanent employees would have access to full employment benefits such as medical insurance, pension or provident funds, study and research leave, among other benefits.

Indicators—such as highest qualifications, teaching and research experience, skills scarcity, satisfying the requirements for internal equity and fairness, strategic priorities, market profiles of individual candidates, and employment equity and benchmarks—are strongly considered in the recruitment and hiring of academics. The combination of these factors is further considered in determining the starting salary. The general practice is to offer new faculty a two- to three-year probationary contract with the possibility of converting to a permanent position on meeting the terms of the contract, which include stipulated research outputs in peer-reviewed publications, satisfactory performance in terms of teaching outputs, and postgraduate supervision for those already holding PhDs. For those employed but not yet holding a PhD, completion of a higher degree, such as a master's or PhD, would be one of the indicators contributing toward satisfying the probationary requirement. However, as earlier figures indicate, the number of permanent positions in universities seems to be declining, with many universities preferring to offer temporary or part-time positions.

Entry-Level Contracts of Young Academics in South African Universities

Different institutions have varied conditions of employment at the entry level for academics, though the two cases presented in this chapter—the University of Pretoria and the University of Cape Town—are fairly representative of the majority of South African universities. For example, at the University of Pretoria, an appointment at entry level for permanent academic staff is subject to a probation period of two years, after which the dean or the head of department submits a motivation report to the nominating committee on the permanent appointment. The committee decides whether to extend the probation period, retain the staff member, or give a month's notice of withdrawal of the appointment. A staff member who is on full-time employment and is not a citizen must apply to be a permanent resident as soon as the South African immigration law allows for it. This includes proof that the applicant possesses exceptional skills and qualifications (DHA 2011). Academics are free to take outside work as long as this does not have any adverse effect on the performance of their work for the university. At the University of Cape Town, probation for academic staff lasts three years, although this may be terminated by both parties with six months' notice. The probation period can be extended or confirmed at the discretion of the university. The appointment can also be terminated if the staff member is found to unsatisfactory.

Full-time and permanent staff have access to benefits, such as retirement and medical schemes. There may be a need to supplement the retirement funds by taking an additional private retirement annuity to sustain quality of life postretirement. Factors such as the salary earned at entry level, promotion opportunities during the career, and the post level at which one retires, have a bearing on the adequacy of the retirement funds to live on at the time of retirement. For example, someone who retires as a full professor will retire with a better retirement fund than someone who retires as an assistant professor or senior lecturer. Membership in the group life insurance scheme of the university is compulsory, as long as the university runs such a scheme. Staff members are entitled to annual leave. Termination of service can be effected by giving one month's notice by any of the parties involved. Each university has entry-level salary guidelines, but these are negotiable based on the qualifications, professional experience, and past salary earned, if the candidate has been previously employed. The normal practice is that candidates would not be offered a salary lower than their immediate past salary.

The teaching loads of young faculty vary according to institutional, faculty-level, or departmental policies and/or practices. The general practice, though, is that young faculty carry mainly undergraduate teaching loads while senior staff members get involved in postgraduate teaching and supervision. For those without PhDs, which in most universities hold the title of "associate lecturer" or "senior tutor" (as in the case of the

University of the Witwatersrand), similar employment conditions and teaching loads as a PhD-qualified lecturer apply. But, most are employed on a one-year, renewable contract—as part-time, sessional, or full-time staff, depending on the teaching roles and responsibilities. The challenge is that many of these academics do not have a sense of job security, and they carry huge teaching loads at the university. Some in this category have a clear vision and understanding of the academic profession and enroll immediately in a PhD program, which (for permanent staff) is fully paid for by their universities. These individuals are automatically considered for a lectureship position on completion of their degree, and a number of the traditional universities consider them to be very vital to the staff development pool, because they have had about four- to five years of work experience at the institution, with an understanding of institutional culture. The probability is high that these individuals will be offered a permanent position, thus leading to the beginning of an academic career for many.

Given the large number of young faculty involved in undergraduate teaching, many of the staff members struggle to balance their teaching and research responsibilities. This is also the case where staff members are involved in postgraduate studies, which require time off. There are normally negotiations between the staff member and the head of department to create time for young faculty to pursue their studies and research priorities. For instance, at the University of Pretoria, staff members, including young faculty who have just completed their PhDs and are on probation or appointed on a permanent basis, can apply for research and development program funds. This amounts to R50,000 (about US$6,000) in seed funding over a three-year period, to help build the recipient's research profile. Staff members also get access to other short courses and staff development programs that are offered on campus.

Strategies to Retain Young Academics in South African Universities

Given the challenge of an aging academic workforce and an undersized pool of young recruits in academia, there are broad institutional and national strategies employed to address this situation, and these are clearly complementary. At the institutional level, there is evidence of institutional initiatives to support young academics in South African universities. For instance, the University of the Witwatersrand in cooperation with international organizations, such as the Carnegie Corporation of New York and the Andrew W. Mellon Foundation, provides funding to recruit and grow a new generation of young academics. Like the Carnegie PhD Fellowship, the Mellon Retiree Mentorship Programme (MRMP) currently provides substantial funding for research and for young faculty to be mentored by retired academics over the three- to four-year period of the doctoral process. The University of South Africa (UNISA) has its own "grow your own timber" program, which focuses on the process of employing promising young graduates as postgraduate assistants and, through their close association with lecturers, these younger individuals are groomed as leaders in their respective fields.

At a national level, there are equally strategic initiatives aimed at addressing the looming crisis of not just recruiting these young academics, but also retaining them. An important example is the South African Young Academy of Science (SAYAS), inaugurated in 2011 by the Department of Science and Technology and the Academy of Science of South Africa. The initiative is "aimed at bringing together young scientists to solve global problems requiring interdisciplinary expertise, encouraging young people into scientific careers, promoting a culture in which research excellence is highly valued and supporting researchers, especially in developing countries" (Makoni 2011, 1).

The National Research Foundation (NRF) also plays a strategic national role in building up a new generation of academic leaders for South African higher education. According to the Act Number 33 of 1998, the object of the NRF is to "support and promote research through funding, human resource development and the provision of the necessary research facilities in order to facilitate the creation of knowledge, innovation and development in all fields of science and technology, including indigenous knowledge and thereby to contribute to the improvement of the quality of life of all the people of the Republic." Indeed, the NRF has greatly facilitated the intellectual project of South African universities to attract and retain young academics. At present, numerous opportunities are available to attract, train, and empower academics in South African universities to compete and collaborate within the African continent and globally. For young faculty members, these opportunities range from funding opportunities for doctoral study, to fully funded postdoctoral fellowships and a rating system that encourages and supports faculty younger than forty.

Examples of the significant NRF funding opportunities for doctoral and postdoctoral support include the Thuthuka Programme, the

Commonwealth Split-Site Doctoral Scholarships, the South African Biosystematics Initiative (SABI) postdoctoral fellowships, and the Y-rating category for young academics below the age of forty. The Thuthuka program has developed two tracks (PhD and postdoctoral work) targeted at South Africans generally under the age of 45 at the time of application. This program aims to "promote the research development of early-career academics employed at South African universities, science councils and other research institutions, and the attainment of an NRF rating by early-career academics, in particular Black and female researchers and persons with disabilities" (NRF 2012, 7).

South Africa has a peer-review rating system of researchers, which is based on an evaluation of the quality of the research outputs of academics. The NRF ratings system, which encompasses five categories for established as well as emerging researchers, provides a valuable tool that not only enables researchers to successfully plot a career path for themselves, but also ensures that they receive the recognition they deserve from their peers for their work. In doing so, "it encourages local researchers to continue their work in South Africa, attract researchers from other countries as well as encourage young, emerging researchers and those who show potential to further their work" (NRF 2012, 7). Rated researchers also play an important role in South Africa's move toward a knowledge economy and are sought after by universities, as the quality and caliber of a university is measured, among other factors, by the number of rated researchers employed.

The National Research Foundation provides incentives to rated researchers in the form of annual awards, which vary according to the rating of each researcher. For instance, an A-rated researcher (which, according to the rating is classified as a "leading international researcher") gets an annual research incentive of about US$18,000, while a C-rated researcher (classified as an "established researcher") gets about US$7,000. In order to encourage research activity and quality research output among young faculty, the NRF has two rating categories that are targeted, respectively, at researchers below 40 and 35 years of age. The Y-rating category (either Y1 or Y2) is for "young researchers" (40 years or younger), who have held the doctorate or equivalent qualification for less than five years at the time of application, and who are recognized as having the potential to establish themselves as researchers within a five-year period after evaluation, based on their performance and productivity as researchers during their doctoral studies and/or early postdoctoral careers. P-rated researchers are young researchers (normally younger than 35 years of age) who have held the doctorate or equivalent qualification for less than five years at the time of application and who have demonstrated "exceptional potential" through such research outputs as turning their doctoral research into peer-reviewed journal articles, book chapters, and/or a book with reputable international and national publishers. As recipients of what is also known as the NRF President's Award, P-rated researchers are likely to become future leaders in their field, a valuable asset in a country where critical knowledge skills are scarce. The NRF rating system can also be viewed as an important avenue through which young faculty are enticed into research or academic careers and are kept incentivized through meaningful forms of recognition.

The Role of Social Networks for Young Academics in South African Universities

Just as in any work environment, social networks play an important role in the life of young faculty. In most cases these networks are established during the period of postgraduate supervision and through faculty advisory interactions at the graduate studies level. On completion of graduate studies, and should the student get appointed at the same institution, the advisor would likely become a mentor for this new faculty member upon assumption of duties. A model that tends to prevail, and is viewed positively, in some universities, is a situation where the mentor and mentee work in a collaborative manner to build teaching and research capacity. At a higher level, this pair also works hand-in-hand to co-author peer-reviewed articles as well as participates in local and international conferences where more networks can be built. Within this academic space, many social networks evolve in which other academics meet—local and international, young and established. This social space helps to build the trust, acceptance, and collegiality necessary for the professional development of the young academic.

Advisors and mentors play an important role in the life of young faculty member, as it is through their mentors that young academics gain access to wider networks, national and international. For example, some mentorship programs entail mentors taking their mentees to conferences where the mentees gain exposure to peers in their fields and their mentor's networks. Mentors also play an important role in the life of young faculty in terms of initiating them into writing for publication. In taking the mentees under their wings, the mentors expose them to different publishing avenues.

At the institutional and faculty level, the dean or head of department can play an important role in providing support to new and young faculty. This can occur through induction programs that assist new faculty in understanding the institutional culture and expectations that are made of them. Induction efforts can also provide access to different sections or aspects of the department, the faculty, and the institution, where they can be provided with help to advance their careers. Some institutions have "grow your own timber" programs, where new faculty gain exposure to peers and mentors that serve as sources of help and support. The "grow your own timber" strategy contributes to inbreeding in various institutions, but this is unavoidable given the scarcity of qualified young people with doctoral degrees and academic skills. Participation in such networks, and the ability to deliver and distinguish oneself in terms of taking advantage of such opportunities, can facilitate promotion. Indeed, including some of these activities on one's curriculum vitae, as well as securing letters of recommendation from mentors, can enhance one's chances of promotion.

Another important activity for the advancement of an academic career in South Africa is participation in university life through membership on university committees, spanning nonacademic and academic spheres. In most instances at the recruitment stage, the university expects the potential new faculty to provide evidence of active participation in the life of the university. In essence, for young academics to secure tenure, a permanent position, and move up the academic ladder, they must demonstrate outstanding teaching, involvement in postgraduate supervision, research outputs through peer-review publications, and active involvement in university life through committee work.

Current Realities of Young University Faculty in South African Higher Education

The current postapartheid South African higher education system has presented the opportunity and space to attract top young academics, both locally and internationally. A number of established, traditional universities—because of their continental and global academic programs—have well-established teaching and research models, which are comparable to some of the best schools around the world. Having said this, the importance of institutional support and competitive, middle-class remuneration are pertinent as incentives to retain and encourage young faculty to dedicate themselves to a long-term academic career. Currently in South Africa, most traditional universities attract young faculty with world-class education, proven research productivity, and loyalty to the academic profession. However, most nontraditional universities (with the exception of the well-paying ones) more easily draw the pool of candidates who are unable to get a job in the traditional universities. In some cases, young faculty in the nontraditional universities have little research experience and use these universities as "incubators" for building their academic profile through teaching experience and peer-review publications. As such, they will be more easily considered by the traditional universities, should there be a vacancy in those institutions. What becomes vital for a young academic to make the transition from working in a nontraditional university to a traditional university is "self-leadership," defined as a clear vision, personal drive, and motivation, which in themselves are essential to sustain an academic career.

In a nutshell, traditional universities offer greater institutional support and career development opportunities through competitive remuneration and research incentives to retain dedicated young academics, as compared to the nontraditional institutions. The only exception to this is the nontraditional universities with huge financial resources; these can easily poach young academics from other traditional universities or recruit them directly through very attractive postdoctoral opportunities. Given their weakened negotiation and bargaining positions for better salaries as a result of a lack of a PhD and other relevant skills for academic work (such as postgraduate supervision and a publication record), many young faculty would normally not earn competitive salaries. A 2012 study by Sehoole (2012) on academic salaries showed that while South African academics have competitive remuneration packages, remuneration at lower academic ranks is not attractive. Individuals drawing these salaries may struggle to sustain a middle-class lifestyle without access to options to augment their salaries through private work.

Main Challenges and Future Trends

The foregoing analysis of the status and future of young faculty in South African universities has revealed the extent to which the academic labor market is intrinsically linked to the South African political economy and the country's broader labor market. The transformation agenda across all spheres of government and the employment sector does have a bearing on recruitment and retention strategies within the academic labor market. What is crucial are regulatory and policy frameworks within which recruitment and employment practices can be implemented without bottlenecks. In this regard, the government directives (through various policies and labor laws that have been passed in pursuit of employment equity goals and targets) are crucial in understanding the (labor) regulatory framework within which higher education institutions are operating.

Higher education in South Africa faces multiple challenges, including an aging senior faculty, the impact of HIV/AIDS, the effects of decades of brain-drain, and the decline in funding for higher education. There is also a need to transform the racial and gender profile of the scholarly workforce; tackle a looming staff crisis, as nearly half of the country's most senior academics will retire in the coming decade; and increase the numbers of academics, as higher education expands to achieve a 20 percent participation rate. Urgent interventions are required, as Badat (2008) warned that "without action, South Africa's efforts to transform the social composition of its scholarly workforce will be undermined, academic quality will be debilitated along with the capacity to produce high quality graduates and knowledge; and the ability of universities to contribute to development and democracy through a new generation of outstanding scholars committed to critical and independent scholarship and social justice will be hampered" (p. 28).

Another major challenge that South Africa faces is the large number of young faculty in higher education institutions without doctoral degrees. This has huge implications for the academic labor market and remuneration practices in this sector, in that it makes the sector susceptible to labor exploitation. A direct consequence is that young academics have weakened bargaining power for better salaries as a result of their poor qualifications. The other challenge associated with this is that, given their lack of doctoral qualifications (which normally comes with capacity and skills to be able to conduct research, produce recognized research outputs, and supervise postgraduate students), young faculty in South Africa find they are vulnerable to possible exploitation because of lack of "clout" in academic standing. The lack of doctoral qualifications and research experience means that the burden of postgraduate supervision and research publication is carried by academics who are White, male, and aging (i.e., over the age of 55). The future challenge, therefore, is not just to replenish the aging academics with younger faculty, but to replace them with young, well-qualified faculty who are able to make substantial and sustained contributions to scholarship.

An additional challenge is the worrying trend observed in employment practices of universities, which finds expression in the form of a bias toward the appointment of part-time and/or temporary staff, who represent 64 percent of all South African faculty. This suggests that only a third of South African academics have permanent full-time appointments. If South African universities are to remain competitive in their employment practices relative to government and the private sector, this trend will have to be reversed.

Remuneration remains a challenge for young faculty, due to some of the factors highlighted earlier. Given the competitive nature of the academic profession, which requires individuals to demonstrate a proven track record of scholarship to survive, the government and higher education institutions may need to develop additional strategies to be able to recruit, invest in, and develop the capacity of these young faculty in order to retain them in academia. In this regard, the contracts and the conditions of employment that are offered to the young faculty should be improved to make a statement about the value attached to these young academics.

Notes

1. In terms of racial classification under apartheid, Colored refers to "mixed race."

2. The countries in the Southern African Development Community (SADC) region are: Angola, Botswana, Democratic Republic of the Congo, Lesotho, Madagascar, Malawi, Mauritius, Mozambique, Namibia, South Africa, Swaziland, Tanzania, Zambia, and Zimbabwe.

References

Academy of Science for South Africa (ASSAf). 2010. *The Phd Study: Consensus Report*. Pretoria: Academy of Science of South Africa.

Altbach, Philip. G., ed. 1996. *The International Academic Profession: Portraits of Fourteen Countries*. Princeton, NJ: The Carnegie Foundation for the Advancement of Teaching.

Badat, Saleem. 2008. "Producing, Transforming the Social Composition of, and Retaining a New Generation of Academics: The Rhodes University Programme of Accelerated Development, Rhodes University." Paper presented at the University Leaders Forum: Developing and retaining the next generation of academics, Accra, Ghana.

Council on Higher Education (CHE). 2004. "Equity." In *South African Higher Education in the First Decade of Democracy*, 59–92. Pretoria: Council on Higher Education.

Council on Higher Education (CHE). 2012. *Vital Statistics, Public Higher Education 2010*. Pretoria: Council on Higher Education.

Department of Education (DoE). 2001. "National Plan for Higher Education." Pretoria: Department of Education.

Department of Higher Education & Training (DHET). 2000–2010. *Headcount of Permanent Instruction and Research Staff, by Nationality, Age, Race and Gender*. Department of Education's Higher Education Management Information System (HEMIS): Department of Higher Education & Training (DHET).

Department of Higher Education & Training (DHET). 2012. *Report of the Ministerial Committee on the Review of the National Student Financial Aid Scheme*. Pretoria: Department of Higher Education & Training (DHET).

Department of Home Affairs (DHA). 2011. "Department of Home Affairs Strategic Plan: 2011–2014."

Fourie, Anco. 2006. *Brain Drain and Brain Circulation: A Study of South Africans in the United Arab Emirates*. Stellenbosch, South Africa: University of Stellenbosch.

Koen, Charlton. 2007. *Post Graduate Student Retention and Success: A South African Case Study*. Pretoria, South Africa: Human Sciences Research Council.

MacGregor, Karen. (December 14, 2008). "Challenges of Equity, Ageing, Expansion." *University World News*, 57. http://www.universityworldnews.com/article.php?story=20081214092139847.

Makoni, Munyaradzi. (October 16, 2011). "Young Scientists' Academy Launched." *University World News*, 85. http://www.universityworldnews.com/article.php?story=20111014203359953.

Moodie, Alison. (December 12, 2010). "South Africa: New Funds to Boost PhD Production." *University World News*, 275. http://www.universityworldnews.com/article.php?story=20101210212934604.

National Planning Commission (NPC). 2011. *National Development Plan—Vision for 2030*. Pretoria: National Planning Commission (NPC).

National Research Foundation (NRF). 2009. *Evaluation and Rating*. Pretoria: National Research Foundation (NRF).

National Research Foundation (NRF). 2012. *Human and Institutional Capacity Development Grants Thuthuka Programme: 2013 Grants Manual*. Pretoria: National Research Foundation (NRF).

National Research Foundation (NRF). 2012. *NRF Honours Rated Researchers*. Pretoria: National Research Foundation (NRF).

Patel, Saliem. 2011. "The Labour Market at a Glance." In *2011 Transformation Audit: From Inequality to Inclusive Growth*, edited by Jan Hofmeyr. Cape Town: Institute for Justice and Reconciliation.

Pillay, PN. 2010. *Higher Education Financing in East and Southern Africa*. Somerset West: African Minds.

PoliticsWeb. 2012. "How Many South Africans Have Left the Country?" http://www.politicsweb.co.za/politicsweb/view/politicsweb/en/page71619?oid=318618&sn=Detail.

Republic of South Africa. 1998. "National Research Foundation Act" (Act Number 33 of 1998).

Sehoole, Chika. 2012. "The Unequal Playing Field: Academic Remuneration in South Africa." In *Paying the Professoriate: A Global Comparison of Compensation and Contracts*, edited by Philip G. Altbach, Liz Reisberg, Maria Yudkevich, Gregory Androushchak, and Iván F. Pacheco, 288–95. USA: Routledge.

Skills Portal South Africa. 2011. "Skills Shortage: Enemy of the State." http://www.thecareersportal.co.za/careers/careers/457-skills-shortage-enemy-of-the-state-.html.

University of Cape Town (UCT). 2012. "Employee Relations: Pass (Professional, Administrative, Support & Service) Staff, Including Scientific and Technical Staff." http://hr.uct.ac.za/service/academic/probation/.

University of Pretoria (UP). "Human Resources Policies and Procedures." http://www.up.ac.za/services/personnel/policies/w97E.html.

University of the Witwatersrand. 2007. "Andrew W Mellon Postgradute Mentoring Scheme." http://www.wits.ac.za/academic/research/general_information_for_researchers/universityresearchfunding/7178/mellon.html.

Chapter 11

"Do I Still Want to be a Professor and, If So, Can I?"

Entering the American Academic Profession in the First Decade of the Twenty-First Century

Martin J. Finkelstein

Introduction

Those who still aspire to become a professor in the American university of the early twenty-first century face a changed landscape and less sanguine prospects than even a generation ago. This chapter focuses initially on how the kinds of jobs available to aspiring academics are changing—as evidenced by the emergence of part-time and limited term full-time appointments—as are the venues for employment, with growth in the nonresearch university sector as well as in the professional fields, in contradistinction to the liberal arts disciplines. The search for initial employment has become longer and more competitive, and working conditions at all but the major research universities have deteriorated. Entering this new landscape is, in many ways, a new breed of career aspirant: new in terms of historical generation (the so-called Millennials) and new in terms of demographics, with the ascent of young women, many of whom are now married (often to other academics or professionals) and seeking to conjoin their strong career aspirations with their equally strong aspirations for parenthood and family life. The net results of this "encounter," we shall argue, is a prolonged period of establishing oneself (with some falling by the wayside), a less secure and predictable career trajectory, and less hospitable working environments—except at a small group of leading research universities.

That being said, we must immediately insist on wrapping these emerging trends in multiple qualifications. The American system of higher education is highly decentralized with major lines of differentiation (institutionally) between the four-year college and university sector, on the one hand, and the prebaccalaureate vocational sector (including two-year community colleges and the for-profit proprietary sector), on the other. Furthermore, within the four-year baccalaureate sector, there are important distinctions between publicly funded and private, nonprofit institutions. Beyond the diversity associated with type of institution, the work life and careers of U.S. academics are shaped both by academic field, reflecting the differential "market" value of academic fields outside the academy, and type of appointment, whether via limited-term contract or promising prospects of permanence, in other words, tenured. Recently, the effects of structural differentiation by institutional type, academic field, and type of appointment on academic work and careers have been further amplified by the powerful impact of the great global recession of 2008.

It is within the context of this increasingly stratified academic workforce and sustained economic dislocation, that this chapter describes the current situation for new entrants into academic careers in the United States. The chapter begins with a more focused examination of the demand side of the academic labor market: What kinds of jobs are available? At what types of institutions? In what fields? How competitive are they and how are they typically filled? The chapter then moves to an examination of the supply side: Who is entering in terms of educational background and demographic characteristics? At what point in the life course? How is that changing? Once having acquired the educational credentials required for entry, what is the entry route into a first academic job? How direct or indirect is it? And how does that vary? Finally, having arrived at entry-level academic jobs, the chapter considers the nature of faculty employment contracts and what new entrants encounter by way of working conditions and career pressures, including compensation, and the principal variations therein. The chapter concludes with a summary of findings and a discussion of their implications for the future of the American academic profession.

The System Context

The higher education system in the United States today includes some 4,000 autonomous institutions currently offering instruction at the post-secondary level to some 18 million students by about 1.4 million faculty members (700,000 of whom are full time).

The university sector offering doctoral education is relatively small in terms of number of institutions: this sector consists of only 273 institutions, although it enrolls disproportionately large numbers of students and employs a disproportionate share of the full-time faculty (nearly 40 percent). Beyond the 273 research and PhD granting universities (two-thirds public, one-third private), the remaining 1,300 institutions in the four-year baccalaureate sector are about evenly divided between master's and free-standing, baccalaureate granting institutions, and are disproportionately (two-thirds) private. Although in the four-year and university sector, private institutions, then, outnumber public institutions in the United States, enrollment in the public sector—led by the research and PhD granting universities—outpaces that in the private sector by 2:1.

Beyond this diverse array of institutional work settings—each with its own unique demands and opportunities[1]—the work roles and prospects for new faculty entering the system are shaped substantially by academic field and by type of appointment. Unlike many other nations where all academic fields are treated equally in the state-regulated reward system, in the United States the working conditions and opportunities for faculty—especially new faculty—are shaped by the market for individual academic fields outside the university. Thus, the status and material conditions of academic departments are a function of the external resources that faculty can attract and the competition offered to universities by nonacademic employment opportunities for faculty. Salaries for academic staff are marketized so that a new professor of accounting likely earns more than a senior full professor of literature.

Historically, academic appointments in the United States were highly uniform and routinized. Faculty were hired to full-time positions for a six- to seven-year probationary period.[2] Following a high-stakes evaluation, they were either granted a permanent (tenured) appointment or dismissed—a process referred to as *up or out*. Beginning in the 1970s, universities began to resort increasingly to the hiring of faculty on part-time (predominantly single course) appointments, and in the 1990s to the hiring of new faculty to full-time, fixed-contract appointments with no prospects for the permanence of tenure. Within a period of barely two decades, the *majority* of all *full-time* new hires in U.S. universities annually—about 45,000 such "new hires" each year[3]—are retained on such fixed-contract appointments. Such appointments offer their incumbents different workloads, working conditions, compensation, and career prospects (Schuster and Finkelstein 2006).

The Demand Side of the Equation: What Kind of Academic Jobs Are Out There?

As late as 1987 (a mere 25 years ago), when the Carnegie Foundation for the Advancement of Teaching administered its national survey of American faculty, the survey instrument only incidentally allowed respondents to identify whether they were employed full- or part time and, if full time, there was no opportunity to describe the type of contract (fixed term versus tenure track or career ladder). Yet, within a decade, the proportion of headcount instructional staff[4] at American colleges and universities employed on a part-time basis had swelled to nearly half—48 percent according to the 1993 National Study of Postsecondary Faculty. Even more strikingly, 1993 was the year in which the National Center for Education Statistics reported in its survey of "new hires" (section G of the biennial Fall Staff Survey) that *more than half* of all new, full-time faculty hires were to noncareer ladder, fixed-contract positions. Over the next twenty years, that annual percentage of fixed-contract appointments has varied only at the margins between 53 percent and 58 percent (Finkelstein, Schuster, and Iglesias 2012). That means that of the 15,000-plus PhD recipients annually over the past two decades who had job offers on receipt of the degree (one-third of the approximately 45,000 annual total PhD recipients), just over half have entered academic work. And among those individuals, fewer than half (i.e., one quarter of the 15,000) have entered into tenure-eligible positions[5]—at least initially (Survey of Earned Doctorates 2011). Overall, including both new hires and continuing appointments, the percentage of *full-time* faculty who are tenured is now about 47 percent—down from about 62 percent in 1970. The percentage of *headcount* faculty (part time plus full time of every kind) who are tenured is now in the neighborhood of 15 percent to 20 percent (Coalition on the Academic Workforce 2011). Leslie (2007) found that these trends were corroborated in institutional responses to the 1999 National Study of Postsecondary Faculty: amid considerable enrollment growth (14 to

18 million between 1993 and 2007) the actual number of tenured and tenureable (probationary) positions declined slightly in all fields outside the physical and life sciences.

This latter point suggests that the broad-based restructuring of demand for faculty at the institutional level has varied by academic field. Off-track appointments (i.e., nontenure-track) are most prevalent in a half-dozen fields, including foreign languages and literature, English composition, mathematics, business, the health professions, and least prevalent in the natural sciences.

One further point about the contours of the academic opportunity structure is the differential growth among institutional types. Historically, the majority of faculty positions in American higher education were at research universities. As late as 1970, nearly half of all faculty positions were located in about 200 universities. By 2010, the center of enrollment growth in American higher education had shifted to the two-year and comprehensive, master's sector and away from the research university. What this means is that the majority of vacancies available to new entrants in 2012 are not at the research universities, but rather in the two-year institutions and the comprehensive, master's level public universities. Although these institutions offer both career-ladder and contingent positions, even the career-ladder appointments typically involve facilities and working conditions that are much less well-resourced in comparison to research universities. Not only is this pattern shaped by differential growth, but also by differential career exit patterns. Faculty at research universities, where teaching loads are lowest and working conditions are best, tend to retire significantly later than their colleagues in other sectors (Schuster and Finkelstein 2006).[6]

Perhaps most critical from the perspective of the nature of the jobs available to newly entering professors—irrespective of institutional type—is the nature of the part-time and full-time, noncareer-ladder positions that are increasingly prevalent. In the United States, traditional academic appointments (at least since World War II) have been constructed on the Humboldtian principle of the integration of teaching, research, and service. Every individual faculty member is expected to perform all three functions and is evaluated for promotion and tenure based on excellence in all three. The growth of part-time appointments has been in positions that are course-based, that is, that are structured around the teaching of a specific course and nothing else.[7] Most part-time faculty teach one or more specific courses, not infrequently at different employing institutions—a significant departure from the historic U.S. model of institutionally anchored careers.[8] Moreover, the available evidence suggests that newly popular fixed-contract appointments tend to be highly specialized in their focus. For example, some are "teaching only," requiring incumbents to teach a large number of typically lower division courses. Some require incumbents to engage in (typically external) grant-funded research, and either not teach at all or teach only incidentally or intermittently. Others may require incumbents to take responsibility for the administration of specialized academic programs, typically ones that are delivered nontraditionally (such as weekend or cohort programs; online or blended programs), involving either no teaching or minimal teaching, and certainly no research and publication.

What this means is that something less than half of the full-time academic jobs with faculty status that are currently available to new entrants provide an opportunity to undertake the full panoply of academic functions—teaching, research, and service—including developing a track record in research and publication, which is most critical to achieving professional recognition and reward. Those more specialized types of fixed-term, full-time appointments pose significant challenges to new entrants seeking to achieve the rewards and recognition in their field that attend research accomplishments. And part-time appointments, especially the "bundling" of several course-specific responsibilities at multiple institutions, clearly detract from career development.

In sum, the last twenty years in the United States have seen a reconfiguration of the academic job market leading to a decline in the number of good jobs, (i.e., tenure-track, career-ladder appointments), and a substantial increase in the number of contingent or temporary jobs that do not offer commensurate opportunities for individual career development and advancement. Those opportunities are differentially available in different academic fields, with the good jobs more plentiful in the natural sciences. Moreover, there is some evidence that the proportion of jobs available in the research university sector (as a proportion of all vacancies) is declining, while the number of opportunities in the master's, baccalaureate, and noncollegiate levels is increasing. The profession has become differentiated, and although there remain traditional jobs in significant numbers at the research universities and top liberal arts college, the situation has changed considerably elsewhere. The top tier is a minority. That means that new entrants will have a harder time locating positions in the most favorable, research-oriented, and well-resourced academic settings.

Processes for Filling Available Jobs

In the United States, the 4,000-plus corporately independent institutions are the buyers that drive the academic job market. Positions are created at the institutional level in response to both *replacement* demand—that is, the retirement of current incumbents or their mobility to other academic institutions or to positions outside academe altogether—and by *growth* demand, that is, changes in student enrollment (Carter and Scott 1998). Historically, the departure of incumbents created a vacancy for the "losing" academic department to fill at its discretion. Over the past decade or two it has become increasingly rare for an incumbent's departure to lead to *automatic* replacement. At most institutions in the United States an academic staff member's departure results in their position being reevaluated and requiring that the unit justify retaining the position. Quite beyond a vacancy created by the departure of a current incumbent, it is not unusual for a new faculty position to be created—either to support a new academic program or some other institutional priority. So, while in the United States there is greater flexibility in generating position vacancies, there is also considerably less systemic (bureaucratic) stability now in the number and distribution of positions.

Even in those cases in which retiring or otherwise departing faculty are replaced with new full-time, tenure-track hires, it is likely that recruitment will be at the entry level. That is, irrespective of the academic rank of the previous incumbent, institutions in the United States tend to adopt the staffing strategy of recruiting at the entry level—where budgeted salary outlays are lowest—and over time "growing their own." Although a few of the major research universities continue to hire world-class scholars at the senior ranks at every opportunity, most prefer to use vacancies as a strategy for budgetary savings and for developing a more malleable junior faculty. This means, for practical purposes, that most faculty recruitment is at the entry level—with a preference for newly minted PhDs.

Once a position is created—either through a vacancy or through a new addition—the search process for full-time academic staff positions, whether in the public or private sector, is typically highly *decentralized*: searches are conducted by individual academic units (departments and even programs) and recommendations are made from the unit to the academic dean supervising the unit in question and ultimately to the campus chief academic officer (Matler 1991). Two aspects of these searches are particularly important: their scope and the legal parameters within which they operate. Regarding scope, most full-time faculty searches at four-year institutions are national in scope, that is, they seek to identify and recruit the most qualified candidates in the United States in the field or subfield in question. At major research universities, the scope of such searches is increasingly international (Bair 2003). Searches at lesser institutions and searches for limited term appointments (even at the research-oriented universities) may be conducted less systematically and may be largely regional or even local in scope.

Historically, faculty searches in the United States were conducted through what sociologists referred to as a sponsorship, in contradistinction to an open, transparent, system (Caplow and McGee 1958; Burke 1988). That is, faculty in hiring departments contacted colleagues at those departments producing the most PhDs in the field and sought recommendations from mentors of their best doctoral students. The primary consideration was to recruit the most promising students from the most prestigious departments (and most prestigious mentors), on the assumption that prestige in venue would likely provide the best guarantee of candidate quality and maximize the prestige value of the new hire.

Beginning with the passage of landmark civil rights legislation in the United States in the 1960s and 1970s, searches for academic staff have been conducted within the parameters of U.S. government antidiscrimination policies reflected in federal legislation protecting against discrimination in employment on the basis of gender, race/ethnicity, age, sexual orientation, and so on. Although informal collegial sponsorship networks still operate, they do so within the parameters of *affirmative action* requirements, which include establishing *availability pools* of minority and women PhDs in the field,[9] mandatory advertising in media designed to reach those nontraditional candidates, mandated reporting on the number of women and minorities included in interviews for a given position, justifications of why a nonfemale or nonminority candidate is preferred over a woman or minority candidate, and so on (Goonen and Blechmen 1999).

In terms of procedure, a hiring academic unit would recommend several candidates to the academic dean supervising that unit (often in some kind of rank order) and the dean would make the actual hiring decision. The dean will not only typically decide which candidate should be selected, but would also negotiate terms and conditions of employment, including rank and salary, directly with the candidate (Twombly 2005). So, in this sense, although the actual conduct of search and screening processes for academic staff is highly decentralized (albeit quite standardized), actual hiring decisions and negotiations are typically conducted more centrally; and academic deans and chief academic officers, especially in the private sector, would have considerable discretion within basic institutional budgetary constraints.

At the point of initial appointment, the *type of contract* or appointment is usually clearly specified. Full-time academic staff contracts differ principally in whether they offer eligibility for the award of tenure (continuous appointment subject to removal only for cause and after due process) after a probationary period of typically six or seven years, or whether they offer a limited-term contract, which may or may not be renewable for one or more succeeding terms (Clark and Ma 2005). The contract letter would make this clear. Irrespective of the type of full-time appointment (tenure-eligible or limited contract), the actual length of the initial employment contract may vary typically between one to three years.

How competitive is the hiring process for full-time positions? What percentage of applicants are interviewed? What is the likelihood of being hired? Stories abound of search committees being overwhelmed by hundreds of applications for individual faculty vacancies. There are no reliable national numbers, but it is clear that competiveness varies by institutional type and academic field. Positions at the most desirable research universities typically generate the greatest candidate interest and activity. Similarly, those fields most afflicted with an oversupply of PhDs relative to employment opportunities, are most likely to generate the largest number of applications. A vacancy in the humanities fields, for example, history or literature, may generate applications in the hundreds—including scores of highly qualified applicants among new, but also recent and more seasoned, albeit underemployed, PhDs. In the natural sciences or professional fields, such as law and engineering, where nonacademic opportunities are plentiful, there may be many fewer applicants. Indeed, in some fields, for example, nursing, it may be challenging to build a robust candidate pool at all! Whatever the size of the pool, most searches reduce the pool to a small group of "most competitive" candidates who are subjected to an intensive screening and interview process. Candidates themselves usually apply to many vacancies with the hope of securing one or more interviews, let alone being hired. The reality that emerges for new PhDs is best described as a job search campaign—characterized by tens of applications, a small number of interviews, and only remote chances of actually being hired. Candidates from all but the most renowned graduate institutions in their field and candidates who have not just earned their doctorates are at a decided disadvantage for most entry-level vacancies.

The Supply Side

Over the past quarter-century, as the U.S. academic labor market tightened and took on the characteristics of a long-term buyer's market (and one substantially restructured in terms of the mix of career-ladder versus temporary opportunities and the mix of institutional and disciplinary venues), the PhD has become the virtually universal entry credential to academic careers of any sort, roughly 90 percent of all tenure eligible appointees to the entry-level rank of assistant professor hold the PhD degree (Clark and Ma 2005). The analogous figure for fixed-term contract faculty would be about 50 percent.[10] Thus, to understand academic supply, one needs to understand trends in the supply of PhDs, their distribution across academic fields, and their demographic and intellectual characteristics.

Doctoral Degree Production

The United States produced 48,000 doctorates in 2010, of which 33,100 (67.5 percent) were in the STEM fields[11] (including psychology and the social sciences, where *N*= 8,200, or about one-quarter of the STEM total), and 14,900 (32.8 percent) were in non-STEM fields. While representing a 16.2 percent increase over the previous decade overall (41,300 in 2000), the non-STEM fields grew by only 0.8 percent. This miniscule increase was led by the humanities fields, where the number of doctorates increased by 2.1 percent,[12] while the STEM fields increased by about 27.3 percent. So, in some sense, doctoral degree production has grown modestly over the past decade. Its differential growth in disciplinary mix has reflected the richer opportunities in the STEM fields and, conversely, the more limited opportunities in the non-STEM fields.

Changing Demographics

Irrespective of the overall numbers, what about the composition of the PhD pool? Three basic highlights are clear from the National Science Foundation's annual Survey of Earned Doctorates (SED). First, the proportion of women has increased over the decade to the point that they now constitute the majority of new PhDs: 52 percent in 2010 compared to 47 percent in 2000. The number of women increased in both the STEM and non-STEM fields—although the increase in the STEM fields was smaller and women still constitute a minority of STEM doctorates (around 25 percent). Second, despite a recent downturn,[13] the number of science and engineering (S&E) doctorates awarded to temporary visa holders grew 8.4 percent from 2005 to 2010.[14] Third, doctoral recipients are getting older: the median age of PhD recipients in 2010 reached 33 (compared to 32 a decade earlier)—and this despite a decline since 1985 of more than a year in the average time to degree from entry into graduate school to degree award.[15] This figure conceals enormous variation by field: in physics the median age was 29, while in the humanities, several of the social sciences, and education, it was closer to 38. That means that, on average, PhD recipients are embarking on an academic career later in their thirties than one or two decades ago.[16]

This later finding becomes particularly significant when we add one other fact to the demographic portrait: women PhDs are more likely to be married than they were one- to two decades ago (Schuster and Finkelstein 2006). Taken together with the increase in median age at PhD receipt and the fact that women actually take, on average, one half to one year longer to earn their degree than men, we see that the increasing pool of PhD women is arriving at the entry portal to an academic career married and near the upper limit of child bearing age. This spawns a heightened "family" consciousness among newly entering academic women and a rising concern about work-family balance issues.

These sorts of concerns are reinforced more generally by the emerging character of the "Millennial Generation"—those born after 1980 and coming to academic age now in the second decade of the twenty-first century. In 1969, the American faculty was dominated by members of the World War II generation and the newest recruits were members of the Baby Boom generation. The members of the Baby Boom generation are now at the end of their careers, being replaced at once by Generation Xers and members of the Millennial generation (Howe and Strauss 2000). This is a generation focused more self-consciously on family and work-life balance issues, a generation focused on teamwork and service in the name of the greater good. They pose a distinct challenge to the traditional norms of blurring lines between work and personal life, and the valorization of professional autonomy above all else (see Howe and Strauss 2000). Anecdotal evidence suggests that they are less willing to sacrifice everything on the altar of work. Moreover, there are behavioral data that suggest that women and minority faculty are leaving academic jobs at a higher rate than white men—although the actual magnitude of that rate is not clear (Trower 2002, cited by Gappa et al. 2007; Leslie 2007).

Intellectual Quality

A generation ago, Bowen and Schuster (1986) first sounded the alarm bells about the risk posed to the future American academic profession of the "best and brightest" young Americans forsaking academic careers for the more rewarding career prospects of business, medicine, and law. To that end, they examined the careers of intellectual elites, including Rhodes and Marshall Scholarship winners, members of academic honor societies (such as Phi Beta Kappa), and the graduates of America's most elite private colleges. Although the evidence was mixed, and although there was no doubt that academic careers were being less frequently chosen by college students than they had been during the 1960s, nonetheless a survey of the chairs of the leading university departments in eight disciplines showed that the quality of new hires continued to be impressive and indeed there had been no perceived decline in the intellectual quality of such new entrants. More recently, Schuster and Finkelstein (2006) resurveyed leading graduate departments at U.S. research universities and reported no perceived decline in the quality of either current doctoral students or recent hires. Moreover, they found that after a serious decline in the 1980s, a slightly growing, and stable, percentage of U.S. college first year students was aspiring to careers as college teachers (albeit still less than 3 percent). They concluded that although the evidence was not conclusive, there was no compelling basis for estimating that the quality of the academic profession was deteriorating in the near or medium term. And, in light of both the continued infusion of foreign talent into American graduate education (typically the global "best and brightest"), as well as the increasing number of doctorally prepared women, the prospects for maintaining the intellectual quality of the new academic generation showed no signs of decline—and perhaps even of strengthening.

From PhD Receipt to First Career Ladder Job: A Long and Winding Road

In the halcyon days of the 1960s and 1970s, prospective academics were often plucked out of graduate school before age 30, while still completing their dissertations, for full-time, tenure-track positions with excellent career prospects. That is no longer the case. Table 11.1 shows the employment sector of doctoral degree recipients with definite employment commitments between 1980 and 2010.[17]

Table 11.1. Employment sector of doctorate recipients with definite post graduation US employment commitments, by broad field of study: Selected years, 1990–2010

Employment commitments and sector	Total	Life sciences[a]	Physical sciences[b]	Social sciences[c]	Engineering	Education	Humanities
				Number			
All US employment commitments							
1990	15,239	1,325	1,780	2,935	1,872	4,020	1,922
1995	15,303	1,456	1,666	2,736	1,890	3,913	2,178
2000	17,246	1,949	2,033	3,116	2,335	3,907	2,575
2005	15,658	1,713	1,785	2,731	2,129	3,550	2,399
2010	14,429	1,763	1,849	2,644	2,025	2,794	1,984
				Percent[e]			
Academe							
1990	51.5	48.5	38.7	50.3	26.3	46.4	83.2
1995	52.4	51.4	41.8	53.4	19.1	48.3	82.8
2000	48.6	46.0	33.7	51.6	14.8	47.9	79.3
2005	54.3	53.2	40.6	61.7	18.5	50.2	83.0
2010	52.6	49.0	35.9	59.9	16.9	53.4	81.7

continued on next two pages

Table 11.1. *Continued.*

Employment commitments and sector	Total	Life sciences[a]	Physical sciences[b]	Social sciences[c]	Engineering	Education	Humanities
	Percent[e]						
Government							
1990	8.8	16.3	8.3	12.8	11.9	7.2	2.2
1995	8.1	14.1	8.6	12.5	10.9	6.0	1.8
2000	7.4	13.6	6.8	11.5	9.0	4.6	2.0
2005	6.9	12.7	6.6	10.1	9.3	4.1	2.3
2010	8.9	14.5	9.8	13.9	12.8	3.5	2.3
Industry/business[f]							
1990	21.9	26.4	50.6	18.4	59.1	6.2	4.7
1995	21.7	24.5	45.3	16.4	66.1	6.0	5.1
2000	26.1	28.9	54.7	17.7	72.9	5.7	6.5
2005	22.8	25.3	48.7	14.4	68.7	4.1	4.2
2010	23.2	24.6	48.1	13.7	64.4	4.5	4.9
Not for profit organization							
1990	6.7	7.3	1.6	13.3	2.2	5.7	5.7
1995	6.3	7.3	2.2	11.5	2.2	5.1	5.8
2000	5.9	6.9	2.0	11.5	1.8	4.6	6.0
2005	5.3	7.1	2.5	8.8	2.3	4.3	6.2
2010	5.2	8.4	2.7	7.2	3.2	4.4	4.9

Other/unknown[g]							
1990	11.1	1.5	0.8	5.2	0.5	34.5	4.1
1995	11.4	2.7	2.1	6.2	1.6	34.6	4.5
2000	12.0	4.6	2.8	7.8	1.5	37.2	6.1
2005	10.7	1.8	1.6	5.0	1.2	37.3	4.3
2010	10.1	3.5	3.5	5.3	2.7	34.1	6.2

[a] Includes agricultural sciences/natural resources, biological/biomedical sciences, and health sciences.
[b] Includes mathematics and computer and information sciences.
[c] Includes psychology.
[d] Non-science and engineering fields not shown separately.
[e] Percentages are based on number reporting definite employment commitments in the United States.
[f] Includes doctorate recipients who indicated self-employment.
[g] "Other" is mainly composed of elementary and secondary schools.

Note: Due to rounding, percentages may not sum to 100.

Source: NSF/NIH/USED/USDA/NEH/NASA, 2010 Survey of Earned Doctorates.

A glance at the table suggests at least two durable trends. First, in the aggregate, there is remarkable durability in immediate postgraduate employment of doctorates over the past twenty years: about half typically enter academe in some capacity, about one-fifth to one-quarter enter industry and less than a tenth enter government or the nonprofit sector. Second, there is enormous variation in employment by academic field: at one end of the spectrum, nearly four-fifths of humanities doctorates enter academe (closely followed by social science doctorates at three-fifths), while at the other end, less than one-fifth of engineering doctorates do so (closely followed by physical science doctorates at one-third). It is important to note that although half of new PhDs move into academe on degree receipt, the move is not necessarily into career-ladder faculty positions (see supra). In 2010, for example, among 13,000 science and engineering doctoral recipients with definite plans, 48.8 percent were planning postdoctoral study; 18.7 percent academic employment; 13.7 percent other employment (in elementary/secondary education, government, or the nonprofit sector); 13.1 percent industry; and 5.3 percent expected to work abroad. Most of the academic sector employment reported—at least initially—is either in postdoctoral fellowship positions or in other nonregular positions including part-time and fixed-contract full-time positions. Although postdoctoral study has always been a significant component of the scientific career in the United States especially in the life sciences, the past two decades have seen a progressive lengthening of this transition phase and an extension to nearly all academe-bound PhDs in the natural sciences. Whereas in the past a single postdoc of one to two years' length was not uncommon, new PhDs now typically hold more than one postdoc and each may last two to three years. This tends to extend the transition phase between graduate study and first full-time academic appointment in a way that does not constructively contribute to workforce training, and may even serve as a career dead end (Ehrenberg et al. 2010).

These aggregated figures are given further specificity and elaboration in a recent national survey of PhDs in the social sciences ten years postdegree receipt. Nerad (2008) reported that it was only after about four years post-PhD that three-quarters of PhD recipients had achieved stable, full-time employment in any sector (academe, industry, government, private-nonprofit) and eight years before 90 percent had done so; less than half had achieved such stable employment in the first two years post-PhD.

Nerad's national sample overrepresented aspirants to academic careers (three-quarters aspired to academic careers). Among them, there was broad pessimism about the job market: one-third characterized their prospects as "fair" and one-fifth as "poor." Only one of eight considered their prospects "excellent." The delayed time to stable, full-time employment was especially acute for those pursuing an academic path. Among the 75 percent of academic hopefuls, only one-fourth had landed a career ladder job within six months of degree receipt, 40 percent within one year. Fully six years out, about three-fourths had secured a tenured or tenure-track faculty position (Nerad 2008). The typical career path began with a temporary position, but typically progressed to a career-ladder position—usually requiring a change of institutional employer and frequently a geographic move.[18] The path to a ladder faculty appointment typically went through such part-time or fixed-contract appointments: the probability of moving from a full-time nonacademic job to a career-ladder position was nearly zero.[19] These results largely match the findings of Ehrenberg et al.'s study (undertaken during the 1990s for the Andrew Mellon Foundation) of successive cohorts of humanities doctorates (Ehrenberg et al. 2010). The concurrent analyses of career mobility data undertaken by Schuster and Finkelstein (2006) and Finkelstein, Schuster, and Iglesias (2013), and based on the National Study of Postsecondary Faculty in both 1999 and 2004, largely corroborate such findings. However, their estimates suggest that mobility between part-time or full-time fixed-contract positions, on the one hand, and tenure track positions, on the other, may be less frequent overall but became somewhat easier between 1999 and 2004.[20]

In this kind of job market, according to Nerad (2008), about one in five who aspired to an academic job changed their career goals within the first five years post-PhD. Sixty percent of these post-PhD "goal shifters" had never been in a tenure-track position. To explain their change of heart, goal shifters usually offered push factors such as "no positions available in academia" rather than pull factors such as attraction to other opportunities. Conversely, people rarely left tenure-track positions. Among those who had ever been on the tenure track, when surveyed, 93 percent were still in ladder faculty positions.

Once the First Stable Job Has Been Achieved

If new entrants spend several years after receiving the PhD transitioning to stable, full-time academic employment, what do they face once they land a relatively good job? In addressing this question, we look at two broad areas: (1) conditions of work life, that is, what kinds of work pressures and commitments do they experience, including required evaluation; and (2) family life and the balance (or lack of) with work life.

Work Life

The work life experience of new entrants, as we have suggested, varies principally by the type of institution in which they are employed and the type of appointment they hold. As we shall see, work life may also vary by gender. The common element to all situations is some kind of performance review—the single factor that dominates early work life experience.

For tenure-eligible appointments, a review typically takes the form of annual assessments of "progress toward tenure" (Twombly 2005). The major high-stakes review for tenure-eligible faculty comes one year before the end of the entire probationary period, at which time a decision is made as to whether to award tenure. That decision is based on an assessment of the performance of academic staff members in their teaching, research, and service responsibilities. At research universities, research performance as reflected in publications and grant awards is emphasized, while at four-year institutions with a predominantly teaching mission, teaching performance is likely to be a more central consideration (although some sort of research or scholarly performance is usually expected).

Tenure review typically involves a year-long process conducted in successive stages by faculty committees at the levels of the individual academic unit, the larger academic "super unit" in which the focal academic unit is embedded, and by senior administrators including the dean of the academic super unit and the chief academic officer and president of the institution (Twombly 2005). Although the recommendations of the faculty bodies are typically dispositive, the final decision is ultimately taken by the president and board of trustees. Typically, about 70 percent of all eligible academic staff who come up for tenure consideration are granted tenure, although that figure drops to about 50 percent at research universities (Dooris and Sandmeyer 2006). In the U.S. system, a negative tenure decision is tantamount to a nonreappointment decision—although in special cases it may be possible to retain such a faculty member on a limited-term, off-track appointment. Academic staff who are denied tenure often seek and accept academic staff positions at less prestigious colleges and universities that set different standards for promotion and tenure, or they may accept full-time positions off the tenure track[21]—although some, no doubt, take a negative tenure decision as the impetus to move out of the academy altogether.

For limited-contract academic staff, major evaluations and reappointment decisions are made in the middle of the year preceding the final year of the contract. They typically involve review by lower level faculty bodies and the deans of major academic units.

In terms of work role and work life, the available evidence suggests that faculty on career ladder appointments—concurrently undertaking teaching, research, and service responsibilities—tend to work longer hours than more specialized faculty on fixed-contract appointments, to the tune of nearly 50 hours weekly, of which about 60 percent is devoted to teaching, advisement, and course development responsibilities (Schuster and Finkelstein 2006). At research universities, they may initially receive a reduced teaching load to enable them to devote more energy to launching a postdissertation research program. They are subject, however, to high, if unclear, expectations for research, publication, and, depending on the field, for securing external grant funding. One of the consistent complaints voiced by tenure-ladder faculty—across all institutional types—was the lack of clear and explicit standards for satisfying tenure requirements (Gappa, Austin, and Trice 2007).

These heightened expectations arise just as many of the new entrants who are women are pushing up against their "biological clocks" and seeking to start or maintain a young family. Indeed, while women social science PhDs in the Nerad study (2008) were equally as likely as men to both land career-ladder jobs and secure jobs at research-intensive universities, gender differences emerged postappointment, including differences in tenure rates and persistence. Among those who had achieved a tenure-track appointment, 33 percent of the men (compared to 28 percent of the women) had been granted tenure at the sixth year post-PhD. Men were slightly more likely to be tenured at more prestigious universities (6 percent versus 4 percent) and half as likely as women to leave career-ladder positions (5 percent versus 9 percent). Indeed, Schuster and Finkelstein (2006) found that among those faculty reporting mobility from tenure-track to fixed-contract positions, the vast majority were women—in part as a means of securing a more manageable workload *sans* research pressures. In their recent comparative study of women in the professions, Mason and Ekman (2007) reported that academe provided a less family-friendly environment than several career specialties in medicine and law (Mason and Ekman 2007).

Among those faculty beginning their careers in nonresearch university settings, research and publications pressures may be less intense, but they are certainly not nonexistent. Moreover, new entrants are likely to have many fewer resources—in terms of graduate student assistance, library and computing facilities, research funds, and so on—to meet the reduced demands, making them perhaps equally onerous (i.e., fewer demands, but with commensurately fewer resources). Once having begun outside the research university sector, it becomes very difficult to move back into it. That is a function both of the fact that career development in a nonresearch setting is likely to suffer, making one less attractive as a prospective job candidate in the research university sector, as well as the tendency of institutions to hire within a band of institutions of either equal or greater prestige (Burke 1988).

In negotiating the stresses of work life, new entrants have historically had to sink or swim on their own. Over the past several decades, many institutions have sought to provide more formal organizational supports to ease early career stresses. Those supports usually take the form of personnel policies that ease family transitions (childcare facilities or family leave for childbirth or eldercare)—some of which are actually mandated by federal legislation. In some cases, formal mentoring programs have been established at the department or school level or, more frequently, department chairs have been encouraged to provide extra support. Formal programmatic approaches, involving release time from teaching for socialization experiences and university-wide peer support programs, remain relatively rare (Gappa, Austin, and Trice 2007).

Family Life

Both men and women increasingly report an unwillingness to sacrifice family life for career—the signature of the millennial generation. But, to pursue their PhD careers, according to Nerad (2008), women made more sacrifices. Although men and women were equally likely to wish for marriage and children, women married and formed marriage-like unions less often; they more often divorced and delayed or relinquished children. Women were almost twice as likely as men to indicate that a job change occurred because of "family needs or responsibilities," or because a "partner's job moved." Women were more likely to be part of a dual-career couple—a situation that is almost uniquely American (Finkelstein 2012)—which may complicate career advancement for doctorate holders because academic careers require geographic mobility (Kulis and Sicotte 2002; Rosenfeld and Jones 1987). Although 59 percent of partnered men reported their partner moved with them to accommodate career advancement, only 42 percent of coupled women did (Nerad 2008).

The Rewards of the Early Academic Career

The rewards of an academic career can be viewed through both a psychic and pecuniary lens. Historically, academic careers came in the nineteenth century to be viewed as something of a "calling" for cultured men of independent means (Veysey, 1965), and competitive compensation did not emerge until after the World War II. How do current aspirants fare?

Psychic Rewards

The available evidence on the psychic rewards of modern academic careers is not straightforward. On the one hand, faculty in the United States consistently express high satisfaction with their career choice—in the neighborhood of 80 percent to 85 percent (and this has been stable for half a century). At the same time early career faculty on the tenure-track are among the least satisfied with their jobs, while early career faculty, especially women, in full-time positions off the tenure track are among the most satisfied (Schuster and Finkelstein 2006). In some respects, these findings follow quite logically from the magnitude and scope of the work pressures on pretenure faculty and the relative diminution of such pressures among those off the tenure track. The mixed picture reflects in real terms the trade-offs that new faculty are required to make between job security, professional recognition, the work environment, family life, and so on. Trower (2011) conducted a study measuring the importance of nineteen job factors to recent graduates of doctoral degree programs. The top five were: (1) institutional support for research; (2) time for family/personal obligations; (3) quality of the department; (4) teaching load; and (5) flexibility of the work schedule. Moreover, the primary considerations of recent graduates when choosing a job were: (1) finding a situation in which they could do meaningful work and strike a balance between teaching and research that suits them; (2) quality of living conditions, for example, affordability of housing, commute, good K–12 schools, community feeling and safety, and job opportunities for spouse or partner; and (3) balance between work and home life. Although quality of department, time for research, and teaching load have always been primary considerations, the rising importance of time for family obligations and work life balance are new: they did not make the list two generations ago (Finkelstein 1984). There thus appears to be something of a revolution in the expectations that new faculty bring to their careers.

Monetary Rewards: Salaries

Table 11.2 shows the median basic annual salary for doctoral recipients in 2010 by field of study and employment sector—probably the best single indicator of relative attractiveness in pecuniary terms of academic careers at the moment of career entry.

When we examine the salaries paid to new doctorates (Table 11.2) across sectors (from academe to industry to government and the nonprofit sector), we see a clear pattern of overall academic disadvantage. At the most extreme, new doctorates entering directly into the business/industrial sector report a 60.5 percent salary premium over those entering academe; at the lower end, new doctorates entering the private, nonprofit sector report a 25.5 percent premium over those entering academe. When we examine individual fields, we find much wider gaps in some fields than others. Thus, in the physical sciences, the salary premium accruing to new doctorates who choose industry over the academy for their first job is 72 percent (101 percent in earth, atmospheric, and ocean sciences), while in the social sciences, the premium accruing to new doctorates choosing a first job in industry rather than academe is 42 percent and in the humanities, a mere 7.3 percent. These data suggest that, across different academic fields, the U.S. academy displays a range of very different positions vis-à-vis recruiting the next generation of PhDs. The competitive compensation challenges remain greatest in the physical and life sciences and engineering, and smallest in the humanities, education, and the social sciences.

When we move to consider the competitiveness of salary levels at the point of entry to the first career-ladder position—the assistant professorship, which typically occurs three- to six years after receipt of the PhD—the most reliable and widely available source of data is the American Association of University Professors' (AAUP) Annual Survey of the Economic Status of the Profession. In 2011, according to the AAUP, the average salary of assistant professors across all four-year institutions was in the range of US$60,000 to US$65,000—although there remained considerable variation by type of institution, with perhaps a 15 percent to 20 percent premium for those employed in the research university sector, especially in the private sector. Impressionistically speaking, that compares to what a newly minted baccalaureate level nurse or mechanical engineer would be offered in their entry-level job or what a newly minted attorney (with at JD degree) would be offered in the public sector. Moreover, recent studies sponsored by the Modern Language Association (MLA) and the American Federation of Teachers (AFT) suggest that these entry-level

Table 11.2. Median basic annual salary for doctorate recipients with definite post graduation plans for employment in the United States, by field of study and employment sector: 2010 (Dollars)

Field of study	Academe	Industry/ business[a]	Government	Not for profit organization	Other/ unknown[b]
All fields	55,720	89,448	77,037	69,940	72,267
Science and engineering	56,956	90,020	77,235	75,873	63,479
Life sciences	58,920	81,493	70,456	78,572	60,0000
Agricultural sciences	55,001	73,334	63,001	60,000	D
Biological sciences	49,250	79,333	64,412	62,501	D
Health sciences	65,605	90,418	80,386	90,501	D
Physical sciences	55,179	94,940	82,667	82,501	67,500
Chemistry	47,396	85,406	68,750	D	D
Earth, atmospheric, and ocean sciences	51,876	104,311	68,000	D	D
Mathematics and computer sciences	59,511	99,382	90,834	88,750	80,000
Physics and astronomy	47,609	88,530	82,858	D	D

continued on next page

Table 11.2. *Continued.*

Field of study	Academe	Industry/ business[a]	Government	Not for profit organization	Other/ unknown[b]
Social sciences and psychology	54,832	77,836	71,598	67,500	61,766
Economics	79,896	96,364	95,358	97,500	D
Psychology	50,993	72,354	61,806	53,612	59,583
Social sciences[c]	53,156	77,250	74,190	72,693	D
Engineering	71,082	91,065	89,575	90,000	85,001
Non-science and engineering	54,819	80,000	76,081	59,000	73,713
Education	57,025	76,500	75,385	66,471	75,868
Humanities	47,157	50,626	65,715	51,112	50,000
Business management/ administration	103,241	110,668	104,001	D	D
Other non-science and engineering fields[d]	54,633	77,778	78,750	50,000	D

D = suppressed to avoid disclosure of confidential information.

[a] Includes doctorate recipients who indicated self-employment.

[b] "Other" is mainly composed of elementary and secondary schools.

[c] Excludes economics.

[d] Excludes business management/administration.

Source: NSF/NIH/USED/USDA/NEH/NASA, 2010 Survey of Earned Doctorates.

salaries (for those who secure career-ladder positions) are considerably higher than those received by either full-time, fixed-contract faculty or part-time faculty. The MLA reported that full-time fixed-contract appointees earned 90 percent of tenure-track average salaries (MLA 2008), while the AFT study reported that full-time, contract faculty earned 60 percent of tenured and tenure-track faculty average salaries combined (JBL Associates 2008). This means that the comparisons we are drawing here are to the best-paid and most advantaged new academic appointees—rather than to the average ones.

The AAUP, MLA, or AFT data do not provide a detailed breakdown by academic field nor is it possible to compare such salaries to those of comparably educated professionals outside academe. Therefore, we have employed data from the U.S. Bureau of Labor Statistics to compare individuals serving as postsecondary teachers (in four-year colleges and universities, but outside two-year community colleges and proprietary institutions) to colleagues working in positions in the same field that are outside academe, but that typically require the terminal degree, or PhD.[22] In order to focus on individuals at the early stages (but not the very beginning) of their career—roughly equivalent to the assistant professor stage—we have examined comparative salaries at the 25th percentile rather than the simple median, with the understanding that any differences may be either accentuated or attenuated at later career stages. Table 11.3 presents the salaries of early-stage postsecondary teachers (25th percentile) as compared to equivalent positions in government, industry, and the private sector in three fields (25th percentile)—chemistry, psychology, and law.[23]

Beginning with chemistry, in the public sector, postsecondary teachers at the 25th percentile earn 7.8 percent more than bench chemists; in the private sector, the figure is 6.1 percent more. In psychology, in the public sector postsecondary teachers at the 25th percentile earn 10.9 percent less than the average for all other psychology job categories; in the private sector, they earn 11.8 percent less. In law, in the public sector postsecondary teachers at the 25th percentile earn 22.2 percent more than the average of all other legal job categories; in the private sector, they earn 17.9 percent less. What these initial comparisons suggest is that there are large differences among fields and between the public and private sector. In chemistry, young postsecondary teachers do relatively well compared to entry-level bench chemists; much less so for entry-level postsecondary teachers in psychology. The situation in law is mixed—varying between the public and private sectors. When considered in the context of the relatively greater security of academic employment, what differences exist

Table 11.3. Salaries of Postsecondary Teachers (Mean and 25th Percentile) and Non-Academic Professionals in Five Fields, and % Academic Differential, 2009

	2009							
	Private		% Diff: Acad versus Non-Acad		Public		% Diff: versus Non-Acad	
Occupation	Mean Sal	25%ile	Mean Sal	25%ile	Mean Sal	25%ile	Mean Sal	25%ile
Chemistry Occupations								
Chemists	$71,780	$49,800	7.3	6.1	$77,640	$50,620	5.5	7.8
Chemistry teachers, postsecondary	$77,030	$52,830			$81,930	$54,5500		
Psychology Occupations	$89,763	$55,437	–19.9	–11.8	$75,860	$59,963	–0.5	–10.9
Clinical, counseling, and school psychologists	$74,200	$46,530	–3.1	5.0	$70,810	$53,050	6.6	0.7
Industrial-organizational psychologists	$108,940	$63,920	–34.0	–23.5	$73,460	$59,880	2.7	–10.8
Psychologists, all other	$86,150	$55,860	–16.5	–12.5	$83,310	$66,960	–9.4	–20.3
Psychology teachers, postsecondary	$71,920	$48,870			$75,480	$53,400		

Legal Occupations	$137,540	$79,720	–20.7	–17.9	$101,175	$62,060	16.8	22.2
Lawyers	$137,540	$79,720	–20.7	–17.9	$98,360	$67,730	20.1	11.9
Judges, magistrate judges, and magistrates	N/A	N/A			$103,990	$56,390	13.6	34.4
Law teachers, postsecondary	$109,020	$65,460			$118,170	$75,810		

Source: US Department of Labor, Bureau of Labor Statistics, 2009 seem rather small and would not seem—at least in the early years—to be a substantial deterrent to the pursuit of an academic career. That may change considerably, however, in the later career years to be sure; but there is little evidence currently or historically that academic career choice has been based primarily on a cold-blooded calculus of economic returns. Moreover, in addition to salary, most universities offer very attractive and competitive fringe benefit packages. In the public sector, those benefits parallel those of public employees and include generous pension programs and health insurance, not infrequently achieved by collective bargaining. In the private sector, benefits may also include tuition benefits for spouses and children as well as subsidized day care. There is some emerging evidence, however, that benefits packages are shrinking (Conley 2012).

Summary and Prospects

The major concluding observation that needs to be made is that the American academic profession as we have known it since World War II—a relatively homogeneous workforce united by a common background, a common mission, a common career trajectory, albeit with significant variation among institutional types and academic fields—has transformed itself, perhaps under our collective radar, into a highly differentiated workforce segmented by diverse backgrounds, career trajectories, motivation, talents, and work roles. The historic core of that workforce—the tenured and tenure-track faculty—is shrinking overall and subject to increased workload pressures. New kinds of part-time and full-time fixed-contract (noncareer ladder) appointments have emerged over the past generation and now constitute the first rung on an increasingly constricted career ladder. The availability of career opportunities varies both by institutional type and academic field—with the best opportunities available in the natural sciences and the most plentiful opportunities outside the research university sector. Current economic crises may further have slowed existing faculty retirements and hence the growth of new positions. This means that career prospects for new recruits are more contingent and differentiated than ever.

The more diverse opportunity structure is matched by a steady, albeit more diverse supply of doctoral recipients and candidates, especially by an increased proportion of women, including married women with family responsibilities. More generally, men as well as women born into this Millennial generation (born post-1980) are approaching their careers with a clearer set of personal requirements for balancing career and family, and a general disinclination to sacrifice everything on the altar of career advancement. The data suggest that over the past one to two decades a period of between two to five years has opened up for most academic career aspirants between PhD receipt and landing the first career-ladder position (for the lucky half that manage to snag them). There is some evidence that a significant minority of aspirants is giving up on academic careers—either during this period or prior to receipt of tenure—and these are disproportionately women. Once having achieved career-ladder positions, early career faculty are confronted with considerable workload pressure and generally declining working conditions (Cummings and Finkelstein 2011). In the face of these challenges, however, faculty consistently report high levels of career satisfaction—although satisfaction with particular jobs varies considerably. The data on academic compensation suggests that the financial disadvantage to working in the academic sector may be exaggerated overall and certainly varies considerably by field and sector of employment (private versus public). In fields such as chemistry and law, for example, academics do relatively well; less so in psychology.

In light of circumstances that are not entirely favorable, the academic profession in the United States faces challenges over the coming generation at the national, institutional, and individual levels.

National Level

At the national level, perhaps the greatest challenge remains that of ensuring the future of a vibrant national intellectual community in the humanities, the arts, and the "softer" social sciences (history, anthropology). Historically, the academic sector has been the primary venue in which professional work takes place in the humanities and, to a lesser extent, the arts. That is threatened by the increasingly dim academic career prospects in the humanities fields and the equally dim prospects for financial support for research in the humanities and the arts. The revolution in academic appointments has hit these areas the hardest; and even major universities are actively considering the wholesale elimination of academic department such as classics, modern languages, anthropology, geography, philosophy, art, and music. Although there has been recently a small increase in PhD production in the humanities, the long-term trend is one of slow and steady decline—although a decline not nearly as precipitous as the decline in the academic opportunity structure.

Institutional Level

At the institutional level, colleges and universities find themselves increasingly home to a very diverse and stratified academic workforce, and shrinking cores of tenured, career-ladder core faculty. The extent to which traditional forms of faculty governance can maintain themselves in light of a more transient faculty is not clear. Nor is it clear how academic departments can continue to operate with a shrinking permanent core and a growing corps of transient colleagues. Both of these developments threaten the prospects for the continued existence of the academic community in the face of the increasing corporatization of higher education. From an operational perspective, the reconfiguration of the faculty body raises major questions about personnel policies. Campuses will need to develop a much more differentiated set of policies in order to accommodate the diversified workforce. Moreover, issues of equity between and among various components of the instructional and/or research workforce are likely to arise and require serious attention.

Institutions need to think long and hard—and collectively—about what kinds of faculty roles support which aspects of their mission. To what extent can the requirements and contours of traditional tenureable positions be modified to accommodate the new Millennial generation of academic women? To what extent ought accommodation be achieved not by modifying traditional faculty roles, but by constructing and strengthening new types of more specialized roles? What is the right proportion of faculty appointments to optimize institutional mission and individual career development and satisfaction? To the extent that the academic workforce is diversifying its background and preservice socialization, what new structures will institutions need to design in order to socialize an increasingly heterogeneous group of professionals to some set of traditional academic norms? Or, to what extent should the traditional norms that bound the tenured faculty simply be allowed to disintegrate? Which norms or elements are mission-critical—in the short- and/or long term? Which are simply gratuitous vestiges of an old order?

Individual Level

At the individual level, the historic structure of academic careers in the United States pursued within a "home" institution rather than within academic fields or geographic regions is, in some respects, under pressure. It is not clear how the traditional academic path on the tenure track will compete with the various emerging alternatives, particularly in meeting the needs of nontraditional academics, including married women with children. To what extent will the traditional academic career (which, after all, only emerged about a hundred years ago) survive as the norm? In a generation, will it stand only as a vestige of a storied past?

As we consider these challenges, it will be important to remember that we are discussing recruitment to "the best job there is" and one for which demand, in its pure form, has been drastically—and, probably, permanently—reduced, relative to the overall size of the enterprise. However precipitous the decline in the academic estate over the past generation, 80 percent of faculty are still satisfied with their jobs and would choose an academic career all over again (Schuster and Finkelstein 2006; Leslie 2007). Moreover, as Christine Musselin has reminded us, it is important to assess contemporary academic careers in the context of the broader restructuring of work in the global economy (Musselin 2007). The overall American economy is losing many good jobs, and, while gaining others, there is very little security in these new positions. The prospect of job security symbolized by tenure is an increasingly rare and precious commodity in the new global economy. The prospect of being able to pursue one's intellectual interests, in a relatively autonomous setting, with some measure of job security, makes academic work, in some sense, a more desirable career choice than ever; and one, presumably, that will continue to attract at least a significant minority of the "best and brightest."

We should also consider the other side of the diversification coin: expanding academic roles and career paths represents not merely potential diminution of the traditional, homogeneous role, but the extension of opportunities to play new and perhaps more personally accessible roles to segments of the population previously excluded from the academic professions. The extent to which the lowering of opportunity for what have been viewed as the "best jobs" translates, in effect, to expansion of opportunity for many different (but nonetheless appealing) jobs, suggests that the calculus of assessing trade-offs between the old and new order may be more complex and nuanced than we first anticipated.

Notes

1. Unlike many national systems, in the United States the observation that "a university is a university is a university" does not apply!

2. Three years in the two-year public community college sector.

3. "New hires" refers to individuals who appear for the first time in the human resource records of their home institutions in a given year.

4. Headcount faculty includes those who are hired on a full-time basis as well as all those hired on a less than full-time basis, usually on the basis of one or two courses taught.

5. "Tenure eligible" refers to positions that lead to an "up or out" tenure decision and subsequent permanent employment.

6. As of 2004, colleges and universities in the United States are no longer permitted by federal law to mandate retirement at a particular age. Although retirement behavior has tended to be fairly stable (most faculty retire around age 65, the traditional retirement age), there is some evidence that the recent economic recession of 2008 led some faculty to delay retirement (TIAA Retirement Confidence Survey 2011), and this trend is accelerated by better working conditions at the major research universities.

7. Only a small proportion of part-time appointments are considered as a percentage of a full-time appointment, for example, half-time with a full range of teaching, research, and service responsibilities.

8. Christine Musselin makes the point in *The Market for Academics* (2010) that while career paths in French and German universities are made within the national discipline, in the United States they are made within the context of the individual university.

9. Availability pools are usually based on numbers and proportions of PhD recipients in a given field by race/ethnicity and gender over previous years, as an indicator of the availability of women and racial ethnic minorities to be hired for vacant positions.

10. Indeed, a large portion of these non-PhD faculty might include master's prepared individuals in health fields such as nursing, or PhD candidates in English or foreign languages or mathematics who are hired on a full-time basis to teach lower division introductory or clinical and remedial courses. Most are in some stage of pursuit of the PhD.

11. STEM is the acronym coined by the National Science Foundation in the United States to refer to the disciplines related to science, technology, engineering, and mathematics.

12. The number of non-STEM doctorates actually declined from 15,400 to 14,900, but that was accounted for largely by the decline in education EdD doctorates, which are no longer counted as research PhDs for NSF purposes. Even after the EdD reclassification, education remained the largest nonscience and engineering field (S&E), reporting 5,294 doctorates awarded in 2010.

13. The number of S&E doctorate recipients with temporary visas decreased 7.4 percent from 2009 to 2010, the second consecutive year of decline after several years of growth.

14. This decline may reflect increased restrictions on temporary visas by the Bush administration following the terrorist attacks of September 11, 2001,

which would have gone into effect in 2002 and 2003 and be reflected in degree production five years or so later.

15. Increasing time-to-degree, especially in the humanities fields, was identified by Bowen and Sosa (1994) as a dual threat to educational efficiency (given low PhD completion rates) and to effectiveness, with evidence that higher time-to-degree was associated with a lack of early career success (see Ehrenberg et al. 2010). A number of initiatives were proposed and undertaken by the Andrew Mellon Foundation and others in the ensuing decade to shorten time-to-degree rates.

16. Although now averaging 7.7 years, there is considerable variation by field, ranging from 6.7 years in the physical sciences to 12.5 years in education, closely followed by 9.3 years in the humanities. Given that individuals typically enter graduate study two years after receipt of the baccalaureate degree, and that the baccalaureate degree is typically earned in the early twenties, doctoral recipients are, on average, in their early thirties at degree receipt—although younger in the physical sciences and engineering and significantly older in education and the humanities.

17. It should be noted that only about one-third of doctoral recipients annually typically have "definite employment commitments" on which to report at the time of degree award.

18. It should be noted that, in the U.S. context, geographic or at least interinstitutional mobility has been a basic ingredient of academic careers. Major research universities typically do not hire their own graduates, requiring at a minimum that they begin their careers elsewhere before considering the possibility of "hiring them back." Although careers in the United States are shaped by the hiring institution, mobility between institutions is the typical pattern in an academic career.

19. There was, however, some reciprocal flow between the contingent academic labor market and stable, full-time positions in industry, government, and nonprofits, as well as to nonfaculty positions in the academic sector.

20. Finkelstein, Conley, and Schuster are currently addressing this question through analyses of more than 21,000 natural and social scientists who responded to the NSF's triennial Survey of Doctoral Recipients at least three times between 1993 and 2008.

21. This tends to be especially true for academic women, who are much more likely than men to move from a tenure track to a fixed-term appointment even prior to tenure review usually for purposes of reducing work demands and restoring a healthier work-family life balance.

22. Insofar as compensation tends to be based on education credentials and years of experience, we have sought to control for both in our comparisons.

23. These fields were chosen because they fulfill two conditions: (1) each offers plentiful nonacademic career opportunities for PhDs; and (2) nonacademic opportunities typically require a PhD or other terminal degree (JD), allowing

comparisons to equate for educational credentials—a principal determinant of salary.

References

Altbach, Philip G. et al. 2012. *Paying the Professoriate: A Global Comparison of Compensation and Contracts.* New York: Routledge.

American Association of University Professors. 2012. "Annual Report on the Economic Status of the Profession, 2011–12." *Academe* (February/March).

Bair, Jeffrey. 2003. "Hiring Practices in Finance Education: Linkages Among Top-Ranked Graduate Programs." *Journal of Economics & Sociology* 62(2): 429–443.

Bowen, Howard, and Jack Schuster. 1986. *American Professors: A National Resource Imperiled.* New York: Oxford University Press.

Burke, Delores. 1988. *The Academic Marketplace Revisited.* New York: Basic Books.

Caplow, Theodore, and Reece McGee. 1958. *The Academic Marketplace.* New York: Basic Books.

Carter, Ralph G., and James M. Scott. 1998. "Navigating the Academic Job Market Minefield." *PS: Political Science and Politics* 31(3): 615–622.

Clark, Robert, and Jennifer Ma, eds. 2005. *Recruitment, Retention, and Retirement in Higher Education: Building and Managing the Faculty of the Future.* Northampton, MA: Edward Elgar.

Coalition on the Academic Workforce, 2011. Preliminary Report.

Conley, Valerie M. 2012. "Eroding Retirement and Benefits: The Wrong Response to Fiscal Crisis." *The 2012 Almanac of Higher Education.* Washington, DC: The National Education Association.

Cummings, William K., and Martin J. Finkelstein. 2011. *Scholars in the Changing American Academy: New Contexts, New Roles and New Rules.* Dordrecht, Netherlands: Springer.

Dooris, Michael J., and Louis E. Sandmeyer. October 2006. "Planning for Improvement in the Academic Department." *Effective Practices for Academic Leaders,* 1(10): 1-16.

Ehrenberg, Ronald G. et al. 2010. *The Education of Scholars.* Princeton, NJ: Princeton University Press.

Finkelstein, Martin J., and William K. Cummings. 2012. "American Faculty and their Institutions." *Change* 44: 48–59.

Finkelstein, Martin J., Jack Schuster, and Kevin Iglesias. 2013. "Faculty Careers in Rapid Transition: The Salience of the Redistribution of Faculty Appointments." *Research Dialogues* 108, Teachers Insurance and Annuity Association.

Gappa, Judith M., Ann E. Austin, and Andrea G. Trice. 2007. *Rethinking Faculty Work: Higher Education's Strategic Imperative.* San Francisco: Jossey-Bass.

Geiger, Roger. 2010. "Impact of the Financial Crisis on Higher Education in the United States." *International Higher Education* 59(Spring): 9–11.

Goonen, Norma M., and Rachel S. Blechman. 1999. *Higher Education Administration: A Guide to Legal, Ethical and Practical Issues*. Westport, CT: Greenwood Press.

Gumport, Patricia. 2000. "Academic Restructuring: Organizational Change and Institutional Imperatives." *Higher Education* 39: 67–91.

Hentschke, Guilbert, Vincente Lechuga, and William Tierney, eds. 2010. *For-Profit Colleges and Universities: Their Markets, Regulation, Performance and Place in Higher Education*. Sterling, VA: Stylus.

Howe, Neil, and William Strauss. 2000. *Millennials Rising: The Next Great Generation*. New York: Vintage Press.

JBL Associates. 2008. *Reversing Course: The Troubled State of Academic Staffing and a Path Forward*. Washington, DC: American Federation of Teachers.

Kulis, Stephen, and Diane Sicotte. 2002. "Women Scientists in Academia: Geographically Constrained to Big Cities, College Clusters, or the Coasts?" *Research in Higher Education* 43: 1–30.

Leslie, David. 2007. "The Reshaping of America's Academic Workforce," TIAACREF *Research Dialogues* 87(March).

Leslie, Larry, and Sheila Slaughter. 1995. "The Development and Current Status of Market Mechanisms in United States Postsecondary Education." *Higher Education Policy* 10, 239–252.

Mason, Mary Ann, and Eve Mason Ekman. 2007. *Mothers on the Fast Track: How a New Generation Can Balance Family and Careers*. New York: Oxford University Press.

Matier, Michael W. 1991. "Recruiting Faculty: Complementary Tales from 2 Campuses." *Research in Higher Education* 32(1): 31–44.

Modern Language Association (MLA). 2008. *Education in the Balance: A Report on the Academic Workforce in English*. Washington, DC: Modern Language Association.

Musselin, Christine. 2007. "Transformation of Academic Work: Facts and Analysis." In *Key Challenges to the Academic Profession*, edited by M. Kogan and U. Teichler. Kassel, Germany: UNESCO Forum on Higher Education.

Musselin, Christine. 2010. *The Market for Academics*. New York: Routledge.

National Science Foundation. 2011. *Survey of Earned Doctorates*. Washington, DC: National Science Foundation.

Nerad, Maresi. 2008. *Social Science PhDs 5+Years Out: A National Survey of PhDs in Six Fields*. Seattle, WA: Center for Innovation and Research in Graduate Education (CIRGE), University of Washington.

Rosenfeld, Rachel, and Jo Ann Jones. 1987. "Patterns and Effects of Geographic Mobility for Academic Women and Men." *Journal of Higher Education* 58: 493–515.

Rudd, Elizabeth, Emory Morrison, Renate Sadrozinski, Maresi Nerad, and Joseph Cerny. 2008. "Equality and Illusion: Gender and Tenure in Art History Careers." *Journal of Marriage and Family* 70: 228–238.

Schuster, Jack, and Martin J. Finkelstein. 2006. *The American Faculty: Restructuring Academic Work and Careers.* Baltimore, MD: Johns Hopkins University Press.

TIAA. 2012. Retirement Confidence Survey, 2011.

Trower, Cathy A. 2002. "Can Colleges Competitively Recruit Faculty Without the Prospect of Tenure?" In *Questions of Tenure*, edited by Richard Chait. Cambridge, MA: Harvard University Press.

Trower, Cathy A. 2006. "Gen X Meets Theory X: What New Scholars Want." *Journal of Collective Bargaining in the Academy* 0.

Trower, Cathy A. 2012. *Success on the Tenure Track: Five Keys to Faculty Job Satisfaction.* Baltimore: Johns Hopkins University Press.

Twombly, Susan B. 2005. "Values, Policies and Practices Affecting the Hiring Process for Full-Time Arts and Sciences Faculty in Community Colleges." *Journal of Higher Education* 76: 423–447.

U.S. Department of Education. 2008. *The National Study of Postsecondary Faculty 2004.* Washington, DC: National Center for Education Statistics.

Veysey, Laurence. 1965. *The Emergence of the American University.* Chicago: University of Chicago Press.

Chapter 12

Future Prospects for Young Faculty Across the Academic World

A Global Comparison and Assessment

Martin J. Finkelstein, Kevin W. Iglesias, Anna Panova, and Maria Yudkevich

Introduction

The preceding chapters have provided a series of portraits of the prospects for newly entering faculty in each of our ten participating countries (Brazil, China, India, France, Germany, Norway, Portugal, Russia, South Africa, and the United States) on a set of common indicators—insofar as these are available. In this chapter, our focus is not on the indicators themselves, but rather on the recognizable patterns in which these indicators coalesce across countries. We propose an analytical framework that focuses our thinking about the questions central to understanding young faculty today and, hence, the future of academia. What kinds of opportunity structures for new entrants are discernable in today's global academic marketplace? What are the types of opportunity profiles (configurations of demand and supply) that exist? What incentives do these provide for recruiting and attracting the "best and brightest" to academic careers? And, by way of counterpoint, what challenges do these pose for the pursuit of academic careers and the recruitment of the new academic generation?

We begin with an overview of our conceptual framework: the key elements that make up what we refer to as the *opportunity structure* for academic careers and our assumptions about how these elements interact to form such a structure. Having done so, we focus briefly on the major elements or indicators before seeking to identify ideal profiles of opportunity structures that emerge among the ten participating countries. We conclude with some assessment of the prospects for recruiting the next academic generation—reflecting the mix of incentives and challenges our analyses reveal.

What emerges impressionistically is a rather mixed picture of contemporary academic systems. Some of them are growing and some are relatively stable (or even shrinking). Some are the recipients of significant and growing government investment, while others are the victims of government cutbacks. Some systems are top-heavy, with a large contingent of aging faculty, while others are relatively unencumbered by seniority. A few national systems offer a clear and predictable path to a secure career, while others offer no discernible career prospects. Some offer attractive compensation vis-à-vis other potential career opportunities, while others barely offer the prospect of financial independence without taking on second and third jobs. Entry requirements also vary substantially across systems. Some systems insist on the doctorate as the entry credential, while others allow for master's and even baccalaureate candidates to enter. Hiring rules and practices differ, as well. In some countries, there are nationwide systems of open competition, while in others entry through sponsorship and social ties flourish and are the main recruitment mechanisms.

The Model

Our analytical framework proceeds from basic concepts of supply and demand as economists have employed these to describe and explain academic labor markets (Carter 1976; Bowen and Schuster 1986; Breneman and Youn 1988; Musselin 2009). We believe that thinking about the different academic systems as representing particular cases of one general model will allow the reader to see more clearly how different features within each system are correlated to each other and how some characteristics of the academic profession in a particular country can be viewed as consequences of some "demand" and "supply" conditions.

Demand for Academic Staff

The main factors that affect the demand for academic staff are the demand for education, the demand for R&D in the country, and technology changes. In terms of demand, it is important to distinguish between "growth" demand and "replacement" demand. Growth demand is driven by growth in student enrollment and the consequent need to staff greater numbers of classes; it is also driven by growth of the demand for R&D. Replacement demand, that is, the demand that is created by the need to replace current academic staff, who (usually for reasons of advanced age) are leaving the system (either in response to mandatory retirement rules or infirmity or obsolescence). Both types of demand assume a stable basic model of delivery of higher education, for example, the organization of instruction in the form of face-to-face course offerings that pair a professor with a group of students over some defined period of time, as typically reflected in student-faculty ratios. Insofar as new models of delivery—including online learning—are emerging, these need to be factored into the demand equation in ways that we cannot yet specify with any degree of certainty. So, there are at least four key elements, or indicators of demand. First is enrollment growth rate (system growth). Second is expenditures on R&D. Third is the age and rank distribution of current faculty (as proxies for likely retirement and replacement demand), as shaped by national retirement policies (whether retirement is obligatory, at what age, etc.). The fourth element includes the existence and scope of new delivery models.

All four elements are playing an increasingly important role in recent years. Indeed, many countries (especially BRIC countries) have experienced considerable massification of higher education, with substantial growth in the share of young people entering universities. This means, inter alia, that the ideal (profile) of the "average student" changes—universities not only need more faculty than in previous decades but they may also need faculty with different qualifications. Both enrollment growth and diversification influence "replacement" patterns in academia. Concurrent with massification, quality of life has improved in recent decades in many countries. Life expectancy has increased and older people are productive and in many cases eager to continue their work. While the potential of technological innovations, the last element in our tetrad, is not fully operationalized at this point, it is important to keep these developments in mind in light of recent debates about the role and potential impact of emerging teaching and learning technologies.

To these traditional indicators of demand must be added what might be described as a cultural component: the value placed on higher education and scientific research as a national imperative. It is usually operationalized as the proportion of total national budget devoted to research and development (R&D) as well as the proportion of general budget expenditures for higher education (especially as a ratio to expenditures for primary and secondary education).

Although the above four indicators reflect the *quantitative* aspect of demand—how many faculty are needed and might be needed soon—there is also the matter of the *quality* of that demand. That is, how good are the jobs that are available and being offered to prospective staff? There are at least three dimensions of *quality of demand*: the extent to which the available jobs offer clear and predictable career prospects (are they jobs that offer clear prospects for advancement and for attaining a stable, permanent position?); the extent to which the jobs offer competitive compensation (both in terms of other, nonacademic options available to entering candidates and more generally in terms of the prospects for a middle-class lifestyle); and the extent to which these jobs assure academic freedom and the possibility to pursue research (in particular, whether entry-level posts assume heavy versus rather reasonable teaching loads).

The competition between universities is important for demand, as well. The demand for faculty is significantly different in situations where only one large institution exists in the country, versus contexts where there are many different competing institutions.

A final aspect of the demand side relates to the general labor market situation of PhDs in a particular country. To what extent does the national economy offer robust alternatives to academic employment for new PhDs in government and industry—in effect, requiring universities to compete for new PhDs? Or to what extent are new PhDs largely limited in their employment prospects to academic opportunities? Such general labor market conditions would clearly shape the demand situation in which universities compete for human capital (i.e., faculty).

Supply of Academic Staff

Factors affecting the supply of labor include: barriers to entry, geographical mobility, occupational mobility, and demand for labor in other industries. In gauging the available supply of potential academic staff, perhaps the most basic threshold question is what are the academic or educational credentials required of entry-level faculty? While some countries require possession of a doctoral degree, or even a postdoctoral credential (which was true until recently in Germany, where the *habilitation* was required), others recruit prospective faculty from the ranks of master's—and even baccalaureate—degree-holders. In some countries, such as Germany and Norway, doctoral study itself is considered to constitute the formal starting point for an academic career. Two fundamental indicators related to supply, then, would include: the national system's reliance on PhD production (operationally defined as the percentage of academic staff already holding the PhD degree) and whether doctoral study constitutes a prelude to—or first stage of—an academic career.

To the extent that the doctorate serves as the career entry point, several general characteristics related to the number and distribution of doctoral degree-holders are relevant to gauging the overall supply situation. There is the matter of the sheer number of doctoral degrees produced annually and, more specifically, the ratio of annual PhD production to the number of new entrants hired within the national system. And connected to this first characteristic, what is the related trend line over the previous 5 to 10 years? Has annual PhD production, that is, supply, been increasing (and, if so, at what rate) or declining (and, if so, at what rate)? Has the ratio of degree production to new entrants hired changed?

Beyond the basic entry credential as a key to assessing the supply side, there is the matter of the demographics of the PhD supply. This includes the birthplace, training, and gender of prospective recruits. To what extent does the national system recruit entry-level academics who are *born or trained abroad*? This is an indicator of the openness of the national system to foreign academic talent as an alternative source of supply for prospective faculty—and must be considered in tandem with indigenous PhD supply. To what extent is supply restricted or amplified by *gender*? Women continue to increase their presence in graduate education globally (Vabo et al. 2013) and although their entry into academic careers has transformed the academic profession in many countries over the past generation, they have been quite restricted in their entry in a number of other countries. Clearly, the openness of the national system to recruitment of women is a major factor in assessing the supply of academic talent. Although the basic indicator of such openness is the overall percentage of women in the national corps of faculty, there may be more nuanced markers, such as the percentage of women in junior ranks (as an indicator of most recent system behavior) or the percentage of women over time (5 to 10 years) in senior ranks (i.e., has the system promoted those women that it has recruited at the entry level?). One can also consider the percentage of women who are part of a dual-career couple (especially in relation to the proportionate frequency of dual-career couples in a general national economy). This latter indicator allow us to assess openness to this rising demographic group in terms of most current recruitment behavior, whether the system accommodates the needs of new and rising demographic groups over time, and what subgroups may be excluded or included.

Another important characteristic of supply is the quality of general and specific training of PhD candidates. One issue here is related to financial conditions of PhD programs. Do candidates get stipends or research grants for their period of study that would make it possible for them to concentrate on research? Or must they teach to cover their tuition and living expenses? Are they forced to look for full-time or part-time jobs to be able to continue their PhD studies? Another issue related to quality is whether PhD programs require candidates to enroll in a structured sequence of courses followed by comprehensive examinations, or whether PhD candidates are mainly focused on preparing their thesis. In the latter case, it is rather difficult to assure the quality of PhD graduates who may lack some necessary skills.

Demand x Supply

Supply and demand intersect at the point of hire. Thus, an important perspective on the labor market for new entrants is the "efficiency" or "effectiveness" of the hiring process. Do national hiring policies and practices maximize the efficiency of the system in recruiting the "best and brightest" into academic careers? Operationally, indicators of efficiency of recruitment would include openness of search and screening processes and the relative competition for new positions. Systems that rely on internal recruitment (of, for example, former students) and limit openness through inbreeding would presumably artificially limit supply, especially top-quality supply, while those that recruit externally at the national and international levels would presumably expand supply, especially the highest quality supply. In general, it depends on whether there is a national academic market and how mature and efficient that market is. Indicators of openness and competitiveness at hire would then include such considerations as whether new positions are filled by open calls or internal-only competition. Also relevant is whether recruitment proceeds at the national and/or international level, both formally and in reality, because in some countries there are transparent and open formal rules of hiring, but rather ad hoc and internally oriented practices are actually applied—Russia is an example of this. The average number of candidates considered for open entry-level positions may also be significant. Finally, it is important to know if it is possible for candidates to be hired without proficiency in the national language.

An Overview of Demand

Table 12.1 provides an overview of the most important indicators of the quantity and quality of demand for each of the ten participating countries. The first column shows the median value of each indicator, followed (in further columns) by the individual country values—the reader can easily see which countries fall above and below the median. A glance at the total column paints a clear picture of overall global expansion in higher education: median enrollment among the ten countries went up nearly 70 percent between 1992 and 2007; median growth in academic staff grew more than 170 percent; and median growth in the gross enrollment ratio, or GER (the percentage of those between 18 and 24 years of age enrolled in postsecondary education), expanded from 29 percent to 55 percent. That said, there has been considerable stability in the percentage of gross domestic product (GDP) expended on R&D as well as on all levels of education, generally, and on higher education, in particular—although there is considerable variation in these metrics across countries.[1] This would suggest that while the size of national systems in terms of students and staff has expanded considerably, system size as a proportion of the national economy has remained relatively stable—meaning that what is spent on national systems has remained proportionately stable as an overall percentage of the economy yet these systems have had to accommodate much larger numbers of students and staff. This tends to be reflected in the growth of the private sector to absorb excess demand (while maintaining relatively stable public expenditures) and in the growth of noncareer ladder, especially part-time faculty appointments that allow for greater budgetary flexibility.

Within this overall picture, there is considerable variation among our ten participating countries. With the exception of Russia, the BRICS (Brazil, China, India, and South Africa) show the most spectacular growth in tertiary enrollment and academic staff, but no increase in the proportion of GDP devoted to education, in general, and below median expenditures on tertiary education as a percentage of all education expenditures. The private sector has mushroomed in Brazil, India, Russia, and even China, with conditions for academic employment largely unregulated and substantially inferior to those in the public sector. Part-time appointments remain the norm in Brazil[2] and temporary appointments dominate both the public and private sector in India—albeit for different reasons.[3] In the BRIC countries, then, growth demand, however robust on the surface, tends to be lower than expected and accommodated by nontraditional

Table 12.1a. Quantity and Quality of Demand, by Higher Education System Characteristics

	Median			Brazil			Russia			India		
Indicator	1992	2007	% Change	1992	2007	% Change	1992	2007	% Change	1992	2007	% Change
Enrollment, total students, tertiary (mn)[1]	1,937	3,776	69,4	1,591	5,273	231,0	4,965	9,370	88,7	4,9[7]	16,9[8]	244,9
Number of academic staff, tertiary (mn)[1]	0,280	0,332	173,5	0,134	0,368	173,5	0,423	0,679	60,6	0,263[7]	0,816[8]	210,3
Gross enrollment ratio[1]	29	55	64,3	11[4]	24[5]	119,7	49	73	49,0	6[4]	13	120,9
Public expenditure on Education as a % of GDP	5	6			4[5]		4.1[4]	3.6[5]	0,4	3.5[4]	3.8[5]	0,2
Total expenditure, Public Education, as a % of GDP per capita. All sources.		1			35,9[5]			10.8[5]			94.7[5]	

Tertiary[2] Educational expenditure on tertiary education as a % of total educational expenditure[1]		23			16,2			23[11]			20,3[12]	
Expenditure per pupil as a % of GDP per capita. Tertiary[2]		33			29,6			14,2[9]			55[10]	
Dollars spent per student, tertiary (PPP$) (thousands)[3]	10,3	10,4		10,3	10,4[6]	0,9				2,3	2,5	6,4

Sources and notes:

[1] OECD/UNESCO
[2] World Bank
[3] Cummings, 2008
[4] 1995, Cummings, 2008
[5] 2005, Cummings, 2008
[6] 2002, Cummings, 2008
[7] 1991
[8] 2011
[9] 2008
[10] 2007
[11] 2008
[12] 2006

Table 12.1a. Quantity and Quality of Demand, by Higher Education System Characteristics *(continued)*

	China			**South Africa**			**France**			**Germany**		
Indicator	1992	2007	% Change	1992	2007	% Change	1992	2007	% Change	1992	2007	% Change
Enrollment, total students, tertiary (mn)[1]	3,660	25,346	592,5	0,490	0,735[6]	50,0	1,840	2,180	18,4	2,034	2,279	12%
Number of academic staff, tertiary (mn)[1]	0,462[4]	1,478	219,9	0,017	0,050[7]	196,4		0,096[8]		0,280	0,295	6%
Gross Enrollment Ratio[1]	3	22	671,2	13	15[6]	19,7	43	55	27,7	35		
Public expenditure on Education as a % of GDP	2.3[5]			6.8[5]	5,3[6]	–22,1	5,9[5]	5,9[6]	0,0	4,7[5]	4,6[6]	–2,1
Total expenditure, Public Education, as a % of GDP per capita. All sources. Tertiary[2]					45.5[6]			1,4			1,1	

Educational expenditure in tertiary as % of total educational expenditure[1]		13,1			21,9			25,4	
Expenditure per pupil as a % of GDP per capita. Tertiary[2]					36,2				
Dollars spent per student, tertiary (PPP$) (thousands)[3]				9,2	9,3	1,3	10,9	11,0	1

Sources and notes:

[1] OECD/UNESCO

[2] World Bank

[3] Cummings, 2008

[4] 2000

[5] 1995, Cummings, 2008

[6] 2005, Cummings, 2008

[7] 2011 (NewFac, South Africa)

[8] 2010

Table 12.1a. Quantity and Quality of Demand, by Higher Education System Characteristics *(continued)*

	Norway			**Portugal**			**US**		
Indicator	1992	2007	% Change	1992	2007	% Change	1992	2007	% Change
Enrollment, total students, tertiary (mn)[1]	0,154	0,215	39,6	0,191	0,367	92,1	14,361	17,759	24,0
Number of academic staff, tertiary (mn)[1]		0,012[5]			0,036		0,826	1,310	59,0
Gross Enrollment Ratio[1]	46	76	64,3	24	57	143,2	78	83	7,2
Public expenditure on Education as a % of GDP	8,3[4]	7,7[6]		5,4[4]	5,7[6]		5,3[4]	5,9[6]	
Total expenditure, Public Education, as a % of GDP per capita. All sources. Tertiary[2]		1,2[7]			1,5			3,2	

Educational expenditure in tertiary as % of total educational expenditure[1]		31,9			22,7			23,7
Expenditure per pupil as a % of GDP per capita. Tertiary[2]		46,5			33,5			21,7
Dollars spent per student, tertiary (PPP$) (thousands)[3]	13,6	13,7		6,9	7,0			

Sources and notes:
[1] OECD/UNESCO
[2] World Bank
[3] Cummings, 2008
[4] 1995, Cummings, 2008
[5] data from 2011. NewFac, Norway
[6] 2005, Cummings, 2008
[7] Public institutions only

Table 12.1b. Quantity and Quality of Demand, by Key Country Indicators

	Median			Brazil			Russia			India		
Indicator	1992	2007	% Change	1992	2007	% Change	1992	2007	% Change	1992	2007	% Change
R&D as a % of GDP[1]	1	1		0,8[2]	1,1	44,1	1,0[2]	1,1	17,5		0,8	
GDP per capita, in PPP$ (constant 2005 international $) (thousands)[1]		15,68			9,18			14,01			2,60	
Internet users (per 100 people), 2007[1]		37			30,9							
Population aged 0–14 (% of total)[1]	22	19	−17,6	34,3	26,8	−21,9	22,6	14,7	−34,7	37,0	31,4	−15,1
Population aged 15–64 (% of total)[1]	65	67	5,1	61,1	66,8	9,4	66,5	71,6	7,7	59,1	63,8	8,0
Population aged 65 and above (% of total)[1]	65	67	5,1	61,1	66,8	9,4	66,5	71,6	7,7	59,1	63,8	8,0
Population growth (annual %)[1]	1	1	−34,8	1,6	1,0	−38,2	0,0	−0,3	−742,9	1,9	1,4	−29,4

Sources:
[1] World Bank
[2] 1996, Cummings, 2008

Table 12.1b. Quantity and Quality of Demand, by Key Country Indicators *(continued)*

	China			South Africa			France			Germany		
Indicator	1992	2007	% Change	1992	2007	% Change	1992	2007	% Change	1992	2007	% Change
R&D as a % of GDP[1]	0,7[2]	1,4	114,7	0,7[2]	0,9	33,9	2,2[2]	2,1	−6,6	2,3[2]	2,5	9,6
GDP per capita, PPP$ (constant 2005 international $) (thousands)[1]		5,24			9,37			30,47			33,40	
Internet users (per 100 people), 2007[1]		16,1			8,2			66,1			75,2	
Population aged 0–14 (% of total)[1]	29,1	19,2	−34,1	37,9	30,3	−20,1	19,7	18,4	−6,6	16,3	13,9	−14,6
Population aged 15–64 (% of total)[1]	65,0	72,9	12,1	58,8	65,0	10,4	65,7	65,1	−0,9	68,5	66,2	−3,4
Population aged 65 and above (% of total)[1]	5,9	7,9	34,3	3,3	4,8	44,6	14,6	16,5	12,9	15,2	19,8	30,8
Population growth (annual %)[1]	1,2	0,5	−57,4	2,1	1,1	−47,4	0,5	0,6	24,3	0,8	−0,1	−117,6

Sources:
[1] World Bank
[2] 1996, Cummings, 2008

Table 12.1b. Quantity and Quality of Demand, by Key Country Indicators

	Norway			Portugal			USA		
Indicator	1992	2007	% Change	1992	2007	% Change	1992	2007	% Change
R&D as a % of GDP[1]	1,7[2]	1,6		0,7[2]	1,2		2,6[2]	2,7	
GDP per capita, PPP$ (constant 2005 international $) (thousands)[1]		48,8			21,99			43,66	
Internet users (per 100 people), 2007[1]		87,1			42,2			73,5	
Population aged 0–14 (% of total)[1]	19,0	19,3	1,3	19,4	15,4	–20,2	21,8	20,2	–7,2
Population aged 15–64 (% of total)[1]	64,7	66,0	2,0	66,4	67,1	1,0	65,6	67,3	2,5
Population aged 65 and above (% of total)[1]	16,3	14,7	–9,5	14,2	17,5	22,9	12,6	12,5	–0,4
Population growth (annual %)[1]	0,6	1,0	79,3	0,0	0,2	987,7	1,4	1,0	–31,4

Sources:
[1] World Bank
[2] 1996, Cummings, 2008

academic appointments. In terms of compensation—insofar as this reflects the "perceived quality" of the available jobs—the evidence suggests that in many BRIC countries entry-level compensation does not allow for middle-class living standards.

As for the four European countries included in this study and the United States, the data show much more modest growth in terms of enrollments and numbers of academic staff, with France and Germany at the low end, Norway and the United States in the middle, and Portugal at the higher end. France, Germany, and Portugal, however, still show lower GERs—between 50 percent and 60 percent—than both Norway and the United States (which stand in the 70 percent to 80 percent range). Moreover, investment in tertiary education, in particular, as a percentage of all education expenditures is highest in Norway.

All countries except Norway tend to offer disproportionately non-career-ladder appointments to new entrants—meaning a relatively low quality of entry-level academic jobs. The United States constitutes a rare example of a higher education system with a well-developed private sector, a proportion of which is demand-absorbing (but a significant proportion of which is not, making for a high variety of employment conditions in that sector, some of the best, but also some of the worst).[4] Although the career prospects for entry-level jobs are, for the most part, limited, the compensation offered as compared to the BRICS, is more attractive—although it varies across the four European countries and the United States. Thus, in terms of the quality of demand, the picture is mixed: relatively unattractive in terms of career advancement, although relatively well-compensated. In sum, the growth demand in Europe is modest, especially insofar as it is moderated by the diminished quality and availability of entry-level positions.

One other long-term factor needs to be considered here, and that is national variation in basic demographic profile. The proportion of youth aged 0 to 14 in all countries except Norway has declined over the past fifteen years—by as little as 7 percent in the United States and France to as much as 34 percent in China and Russia—with a median decline of about 17 percent. These demographic realities will provide a sustained break in enrollment-driven demand across the board—at least insofar as that demand is driven by the traditional youth population.

When we turn to replacement demand, there are several divergent patterns that span the BRICS, the United States, and the European countries. More than 40 percent of the faculty in Russia, Germany, Portugal, and the United States are over 50 years old, compared to about 25 percent to 33 percent in France and Norway. On the other hand, China, India, and South Africa report substantial cohorts of younger faculty in their thirties and forties, and in Brazil the share of young faculty has been growing in recent years. This suggests that for most of our ten participating countries, the prospects for replacement demand are good—assuming that mandatory retirement policies continue in all countries except in the United States, and that departing academic staff are actually replaced by full-time career ladder appointees. The latter assumption regarding replacement seems particularly tenuous. Moreover, retirement ages continue to rise almost everywhere and, in those countries with substantial private sectors (the United States, Brazil, India, Portugal), many of the available positions in the private sector will be filled by academic staff who retire from the public sector. Ironically, it is in the high growth systems of China and South Africa where relatively young faculty cohorts may crowd out new entrants.

Supply Prospects

The data in Table 12.2 suggest that the majority of our ten countries—all but China and South Africa—recruit most of their full-time academic staff from the ranks of newly minted PhD degree recipients, although the proportion ranges from half to nearly three-quarters.[5] Moreover, at least three of the ten study countries—Norway, Germany, and Russia—consider that PhD students are already in the first stage of an academic career. Indeed, in Russia, the beginning of an academic career is normally associated with the start of a PhD program but not vice versa: many full-time PhD students do not even seek to pursue an academic career and consider the PhD degree as an important supplemental credential in the nonacademic labor market.

Among the ten countries, six—the United States, Germany, France, Russia, Brazil, and China—supply substantial numbers of "native" PhDs to their respective systems, although Germany, Brazil, and China to some extent draw on foreign trained PhDs as well.[6] South Africa draws particularly heavily on foreign PhDs. In virtually all cases, then, a supply of PhDs—native or foreign—is available, if not willing, to serve. Moreover, with the exception of Germany, the study countries all draw on women[7]—the new majority of PhD recipients globally except in the natural sciences and engineering—for anywhere between 40 percent and 50 percent of their newly entering academic staff. Only the United States and Germany tend

Table 12.2a. Supply of PhDs

	Brazil		Russia		India		China		South Africa	
Indicator	1992	2007	1992	2007	1992	2007	1992	2007	1992	2007
Number of PhDs			43100[2]	54558[3]			67293[4]	258950[6]		
% PhD among f/t faculty	57[10]		71[11]				6,1[5]	14,9[7]		19,7[9]
% non-native born[1]		1,95		0,2				0,03		8,93
% foreign trained[1]:										
First-Degree		1,40						0,08		8,31
PhD		12,90						6,49		83,78

Sources and notes:

[1] CAP 07

[2] Data from 2000 indicates students enrolled in doctoral program (NewFace, Russia)

[3] Data from 2010 indicates students enrolled in doctoral program (NewFace, Russia)

[4] 2000 (NewFac, China). Enrollments

[5] 2000 (NewFac, China)

[6] 2010 (NewFac, China). Enrollments

[7] 2010 (NewFac, China)

[8] 2008 (NewFac, China)

[9] 2011 (NewFac, South Africa)

[10] NewFace, Brazil

[11] NewFace, Russia

Table 12.2a. Supply of PhDs *(continued)*

	France		Germany		Norway		Portugal		US	
Indicator	1992	2007	1992	2007	1992	2007	1992	2007	1992	2007
# PhDs					4476[4]	9041[5]			41000[10]	48000[10]
% PhD among f/t faculty			64		53		48[6]	68[7]	59[11]	77[1]
% non-native born[1]				13,88		22,65		7,47	13,9	17,49
% foreign trained[1]:										
First-Degree				6,94				4,19		13,16
PhD				6,23				24,79		3,14

Sources and notes:

[1] CAP 07

[2] 2004 (NewFac, France)

[3] 2011 (NewFac, France)

[4] 2003. Number of Doctoral Candidates. NewFac, Norway

[5] 2011. Number of Doctoral Candidates. NewFac, Norway

[6] 2001. Public Universities. NewFac, Portugal

[7] 2009. Public Universities. NewFac, Portugal

[8] SecG-IPEDS

[9] National Study of Postsecondary Faculty, 1993

[10] National Science Foundation, 2007, Survey of Earned Doctorates

[11] National Study of Postsecondary Faculty, 1993

Table 12.2b. Female Participation

	Brazil		Russia		India		China		South Africa	
Indicator	1992	2007	1992	2007	1992	2007	1992	2007	1992	2007
% female, all[1]		47,1		55[2]				37,0	42,5	47,0
% female, junior[1]		47,9		~70[2]				45,7		47,1
% female, married[1]		64,9						85,0	70]	67,1
% female, with children[1]		57,2						68,2		57,5
% dual career couple[1]		62,5		70				92,0		71,8

Sources:
[1] CAP 07
[2] NewFaculty, Russia, 2009–2010

Table 12.2b. Female Participation *(continued)*

	France		Germany		Norway		Portugal		US	
Indicator	1992	2007	1992	2007	1992	2007	1992	2007	1992	2007
% female, all[1]			34,70	28,7	44,10	37,8	49,60	43,6	38	41,9
% female, junior[1]				35,2		52,4		46,4		49,5
% female, married[1]				83,1		83,1		73,3	83	66,9
% female, with children[1]				39,8		55,4		65,1		30,5
% dual career couple[1]				46,1		80,8		87,1		61,5

Source:
[1] CAP 07

to draw less on married women with children than the others (Finkelstein 2013). However, the general pattern in all countries is that at the higher academic and administrative ranks there are substantially fewer women than at the bottom of the academic hierarchy.

Overall, there is a reasonably robust supply of PhDs theoretically available (either native or foreign) and the largest emerging demographic in the supply—women PhDs—is being tapped, for the most part.

Hiring Processes

What can we say about how hiring mechanisms mediate the demand and the available supply? Table 12.3 suggests that although the majority of our ten participating systems employ open, competitive recruitment and hiring strategies, at least three systems (Russia, China, and India) employ less open and competitive processes throughout most of the system.[8] To the extent that local social ties shape recruitment and hiring processes, we can assume that, in these three countries, the opportunities for the "best and brightest" to find their way into available positions is likely not optimized. To a large extent, this could be explained by the lack of national academic markets, in which case social networks substitute as market mechanisms for distribution and price determination.

At the other end of the spectrum, countries such as France, Germany, Norway, and the United States typify open, nationwide recruiting strategies for academic staff. Only the United States is likely to extend recruitment internationally, if for no other reason than its use of English (the French and German systems are somewhat limited in international recruitment by language barriers). Universally, international recruitment affects mostly top research universities and, in most cases, involves only the upper echelon of young academics. Most fresh PhDs (who stay in academia) are hired within the national market and do not even enter the international market.[9] Moreover, countries differ in their levels of inbreeding—which is rather common in Russia, China, and Portugal, and quite low in the United States, France, and Germany.

In many countries, the first positions available for young faculty do not offer permanent status or even the prospect of promotion to a permanent position at the same university. Although the United States with its tenure-track system seems to be an exception, in recent years the share of young faculty that gains access to the career ladder has diminished substantially. Moreover, postdoc positions—which until recently did not

Table 12.3. Quality of Hiring

Indicator	Brazil	Russia	India	China	South Africa	France	Germany	Norway	Portugal	US
Hiring: Open or closed?[1]	Lo-Hi	Lo	Lo	Lo-Hi	?	Hi	Hi	Hi	Hi	Hi
% Inbreeding[1]	Lo-Hi (?)	Hi	Hi	Hi	Hi	Lo	Lo	Lo	Hi	Lo
Scope: Local vs Nati/Intl[1]		local	local(?)	Nati	Nati/Intl	Nati	Nati	Nati/Intl	Nati	Nati/Intl

Source:
[1] NewFaculty

exist at all in some countries and, where they did, were limited to a few life science disciplines—have emerged in some countries (like France and Germany) and become more widespread, even dominant, in others (such as the United States). This means that the age at which a permanent position is secured—if it is secured—is substantially higher.

Patterns in Country Profiles

Based on the earlier analysis, it is possible to construct country profiles showing levels of growth and replacement demand, quality of available positions (both in terms of career advancement and compensation), availability of native—and openness to foreign—PhD supply, openness to women, and the openness/competitiveness of hiring processes. Table 12.4 attempts to provide a summary profile for our ten participating countries on the various indicators of demand and supply as well as hiring processes.

A glance at Table 12.4 suggests a few discernible patterns. First, there is no single nation that offers both high-growth and high-replacement demand for academic staff. Only two nations offer high-growth demand (Brazil and India) and only two offer high-replacement demand (Russia and Germany). The dominant pattern is one of low to moderate demand from both sources. Such demand must be considered in the context of the quality of that demand—in terms both of advancement potential and compensation. Only Norway displays high potential on both dimensions of demand quality—although the United States is close with relatively attractive compensation, but increasingly compromised career advancement possibilities. China offers a split: the central government-funded research university sector offers both attractive compensation and advancement opportunities, while the bulk of the system offers unattractive compensation and uncertain advancement opportunities.

When it comes to supply, the ten nations split in terms of those that do not employ the PhD as the entry criteria (South Africa, China) and the majority that do—although there are variations across the various sectors of the systems. All have ready access to PhD supplies—although in the case of South Africa, these supplies are not indigenous. Moreover, the available evidence suggests that all systems—with the possible exceptions of Germany and the United States—are exploiting the full potential of academic women, who are increasingly becoming the new majority of PhD recipients.

Table 12.4. Country Profiles, by Supply and Demand Indicators

Indicator	Brazil	Russia	India	China	South Africa	France	Germany	Norway	Portugal	US
Growth demand	Hi	Lo	Hi	Med	Med	Lo	Lo	Lo	Lo	Med
Replacement Demand		Hi		Lo	Lo	Med	Hi	Med	Med	Med-Lo
Job Quality: Hi(ft) Career ladder	Med Lo(p)	Lo	Hi	Lo	Lo	Lo	Hi	Lo	Med	
Job quality: compensation	Lo-Med	Lo	Lo	Lo- Hi	Lo	Med	Hi	Hi	Med	Hi
Supply of PhDs[1] (Number of PhD awarded)	9700	8900	11051	47407	1576	12000	26981	1300	1414	49500
Female Participation[2] (percent of Ph.D.'s in country are awarded to women)				<50 47,9[3] 2010			<50 44 2010	50 50[3]	50 50 2000–2009	>50 52 2010
Openness of hiring	Lo-Hi	Lo	Lo	Lo-Hi	Lo-Hi	Hi	Hi	Hi	Hi	Hi

Sources and notes:

[1] Data from the experts (country chapters)

[2] New Faculty Study (tables)

[3] Percent of women among PhD students, 2010

[4] CAP 2007

Finally, the ten participating countries are split between those that tend to hire locally and depend on social ties (the BRICS, including Russia, China, India), and those that hire openly and competitively, including the European countries and the United States. The countries in the latter category are most effectively positioned to recruit and attract the "best and brightest"—although it must be noted that the BRICS countries show considerable differentiation within their systems between the research and the nonresearch sectors.

The country analyses presented in this book show that the opportunities for young graduates to build a career have changed significantly in recent years, as working conditions have become less stable and the career ladder has become unpredictable. The proportion of permanent positions has decreased in many countries, including the countries where growth-driven demand for new faculty is high (e.g., in India). In several countries (the United States, Norway, Portugal, Germany, etc.), the period between being awarded a PhD degree and obtaining a permanent position has become substantially longer. In these countries, the time available for developing an academic career has inevitably shortened. In addition, the teaching loads for young faculty have increased, and in some countries the administrative load has increased, as well (e.g., in Brazilian regional public universities). Such tendencies can potentially constrain the professional development of young faculty as researchers. New career paths have appeared, but some temporary positions never lead to permanent posts, and universities often have no interest in what happens to faculty in a temporary position after their contract expires. In addition, the scope of work of the faculty in such positions is often severely constrained and administratively determined in rather narrow ways. For example, it may assume a heavy workload or a very specific research topic.

The competition for permanent positions among young PhD holders has increased. In such a situation, young PhD holders must take responsibility for their career and have a clear career strategy, including their choice of postgraduate studies, and the choice of their first job. It becomes critically important for young professionals to obtain relevant research skills, acquire useful academic connections, and integrate themselves into international academic networks. It is desirable for this to happen during their postgraduate studies and while holding their first position. It becomes important not only to be bright and productive but also to be fast, establishing oneself quickly in the field.

In a number of countries, there is a significant change in the system of postgraduate studies that aims to enhance competitiveness and increase the attractiveness of academic work. In particular, several governments assist postgraduate students financially and provide young PhD holders the opportunity to accept internships abroad (for example, China, South Africa, Norway). Thus, national governments encourage the international integration of young faculty. It is extremely important for the professional socialization of young researchers to allow them to expand their knowledge and integrate themselves into academic and scientific networks. Currently, postgraduate study in several countries is acquiring more formalized structures. This concerns not only the writing of the thesis itself; students are also required to fulfill structured coursework requirements in order to get a better understanding of research methods (for example, in Germany and in France).

It is critical for young professionals to build relationships, and reforms in Germany and France endeavor to provide more appropriate conditions for that. These reforms are aimed at reducing the dependency of doctoral candidates on their supervisors and establishing professional networks among doctoral candidates and young faculty. At the same time, in countries where a strong academic environment has not yet been built, the only path to integration into the academic network and to getting necessary resources is via close interaction with supervisors. In South Africa, because of the low supervisory capacity, such paternalism is encouraged, and this plays an important role in the experiences of young academics.

Some PhD holders cannot find a permanent position in academia and are forced to seek employment outside of the academy; others initially seek a nonacademic job. Therefore, in some countries, postgraduate studies have begun to change so that PhD holders have more opportunities for employment outside academia. The main limitations for PhD holders to find a job outside academia is that companies in the private sector often do not understand why they should pay more for a PhD holder, when they can hire a master's degree holder (e.g., France). Often, companies do not have sufficient infrastructure or resources (material and technical facilities, for example) for innovative activities that could be undertaken by PhD holders (Portugal offers a case in point of this kind of situation). External employment opportunities for PhD holders strongly depend on their field. In order to address these issues, it is necessary to raise the prestige of postgraduate studies, and as well increase employment opportunities outside academia for PhD holders. For example, French universities are beginning to open joint postgraduate studies with industrial companies, and universities in Portugal encourage PhD holders to open their own private laboratories. As a result, these universities are increasing the competitiveness of PhD holders.

Recruitment procedures play an important role in the career development of young professionals, as we discussed before. In some countries, hiring is transparent at all levels; in other countries this is not the case. For example, in Germany, hiring for entry-level positions is often the personal decision of a professor; in India, even though the procedure is formalized, personal relations play an important role. Transparent hiring based on clear criteria would allow young faculty to develop a better strategy for their career development and more effectively build their own professional networks. Such procedures would weaken the influence of social (paternalistic) networks and would encourage the career development of talented PhD holders. Governments in several countries are seeking to open up such recruitment procedures.

The conditions that are provided to young faculty in entry-level positions are crucial for their future career development. It is necessary to develop programs that would allow younger faculty to integrate into academia and further develop their professional skills. In some American universities, mentoring programs were established to allow experienced professors to share experiences with new faculty. In France, some universities reduce the teaching load for young faculty who hold a permanent position. Some French universities also support young faculty in finding external funding, helping them to submit competitive applications for grants. In China and India, universities provide special training courses for young faculty that focuses on theoretical aspects of teaching.

Despite the demonstrable instability and not altogether sanguine prospects, the academic career remains attractive globally. This is because academia still gives young people the freedom to manage their time, and to choose the precise career path that best suits their interests—in a context where all employment relationships are increasingly tenuous and performance-based.

Conclusions

In this chapter, we have attempted to summarize important aspects of the demand and supply sides of the national academic systems as well as to provide a comparative portrait of the hiring mechanisms that bring together demand and supply. We believe that our analytical model provides the reader of this book with a means to put ten different national "young faculty portraits" into recognizable patterns.

Several features and trends seem common to the contemporary situation of young faculty in different countries. The age at which one secures a first permanent or stable job is increasing, giving rise in many cases to new institutional arrangements such as postdocs. Many national systems are experiencing the impact of massification in higher education. The number of available posts grows as enrollments increase. However, growth does not come without costs: the quality of jobs in some cases goes down (due to higher teaching loads and less well-prepared students who in previous decades might never have been admitted). The change is not uniform: while average institutions in the country may experience severe problems trying to "chew and swallow" larger student enrollments, top research universities may still enjoy the fruits of selectivity and exclusivity.

Finally, while the situation of the private sector of higher education varies in different countries, in all cases the private sector does affect the prospects for new faculty—at least in terms of providing extra opportunities, albeit largely unregulated.

Without doubt, our analysis has important limitations in several areas. First, our aggregated data do not differentiate by academic field. The situation in the natural sciences and engineering may be different, and in some countries (such as the United States) this difference is enormous. Career prospects, job conditions, and faculty demographic profiles could be dissimilar in different segments within one national system. Top research universities or institutions with special support from the federal government can provide quite different conditions from those in the rest of the system. However, our framework may be quite useful for the general understanding of common challenges and national differences that young faculty in different countries face today.

Notes

1. It should be noted that median overall economic expansion in the ten countries over the period 1992 to 2007 has been about 17 percent, suggesting that the relatively stable proportion of expenditures on tertiary education do not represent a windfall of absolute additional dollars attributable to wildly high general economic expansion.

2. Though Brazil has a higher proportion of full-time faculty than other Latin America countries, in recent years the share of such contracts has diminished in the public sector. Full-time contracts are now more widespread in Brazil's private higher education sector (i.e., about 67.5 percent of contracts in the private sector are now full time).

3. In the public sector, a quota system for lower castes and tribes leads to many entry-level positions going unfilled, and a variety of temporary positions created to meet teaching demands. In the private sector, mostly for-profit providers offer temporary contract employment.

4. Of the 800 to 900 private institutions in the United States, about one quarter would be considered elite and 50 percent or so primarily demand-absorbing.

5. In the case of Brazil, this applies only to full-time faculty and not to the vast majority of academic staff who remain part time. In India, a PhD degree is not a strict requirement, but is an important factor in hiring decisions.

6. The United States draws on foreign-born students for its doctoral programs, especially in the natural sciences, engineering, and mathematics.

7. In Germany, the share of women at entry-level rank is lower than in other countries.

8. In China and India, open and competitive hiring characterizes the very top of the system, that is, the most prestigious research universities.

9. It should be noted that in response to the recent depression in the academic job market in both Europe and the United States, new PhDs have increasingly begun to look to Asia, including Australia and New Zealand, as a first job destination.

References

Bowen, Howard, and Jack Schuster. 1986. *American Professors: A National Resource Imperiled*. New York: Oxford University Press.

Breneman, David, and Ted I. Youn, eds. 1988. *Academic Labor Markets and Careers*. Philadelphia: Falmer Press.

Carter, Alan M. 1976. *PhDs and the Academic Labor Market*. New York: McGraw Hill.

Finkelstein, Martin. 2012. "American Faculty and their Institutions: A Multinational Comparison." *The NEA 2012 Almanac of Higher Education*. Washington DC: National Education Association

Musselin, Christine. 2009. *The Market for Academics*. New York: Routledge.

Vabo et al. 2013. "Internationalization and Women Academics." In *The Internationalization of the Academy: Changes, Realities and Prospects*, edited by Futao Huang, Martin J. Finkelstein, and Michele Rostan. Dordrecht, Netherlands: Springer.

Contributors

Philip G. Altbach is research professor and director of the Center for International Higher Education in the Lynch School of Education at Boston College. He was the 2004 to 2006 Distinguished Scholar Leader for the New Century Scholars initiative of the Fulbright program. He has been a senior associate of the Carnegie Foundation for the Advancement of Teaching. He is author of *Turmoil and Transition: The International Imperative in Higher Education, Comparative Higher Education, Student Politics in America*, and other books. He co-edited the *International Handbook of Higher Education.*

Elizabeth Balbachevsky is associate professor in the Department of Political Science at the University of São Paulo, São Paulo, Brazil, and deputy director of the University of São Paulo's Center for Public Policy Research (Núcleo de Pesquisa de Políticas Públicas—NUPPs-USP). Additionally, she is a fellow of the University of Campinas' Center for Advanced Studies (CEAv). She was a Fulbright New Century Scholar in 2005 to 2006 and an Erasmus Mundus Scholar in the European Master's in Higher Education Program (2009). In 2007 and 2008 she directed the National Survey on Brazilian Academic Profession for the international research network, the Changing Academic Profession. Her recent publications include: *Brazil: Diverse Experience in Institutional Governance in the Public and Private Sectors* (Springer), *Job Satisfaction in a Diverse Institutional Environment* (Springer), and "Incentives and Obstacles to Academic Entrepreneurship" in *University and Development in Latin America: Successful experiences of Research Centers* (Sense Publishers, 2008).

Martin J. Finkelstein is professor of Higher Education at Seton Hall University, South Orange, NJ. He received his PhD from the State University of New York at Buffalo and has taught at the University of Denver and Teacher's College, Columbia University and has served as a visiting scholar at the Claremont Graduate University, the Research Institute for Higher Education, Hiroshima University, Japan and visiting professor at the University of Hong Kong. He is the author of *The American Academic Profession* (Ohio State University Press, 1988) and co-author of *The New Academic Generation* (with Robert Seal and Jack Schuster, Johns Hopkins University Press, 1998), and (with Jack Schuster), *The American Faculty: The Restructuring of Academic Work and Careers* (Johns Hopkins University Press, 2006). His most recent book is *Scholars in the Changing American Academy: New Contexts, New Roles and New Rules* (Springer, 2011). He has served as co-director of the U.S. component of the Changing Academic Profession Survey 2007, a reprise of the 1992 Carnegie International Survey of the Academic Profession (Boyer and Altbach, 1996).

Sandra Hasanefendic is a PhD student at the Instituto Superior de Ciências do Trabalho e da Empresa—University Institute of Lisbon (ISCTE-IUL) and the Center for Innovation, Technology and Policy Research at the Instituto Superior Técnico (IN+/IST) in Lisbon, Portugal. She completed her undergraduate studies in Serbia and obtained a master of arts in languages, literature and culture from the University of Aveiro (Portugal). Sandra's PhD project focuses on the influences of the new economy and globalization—specifically, academic capitalism and new managerialism—on the academic leadership at universities of applied sciences in Portugal, the Netherlands, and Finland, and examines faculty responses to changed institutional environments.

Hugo Horta is a researcher at the Center for Innovation, Technology and Policy Research at the Technical University of Lisbon, Portugal. He returned to academia after serving as advisor to the Secretary of State of the Ministry of Science, Technology and Higher Education, from 2010 to 2011. Prior to this, he held a postdoc position in Japan, examining academic inbreeding from a comparative perspective. He is also the Portuguese National delegate to the European Research Area (ERA) Steering Committee on Human Resources and Mobility, participating in several ERA workgroups.

Kevin W. Iglesias is a senior research associate with the Center for College Readiness at Seton Hall University. In addition to his work with the center, Mr. Iglesias has also taught numerous courses in directed research and statistics at the graduate level. Currently, he is a PhD candidate in

Education Research, Assessment and Program Evaluation at Seton Hall University.

Narayana Jayaram has taught sociology in various capacities at Bangalore University (1972–1999) and Goa University (1999–2003), and research methodology at the Tata Institute of Social Sciences, Mumbai (since 2003). He was director of the Institute for Social and Economic Change, Bangalore (2006–2008) and was a fellow at the Indian Institute of Advanced Study, Shimla. His recent publications (as author or editor) include: *Social Conflict* (co-edited with Satish Saberwal); *The Indian Diaspora: Dynamics of Migration*; *Keywords: Identity* (with Aziz Al-Azmeh, Wang Bin, David A. Hollinger, Mahmood Mamdani and Emmanuel Renault).

Barbara M. Kehm is a professor of higher education at the University of Glasgow in Scotland. She was professor and researcher at the University of Kassel's International Center for Higher Education Research (INCHER). From 2004 until 2011 she was the Director of INCHER. Her expertise is focused on new forms of governance in higher education, internationalization of higher education (especially in the context of the European Bologna Process), reforms of doctoral education, and issues of professionalization in academia. Kehm's publications include more than 25 authored, edited, and co-edited books and more than 200 journal articles and book chapters.

Svein Kyvik holds a PhD in sociology and is currently a research professor at NIFU (Nordic Institute for Studies in Innovation, Research and Education) in Oslo, Norway. For more than three decades, he has undertaken research in the fields of sociology of science, academic careers, and higher education policy. His latest books are: *The Dynamics of Change in Higher Education. Expansion and Contraction in an Organisational Field* (Springer, 2009); and (with B. Lepori) *The Research Mission of Higher Education Institutions outside the University Sector. Striving for Differentiation* (Springer, 2010).

Yi Li is the general office director and human resources specialist of the Graduate School of Education at Shanghai Jiao Tong University. She completed her master's thesis in higher education and has had 13 years' work experience in higher education administration. Between 2006 and 2007, Yi Li achieved a visiting scholarship opportunity from the Croucher Education Foundation, Hong Kong, for six months. Her research focuses on higher education administration, student counseling, and faculty development.

Nian Cai Liu obtained his master's and PhD degrees in polymer science and engineering from Queen's University at Kingston, Canada. Professor Liu worked as an associate and full professor at the School of Chemistry and Chemical Engineering of Shanghai Jiao Tong University from 1993 to 1998. He moved to the field of higher education research in 1999. He is now the dean of the Graduate School of Education and the Director of Center for World-Class Universities, Shanghai Jiao Tong University. His current research interests include world-class universities, science policy, and strategic planning of universities. He has published extensively in both Chinese and English journals. The *Academic Ranking of World Universities*, an online publication of his group, has attracted attention from all over the world. He is on the advisory boards of Scientometrics, *Research Evaluation*, and the *Journal of Engineering Education*.

Christine Musselin is vice rector for research at Sciences Po in Paris, France. She has been the director of the Centre de Sociologie des Organisations, a research unit of Sciences Po and the Centre national de la recherche scientifique (CNRS) in France. She leads comparative studies on university governance, public policies in higher education and research, and academic labor markets. Her book, *La longue marche des universités françaises* published by the Presses Universitaires de France in 2001 has been edited in English as *The Long March of French Universities* (Routledge, 2004). Her book, *Le marché des universitaires,* was published by the Presses de Sciences Po and issued in English by Routledge.

Emmanuel Oluseun Ojo is a lecturer in the School of Education, University of the Witwatersrand, South Africa. He currently teaches economics, methodology in the teaching of economics, and qualitative research methodology (phenomenography). Emmanuel has a master's of education in educational leadership and policy studies from the University of the Witwatersrand. He has published a book on internationalization of higher education in South Africa and a number of articles in international peer-reviewed journals focusing on the same topic. He is currently a PhD candidate at Witwatersrand and a recipient of the Andrew W. Mellon Foundation's Mellon Retiree Mentorship Program for Humanities.

Anna Panova is a researcher at the Center for Institutional Studies at National Research University—Higher School of Economics. She received her master's in economics from HSE. Her current research interests include academic contracts and governance system of universities.

Laura E. Rumbley is associate director of the Boston College Center for International Higher Education (CIHE) and a lecturer in BC's graduate program in higher education administration. She was previously deputy director of the Academic Cooperation Association (ACA), based in Brussels. She has authored and co-authored a number of publications, including the foundational document for the 2009 UNESCO World Conference on Higher Education, *Trends in Global Higher Education: Tracking an Academic Revolution* (with Philip G. Altbach and Liz Reisberg). A former U.S. Foreign Service Officer, Laura currently serves as co-editor of the *Journal of Studies in International Education.*

Chika Sehoole is an associate professor and chair of the Department of Education Management and Policy Studies at the University of Pretoria, South Africa. He holds a PhD from the University of the Witwatersrand, Johannesburg, South Africa. In 2003 to 2004 he was a visiting Rockefeller postdoctoral fellow at the Center for African Studies at the University of Illinois in Urbana Champaign. In 2005 to 2006 he was a New Century Fulbright Scholar. His publication highlights include *Democratizing Higher Education in South Africa, Constraints of Reform in Post-Apartheid South Africa* (2005), Routledge. Chika Sehoole is chair the board of the African Network for Internationalization of Education (ANIE).

Qi Wang is an assistant professor at the Graduate School of Education of Shanghai Jiao Tong University, China. She received her MA in education (International Education) and PhD in education from the University of Bath, UK. Her research interests include building world-class universities, skill formation and national development, and comparative and international education. Recently, she has been one of the key researchers involved in a research project on international competitiveness and research university development funded by the Science and Technology Commission of the Chinese Ministry of Education.

Maria Yudkevich is a vice rector of the National Research University Higher School of Economics in Moscow, Russia (HSE) and associate professor of economics at HSE. She also chairs the HSE Center for Institutional Studies and Laboratory for Institutional Analysis, a research center for young scholars who focus on both theoretical and applied economic analysis of educational institutions. The main areas of her interest and research work are contract theory with a special reference to faculty contracts, universities, and markets for higher education.

Index